ESSAYS IN CANADIAN ECONOMIC HISTORY

Essays in

Canadian Economic History

HAROLD A. INNIS

Edited by Mary Q. Innis

UNIVERSITY OF TORONTO PRESS

The editor wishes to acknowledge the permissions granted by the following for the use of copyright material: McClelland and Stewart Limited, for the passage from A. A. Milne's *Winnie the Pooh* quoted on pages 240–1; The Society of Authors, as the Literary Representatives of the Trustees of the estate of the late A. E. Housman, and Messrs. Jonathan Cape Ltd., for the lines from A. E. Housman's *Collected Poems* quoted on pages 292 and 308; and Mr. A. D. Peters, Literary Agent representing the estate of the late Hilaire Belloc, for the lines from Hilaire Belloc's *Cautionary Verses* quoted on pages 292 and 307.

Foreword

SCHOLARS familiar with the work of the late Harold A. Innis will need no introduction to the essays that follow. The committee advising Mrs. Innis on what should be done to make more available Professor Innis's published and unpublished writings early decided on new editions of *The Fur Trade in Canada* and *The Cod Fisheries*. These two books represent clearly Professor Innis's chief findings in the field of Canadian economic history. In them are worked out most of his ideas of how Canada's economic development took place. From these two books alone, however, one cannot get a clear picture of the development of Innis's thought. *The Fur Trade in Canada* was not published until ten years after he had begun serious work on Canadian economic history, *The Cod Fisheries* not for another ten years. In between, he had written a great number of papers, forewords, and articles in which he had set forward ideas with which he was currently grappling and conclusions to which he had been led from work he was then engaged upon. Some of the themes he had taken up in this way were never further developed; many of them were pursued in the later larger undertakings but not in a way that involved the full incorporation of their contents. The scholar seeking to understand Innis's interpretation of Canadian economic history could not stop short of reading the many scattered papers and forewords he had written over his lifetime. This work was a highly important part of his total work.

In planning the present volume the committee faced an extremely difficult problem of selection. Obviously not all these scattered pieces of writing could be brought together in one reasonably sized book; much had to be left out. It was decided from the first that the essays selected would be those bearing on Canadian economic history. A good deal of Innis's writings in the latter years of his life are not included. Unfortunately, however, it was necessary to go even further in the way of selection: essays which appeared inordinately long or which were reasonably accessible were left out. Painful deletions were made even at the very last moment in the interest of keeping the book from being too long.

Not all of Innis's friends will agree on the selection that was finally made, but the committee believes that apart from one or two essays which were excluded solely because of length the essays here published represent the best of Innis's scattered writings in Canadian economic history. The *Essays* should be thought of as a companion volume to *The Fur Trade in Canada* and *The Cod Fisheries*. The three, together with Part II of *Settlement and the Forest and Mining Frontiers* (Toronto, 1936), provide for the student a solid background of reading for an understanding of the economic history of Canada.

The committee, consisting of Professors D. G. Creighton, W. T. Easterbrook, D. Q. Innis, and S. D. Clark, must accept responsibility for the selection of the essays contained in this volume, but credit for the work of preparing the essays for publication goes to Mrs. Innis. The work she did throughout made the task of the committee a very light and pleasant one. A great obligation is also owed to Mrs. Jane Ward of the Department of Political Economy and to Miss Houston and the other members of the editorial staff of the University of Toronto Press.

S. D. Clark

Contents

1

The Teaching of Economic History in Canada[1]

I T is the ambition of this paper to outline the subject of economic history as the core of Canadian economics. The central position must of course always be accorded to economic theory, but economic history is always an attempt to test the validity of principles of economic theory, and to suggest necessary emendations. A new country presents certain definite problems which appear to be more or less insoluble from the standpoint of the application of economic theory as worked out in the older highly industrialized countries. Economic history consequently becomes more important as a tool by which the economic theory of the old countries can be amended. On the other hand, the fashioning of this tool requires skill of a high order and, in a new country, superabundant energy, because of the immediate and heavy demands of teaching or of giving expert advice in the solving of practical problems of a pecuniary character. The rapidity of the development of new countries in the latter stages of industrialism has placed the economist under serious handicaps. The heavy demands of teaching make research and postgraduate work difficult and dependence on outside textbooks inevitable. For example, the textbooks of the United States and England pay little attention to the problems of conservation and of government ownership which are of foremost importance in a new country such as Canada. Canadians are obliged to teach the economic theory of old countries and to attempt to fit their analysis of new economic facts into an old background. The handicaps of this process are obvious, and there is evidence to show that the application of the economic theories of old countries to the problems of new countries results in a new form of exploitation with dangerous consequences. The only escape can come from an intensive study of Canadian economic problems and from the development of a philosophy of economic history or an economic theory suited to Canadian needs.

It is proposed to present a survey of the work done in economic

[1] This paper was read before the sub-conference of economics and commerce teachers of the National Conference of Canadian Universities at the Chateau Laurier in Ottawa, May 22 and 23, 1929. [It was published in *Contributions to Canadian Economics*, II, 1929 (University of Toronto Studies, History and Economics, 1930), 52–68.]

3

history in Canada or in Canadian economics in order to appreciate weak points in the line of attack and to suggest possible remedies. And we may begin with the actual teaching of economic history in Canadian universities. The calendars of various universities over a long period of years are not adequate guides, but they will serve as indications, and the calendars of the current academic year are valuable indices. In some universities the subject of economic history is not referred to, although one gains the impression that it is not altogether neglected, since the names of textbooks by such authors as Cheyney and others are included in the references. In western Canada, Manitoba has provided, for a long period of years, courses in mediaeval and modern economic history for undergraduates and graduates. Saskatchewan has an ambitious programme of three courses: Great Britain prior to 1763, the British Empire after that date, and Europe and the United States. In eastern Canada, the University of Western Ontario has had courses on the industrial and economic history of Great Britain, Europe, and the United States, and, beginning in 1923–4, on Canada since Confederation, and after that date on Europe and North America. The University of Toronto at present gives two courses, one on British economic history after 1700, and one on Canadian economic history. McMaster University has a course on industrial history and labour problems, referring chiefly to Great Britain. Queen's University provides courses on the economic history of Europe, Canada, and the United States, and appears to have been the first university, with Professor Swanson as the first professor, to offer a course on the financial history of Canada, beginning in 1915–16, and on the economic history of Canada, beginning in 1920–1. McGill University attaches considerable importance to the subject, and gave at an early date courses on the industrial revolution in Great Britain and the United States, and later two courses on economic factors in the evolution of society, the dividing line being 1800. More recently it has offered two courses for graduates on the development of public policy in Canada since 1867. Dalhousie University provides courses on the economic history of the United States, Europe, and Canada. New Brunswick, Mount Allison, and other Canadian universities give economic history a much less important place in their curricula. The subject is also taught by history departments, but largely as an incidental course.

In the main, it will be seen that economic history, as taught in Canada, is concentrated about the standard texts of Ashley, Cunningham, Knowles, Lipson, Clapham, Fay, Toynbee, and others for Great

Britain, of Faulkner and Lippincott for the United States, and probably, in the future, of Knight, Barnes, and Flugel for Europe. It is probable that in some universities the work of Tawney and Unwin in England, of Sombart and Weber in Germany, of See and Pirenne in France and Belgium, and of Gras in the United States, are given special consideration. The stress is chiefly on modern economic history, on the economic history of the industrial revolution, and on the United Kingdom and the United States. Apparently some attention is being paid to the possibilities of widening the subject and of extending it to include Greek and Roman civilizations following the publication of such important volumes as Rostovtzeff's *Social and Economic History of the Roman Empire* (Oxford, 1926). The rapid expansion of the subject and the appearance of important periodicals[2] will call for a thorough realignment of the courses.

The courses in the curriculum are given generally in the later years. Professor Ashley, who might have done so much for economic history in Canada had he remained in Toronto, and who was appointed to the first chair of economic history in the world, at Harvard, advocates for commerce schools an introductory course in economic history paralleling an introductory course in economic theory.[3] The advanced work requires a competent knowledge of French, especially for Canada, of German, and, Professor Ashley adds, of Latin. From the standpoint of advanced work in Canadian economic history, familiarity with the excellent work of French economic historians in the seventeenth and eighteenth centuries, of the economic history of the United Kingdom after the industrial revolution, and of the United States especially after the Civil War, must be assumed.

The extent of the research work in Canadian economic history, based on the teaching of these subjects, is difficult to estimate as by far the most important work has been done by Canadian students doing graduate work in the United States. For example, competent and thorough doctoral theses done in American universities on Canadian subjects include those of D. A. MacGibbon, *Railway Rates and the Canadian Railway Commission* (New York, 1917), J. Viner, *Canada's Balance of International Indebtedness 1900–1913* (Cambridge, 1924), H. S. Patton, *Grain Growers' Co-operation in Western Canada* (Cambridge, 1928), W. A. Mackintosh, *Agricultural Co-opera-*

---

[2] *Agricultural History; Journal of Economic and Business History; Economic History Review*; and economic history supplement to the *Economic Journal*.

[3] W. J. Ashley, "The Place of Economic History in University Studies," *Economic History Review*, I, no. 1 (1927), 1–11.

tion in Western Canada (Kingston, 1924), W. J. Donald, *The Canadian Iron and Steel Industry* (Boston, 1915), H. A. Logan, *The History of Trade Union Organization in Canada* (Chicago, 1928), E. W. Bradwin, *The Bunkhouse Man* (New York, 1928), R. M. Breckenridge, *The Canadian Banking System* (Toronto, 1894), S. Vineberg, *Provincial and Local Taxation in Canada* (New York, 1912), and others. This is not to say that there are not a large number of graduate theses resting in the vaults of Canadian university libraries and that a great deal of valuable work has not been done, but it has not been such as could be made available by publication in such a way as to be comparable with those noted. McGill University has done commendable work in publishing masters' theses, and numerous valuable articles have been published in such periodicals as the *Canadian Historical Review, Economic Geography,* the *Journal of Political Economy,* and the *American Economic Review.* In the main, graduate work in Canada has been restricted to practical problems, and Canadians have not been in a position to take the detached view which makes for successful and extensive graduate work. Those engaged in the teaching of economics in Canada have done important work, but it is significant that much of this is buried in government reports, to mention only that of Professors MacGibbon, Swanson, Clark, McLean, Mavor, and Jackman. The demands of government work in a new country are shown not only in the investigations of commissions, but also in the number of economists who have been engaged in the works of government departments such as the Bureau of Statistics, the Tariff Advisory Board, the Board of Railway Commissioners, the Public Archives, the Department of External Affairs, and other branches of the provincial and federal governments. The demands of business are becoming more insistent, and year after year brings new departures from the ranks. Not only has there been this direct weakening of the staff, but also indirectly economics departments are being burdened to an increasing extent with the task of teaching students who enter universities with no interest in graduate work and only for the purpose of being trained for a job to be provided for them at the end of their course. This involves teaching larger numbers of weaker students the subject of price economics with consequent direct and indirect losses to the subject of economics as a whole.

We have been handicapped also by the relatively slow growth of economics and its emergence as a subject separate from history and political science. The important position of the government in Canada and its relation to France and Great Britain and the interest in the development of responsible government have given political science a privileged position. Much of the best work in the field of Canadian economic history has been done on subjects marginal to economics, political science, and history. Dr. Adam Shortt's *Documents Relating to Canadian Currency, Exchange and Finance during the French Period* (Ottawa, 1915) and *Lord Sydenham* (Toronto, 1926), W. B. Munro's *Documents Relating to Seigniorial Tenure in Canada, 1598–1854* (Toronto, 1908), Stephen Leacock's *Mackenzie, Baldwin, Lafontaine, Hincks* (Toronto, 1926), and O. D. Skelton's *Life and Times of Sir A. T. Galt* (Toronto, 1920) and *Life and Letters of Sir Wilfrid Laurier* (Toronto, 1921) may be cited as examples of the importance of political science. In the field of history, H. P. Biggar, *Early Trading Companies of New France* (Toronto, 1901), J. S. McLennan, *Louisbourg from Its Foundation to Its Fall* (London, 1918), G. C. Patterson, *Land Settlement in Upper Canada 1783–1810* (Toronto, 1921), G. C. Davidson, *The Northwest Company* (Berkeley, 1918), G. Bryce, *Remarkable History of the Hudson's Bay Company* (London, 1900), H. I. Cowan, *British Emigration to British North America* (Toronto, 1928), Chester Martin, *Lord Selkirk's Work in Canada* (Oxford, 1916), W. Smith, *History of the Post Office in British North America 1639–1870* (Cambridge, 1920), A. S. Morton, *Journal of Duncan McGillivray* (Toronto, 1929), D. C. Harvey, *The French Regime in Prince Edward Island* (New Haven, 1926), and C. D. Allin and G. M. Jones, *Annexation, Preferential Trade and Reciprocity* (Toronto, 1911) may be cited.

It is possible to go into various other marginal subjects and to note valuable contributions to economic history made by scientists in Canada and other countries. M. I. Newbigin, *Canada: The Great River, the Lands and the Men* (New York, 1926), F. W. Wallace's two volumes on wooden shipbuilding, B. M. Selekman's *Postponing Strikes* (New York, 1927), E. S. Moore, *Mineral Resources of Canada* (Toronto, 1929), R. Drummond, *Minerals and Mining in Nova Scotia* (Stellarton, 1918), the publications of the Commission of Conservation, J. W. Jones, *Fur Farming in Canada* (Ottawa, 1914), B. E. Fernow, *Forest Conditions of Nova Scotia* (Ottawa, 1912), and H. M. Whitford and R. D. Craig, *Forests of British Columbia* (Ottawa, 1918) are examples. The names of the authors of the economic sections in *Canada and Its Provinces* include Dafoe, Lugrin, Chapais, E. T. W. Chambers, F. D. Adams, and others. We have gained materially from the work of students outside Canada—E. Salone, *La Colonisation de la Nouvelle France* (Paris, 1906), G. Vattier, *Esquisse historique de* la colonisation de la Nouvelle France (Paris, 1928), J. F. W. Johnson, Report on the Agricultural Capabilities of the Province of New Brunswick (Fredericton, 1850), and others—but to a certain extent these must be offset by the work of Canadians on outside subjects—J. Mavor, An Economic History of Russia (London, 1914), W. T. Jackman, The Development of Transportation in Modern England (Cambridge, 1916), J. C. Hemmeon, The History of the British Post Office (Cambridge, 1912), L. W. Moffit, England on the Eve of the Industrial Revolution (London, 1925), A. Brady, William Huskisson and Liberal Reform (Oxford, 1928). All of these men have done excellent work in the Canadian field, to cite only W. T. Jackman, Economics of Transportation (Toronto, 1926), as a result of their studies on outside subjects. On the whole, we have a competent body of work on which to rely for the development of an economic history of Canada, although there are large and obvious gaps. Early trade, labour, transportation, business organization, marketing, public finance, agriculture, and industry are among the more obvious. The appearance of J. N. Fauteux's Essai sur l'industrie au Canada, sous le régime français (Quebec, 1927) is significant of a probable development of research along these lines.

In the social sciences, economics must be brought level with history and political science and especially with the so-called natural sciences for the advantage of the subject as a whole. Canadian economic history is in a sense at the root of the problem. Its elaboration will strengthen the anchorage of economics which is so essential to a rapidly growing young country such as Canada. Our economic and social organization has lagged far behind our material expansion.

In the improvement of the position of economics several lines of attack are open and among these the development of research is of foremost importance. One of the most serious handicaps to research has followed from the lack of library facilities and an inadequate bibliography. The archives of the Dominion and of the provinces and older cities contain invaluable material for the study of economics. The reports of a large number of able men who represented France and Great Britain in governing Canada have been preserved in the archives of London and of Paris as well as of the smaller towns. The Public Archives of Canada has made transcripts of most of these documents, and they are available to students who can afford to purchase tickets to Ottawa. Moreover, important data have been published in its reports and special publications. The archives department of Quebec has also made material in its possession available in numerous publications. State historical societies in the United States, especially New York,

Wisconsin, and Michigan, have published numerous documents relating to Canada. The wealth of this material has given the political scientist and the historian a decided advantage as we have seen. Unfortunately, Canada is not in the same happy position as to the records of various important business firms, which, following the recent work in economic history, must become increasingly important. Progress is being made in this direction, as shown in Dr. Shortt's work on the Baring papers, and the Canada Company papers, and in the recent proposal to make the papers of the Hudson's Bay Company accessible. The archives of the Grand Trunk are a further case in point. Perhaps the wealth of this material has blinded our eyes to the value of business records of Canadian firms. It is significant that some of the most valuable work in this direction is being done in Saskatchewan under the able direction of Professor Morton in history. The difficulties are partly the result of the lack of attention to these invaluable records on the part of archivists, historians, economists, and especially librarians, and partly the lack of pride among business firms in their own records. One can think of no more valuable work that a newly formed Political Science Association could undertake than the advocacy of ways and means by which these records could be preserved and made available for the student in Canadian economics. These records must form the basis of a sound development of economic history and we must attempt to stimulate the interest of local libraries, of historical societies, and of the archives in the preservation of these invaluable documents.

We are seriously limited in effective work in the accessibility of printed material. Again the governments of various countries interested in Canada, especially the United Kingdom and the United States, have published the reports of commissions, to mention only the valuable material to be found in the Commission reports on the Hudson's Bay Company in 1749 and 1857, Lord Durham's *Report on the Affairs of British North America*, and I. D. Andrews' *Report on the Trade and Commerce of the British North American Colonies 1851* for the United States. The imperial, federal, and provincial governments have published innumerable reports and records in the sessional papers, the census, and such invaluable compendiums as the *Canada Year Book*. Canada has also been fortunate in having a large number of competent visitors who wrote down the results of their observations in numerous works. These range from Lahontan, Charlevoix, Peter Kalm, Weld, Heriot, Gray, Mackenzie, and La Rochefoucauld to John A. Hobson. Various individuals have written valuable and detailed surveys, such as Gourlay, *Statistical Account*, T. C. Haliburton, *An His-*

torical and Statistical Account of Nova Scotia (Halifax, 1829), and J. Bouchette, *The British Dominions in North America* (London, 1832). Several of these volumes have been made accessible by reprints and especially by societies such as the Royal Society of Canada and the Champlain Society. Numerous libraries have been industriously engaged in the collection of Canadiana and valuable collections are in the possession of the parliamentary library and the archives library in Ottawa, the Toronto Public Reference Library, the Bibliothèque Saint-Sulpice of Montreal, and the legislative libraries of Manitoba, British Columbia, and other provinces. But again Canadian libraries have been notoriously delinquent in their attention to economic material, and Canada has no library which makes any pretence at keeping abreast of the material published on the economic conditions of Canada and other countries with the exception of the Higher School of Commercial Studies under Dr. Laureys in Montreal. In the publication of bibliographies economists are under heavy obligations to historians, to mention P. Gagnon, *Essai de bibliographie canadienne* (Quebec, 1895), N. E. Dionne, *Inventaire chronologique* (Quebec, 1905), the *Review of Historical Publications* (now the *Canadian Historical Review*), *Canada and Its Provinces,* and R. G. Trotter, *Canadian History* (Toronto, 1926). Another task which a newly formed association could well undertake is that of preparing a bibliography of Canadian economics. This problem is closely related to that of a Canadian journal of economics in which shorter articles dealing with Canadian economics can be published, and in which a bibliography on the subject can be built up. It would afford moreover a medium for self-criticism of which Canadians are very much in need.

Perhaps the most serious obstacle to effective work in Canadian economics and economic history is the lack of a philosophy of economic history applicable to new countries. The great bulk of effective work is conducted under the direction of American graduate schools or in the related fields of political science and history. Much of the work has been defective through the attempt to fit the phenomena of new countries to the economic theories of old countries; or to give it a slant or bias toward this or that school of political science or history. These difficulties persist in the attempts which have been made so far to present an economic history of Canada or to present a textbook in Canadian economics.[4] They are evident in S. A.

---

[4]I have attempted in the introduction of *A History of the Canadian Pacific Railway* (London, 1923) to give a sketch of Canadian economic history before 1867 from the standpoint of geography, as does also Professor O. D. Skelton after that date, but the limitations are obvious.

THE TEACHING OF ECONOMIC HISTORY IN CANADA

Cudmore's *Economics for Canadian Students* (Toronto, 1912), D. A. MacGibbon's *An Introduction to Economics* (Toronto, 1924), R. E. Freeman's *Economics for Canadians* (Toronto, 1928), H. Heaton's *A History of Trade and Commerce* (Toronto, 1928), Professor Mavor's and O. D. Skelton's *General Economic History of the Dominion 1867–1912* (Toronto, 1913). It may be worth while to criticize the weaknesses of some of the more pretentious of these works in order to suggest possible remedies. Undoubtedly we have been very much influenced by Germany in our economic history, and the interest was shown in the translation of Carl Bücher's *Industrial Evolution* (New York, 1912) by S. M. Wickett. Professor Mavor has attempted to divide Canadian history on the basis of four periods: barter with the Indians, settlement producing for its own consumption, the exploitation of field and forest for export, and finally the specialization of East and West and its integration by transport and finance.[5] His analysis is too simple and tends to throw too much emphasis on finance. Professor Mavor was seriously handicapped by his stern background of Scottish individualism in his interpretation of Canadian phenomena. Professor Heaton has approached the subject from the standpoint of expansion from a period of self-sufficiency, but the development of a new country means above all things continued relations, especially trade, with the old country. However useful the scheme may be in a study of the evolution from the manorial economy it means little in the study of a new country which of itself belongs to a different stage, and to the beginnings of international economy. Canada has never been self-sufficient, and her existence has depended primarily on trade with other countries. New countries must be considered in relation to old countries. Professor Heaton has been handicapped by the preconceptions formed from the study of English economic history. Work done in the United States has also had a strong influence on Canadian economic history and historians have been insistent on the possibilities of Professor Turner's frontier school.[6] But Canada had no gradual development by which the frontier could exercise any continued and pervasive influence and the limitations of the frontier school are numerous. Professor Gras's work on the metropolitan economy has also been the object of considerable attention,[7] but Canada has

[5]*Contributions to Canadian Economics*, I (1928), 7–16.
[6]W. N. Sage, "Some Aspects of the Frontier in Canadian History," *Canadian Historical Association Report*, 1928, pp. 62–72.
[7]N. S. B. Gras, *Introduction to Economic History* (New York, 1922); M. L. Hartsough, *The Twin Cities as a Metropolitan Market*, Research Publication of the University of Minnesota, Social Sciences, no. 18; C. R. Fay, "The Metropolitan Market," *Journal of the Canadian Bankers' Association*, XXIV (1927), 181–92.

established metropolitan areas only with the greatest difficulty and in the face of geographic handicaps, and city growth in Canada has been the result of factors different from those characterizing the United States. It is probable that we should find Canadian metropolitan centres following quite a different course from that suggested by Professor Gras, for example in the Twin Cities. These schools are based on the development of English and American industrialism and commercialism and the strong sweep of the westward movement in the United States. It is scarcely necessary to dwell on the work of Gustavus Myers, *History of Canadian Wealth* (Chicago, 1914), who has treated Canadian history as an evolution of the predatory culture. Professor Mackintosh has done suggestive work as a Canadian in pointing out that Canada only developed as a nation with the production of wheat as a staple.[8] Unfortunately this theory only relates to the later stages of Canadian development and does not pretend to cover the development of Canada as a whole.

From the analysis it would appear that Canadian economic history must be approached from the standpoint of trade with other countries, France in the beginning, later Great Britain and the United States, and finally the Orient and the world generally. Economists will be safe in following the political scientist and the historian in their studies of the relationship of Canada to other countries. Canada's development in relation to other countries meant the development of trade from the Atlantic seaboard in commodities accessible by water transport. With primitive transportation fish and furs occupied a dominant position and the exhaustion of furs was followed by lumber. Economists cannot pretend to an understanding of Canadian economic history without an adequate history of transportation. A history of transportation must be accompanied by a history of trade and especially of the trade relations between Canada and old countries. Further, Canadians will find it necessary to work out the economic history of each industry, especially in technique and capital organization. It is hardly necessary to point out the difficulties in studies of this character as the great mass of Canadian material is related to governmental problems and the bulk of the economic material is *obiter dicta*.

The economic history of Canada from the standpoint of transportation might be divided into two periods: those of water transport and of land transport. In the first period fishing, the fur trade, and the lumber trade were conducted primarily by water transport and in the

[8]W. A. Mackintosh, "Economic Factors in Canadian History," *Canadian Historical Review*, IV (1923), 12–25.

second period wheat, minerals, lumber, and pulp and paper were handled primarily by railways. The difficult period of transition from water transport to land transport which dates roughly from the canals of the 1840's to the completion of the Canadian Pacific in 1885 is marked by the struggle for responsible government, the decline of the mercantile system, and Confederation, and these developments were more than a coincidence.

I have tried to trace elsewhere[9] the development of the fur trade in the first period, and to show the evolution of the present geographic entity of northern North American in response to the demands of trade. The expansion of the fur trade up the St. Lawrence and the Ottawa, along the Great Lakes, northwest along the edge of the Canadian shield, and westward to the Pacific, under the French, the English Canadians and the Northwest Company, and finally the Hudson's Bay Company, was a logical development from the exhaustion of supplies of beaver and from the production of the best grades of fur in northern latitudes. Having shown that the present boundary lines of the Dominion were largely determined by the fur trade, some of the main lines of economic development may be suggested. The fur trade was carried on with the Indians, who demanded the manufactured goods of Europe. The growing efficiency of industrial England gradually weakened French control of the trade through the supply of cheap, well-made manufactured goods and, after the conquest of New France, made impossible the control of northern North America by the American colonies. Montreal held its supremacy over New York. The fur trade not only laid down our political boundaries, but was basic to our connections with England. The fact that the trade was prosecuted throughout the northern half of North America, largely under one control, was responsible for the establishment and maintenance of British connections. It was responsible also for the organization of economic activities throughout Canada which were kept alive until later industries were developed. Capital from the fur trade fertilized the economic beginnings of Ontario and other parts of Canada, and the trade and industry of Montreal. The trade was conducted by the waterways of the Canadian shield primarily with the canoe from Montreal, but later with the York boats from Hudson Bay. Its extensive transport system necessitated the organization of food supply, chiefly from the agricultural areas of Ontario and Quebec and the buffalo of the plains. The parts of northern North America suitable to the fur trade were

[9]H. A. Innis, *The Fur Trade in Canada: An Introduction to Canadian Economic History* (New Haven, 1930).

the Canadian shield and the territories immediately to the south, which furnished ample supplies of food. Canada included the Canadian shield, the northern portions of the Great Plains, and the northern sections of the Rocky Mountains along the Pacific coast.

The development of the fur trade along the water routes and the decline of exports from Montreal were accompanied by an increase in the exports of a new staple adapted to water transport and available on the St. Lawrence and its tributaries, namely lumber. The coming of the railway with the weak economic development of northern North America brought in its train the phenomena of government ownership, the rapid growth in the export of wheat from the West, and finally of minerals and pulp and paper from the Canadian shield. The rapidity of development in Canada after 1900 presents a fascinating problem to the student of Canadian economic history. The peculiar characteristics of Canada's development as shown in the sudden plunges of economic life warrant careful study.

Water transport was of vital importance in the handling of certain commodities, a light valuable commodity such as fur obtainable along the water routes across Canada and a bulky commodity such as lumber produced in the areas immediately available to main water courses. Both commodities were exported to Europe and involved the exploitation of virgin plant and animal resources. Furs were essentially a product in demand as luxuries and adapted to the mercantile policy, whereas lumber was required to bridge the gap in the shift from a relatively non-industrial to an industrial community, and from mercantilism to free trade. The rapid growth of towns and ships depended on lumber. This commodity furnished the scaffolding and moulding on which the present industrial equipment of Great Britain and the United States was built up. It served until industry could shift from organic to inorganic materials. With the dominance of water transport the economic development of Canada was particularly susceptible to the demands of outside markets. The instalment of the modern industrial equipment of Great Britain and more recently of the United States and other countries led to the exhaustion of raw materials and to the search in new countries for new sources of commodities produced in the hinterlands and not accessible by water transport. Moreover, it made available quantities of material for railroad construction and machinery for exploitation, and the depletion of raw material released skill and experience. The shift to land transport was a phenomenon of intensified industrialism. The immediate demands of the new industrial populations for foodstuffs intensified the importance of wheat.

The immediately available experience of the United States in the handling of this product, especially shown in the invention of grain binders, and the vast level stretches of prairie were factors contributing to the rapid increase in production of that commodity. Moreover, the modern industrial equipment created new demands for inorganic materials, and especially for metals, copper, lead, zinc, and nickel. Again it made available the materials for the exploitation of the mines—carbide, explosives, and hydro-electric power. The immediately available experience of the United States and the vast relatively level stretches of the Precambrian shield were factors contributing to the rapid increase in production of these commodities. Finally, the overwhelming efficiency of the new industrialism has necessitated the development of effective methods of disposing of the products to the unappreciative consumer. The rapid rise of advertising has been largely responsible for development of the pulp and paper industry. Land transport and the efficient handling of heavy bulky commodities have given Canadian economic development a fundamentally different trend from that of water transport. It cannot be over-emphasized that Canadian problems cannot be answered in terms of the economics of older countries. The concentration of control of capital in the branch bank system and of transport in the transcontinental railway system are essentially Canadian and fundamentally different from the United States.

It is not the task of this paper to suggest the interrelations of these lines of development and their ultimate effects on Canada. But it is possible to conclude that Canada as one of the most recent products of industrialism offers vast fields for research of the most significant character, not only for her own needs but also for those of highly industrialized countries. The fields of labour, and finance, and every phase of economic activity will gain from an understanding of the general economic background. The study of economic history should enable Canadians to see more clearly the course of the economic growth of Canada and possibly to guide it with more intelligence and should aid them in determining their own destinies from an economic point of view as they have succeeded in gaining control over them from the constitutional standpoint.

In conclusion, I should like to suggest as a means of promoting the interests of economic history in a new country two lines of attack. In the first place the curriculum should have courses including a general introduction to economic history, French economic history in the seventeenth and eighteenth centuries, the British Empire after 1763, the industrial revolution in other countries, including the United

States, and Canadian economic history. To parallel these courses, other subjects in the curriculum should have a Canadian background to provide for a continued widening and intensification of the content of courses with reference to Canadian economics.

It is advisable further that the student should have a knowledge of French, German, and Latin, and of certain of the sciences, especially biology and geology and the applied sciences, electricity, metallurgy, and mechanics with relation to Canadian development. In the second place, an economic association and an economic journal might do much to hasten the development of a bibliography and the collection of business records. Perhaps after the more obvious gaps have been filled someone will write a textbook on Canadian economics for use in the secondary schools and in the universities. Once economists have made this progress their task should become cumulatively less difficult. Undergraduate work will be strengthened and graduate work will become more effective. An intelligent perspective is a prerequisite to the development of Canadian economics.

The Work of Thorstein Veblen*

THE appearance of a doctoral thesis from the University of Paris by William Jaffé entitled *Les Théories économiques et sociales de Thorstein Veblen* (Paris, 1924) is a reminder that the work of Thorstein Veblen may be regarded as practically complete and that the time for review and criticism of the main body of that work has arrived. That Mr. Veblen has regarded his main work as complete is evident in the publication of his works in the more popular journals such as the *Dial* and the defunct *Freeman*. He has approached the point at which popularization could be safely undertaken and his most recent work, *Absentee Ownership and Business Enterprise in Recent Times: The Case of America* (New York, 1923) is his most effective literary work and probably his least effective scientific work.[1] We may safely launch upon a survey of his work without fear of the necessity of serious revision through the appearance of later publications. Some such approach is necessary at an early date lest the importance of his contributions should be obscured by the violence of the controversies which have raged about them. Already the ablest of his critics have tended to neglect the significance of his main contribution.

Characteristically Mr. Thorstein Veblen has refused to contribute information to *Who's Who* and so far as I am aware the date of his birth is unknown. He is a descendant of the Scandinavian settlers of the northwestern states. Doubtless he would describe himself as belonging to the dolichocephalic blond race, the race which—according to his description of the theory—followed the retreat in the last glacial period and which because of the severity of the environment was subjected to appreciable mutation.[2] It was the race which had been least subject to the hybridization which had characterized European peoples

*From the *Southwestern Political and Social Science Quarterly*, X (1929), 56–68.

[1]J. M. Clark, "Review of Absentee Ownership," *American Economic Review*, XIV (1924), 289–93. The publication of *Laxadaela Saga*, tr. T. B. Veblen (1925), is further evidence of a completion of the main economic work.

[2]See *The Place of Science in Modern Civilization and Other Essays* (New York, 1919), pp. 455–76, 477–96.

in recent times. Grant[3] has emphasized the importance of the contributions of this race to European culture perhaps unduly, as Kroeber, a defender of the Mediterranean races, has pointed out.[4] Nevertheless this people has left its stamp on European races and on European culture, as a study of the inroads of the Danes, the Vikings, and the North Germans would show.[5] In some sense Mr. Veblen has shown evidence of this lineage in his devastating attacks on the established economic theories of the current period. But Mr. Veblen has, on the whole, disregarded the importance of races in studies on European culture, chiefly on the ground of the wholesale hybridization[6] which has taken place— taking strong ground that even the Jews have not escaped this tendency.[7] He has regarded this hybridization as important in its increasing the number of combinations of unit characters described under the Mendelian theory[8] but it provides no significant basis in the explanation of the trends of European cultural growth. For an explanation of Mr. Veblen's work we must turn to environmental influences.

Of these early and direct influences little is known, other than the information given to me by Mr. S. J. McLean and others that he lived a hard, energetic life in Wisconsin, the state in which he was born. He graduated from Carleton College, Minnesota, in 1880. His interests after graduation were apparently in philosophy, as he continued with graduate work at Johns Hopkins University in that subject, but, as his description has it, suffering a breakdown in health he decided to study economics and secured his doctorate from Yale. His study of philosophy was confined chiefly to Kant, Comte, Spencer, and Darwin or the positivistic school.[9] In 1884 his first article on Kant's *Critique of Judgment* was printed in the *Journal of Speculative Philosophy*. He regarded himself in some sense as a disciple of Spencer.[10] With Darwin he was obviously impressed with the importance of evolution but he was not convinced of the finality of materialism and mechanism and he was among the first to detect the relation between the industrial

[3]Madison Grant, *The Passing of the Great Race or the Racial Basis of European History* (New York, 1916).
[4]A. L. Kroeber, *Anthropology* (New York, 1923–4).
[5]M. W. Williams, *Social Scandinavia in the Viking Age* (New York, 1920).
[6]*Imperial Germany and the Industrial Revolution* (New York, 1915), pp. 5ff.
[7]"The Intellectual Preëminence of the Jews in Modern Europe," *Political Science Quarterly*, XXXIV (1919), 33–42.
[8]*Imperial Germany*, pp. 5ff.
[9]William Jaffé, *Les Théories économiques et sociales de Thorstein Veblen* (Paris, 1924). This volume has an excellent bibliography.
[10]*Annals of the American Academy of Political and Social Science*, II (1891–2), 57ff.

revolution and the Darwinian theory and the later theories of physics and chemistry.[11] Like the positivists he was willing to test the theory of evolution and to attempt to work out scientific laws for economics, always remaining critical, however, and prepared to check the validity of any line of approach. It cannot be urged with satisfaction that his philosophy is determined by Hegel and Karl Marx.[12] He was influenced by these men but the roots of his philosophy are to be found in Kantianism, possibly in Comte but rather in Hume, Locke, and Spencer and post-Darwinian philosophy; he had little sympathy with Bergson[13] and the *élan vital*. It is because of the background of philosophy that he has been referred to as the most important economist to come out of America.

With this philosophical background Veblen approached the subject of economics. His approach was from the inductive side in keeping with his philosophy. He was interested in dynamics and his first important published work on economics, printed in the first number of the *Journal of Political Economy* in 1892, was entitled "The Price of Wheat since 1867." In a later number in the same year he published an article on "The Food Supply and the Price of Wheat."[14] These articles were models of analysis of economic facts. One is immediately struck by the similarity, in character of analysis and in range, between these articles and the volume on *Business Cycles* by Wesley C. Mitchell. They were models for the work of later economists in analysing the relationship of complex factors.

The close attention to dynamic factors in these articles warrants a further consideration of Veblen's environment. His discussion covered the important period after the Civil War in which American industrialism came into full bloom. The phenomena of that period with its essential dynamic features left a strong impression on Veblen's work.

He was influenced not only by the dynamic factors of his immediate environment but also by the school of German economic historians. The German economists found themselves in a similar environment following the Franco-Prussian War of 1870 and the rapid spread of the industrial revolution. The American economists of the middle west had much in common with the German economists of the period after 1870. This influence was strengthened as a result of the close relationship between German universities and American uni-

---

[11]"The Evolution of the Scientific Point of View," *The Place of Science*, pp. 32–5. See C. E. Ayres, *Science the False Messiah* (Indianapolis, 1927).

[12]"The Socialist Economics of Karl Marx and His Followers," *The Place of Science*, pp. 409–56.

[13]*The Instinct of Workmanship* (New York, 1914), pp. 334n., 335n., 336n.

[14]Vol. I, no. 1 (Dec. 1892), 68–103, and no. 3 (June 1893), 365–79.

versities through which large numbers of American students prosecuted their studies in Germany.[15] The influence of Schmoller and especially of the German historical school and their break with the English classical school is important to an appreciation of Veblen. If one were a disciple of the frontier school one might say that Veblen's influence on economic theory was a result of the frontier but it was the frontier of the industrial revolution which influenced his thought and not that of American agriculture, important as this may have been.

At this point it is advisable to present a brief survey of Mr. Veblen's academic record. He was elected fellow at Cornell in 1891–2. For the *Quarterly Journal of Economics* in 1892 he wrote an appraisal of Bohm Bawerk's work[16] praising him for his distinction between social and private capital but charging him with adherence to the wage fund doctrine, and an article on overproduction,[17] holding that it was a description of production at a lower price level. In the same year in an article on socialism in the *Annals of the American Academy*[18] he attempted to explain the causes of discontent which he regarded as due to jealousy and envy. One passage was a prelude to the *Theory of the Leisure Class*: "As we are all aware the chief element of value in many articles of apparel is not their efficiency for protecting the body but for protecting the wearer's respectability and that not only in the eyes of one's neighbors but even in one's own eyes. Indeed it happens not very rarely that a person chooses to go ill-clad in order to be well-dressed. Much more than half of what is worn by the American people may confidently be put down to the element of dress rather than to that of clothing."[19] Socialism could not claim inadequate production as a ground for condemning modern society. On the other hand, private property was the cause of waste. Moreover, socialism, like the British constitution, suggested a way out from the two horns of the dilemma of status and contact which were supposed to dominate all civilizations in the writings of Maine and Spencer.

As a result of these articles J. Laurence Laughlin, under the direction of President Harper in the founding of the University of Chicago, included Veblen in his raids and captures on the brilliant younger men of the older eastern universities. He was appointed reader in 1892

[15]See H. R. Seager, "Economics at Berlin and Vienna," *J.P.E.*, I (1892–3), 236–62, and C. F. Thwing, *The American and German University* (New York, 1928).

[16]"Bohm Bawerk's Definition of Capital, and the Source of Wages," *Q.J.E.*, VI (1891-2), 247–50.

[17]"The Overproduction Fallacy," *ibid.*, pp. 484–92.

[18]"Some Neglected Points in the Theory of Socialism," *Annals of the American Academy of Political and Social Science*, II (1891–2), 57–74.

[19]*Ibid.*, pp. 63–4.

and became tutor in 1894, instructor in 1895–6 and assistant professor in 1901, at which rank he remained until his resignation in 1905. Throughout his term at Chicago he gave a course on the history of socialistic theories. In 1895–6 he began a course on the scope and method of political economy with special reference to the German historical school. His early articles on wheat were obviously on a subject with which he had first-hand acquaintance and his analysis is strictly a price analysis with great emphasis on the state of the industrial arts—on the introduction of railroads, the ocean steamship, and agricultural machinery. He predicted that the price of wheat would remain below 91 cents for the next decade and with the exception of 1898, when it was 93 cents, his prediction was fulfilled. It is suggestive in this connection that Veblen and his followers who have protested most against the inclusiveness of price economics have done most in the study of price phenomena. On the basis of these papers he began a course on problems of American agriculture in 1895–6 which continued until 1900. In 1896–7 a course on the history of political economy was added and in 1897–8 his famous course on the economic factors of civilization was begun. This course was given in Leland Stanford to 1911, in the University of Missouri to 1918, and in the New School for Social Research which he joined at the later date. When it was suggested that the material should be published he replied in a way which all lecturers will appreciate, that one could beat about the bush in a lecture but it was difficult to get sufficient accuracy to warrant publications. In 1904–5 he gave his first course in trusts. In Leland Stanford and Missouri he continued with courses on the history of socialism and the history of economic theory. At Leland Stanford he was associated with Professor Allyn Young as acting head, and at Missouri with Professor Davenport. At the New School he came and worked with Professor Wesley C. Mitchell. At Chicago he was editor of the *Journal of Political Economy* from 1895 to 1905. It is interesting to note the policy followed by him in the *Journal of Political Economy*[20]—the absence of articles on abstruse points of theory, the inclusion of a wide range of subjects on descriptive economics, and especially of articles on Europe, Germany, and Austria, and the number of reviews of German works. In 1895 he translated for publication Gustav Cohn's *System der Finanzwissenschaft.*[21]

It was in the last years of that decade that his most important con-

[20]"The Journal is established primarily to promote the scientific treatment of practical problems." *J.P.E.,* VI (1897–8), title page; *American Journal of Sociology,* XIV (Sept. 1898), 187–201; (Nov. 1898), 352–65; (Jan. 1899), 503–19.

[21]Gustav Cohn, *Science of Finance,* tr. T. B. Veblen (Chicago, 1895).

tributions began to be published. Three articles were printed in the *American Journal of Sociology*, 1898–9, on the "Instinct of Workmanship and the Irksomeness of Labour," "The Beginnings of Ownership," and the "Barbarian Status of Women."[22] These were introductory to the *Theory of the Leisure Class: An Economic Study of Institutions* (1899). Unfortunately this proved his most popular work, as shown in the number of editions through which it has run. It was written at the period when the gilded age was at its height and it marked the beginning of the revolt which has since culminated in the works of Upton Sinclair, H. L. Mencken, Sinclair Lewis, and a host of modern writers. The environment was certain to evoke some such work from a man who had to do with such practical affairs as wheat farming. Its style was unfortunate, not because of its difficulty, but because of the manner in which the phrases stuck. From that work Veblen's reputation never recovered. He was regarded as the satirist with barbed phrases. Conspicuous consumption, pecuniary emulation, became "Veblenian" terms. In spite of its popularity the volume was a direct and devastating attack on the marginal utility theory. It was precisely a clash between the viewpoint of the German historical school with its stress on the evolution of institutions and the classic theory. In this work Veblen attacked economics from two angles—consumption and production. His first important volume was designed to show the weakness of economic theory on the consumption side. He delivered a more reasoned broadside in the article on the "Limitations of Marginal Utility" in the *Journal of Political Economy* for 1909,[23] but the main task had been done. In some sense this was his most important service, and it is probably what Graham Wallas was thinking of when he described him as a genius comparable to Jeremy Bentham. He attempted to destroy the hedonistic calculus which Jeremy Bentham had done much to set up.

Not only was the gilded age at its height in the gay nineties and conspicuous consumption most conspicuous, but also there reached a peak in the United States, in that decade or in the beginning years of 1900, another phenomenon which became conspicuous on the side of production. The United States Steel Corporation was formed in 1902. The rapid strides of machine industry after the Civil War produced more goods than could be consumed without resort to conspicuous consumption, and a situation of overproduction, from the standpoint of the market, resulted in the rapid formation of trusts after

[22]Graham Wallas' review of *Imperial Germany and the Industrial Revolution*, *Q.J.E.*, XXX (1916), 186.
[23]Vol. XVII, 620–36.

the seventies. After 1900 Veblen became intensely interested in this phenomenon of production. An article on "Industrial and Pecuniary Employment" appeared in the *Publications of the American Economic Association* in 1901,[24] and a most satiric article on "An Experiment in Trusts"[25] appeared in the *Journal of Political Economy* in 1904. In the same year his chief contribution on the side of production, *The Theory of Business Enterprise*, was published. An article on "Credit and Prices" appeared in the *Journal of Political Economy* in 1905[26]—again it was the attitude of a practical wheat grower which predominated and production was regarded from the standpoint of the expert engineer. This prediction from *The Theory of Business Enterprise* is worth quoting: "Barring accidents and untoward cultural agencies from outside of politics, business or religion, there is nothing in the logic of the modern situation that should stop the cumulative war expenditures short of industrial collapse and consequent national bankruptcy such as terminated the carnival of war and politics that ran its course on the Continent in the sixteenth and seventeenth centuries"[27]—a prophecy amply fulfilled ten years later. With the publication of this volume his interests appear to have continued with the problems of production, and his next important work was *The Instinct of Workmanship and the State of the Industrial Arts,* published in 1914. This was followed by *Imperial Germany and the Industrial Revolution* (1915), *An Inquiry into the Nature of Peace and the Terms of Its Perpetuation* (1917), *The Vested Interests and the State of the Industrial Arts* (1919), *The Engineers and the Price System* (1921), *Absentee Ownership and Business Enterprise in Recent Times: The Case of America* (1923). His main argument was logically developed in each of these volumes—namely, that machine industry was overwhelmingly and increasingly productive, and that the problems of machine industry were incidental to the disposal of the product.

The constructive part of Veblen's work was essentially the elaboration of an extended argument showing the effects of machine industry and the industrial revolution. Veblen's interest was in the state of the industrial arts which had got out of hand—a point similar to that urged by Samuel Butler. The destructive part of his work, contrary to general opinion, is slight, and confined to articles and reviews written in the latter period. They were chiefly concerned with contemporary economic theory, being directed as criticism of the classical and neo-

24Series 3, vol. II.
25"An Early Experiment in Trusts," *The Place of Science*, p. 497.
26Vol. XIII (1905), 468–72.
27*Theory of Business Enterprise*, p. 301.

classical economists, and partly as support of the historical school. On this side he was also interested in the effect of the industrial revolution on economic theory. In the articles in the *Quarterly Journal of Economics*, 1899–1900, on "The Preconceptions of Economic Science," he suggested the effects of the handicraft system on the science.[28] He attempted to trace the effects of industrialism on economic theory in the later reviews and articles.[29] In a review of Schmoller's *Grundriss*, he spoke favourably of the work but criticized it for the bias which it evinced against modern tendencies.[30] In 1906–7, he presented a paper on Karl Marx showing the dependence of his work on Hegel.[31] In 1908, by which time he had rounded out his work on consumption and production, he waged his onslaught on static economics by a review of Professor Clark's works.[32] In the next year he reviewed Fisher's *Capital and Income*,[33] and in 1909 his *Rate of Interest*,[34] characterizing them, as would be expected, as most effective work in the sphere of taxonomy. Contemporary economic theorists, from his point of view, were engaged in the business of classifying, and the science under Marshall was in much the same position as botany under Asa Gray.[35] If modern economic theorists were taxonomists, Veblen attempted the study of the embryology, morphology, physiology, ecology, and aetiology of economics. Like Professor MacIver[36] and Professor Unwin, he insisted upon the existence of laws of growth and decay of institutions and associations. His life work has been primarily the study of processes of growth and decay. It is much too early to appraise the validity of this work—certainly he attempted far too wide a field for one individual—but it is the method of approach which must be stressed, and not the final conclusions. It has been unfortunate that the slight character of the work in criticism has been responsible for the violence of modern controversy and that, in consequence, the main constructive work has been forgotten.

The net results are extremely difficult to estimate. Certainly the most virile of the younger economists have been strongly influenced by his work. The intense work on descriptive economics in the United States has

---

[28]*The Place of Science*, pp. 82–179.
[29]"Why Is Economics Not an Evolutionary Science?" *ibid.*, pp. 56–81.
[30]*Ibid.*, pp. 252–78.
[31]"The Socialist Economics of Karl Marx and His Followers," *ibid.*, pp. 409–56.
[32]"Professor Clark's Economics," *ibid.*, pp. 180–230.
[33]*Political Science Quarterly*, XXIII (1908), 112–28.
[34]*Ibid.*, XXIV (1909), 296–303.
[35]*The Place of Science*, pp. 175ff.
[36]R. M. MacIver, *Community* (London, 1917), *The Modern State* (Oxford, 1926).

been partly a result of the suggestiveness of Veblen.[37] He has been largely the cause of a split in American economics, with the classical and the neoclassical students ranged and opposed to the "evolutionists." In England the intelligentsia of the British Labour party have each in turn paid tribute to Veblen's influence.[38] It would probably be unwise to draw comparisons, but his position in the industrial revolution is, to a large extent, similar to that of Adam Smith at the beginning of the revolution. He has been the first to attempt a general stocktaking of general tendencies in a dynamic society saddled with machine industry, just as Adam Smith was the first to present a general stocktaking before machine industry came in. As with Adam Smith, nothing is more conspicuous in Veblen's work than his attention to current events and his interests in dynamics.[39] Only less conspicuous was his attempt to maintain an unbiased approach—a point on which he had criticized Schmoller. His interest in anthropology, his terrific irony, and his fearlessness were weapons protecting him from absorption into the partialities of modern movements. His anxiety has always been to detect trends and to escape their effects. On being charged with bias against existing institutions by a reviewer of the *Theory of the Leisure Class*, he replied characteristically, "If one would avoid paralogistic figures of speech in the analysis of institutions, one must resort to words and concepts that express the thoughts of the men whose habits of thoughts constitute the institutions in question." It was this emphasis on the importance of the scientific point of view which led him to write *The Higher Learning in America or a Memorandum on the Conduct of Universities by Business Men* (New York, 1916), and which encouraged him along with his disciples, especially Wesley C. Mitchell, to found the New School for Social Research in which no degrees were to be given, and the only sustaining motive was the stimulus to research. Like Adam Smith, he is an individualist, and like most individualists in continental countries, in which the industrial revolution made such rapid strides, he is in revolt against mass education and standardization. Veblen has continued with Unwin, MacIver, Fay, and Tawney the work begun by Adam Smith on behalf of the individual and the common man. Veblen's satire, on the other hand, is a product of America, or of the industrial revolution with a continental background. As Veblen has pointed out, England, although the first to feel the effects of the industrial revolution, has never been

---

[37]Paul T. Homan, *Contemporary Economic Thought* (New York, 1928).
[38]Sidney and Beatrice Webb, *The Decay of Capitalist Civilization* (London, 1923).
[39]R. H. Tawney, *The Acquisitive Society* (New York, 1921).

conquered by it. America and the new continental countries have been less fortunate.

In conclusion, his work is a consistent whole, and springs essentially from a post–Civil War environment, when the terrific increasing efficiency of machine industry brought problems of conspicuous consumption and of checking of production. It stands as a monument to the importance of an unbiased approach to economics and as an incentive to research in the current problems of the industrial revolution. In the perennial struggle between standardization and dynamic growth, between static theory and dynamic history, between Frankenstein's monster and Frankenstein, between mechanization and the instinct of workmanship, Veblen has waged a constructive warfare of emancipation against the tendency toward standardized static economics which becomes so dangerous on a continent with ever increasing numbers of students clamouring for textbooks on final economic theory. He attempted to outline the economics of dynamic change and to work out a theory not only of dynamics but of cyclonics.

Any substantial progress in economic theory must come from a closer synthesis between economic history and economic theory. The extensive work being done in economic history in the origin and growth of institutions by the late Professor Unwin, and his school, Professor Fay,[40] Professor Tawney, and Professor Gras, will call for more diligent application in the synthesis with economic theory. It is to be hoped that economic theory will not disappear through neglect or through the deadening influence of specialization, and that Veblen's attempts at synthesis may be revised and steadily improved. The conflict between the economics of a long and highly industrialized country such as England and the economics of the recently industrialized new and borrowing countries[41] will become less severe as the study of cyclonics is worked out and incorporated in a general survey of the effects of the industrial revolution such as Veblen has begun and such as will be worked out and revised by later students.[42]

[40]See especially C. R. Fay, *Great Britain from Adam Smith to the Present Day* (London, 1928).

[41]J. A. Hobson, *Free-Thought in the Social Sciences* (London, 1926).

[42]This paper is directly opposed to the conception that Mr. Veblen's work is to be regarded in the biological sense as that of a sport and is intended to stress the importance of the environmental factor. Having actually lived through one of the economic storms of new countries, he has attempted to work out some of their important characteristics. His contribution to economics is directly in relation to this background.

An Introduction to the Economic History of the Maritimes, Including Newfoundland and New England*

A T a period in the history of the Empire when economic aspects are the subject of so much discussion it is perhaps necessary to apologize for attempting to contribute further to an understanding of the causes of the Empire's growth from that point of view. My excuse follows from a continued interest in the subject arising out of the conclusions of a study on the fur trade. This paper is presented therefore as an analysis of the growth of the fishing industry, and as an attempt to apply conclusions reached in a study of the fur trade, to a study of the relationships between that industry and the expansion of the Empire.

We may begin by noting briefly the outstanding changes of the period prior to 1783. By that date realignments in control over North America had resulted in the practical disappearance of France from the continent, the control by England of the northern portion of the continent formerly controlled by France, and the emergence of an independent power in the southern portion formerly controlled by England. Control of the northern area concerned primarily in the production of fur as a staple, of a portion of the seaboard (especially Newfoundland) concerned primarily in the production of fish, and of the tropical regions in the British West Indies producing sugar, remained within the highly efficient industrial area of Great Britain.

In this paper we are more immediately concerned with the area which has been dominated by the fishing industry and again we may note that at present four separate governments are interested in the fisheries of the North Atlantic: the United States in New England, Canada in the Maritime Provinces, France in the islands of Saint-Pierre and Miquelon, and Newfoundland. It is significant that Newfoundland has continued throughout its history in allegiance to Great Britain and that New England played an active role in the struggle against the control of Great Britain. These developments on the seaboard suggest striking contrasts with development on the continent.

*From the *Canadian Historical Association Report*, 1931, pp. 85–95.

The fur trade, for example, was characterized by centralization of organization whereas the fishing industry has been characterized by decentralization.

A brief survey of the geographic background is essential to an understanding of the general developments of the period. The cod has been of central importance in the development of the fishery. It is one of the most prolific of fishes and a female thirty to forty inches long will produce 3,000,000 eggs. Generally the cod spawns in less than thirty fathoms of water and the eggs hatch on the surface, the most favourable temperature being between 40° and 50° F. To float, the eggs require a fairly high salinity such as is provided in the open sea rather than in the Gulf of St. Lawrence. The newly hatched fry feed chiefly on plankton near the surface of the water for probably two months and then take to the bottom, and the range through later stages of growth varies from twenty to seventy fathoms. As a result of these characteristics the industry is restricted as to areas and seasons. The range of depth restricts the industry to the vast submerged portion of North America known as the continental shelf and to certain portions of the coast line. The coastal plain which, to the south of New York, became important for the production of the staple products of cotton and tobacco was submerged to the northeast of New York within recent times to a depth of about 1,200 feet and became important for the production of fish. The cuestas of this plain have survived as the banks of the fishery, and the high ridges of more resistant rocks have survived in the coast of New England, the peninsula of Nova Scotia, and the island of Newfoundland. The plain extends northeast from the Gulf of Maine to the Grand Banks of Newfoundland. Temperature is scarcely less important than depth and the Labrador Current from the north and the Gulf Stream from the south are important determining factors. The disappearance of ice along the coast of Labrador and Newfoundland in spring is followed by the migration of cod to the north. Fishing may begin during the winter months on the banks of the Gulf of Maine, in April on the Grand Banks, and in June along the coast of Newfoundland. A further geographic factor should be noted from the standpoint of technique. Contact between the Gulf Stream and the Labrador Current is responsible for the greater frequency of fogs on the coast between the State of Maine and Nova Scotia, in the neighbourhood of the Grand Banks, and in the Straits of Belle Isle. These areas are consequently more favourable for the prosecution of the green fishery while areas without fog in Newfoundland and the Gulf are more favourable to the dry fishery.

The technique of the industry is scarcely less important than its geographic background. Dry fishing involved catching the smaller fish near the shore with boats, or the larger fish on the banks with ships, salting the product and finally washing out the salt, and drying the fish on the beach or on specially built staging. Wet fishing involved catching the fish near the shore or on the banks, but chiefly on the banks, salting it and sending it to market. The larger bank fish were less suited to drying. In the main the fish were carried to market, in the case of the bank fishery by the ships which caught the fish, especially if the ships came from Europe, or in the case of the dry fishery by the ship bringing the men and boats from Europe, or by trading ships. In both types the unit of the industry was small and depended ultimately for its efficiency on the individual fisherman. But the bank fishery required large ships whereas the dry fishery on shore was prosecuted by small boats. Since the ship was the largest technical unit and the initiative of the individual fisherman was of paramount importance large central organizations, such as characterized the fur trade, were absent. As a result the history of the fishery was characterized by slow and gradual movements in which the underlying factors included the relative efficiency of fishing areas, especially in relation to nearness to the fishing grounds, technique, and markets. Moreover, the supplies of fish were practically inexhaustible. The ultimate developments were the result of the continuous and powerful operation of economic forces and were not subject to the sharp changes which characterized the fur trade.

With this brief survey of the geographical background and of the technique of the fishery we may attempt a survey of the outstanding characteristics of the history of the fishery. The first century in the history of the contact between the New and the Old World witnessed far-reaching changes of fundamental importance to the fishery. The French fishery became relatively important early in the century and was carried on by ships from the channel and Bay of Biscay ports to the north in the neighbourhood of the Straits of Belle Isle and to the south of Newfoundland and probably in the gulf. Apparently about 1540 the bank fishery was added. The Portuguese prosecuted the fishery to the south of Newfoundland throughout the period. The Spanish fishery increased rapidly after about 1545 but declined rapidly toward the end of the century. It is significant that these countries were primarily concerned with the development of wet fishing and with supplying the home market. They developed the fishery in the neighbourhood of the banks and in areas less suitable to dry fishing. Located in more southerly regions they had access to cheaper supplies of salt which was obtained by evaporation from the ocean and as continental countries they sent out ships from a relatively large number of scattered ports and brought back the larger fish for an important home market.

Toward the end of the century the rise in prices in Spain which followed the influx of treasure led to the development of an import trade in fish and to a decline of the Spanish fishery. Consequently countries formerly engaged in producing for the home market began to produce dry fish for the Spanish market. The technique of fishing changed from a direct importation of salt green fish to be dried at home for the home market to the drying of fish in the producing area to be exported direct to Spain. The rise in importance of dry fishing in the New World corresponded closely to the decline of the Spanish fishery in Newfoundland and the opening of the Spanish market. French ports, especially Saint-Jean-de-Luz and La Rochelle, became interested to an increasing extent in the Spanish market. England suddenly found that a disadvantage in the lack of a cheap supply of salt in green fishing became very much less serious because of the smaller demands for salt in dry fishing. Ports in the west country dried the smaller cod of the Newfoundland coast, sent the finished product to Spain, and returned to England with iron, specie, and Spanish goods. The fishery began its long history as a nursery for seamen, a market for English manufactured products, especially woollen goods, and a means of securing specie from Spain.

By the end of the century the west country ports had become established in the Avalon Peninsula in Newfoundland and French ships had penetrated to the areas of the gulf, expecially the Gaspé Peninsula, suitable for the production of dry fish. In developing the dry fishery France came in contact with the resources of the interior and after 1600 the fur trade[1] was added to the fishing industry. The revolution which followed the influx of treasure into Spain ended with the development of trade in the dry fishery and with the entrenchment

[1]For the relationship between dry fishing and the fur trade, see H. P. Biggar, *Early Trading Companies of New France* (Toronto, 1901). It is interesting to note that the northern ports were interested primarily in the green fishery and the Paris market, and that the capital acquired through this fishery was adequate to support the dry fishery to Gaspé and Spain, and in turn the fur trade. The early fur trading companies originated in Rouen, Dieppe, and northern ports and included the southern ports after strong protest had been made. Indeed the early difficulties of the fur trade followed from the widespread prosecution of the fishery by the ports of France. The fur trade developed along its own lines only after the amalgamations had been achieved by Champlain. The decentralized organization of the fishery was adapted with difficulty to the centralized organization of the fur trade.

of England in Newfoundland, and the penetration of the French into the gulf and the continent. A final result followed with the expansion of the English fishery to the shores of New England early in the seventeenth century.

The outstanding characteristics of the fisheries of France and of England were evident in the developments of the sixteenth century. The French fishery was essentially the result of the continental character of France by which a large number of ports scattered along the coast were engaged in producing for a large home market. The bank fishery tended as a result to predominate and the dry fishery was added as a minor branch. Protestant England on the other hand was an island with a relatively small and declining market for fish and trade in fish was fundamental to the expansion of the British fishery. The dry fishery consequently was of paramount importance. Dependence on trade tended to emphasize geographic advantages of distance and the west country assumed a key position in the development of the fishery on the coast of the Avalon Peninsula in Newfoundland. Whereas ships from the numerous scattered ports of France carried on the fishery over a wide territory in the New World the ships of the narrow portion of England in the west country concentrated on a small portion of Newfoundland. With the dry fishery and trade the west country became rooted to the coast line of Newfoundland. The Avalon Peninsula became in some sense a cornerstone of the British Empire from the standpoint of territory, trade, shipping, seamen, industry, agriculture, and finances. England with limited resources especially in salt concentrated on dry fishing for foreign trade in a restricted area of Newfoundland nearest to herself, whereas France with diverse resources and cheap supplies of salt prosecuted the fishery over a wide area with special emphasis on the home market. The self-sufficiency of a continental area contrasted strikingly with the essential demands for trade of an island area. The characteristics of France as a self-sufficient area pointed out by Montchretien in 1615 and elaborated by Vidal de la Blache[2] were of fundamental importance to her position as an empire on the Atlantic. A large land area with diversity of resources dependent on wide ranges of climate and other geographical factors tended toward self-sufficiency in contrast with a relatively small island with scarcity of raw material, an inadequate home market, and essential dependence on trade.

[2]Antoyne de Montchretien, *Traité de l'économie politique dédié en 1615 au Roy et à la Royne Mère du Roy*, par Th. Funck-Bretano (Paris, 1889); Vidal de la Blache, et L. Gallois, *Géographie universelle*, vol. VI, part 1, *Figure et personalité de la France* (Paris, 1927–48).

The second century in the history of the English fishery was marked by a sharp bifurcation in New England and Newfoundland. The history of Newfoundland stood in sharp contrast to that of New England. The short fishing season in Newfoundland and the limitations of the area from the standpoint of agriculture and lumber were factors militating against settlement. Companies for the establishment of colonies from England failed as decisively in the first half of the seventeenth century as in the early years of the sixteenth. Throughout the century settlement increased slightly and the fishery was conducted by fishing ships which returned annually with their complement of fishermen to the west country. The Act of 10 and 11 Wm. III, c. 25, "An act to encourage the trade of Newfoundland," passed in 1699, outlined and sanctioned the position of the fishing ships from the west country in Newfoundland.

Although the century was characterized by control over the Newfoundland fishery from England, certain suggestive tendencies of divergence were in evidence. In spite of legislation dominated by the west country, settlement had increased. Fishing ships arrived with a larger number of men for the conduct of the fishery than were necessary for the handling of the ship. In contrast to the fur trade ships tended to come out light and to return loaded with dry fish, and whereas the fur trade attempted to restrict outward bound cargo and increase homeward bound cargo the fishing industry attempted to increase outward bound cargo to balance homeward bound cargo. In spite of the cost of providing supplies to carry residents over the winter in Newfoundland the tendency toward settlement was shown in the rise of the byeboatkeeper. With the expansion of the fishery and the cutting off of timber suitable for building stages and flakes, men were left over the winter to watch the increasingly valuable property. The importance of individual initiative in the fishery led to the emergence of the byeboatkeeper as a separate owner for whom ships brought out labourers as passengers. Even the legislation of 1699 was forced to recognize his position.

The inevitable tendencies of the fishery which became evident in Newfoundland were of overwhelming importance in New England, and indeed through New England contributed to further changes in Newfoundland. The marked migration to New England was stimulated by fishing vessels anxious to take out a cargo of colonists. The effects of the fishery on settlement in New England in the first half of the sixteenth century were similar to the effects of the lumber industry on settlement in Canada after 1820 and in striking contrast to the effects of the fur trade in discouraging settlement. In relation to the imports of bulk raw materials settlers provided an excellent return cargo. The striking contrast between New England and Newfoundland was a result of the abundance of supplies characteristic of a more southerly location. Agriculture, lumbering, and shipbuilding flourished in New England in response to the demands of the fishery. The importance of the control of the Newfoundland fishery in the west country was paralleled in the importance of direct control in New England. Industry, trade, a nursery for seamen, a means of acquiring specie were as important to New England as to England. The possession of diversified resources led to a profoundly different type of development from that which characterized Newfoundland. Indeed, the growth of New England contributed to the establishment of settlement in Newfoundland. Provisions and supplies were sold in Newfoundland in return for bills of exchange, and Newfoundland became a channel by which fishermen migrated from England to New England. The results were described by Sir Josiah Child in his *A New Discourse on Trade*, written in 1665, with several editions to 1694:

Certainly it is the interest of England to discountenance and abate the number of Planters at Newfoundland for if they should increase it will happen to us as it hath to the fishery of New England which many years since was managed by English ships from the Western ports, but as plantations there increased fell to the sole employment of the people settled there and nothing of the trade is left the poor old Englishmen but the liberty of carrying now and then by courtesie or purchase a ship-loading of fish to Bilbao when their own New England ships are better employed or not at leisure to do it. New England is the most prejudicial to this kingdom because of all the American plantations His Majesty has none so apt for building of shipping as New England, none comparably so qualified for the breeding of seamen not only by reason of the natural industry of that people but principally by reason of their cod and mackerel fisheries and in my poor opinion there is nothing more prejudicial and in prospect more dangerous to any mother country than the increase of shipping in her colonies, plantations or provinces. . . . All our American plantations except that of New England produce commodities of different natures from those of this kingdom as sugar, tobacco, cocoa, wool, ginger, sundry sorts of dyeing woods, etc. Whereas New England produces generally the same we have here viz., corn and cattle, some quantity of fish they do likewise kill, but that is taken and saved altogether by their own inhabitants, which prejudices our Newfoundland fish. . . . the other commodities we have from them are some few great masts, furs, and train oil, of which the yearly value amounts to very little, the much greater value of returns from them being made in sugar, cotton, wool, tobacco and such like commodities which they first receive from some other of His Majesty's plantations, in barter for dry codfish, salt mackerel, beef, pork, bread, beer, flower, peas, etc., which they supply Barbadoes, Jamaica, etc., with, to the diminution of the vent of those commodities from this kingdom; the great experience of which in our own West India plantations would soon be found in the advantage of the value of our lands in England, were it not for the vast and almost incredible supplies those colonies have from New England. The people of New England, by virtue of their primitive charters being not so strictly tied to the observation of the laws of this kingdom do sometimes assume the liberty of trading, contrary to the Act of Navigation by reason of which many of our American commodities especially tobacco and sugar are transported in New English shipping directly into Spain and other foreign countries without being landed in England or paying any duty to His Majesty, which is not only a loss to the King and a prejudice to the navigation of old England; but also a total exclusion of the old English merchant from the vent of those commodities in those ports where the New English vessels trade, because there being no custom paid on those commodities in New England and a great custom paid upon them in Old England it must necessarily follow that the New English merchant will be able to afford his commodity much cheaper at the market than the old English merchant; and those that can sell cheapest will infallibly engross the whole trade sooner or later. . . .—of ten men that issue from us to New England and Ireland what we send to or receive from them does not employ one man in England.

But Child was an ancestor in direct line of Adam Smith:

. . . to do right to that most industrious colony, I must confess, that though we loose by their unlimited trade with our foreign plantations, yet we are very great gainers by their direct trade to and from Old England. Our yearly exportations of English manufactures, malt, and other goods from home thither amounting in my opinion to ten times the value of what is imported from them—and therefore whenever a reformation of our corresponding in trade with that people shall be thought on, it will in my poor judgment require great tenderness and very serious circumspection.

Such "great tenderness and very serious circumspection" were not at hand.

It is unnecessary to emphasize to historians, certainly to economic historians, the difficulties of deciding upon any precise date at which a given period ends or begins and the century mark can only be suggested for purposes of convenience. The constitutional historian or the military historian may perhaps choose the dates of treaties, acts, and battles as precise measuring points but the economic historian is interested rather in the slow accumulation of forces which gather headway long before they have been crystallized in events which are of special interest to the constitutional historian. The cumulation of forces responsible for the important developments in the eighteenth century has its roots deep in the seventeenth and in the sixteenth centuries.

Before the end of the seventeenth century the New England fishery had expanded to the outlying banks and to the shores of Nova Scotia. With year-round open ports, earlier fishing, and larger fish, New England had expanded her production and her markets. The advantage of a base in close proximity to the fishing grounds and the possibility of using small fishing vessels provided New England with an elasticity and a flexibility in her fishery which was impossible for France or for England. Consequently pressure both in markets and in the fishing grounds from Newfoundland in the north and New England in the south forced the French in the Treaty of Utrecht to retreat in Newfoundland and Nova Scotia to Cape Breton. Nova Scotia became what Mr. Brebner has happily called "an outpost of New England." The importance of the bank fishery for the French, as Denys found to his cost, proved a serious check to the establishment of settlement.

The expansion of the New England fishery and in turn of the shipbuilding industry and trade was accompanied by an extension to the south as well as to the north. Trade began with the southern colonies and in their staples, and with the British West Indies, which started in the second half of the seventeenth century to produce sugar as a staple product. With the importation of slaves from Africa, an additional market was opened for dried cod, especially the poorer grades, and for agricultural products and lumber and, in the transport of these products, for ships. New England had developed an important trading nucleus with characteristics similar to those of England and with the same advantage of cheap, year-round ocean transport. In certain markets such as the West Indies and indeed in Newfoundland she had the advantage of location over England.

The advantages of these two areas in the growth of shipbuilding, industry, and trade were basic considerations behind the increasing competition which became an outstanding feature of the eighteenth century. The earlier advantage of England in more advanced industrial technique became steadily less important in competition with New England. The Navigation Acts formulated in the latter part of the sixteenth century contributed to the expansion of New England and in turn were outgrown. The political structure of the old Empire hardened and became inadequate to meet the demands of a slowly shifting economic structure. The signs of strain became evident in the West Indies. Pitman in his able work, *The Development of the British West Indies 1700–1763* (New Haven, 1917), has pointed out the importance of the increasing influence of the West Indies planters in Great Britain and the clash which arose between the interests of the planters and of the North American colonies in the Molasses Act of 1733. And in turn he has suggested forcibly the difficulty of confining an expanding producing area such as a New England to a small group of islands for the marketing of its products or for the purchasing of its returns. The results were not immediately decisive but led to an increase in smuggling and disrespect for political control.

The expansion of New England shipping and trade to the south which contributed to the difficulties of the old Empire was accompanied by an expansion to the north which led eventually to the disappearance of the French Empire in North America. As in the interior of North America the French fur trade was being pinched out to the north from Hudson Bay and to the south from the British colonies, so in the fishing areas the French fishery was faced with competition from Newfoundland in the north and New England in the south. The expansion of New England in the fishery was hastened by the invention of more efficient vessels, such as the schooner about 1713, and the retreat of the French from Nova Scotia. The activity of New England in the capture of Louisburg[3] in 1745 was an indication of pressure from that direction and the inevitable disappearance of France followed in 1763. The disappearance of France was followed with equal inevitability by increasing competition between England and New England. The political structure became more rigid and the Molasses Act was followed by the Sugar Act of 1764, the Quebec Act of 1774, and Palliser's Act of 1775. The result was the emergence of the colonies as an independent unit.

The realignment of boundaries in 1783 especially in the Maritimes is a source of continual interest. The marginal ground of Nova Scotia ceased to be an outpost of New England and we may hope that Mr. Brebner will at some time give us a complementary history of Nova Scotia as an outpost of England. The developments in the period after 1713 which characterized the New England fishery at Canso and the French fishery in Cape Breton are suggestive. It is significant that the New England fishery proved unable to establish itself successfully in the face of Louisburg competition. The evidence suggests strikingly that New England had not solved the problem of combining small schooners with a boat fishery. Consequently New England schooners were engaged on the banks near Canso but the dried fish was inferior to that produced by the adjacent boat fishery at Louisburg and was not satisfactory for the high-priced Spanish market. New England had

[3]See J. S. McLennan, *Louisbourg from Its Foundation to Its Fall* (London, 1918), *passim.*

in some sense reached a geographic limit with her specialized technique for the production of the best grades of fish. The geographic limitations of the New England fishery in view of the requirement that for the greatest efficiency the fishery be conducted from the land nearest the fishing grounds, led to the establishment of Nova Scotia as a separate unit. New England tended to become more effective in trade to Cape Breton and to Newfoundland than in the fishery.

Aside from the general trends already described which led to the disappearance of the French the fishery at Louisburg had interesting characteristics. The attempt to establish a sedentary fishery contrasted sharply with the attempt to check a sedentary fishery in Newfoundland. The fishing ship fishery, especially from Saint-Jean-de-Luz and the Biscay ports, continued to demonstrate its efficiency, because the lack of supplies, other than those obtained chiefly by smuggling from the English colonies including Acadia, reduced the boat fishery dependent on those areas to an uncertain existence. The boat fishery continued to increase in Newfoundland because of larger supplies of provisions obtained from New England. France, having begun to retreat from the dry fishery and to concentrate on the bank fishery, found it impossible to return to Cape Breton and Louisburg. The attempts to increase settlement in Louisburg failed in the face of the efficiency of fishing ships from France while the attempts to check settlement in Newfoundland failed in the face of the increasing efficiency of the boat fishery. The contrast between France as a self-sufficient unit dependent on the bank fishery and the home market and England as a trading unit dependent on the dry fishery and the foreign market becomes increasingly sharp throughout the period.

By the end of the eighteenth century the ultimate effects of the fishing industry had been worked out as seen in the American Revolution, in the settlement of the Maritime Provinces, and in the expansion of settlement in Newfoundland. The Revolution practically brought the fishing ship fishery in Newfoundland to an end and in turn was responsible for the marked growth of settlement. Newfoundland saw the beginning of the end of a policy described by William Knox in 1793: "The island of Newfoundland had been considered in all former times, as a great English ship moored near the Banks during the fishing season for the convenience of English fishermen. The governor was considered as the ships captain, and all those who were concerned in the fishery business as his crew, and subject to naval discipline while there, and expected to return to England when the season was over." The Judicature Act was passed in 1791 and eventually a permanent court was established in 1809 (49 Geo. III, c. 27). The position of private property was steadily strengthened (54 Geo. III, c. 45, 1811).

Throughout the whole area the outstanding characteristic of technique proved of first importance. The fishery was conducted with greatest efficiency in the area nearest the fishing grounds. The period is marked by a gradual drift in which New England assumed independence rapidly and Newfoundland very much more slowly. The importance of the individual fisherman was emphasized throughout. Coke's argument early in the development of the New England fishery regarding the monopoly of Sir Fernando Gorges was typical of the history of dry fishing: "Your patent contains many particulars contrary to law and the liberty of the subject; it is a monopoly and the ends of private gain are concealed under colour of planting a colony; to prevent our fishermen from visiting the sea coast for fishing is to make a monopoly upon the seas which are wont to be free; if you alone are to pack and dry fish you attempt a monopoly of the wind and sun." It is significant that Faneuil Hall, the cradle of American liberty, was built from the profits of a successful merchant in the fishing industry. The scattered character of the fishing grounds, the importance of individual initiative, the relatively short seasons, and dependence on a foreign market were factors leading to the growth of a strong sense of local importance in scattered communities. Metropolitan centres grew up with difficulty in fishing areas and were subject to continual competition by cheap water transportation from other centres. It was not an accident that the strong sense of economic and political independence led to the growth and establishment of representative institutions in New England and in turn, as Livingston and Martin have pointed out,[4] to the evolution of responsible government in Nova Scotia. But if the trend toward responsible government which contributed to the breaking up of the old Empire in New England and to the establishment of the new Empire through Nova Scotia characterized those areas, the weakness in the growth of metropolitan centres contributed to the control of the west country in England over Newfoundland and to the long and painful character of Newfoundland's evolution. It is important to emphasize these characteristics of the Maritimes to understand their position in Confederation and their attitude toward central Canada which has in its turn emerged from

[4]Chester Martin, *Empire and Commonwealth: Studies in Governance and Self-Government in Canada* (Oxford, 1929), *passim*; W. R. Livingston, *Responsible Government in Nova Scotia: A Study of the Constitutional Beginnings of the British Commonwealth* (Iowa City, 1930), *passim*.

a fundamentally different background. The tendency toward centralization in continental Canada is in sharp contrast with the tendency toward decentralization in the Maritimes. It is unnecessary to refer to the part which individuals from the Maritimes have played as a result of their outlook in leavening the lump at the centre.

Throughout this paper an attempt has been made to emphasize the continuous and powerful effects of the underlying technique of industry on the economic, social, and political activities of the communities concerned. It has been assumed that the pull has been outwards from the land and that the frontier of New England history was toward the sea and not, as Turner has suggested, toward the land.[5] The Appalachians have been given an unnecessarily important position as a barrier to New England expansion to the interior. The fishing industry provided a direct outward pull to the activities of the Maritimes and it is significant that exploration to the interior of Canada became important only at the end of a century and that the interior of Newfoundland[6] is still largely an unknown land. An incidental result of this tendency was shown in the hostilities with the native populations. The bitter wars of New England and the extermination of the Beothic in Newfoundland contrasted strikingly with the fur trade and its dependence on friendly relations with the Indians. The activities of the Maritimes area were concerned with the coast and the submerged continental shelf and not with the interior.

The fishing industry especially as related to the production of dried cod and in turn to trade was of fundamental importance to the development of diverse activities. As a food product dried cod was in constant demand and as a product of the sea the supply was continuous. It was consumed chiefly in non-agricultural tropical areas and its production involved ships, sailors, a highly industrialized com-

[5]See F. J. Turner, *The Frontier in American History* (New York, 1921), esp. chap. II.
[6]"Horses cannot go far in because there is no grass except on a few of the more slow-moving rivers, and men can only carry on their backs supplies for a short journey. But the principal reason, at least it seems so to me, is that the Newfoundlander being purely a fisherman, and delighting only in the acquisition of the harvest of the sea, knows and cares little about possible farm lands. Moreover he has always been unable to build light draught canoes of tough wood, because no wood capable of withstanding the rocks of the rivers is to be found in the island. He is also clumsy in the rivers, and unable to use a pole like the Indians. Perhaps he gets a few miles up an easy river in his punt, but on meeting with difficulties, such as the breaking of his soft wood boat, readily gives up the task. He has any amount of pluck but no skill on the rivers. Though all at home at sea, he is all at sea at home." J. G. Millais, *Newfoundland and Its Untrodden Ways* (London, 1907), pp. 228–9.

munity, an agricultural community, and trade with tropical areas. The old captain in Sarah Orne Jewett's *The Country of the Pointed Firs* emphasized the importance of agricultural products to a fishing community: "It ought to read in the Bible 'Man cannot live by fish alone' if they'd told the truth of things; t'aint bread that wears the worst on you." Through the fishery, trade between tropical and north temperate countries or between areas with an absolute advantage in production was stimulated. Specie was added to the temptation of the advantages provided by sugar and salt. In addition to building up a fleet for the carrying trade as well as for the support of the navy and to serving as a nursery for seamen it provided specie by which England and New England were able to build a money economy and a highly integrated trading and industrial community. Capitalizing the advantages of cheap water transport the relatively small unit of the fishing or the trading ship was a powerful driving force for trade. Ships managed by individuals were continuously searching for cargo and seeking out new commodities and channels of trade. Cod was the basis for a strong and flexible economy which demanded and provided a wealth of individual initiative.

Its social effects may be suggested in the following monologue of our sea captain in his lament over its disappearance.

I see a change for the worse even in our own town here; full of loafers now, small and poor as it is who once would have followed the sea, every lazy soul of them. There is no occupation so fit for just that class o' men who never get beyond the fo'cas'le. I view it, in addition, that a community narrows down and grows dreadful ignorant when it is shut up to its own affairs, and gets no knowledge of the outside world except from a cheap, unprincipled newspaper. In the old days a good part o' the best men here knew a hundred ports and something of the way folks lived in them. They saw the world for themselves, and like 's not their wives and children saw it with them. They may not have had the best of knowledge to carry with 'em sight-seein' but they were some acquainted with foreign lands an' their laws, an' could see outside the battle for town clerk here in Dunnet; they got some sense of proportion. Yes, they lived more dignified, and their houses were better within and without. Shipping's a terrible loss to this part o' New England from a social point o' view ma'am. . . . No there's nothing to take the place of shipping in a place like ours. These bicycles offend me dreadfully; they don't afford no real opportunities of experience such as a man gained on a voyage. No: when folks left home in the old days they left it to some purpose, and when they got home they stayed there and had some pride in it. There's no large-minded way of thinking now; the worst have got to be best and rule everything.

In the emphasis on the type of economy built up in relation to the fishery and its independent growth we are led to consider the position of the Maritimes in the British Empire after the main alignments had been reached. The new Empire included on the Atlantic two staple-producing areas, Newfoundland and the British West Indies, producing respectively cod and sugar. After some debate as to whether an addition should be made in the production of sugar by taking Gaudaloupe it was finally determined that Canada, with a new commodity, fur, should be taken. The experience of the old Empire in relation to Newfoundland and the British West Indies is suggestive. In Newfoundland the control of the west country was of paramount importance in the development of the fishery, and legislation was guided in the interests of such towns of the west country as Dartmouth and Poole.[7] Such control was possible because of the dependence of Newfoundland on one staple commodity. In the West Indies Pitman has shown again that the planters were able to obtain similar legislation in their favour. In the fur trade similar direct relationships developed with astonishing rapidity. The mercantile interests concerned with the staples had sufficient influence to mould legislation in their favour. The political structure was not sufficiently elastic to meet the demands of a rapidly expanding and competing economic organization such as was involved in New England. Legislation concerned with the conservation of the staple industries grew increasingly important with the expansion of communities becoming less dependent on staples. In a sense vested interests wrecked the old Empire and saved the new. The dominant forces, however, go much deeper. Great Britain as an island with a relatively small population and low consuming power became efficient in the handling of staples for trade as well as for home consumption. Fish was sold to a large extent in Spain, Portugal, and the Mediterranean, fur and sugar were re-exported to the continent. Lumber was given a preference, chiefly for the home market. The weakness of areas depending on a staple necessitated an efficient marketing system and supplies of capital from the consuming and trading areas. Concentration on staples assumed consumption of manufactured products imported from more efficient producing regions. The production and export of staples assumed efficient water transportation. The relation between the production of staples in outlying areas and the political control at the centre exercised by mercantile interests directly concerned with trade in staples was an important factor in the period after the American Revolution, but Great Britain became to an increasing extent an industrial as well as a trading area,

[7]See D. W. Prowse, A *History of Newfoundland* (London, 1895).

especially with the development of railways, and the demand for cheaper raw materials became an increasingly powerful factor. Adam Smith wrote: "As it is the power of exchanging that gives occasion to the division of labour, so the extent of this division must always be limited by the extent of that power, or in other words, by the extent of the market."[8] Capital began to pour out in increasing quantities to new areas after the Napoleonic wars to provide new supplies of raw material and new demands for manufactured goods. The strongly rooted individualism which led, through New England, to the break-up of the old Empire, and which contributed to the French Revolution, finally provoked the passage of the reform bills in England and the growth of responsible government. The reform bills cleared the way for the destruction of privileges enjoyed by staple-producing areas in the political structure and even the protests of the lumber interests were of little avail in the steady revision which led to the emergence of free trade and the disappearance of the Navigation Acts.

The influence of the sea and its industries has declined with the growing importance of land and the railways. The staple producing areas have continued and increased in strength with their dependence on railways, to mention only the case of wheat in Canada. It remains to be seen whether the new Empire will be endangered by the inelasticity of economic and political structure created by a new and more powerful set of vested interests or whether the elasticity and flexibility of the political and economic structure which has been an important contribution of the fishing industry will prevail.

[8]L. H. Jenks, *The Migration of British Capital to 1875* (New York, 1927), chap. II.

The Rise and Fall of the Spanish Fishery in Newfoundland*

THIS paper is intended to throw further light on the history of the Spanish fishery especially in the sixteenth century and in relation to the fisheries and economic development of other countries. It is based largely on papers from the Coleccion Vargas Ponce, kindly loaned to me by Dr. H. P. Biggar. These papers are confined to the period from 1549 to 1652 and are concerned to a large extent with the fishery of San Sebastian and the province of Guipuzcoa. As a border province of Spain it fortunately illustrates in most striking fashion the effects of competition, especially from the border province of the lower Pyrenees in France, the sixteenth-century Labourd (Labort), and its principal town Saint-Jean-de-Luz. It is hoped that by a consideration of the details of the fishery during this period and for this area, suggestions as to the general trend of the Spanish fishery may be indicated. This paper includes, in the first part, a general survey of the fishery, chiefly contained in the documents, and, in the second part, an analysis of the changes in the fishery.

Abundant evidence exists to show the development of the French and the Portuguese fishery in Newfoundland in the first half of the sixteenth century. Bayonne in France was apparently sending out fishing ships as early as 1520. There is almost no evidence, however, to show an active interest in the fisheries on the part of Spain until at least 1540. Prowse[1] had cited extracts from C. F. Duro, *Arca de noé*, which will bear repeating. The first is a "Memorial from the son of Matias de Echevete saying that he was the first Spaniard who went to the Newfoundland fishery in a French vessel 1545, and afterwards made 28 voyages up to 1599 being the founder of the Basque fishery there." From the records of San Sebastian, near the French boundary, he cites:

In 1561 a dispute arose about the payment to the church of two per cent on the products of the Newfoundland fishery, at which time witnesses were

*From *Transactions of the Royal Society of Canada*, third series, vol. XXV (1931) Section II, 51–70.
[1]D. W. Prowse, *A History of Newfoundland* (London, 1895), p. 44; also Vera Lee Brown, "Spanish Claims to a Share in the Newfoundland Fisheries in the Eighteenth Century," *Canadian Historical Association Report*, 1925, pp. 66–7.

asked if they knew if the Newfoundland fishery had been followed for only a few years. Amongst the declarants were some old men of seventy, who all agreed that this fishery was not more than from seventeen to twenty years established before then. That is to say that they frequented Newfoundland from 1541 to 1545, and on account of the very much gain in these voyages they had abandoned their fishery in Flanders, England and other places. Some of the witnesses said that the fishery of Newfoundland had been discovered since the year 1526 and that the Guipuscoans carried it on since 1540.

It is probable that the fishery had developed at a late date[2] and had only become important enough by 1561 to warrant the more immediate interest of the church in tithes.

The relatively late development of the Spanish fishery probably placed it under a handicap in its competition with rival fisheries. A shift from the Irish fishery[3] to the Newfoundland fishery probably meant the application of similar technique. The abundance of salt made it possible for Spain to engage in the more inefficient type of wet fishing. Parkhurst reported in 1578 regarding the Spanish "who make all wet and do drie it when they come home." Large cargoes of salt were taken out, the fish taken, probably on the banks, and salted, and the return voyage made with the green fish to be dried on arrival at the home port. This was necessarily an inefficient type of fishing and produced a relatively inferior product. Nevertheless this fishery expanded rapidly in the second half of the century and the product was favoured in the home market. It becomes the task of this paper to trace the factors responsible for its rise and decline.

On April 21, 1553,[4] an order was issued prohibiting any vessel from leaving Guipuzcoa without a special licence from Don Luis Carvajal, Captain-General of the fleet. On June 3[5] a petition was presented by the council of Vasarte, urging that the season was too far advanced to make it possible for the fishing vessels to wait to proceed under the protection of the Captain-General and that more satisfactory results could be obtained by proceeding in groups of two and three. The vessels were able to earn 200,000 ducats in the fishery and further delay was regarded as serious. A second petition[6] in the same month

---

[2]In 1549 the master of a vessel of Echaviz provisioned for Newfoundland asked for a chalice with which to celebrate mass. leg. iii, no. 2.

[3]See Prowse, p. 44.

[4]See V. L. Brown, p. 77. Prowse estimates 200 ships and 6,000 men in 1553.

[5]Minuto entre los documentos de la junta particular de Tasarte de este año en el archivo de Tolosa.

[6]Minuta de las cartas de favor que a los magnates y paysanos escribio la Provincia de Guipuzcoa despues de un junta de Vasarte para anular las dos cedulas sobre navios a Terranova de que habla el registro deste año. En el archivo de Tolosa entre los documentos de la junta particular de Vasarte.

continued by stating that Newfoundland was the only region from which a supply of fish could be obtained. The result of these petitions was a royal cedula of July 15, 1553, reversing the earlier order.

The first combat in a long struggle between the royal naval authorities and the fishery was decided in favour of the province. A decree of April 21, 1557, forbade the fishing fleet going to Newfoundland without being armed. As a result of a plea from Biscay, Guipuzcoa, and the four coast towns that this decree would prevent them from going and that since they had prepared for the voyage great loss would follow, the decree was revoked (July 15, 1557, Valladolid) and people in the Basque country were allowed to go to Newfoundland. The Spanish fleet was employed, however, in the early period in support of the fishery as well as in opposition to it and especially in its attacks on the French. In 1555(?) for example Don Luis[7] had been successful in taking a French prize of 130 tons loaded with cod. It was reported that from one fleet of forty-two ships from Newfoundland, four French ships of a value of 8,000 ducats had been captured. From another eight ships, four were captured; of five ships from Saint-Jean-de-Luz two were taken worth 3,000 ducats. Two vessels captured seven ships from Newfoundland worth 12,000 ducats, another vessel captured six ships with cod worth 12,000 ducats, and still another took three small ships valued at 5,000 ducats. In fifteen days prizes valued at 47,000 ducats had been captured.

By 1564[8] peace had been restored and apparently plans were inaugurated for the development of trade between French and Spanish vessels at Placentia in Newfoundland. Reference is made in a note dated Biarritz, February 10, 1564, to letters which had passed between Saint-Jean-de-Luz, Cape Breton, and Biarritz regarding trade especially in salt to be supplied from Spain. Apparently no agreement was reached, as a letter dated Cape Breton, February 8, 1564, stated that an attempt had been made to bring together the ships of that locality but of sixteen ships only two had reported, the remainder having left for Newfoundland. The difficulties of arranging for co-operation were seriously enhanced by a decree dated August 5, 1567, prohibiting French, English, Scotch, Portuguese, or Levantine (from Murcia) ships from carrying merchandise or supplies outside of the kingdom or engaging in coastal trade with a penalty of confiscation of ships and cargo.

[7]Archivo general de Indias.

[8]Cartas a la ciudad por villas de Cabreton, San Juan de Luz, y Bearris del año de 1564 sobre el tratamiento que havian de tenor los vecinos de aquellos pueblos, y los nuestros empleados en las pesquerias del Puerto de Plasencia y Terranoba. Originales en el archivo de S. Sebastian.

It is probable that the Spanish fishery reached its peak in the decade from 1570[9] to 1580. The fishing and whaling fleets had become important additions to the industries of the ports of the Spanish Basques. In 1574 the ships were described as leaving the coast for Newfoundland about the end of March or the beginning of April and returning the middle of September and October.[10] The whale fishermen left about the middle of June and returned in December or the beginning of January. Anthony Parkhurst in 1578 reported "above 100 saile of Spaniards that come to take Cod—besides 20 or 30 more that come from Biskaie to kill whale for traine.[11] These be better appoynted for shipping and furniture of munition than any nation saving the Englishmen." They were described as coming from most parts of Spain.[12]

But signs of difficulty were in evidence. In 1577 San Sebastian presented strong protests[13] against the decree of August 5, 1567. It was held that foreigners prohibited from taking cargo at San Sebastian went to the neighbouring French port of Saint-Jean-de-Luz to unload their cargoes, and that small Spanish vessels went to that port for goods. The results were serious as this change tended to break down the whole position of the port of San Sebastian in relation to its trade with the hinterland as well as with its external markets. The province of Guipuzcoa consisted chiefly of sterile land which gave little possibility of producing foodstuffs adequate to the growth of a port. Bread and provisions could be produced locally to support the population for about two months. Consequently San Sebastian was particularly dependent on trade and the shift of foreign vessels to Saint-Jean-de-Luz was a direct and serious blow. The merchandise of the interior, and especially the important commodity wool from Aragon and Navarra, was sent to Saint-Jean-de-Luz rather than San Sebastian, as the province of Guipuzcoa was subject to a royal tax on wool of one ducat for each sack. The shifting of internal trade to Saint-Jean-de-Luz provided foreign ships with a return cargo. The trade in provisions for the supply of foreign ships as well as for local needs was shifted to Saint-Jean-de-Luz. As a result of the shortage of provisions prices

---

[9]In 1570 a ship from Vizente de Eschave was lost near a harbour in Newfoundland. The crew were from Pasages and Lego, and were brought back by another Spanish ship.

[10]Coleccion Navarette, tome 28, no. 22.

[11]Prowse has reference to the loss of 540 men in the Basque whaling fleet through being frozen in on the Labrador in 1577.

[12]R. Hakluyt, *The Principal Navigations* (Glasgow, 1904), extra series, VIII, 9.

[13]Coleccion Vargas Ponce, V, no. 8.

were high which with the decline of a market for exports led to a steady drain of specie. Goods including wheat and provisions were sold, but only in return for money. The iron foundries declined more particularly as wars with England had been directly effective in cutting off demand. The effects were cumulative. Shipbuilding in Spain declined with trade in San Sebastian and increased in France with trade in French ports. Moreover, the French in retaliation forbade Spanish ships to load in their harbours and consequently injured Spanish shipping and trade. The cost of shipbuilding was increased with the decline of trade; and cordage, tar, rigging, elm, and supplies for boatbuilding imported from foreigners had increased in cost by one-third. From the standpoint of the government it was pointed out that the royal taxes on wool had declined, provisions for the fleet had increased in price, and ships and seamen were on the decline.

San Sebastian occupied a position of paramount importance from the standpoint of the Newfoundland fisheries. These fisheries provided an important supply of food to a deficient area and served as an important basis for trade and shipping. Other Spanish ports were less concerned with the fishery and supported regulations against which San Sebastian protested. They protested against lack of enforcement which favoured San Sebastian. For example, they objected to San Sebastian using French ships, as a substitute following the decline of her own shipping, to go to the Newfoundland fishery. It was argued that the marked decline in the large number of ships owned by the province of Biscay and the dangers which followed from loss of control to foreigners, especially from pirates who would attack the land fleets from New Spain, could be remedied by reducing the number of vessels owned by foreigners. This result could be obtained by forcing foreign ships to return empty and encouraging Spanish ships to go to foreign ports with cargo even if they were obliged to return empty. It was held that no nation would dare to inflict injury on Spanish ships taking cargo to its ports and that foreign traders would respond to the guarantee of fair treatment from Spain in loading these ships. The great value of cargoes from Spain would place that nation in a position to force foreigners to sell their ships to her. Vessels belonging to French frontier towns—Saint-Jean-de-Luz, Zibura, Azcavin, Urnia—would be sold to Spain after all their advantages had been eliminated. Moreover the profits of these towns from the Newfoundland fishery estimated at 60,000 ducats would accrue to Spain. The apple orchards of Spain would thrive with the demands of the fishery for cider and the French orchards would be displaced. The dangers arising from the simultaneous arrival of from a hundred and fifty to two hundred foreign ships with four to six thousand men at San Sebastian would disappear. With more native ships, freight charges would be lowered, and competition would be stimulated. It was urged, therefore, that in spite of the protests of San Sebastian the regulations should be enforced. San Sebastian claimed that Newfoundland ships were not included in the regulations as they carried only provisions for the voyage but it was held by the other ports that the exemption was seriously abused and should not be permitted. They asked for a more rigid inspection over imports and exports. Ships bringing fish from Newfoundland to Spain should be forbidden to take money and only allowed to take foodstuffs and provisions needed on the voyage. With specie remaining in the kingdom and an increase in the shipments of iron and other merchandise, the native ships would obtain both the money and trade which was formerly held by foreigners. A careful inspection of the cargo books would insure the increased export of iron and merchandise. Trade within the kingdom would be increased. Portugal and Andalusia would become to an increasing extent sources for wheat and imports of these products would decline. As always there were vested interests. Under the regulations Renteria was engaged in building ships and a removal of the regulations would create serious injury. The remedy to the difficulties would be found in more rigid enforcement and in introducing new arrangements such as that of prohibiting the sailing on foreign ships of natives and on Spanish ships of foreigners.

A decree of August 1578, by which foreigners were not allowed to load their ships,[14] was a direct challenge to the protest of San Sebastian and was responsible for continued difficulties. In spite of the claims of the other ports, ships and seamen were not available. Foreign ships with merchandise were forced to return without cargo and exports were confined to Spanish ships. If no Spanish ship was available no means of shipment was at hand. In 1580, Renteria protested that since the earlier decrees did not include ships going to Newfoundland, Ireland, and elsewhere for fish and oil but that these ships went to the grounds empty except for provisions and fishing supplies, it was particularly important in view of the extent of the Newfoundland fishery that the Spanish should not go with French vessels.[15] It accordingly asked for a new decree prohibiting Spaniards from taking foreign

14Archivo general de Indias.
15Copiado a la letra del registro de la junta general de Renteria por Abril de 1580 que existe en el archivo de Guipuzcoa situado en Tolosa.

vessels to the fishery. San Sebastian replied in a petition of March 21, 1580, with the usual arguments—the sterility of the province and the inability to supply itself with barley, bread, wine, or meat while ancient rights permitting French and English vessels to come even in time of war because of the scarcity of provisions placed it in a peculiar situation. If foreign vessels were not allowed to take return cargoes it was difficult to encourage French and English vessels to bring provisions and merchandise. If exports and the Newfoundland fishery were to be limited to Spanish ships Saint-Jean-de-Luz and other French towns would gain at the expense of San Sebastian. Guipuzcoa was forced to get its revenue from the trade by sea and the position of the fishery was of first importance. The position of Spain in the Newfoundland fishery was in danger of being jeopardized by the ship-building interests. It was difficult from the standpoint of the mercantile policy to decide whether shipbuilding was more important than the fishery.

The position of Spain in the fishery was being steadily weakened. In 1584 it was reported[16] that Saint-Jean-de-Luz and Sibiburo had over fifty large ships going to Newfoundland in the cod and whale fishery. The majority of these ships brought their cargo of fish and oil to San Sebastian although some was delivered at Bilbao and Castrio. It was estimated that these deliveries totalled over 140,000 ducats and although they were required to take merchandise in return there was a heavy drain of money from Guipuzcoa with serious results to trade. Saint-Jean-de-Luz and Sibiburo were estimated as having more ships than the entire provinces of Biscay and Guipuzcoa. In spite of pro-hibitions and heavy fines French ships took many Spanish sailors from Biscay and Lequestio. An important contributing factor in the decline of Spanish shipping was the increasing scarcity of timber[17] and the inability to build large ships. Determined protest was lacking and protest was entered only with a view to increasing exports of merchan-dise. It was suggested that the amounts of codfish and oil brought by each ship should be carefully recorded so that particular care might be taken to force vessels to purchase iron and other supplies, provisions and merchandise of San Sebastian and Guipuzcoa.

The Armada has been regarded as the critical point in the history

[16]Original en el registro de Tolosa de este año, no. 35.

[17]Sir Thomas Chamberlain reported in 1561, "In Biscay they had for a long time felled timber for building ships and planted none, so there was scarcely any now, and that double the price it was thirty years ago. Those of Biscay frankly declared that their ships had been so often stopped for the king's service and so badly paid, that they had to turn to other trades." Cited Prowse, p. 48.

of the Spanish fishery to Newfoundland. It only hastened, however, a tendency which was already marked. The decline of the Spanish fishery had followed in part from unfortunate regulations and from the difficulty of developing an adequate shipping industry. Again the fishery had apparently never taken sufficient root to weather the protests of hostile interests and its decline proved certain with the growth of the neighbouring French Basque towns. Moreover, no development had taken place in Newfoundland. Little evidence is available as to the points from which the Spanish fishery was carried on, but Sir Humphrey Gilbert saw twenty Spanish and Portuguese vessels in August 1583 at St. John's and we have already noted that Placentia was another rendezvous. They were apparently interested in the bank fishery off the southern coast of Newfoundland and confined themselves to green fishing. The type of fishing gave little possibility of permanent settlement.

The hostilities preceding the Armada had serious effects on the Spanish Newfoundland fishery. In 1585 Sir Bernard Drake carried out an attack on Spanish ships in Newfoundland and apparently captured six hundred Spanish prisoners and probably fifty thousand quintals of fish.[18] In 1586 complaints were lodged against the rigid enforcement of the regulations as to vessels going to Newfoundland[19] and Guipuzcoa protested against the overriding of its authority in the impressment of men for the navy. An embargo on the ships had resulted in the cessation of trade and the cod fishery was completely checked. The whale fishery, which was estimated as worth about 200,000 ducats, was also threatened. A petition asked that the ships commandeered should be allowed to go and they were finally given permission about the middle of June to proceed, provided no men belonging to the navy were taken. Guipuzcoa complained further against a regulation making English goods contraband and requiring that they should be consumed within thirty days. Soldiers had been stationed at the mountain pass in Beobia in Guipuzcoa through which English goods had been smuggled. A petition asked that the soldiers should be removed, and that the limit for consumption of goods should be extended for a year on the plea that they were in the possession of widows and the poor, and the city again protested against the overriding of its ancient rights by the central authorities. The effectiveness of political power in checking economic activity was an outstanding feature in the problems of the fishery. The strong political power contributed to the decline of the fishery and suggested a striking contrast to the strength of eco-

[18]Prowse, p. 79.   [19]Original en el archivo de Guipuzcoa.

nomic power in England and in New England. The British Empire became possible with the overriding of political power by economic power, but Spain as illustrated in the fishery was limited by the overwhelming strength of political control. The position of Guipuzcoa contrasted strikingly with that of the west country in England. Elasticity was a characteristic of the northern countries in its fishing and contrasted with the rigidity of central control in Spain.

In the following year, 1587, the problem became more serious. On March 23, 1587 (San Lorenzo), an order was issued to warn ships that English pirates from La Rochelle and other centres were arming boats to prey on ships proceeding from Guipuzcoa to the cod and whale fisheries and advising them to go out well armed and heavily manned and in groups rather than singly. The problem of securing a sufficient number of sailors was becoming serious. It was proposed to raise men from Biscay to mix with the skilled fishermen of Guipuzcoa and in this way to secure sufficient men for the navy as well as for the fishery and for trade.[20] A further proposal suggested including thirty experienced men in every hundred.[21] It is significant that the Newfoundland fishery was referred to as "de Terranoba que es la grangeria de ella," the granary of Guipuzcoa. Even the whale fishery was becoming less certain and a report of the same year (1587) stated that since the whales migrated to the south in the late fall to give birth to their young in warm waters and returned to the northeast in the spring when they were hunted by the Biscayans in the vicinity of Newfoundland, an attempt should be made to establish a whale fishery in the neighbourhood of St. Helena and St. Augusta and in this way to avoid Newfoundland.[22] The year of the Armada was noted chiefly for the activities shown by Spanish ships in capturing French prizes.[23] A ship from Pasage captured twenty French ships and brought into the port six loaded with codfish. One captain had a record of over one hundred and fifty French ships large and small, and others took large numbers.

References to the Spanish fishery after the Armada are few. In 1594 eight Spanish ships were reported at Placentia and in 1597 Spanish vessels were reported at the Bay of St. Lawrence and the south shore of Newfoundland, at the Magdalen Islands, and at Cape Breton. Hostilities between the Spanish and the English continued with the

[20]Madrid, April 20, 1587.　　　　[21]Toledo, April 25, 1587.
[22]Relación que da Pedro de Arpide pilocto de la carrera de las yndias natural de la provincia de Guipuzcoa del curso que acen los ballenas que matan los bizcaynos en tierra nueba es lo siguente.
[23]Coleccion Vargas Ponce, V, no. 13.

result that the Spanish were steadily forced to give ground. Similarly La Rochelle and French towns were accustomed to capture Spanish vessels as prizes and the latter retaliated.[24] In 1600 reference was made at Motriso to the importation of large quantities of wheat at low prices to provision the ships going to the Newfoundland fishery, and to complaints of engrossing.[25] In 1602 Prowse refers to seven whaling vessels and several cod fishing vessels.[26]

By 1600 the position of the Spanish fishery had been seriously weakened. The French were commandeering Spanish vessels calling at French ports with little possibility of redress.[27] In 1603 San Sebastian protested effectively against a 30 per cent tax on exports on the ground that it was necessary to obtain foodstuffs, especially wheat and barley, from France and allied territory to maintain its trade, finance, and shipping.[28] Vessels bringing in grain were allowed to proceed out without giving bonds and to take in return, exempt of taxes, local products such as cider, millstones, chests, staves, puncheons, wine casks, iron in bars, and wrought linen, as well as oil, whalebone, and fish brought in by natives of Guipuzcoa and not others from Newfoundland. The decline of the fishery was hastened further by the peace of 1604 which made it possible for the English to export fish without difficulty to Spain. The signs of decay are not striking but the evidence presented in the documents to 1615 is cumulative. In 1605 protests were made by Motriso that San Sebastian compelled the ships of the province to come to Pasage to unload and distribute their cargoes of codfish from Newfoundland and prevented them from returning to their own ports.[29] San Sebastian regulations for the dumping of ballast for ships loading for Newfoundland were regarded as detrimental. Moreover, San Sebastian forbade ship owners and captains to use their own supplies of cider but forced them to buy from the stock of that city. The dominant centre was attempting to maintain its share of the returns from the fishery at the expense of other towns in the province.

In 1608 renewed evidence of the old difficulties appears. Whalers proceeded to Newfoundland in French ships[30] contrary to regulations.

---

[24]Minuta en el archivo de Guipuzcoa entre los documentos de esto año (1593).
[25]Original en el archivo de Guipuzcoa, registro 1.
[26]Prowse, p. 48.
[27]Original en el archivo de Guipuzcoa, registro 1.
[28]Ventosilla, Oct. 17, 1603.
[29]Hernani, Nov. 17, 1605.
[30]San Lorenzo, Nov. 3, 1608. In 1609 permission was given a citizen of San Sebastian to use a French ship on the ground that two years before he had lost

Rigid enforcement of regulations prevented foreigners from obtaining supplies in Guipuzcoa for the Newfoundland fishery and foreign boats bringing supplies were not allowed to take out goods. A petition held that, since the Newfoundland fishery involved the heaviest trade in the kingdom, regulations preventing foreign ships bringing supplies from taking back goods were the cause of serious loss.[31] In the following year (1609) warning was issued against the danger of English pirates in Newfoundland,[32] and two years later Spanish vessels were charged with collusion with pirates in the Newfoundland fishery.[33] In 1613 the Newfoundland whale fishery was reported on the decline as a result of persistent hunting. San Sebastian was subject to serious losses from bankruptcies. An attempt to revive the fishery by going to Norway proved unsuccessful because of the pretensions of the English.[34] Of more significance was the statement that in the four towns accustomed to send men to Newfoundland impressment for the navy had been extensive and no expedition proceeded to Newfoundland in that year.[35] A significant corollary was a statement showing thirty ships from Saint-Jean-de-Luz coming to Pasage to unload codfish and oil to the extent of 16,000 cargas (4 bushels each) of codfish and 150 cargas of oil for the town of Bilbao.[36] A few English ships also brought cod to Bilbao. A document dated San Sebastian, March 20, 1615, stated more explicitly that sailors to Newfoundland and Norway as in former years had made little returns and that many were anxious to join foreign ships. In 1616 Spanish citizens complained that even the towing of ships in the harbour of Pasage was being monopolized by French citizens in small boats and asked that a preference should be given to Spanish pinnaces in unloading and lightering.[37]

The available evidence suggests that the Spanish fishery continued in relation to whaling rather than cod. The members of St. Peters guild of sailors in San Sebastian in 1615 complained that a preference given on oil from Newfoundland had been responsible for the sale of large

a ship through impressment in the navy. Although given permission to go to the Newfoundland fishery, because of the failure of that fishery he asked permission to use the vessel for other purposes. Madrid, Feb. 8, 1609.

[31]Coleccion Vargas Ponce, III, no. 34.
[32]San Lorenzo, June 2, 1609.
[33]San Sebastian, Oct. 20, 1611.
[34]Mondregon, Nov. 16, 1613.
[35]Parece que se deduce del concepto de esta real orden que tambien iban muchos marineros a las pescas de Terranoba por estos años desde los quatro villas de la costa.
[36]Las naves francesas de Sant Juan de Lus que an venida a esta canal del Pasage descargades su carga de bacallao y grasas en la ville de Bilbao.
[37]Coleccion Vargas Ponce, VI, no. 27. Original en el archivo de Guipuzcoa

quantities of oil by the French in Bilbao, and asked that an embargo should be placed on all oils coming to Biscay from foreign countries with the exception of that brought by ships from Labort.[38] As ever the importance of the fishery to the navy was the basis of the general plea. A similar petition dated San Sebastian, July 25, 1618, was presented asking that oils brought by natives from Newfoundland should be preferred.[39] In the same year the argument was reinforced with a second petition stating that Flemish and English competition had checked the Spanish whale fishery in Norway and that in retaliation preference should be given to oil produced by natives in Newfoundland.[40] The preference was granted and apparently rigidly enforced as a request was made to exempt the people from Labort because of their close relations with the people of Guipuzcoa and the small amount of oil sold to Spain. The plea was apparently unsuccessful as Saint-Jean-de-Luz, Sibiburo, and neighbouring towns petitioned for exemption, stating that they should be treated as neighbours and not as strangers and that a precedent had been created earlier in exempting Labort from the 30 per cent tax.[41]

In 1625 an estimate of the number of ships at San Sebastian interested in the Newfoundland fishery gave 41 ships with 295 shallops and 1,475 men.[42] For this number of men 3,680 barrels or 5,315 cargas of cider were to be purchased, if possible from the city. Guipuzcoa continued to suffer from interference of the central authorities. Citizens protested in 1625 that ships which had returned from Newfoundland had been commandeered at great loss to those interested and that an embargo had been placed on French goods.[43] Fuenterabias authorities had seized ships bringing supplies from France for debts, the pass of Beobia was closed again, and the trade of Guipuzcoa by land and sea was at a standstill. On the strength of earlier precedents the arguments based on the sterility of the province prevailed and permission was granted for free transport by land or sea of bread, wheat, barley, oats, wine, meat, and other provisions for the maintenance of the province. Free entry was provided to supplies from France, England, Navarre, and other parts. A decree of August 24, 1625, was confirmed on January 21, 1626, to emphasize the point that all ships were to be permitted free entry to the harbours of Guipuzcoa and that codfish

[38]Coleccion Vargas Ponce, V, no. 45. Original en el archivo de Guipuzcoa.
[39]Coleccion Vargas Ponce, III, no. 50.
[40]Ibid., no. 51.
[41]Ibid., III, no. 53.
[42]Carta a la ciudad de San Sebastian por su Regidor Torrero de Pasage. Coleccion Vargas Ponce, III, no. 30.
[43]Coleccion Vargas Ponce, III, no. 30.

should be included provided that the returns were made in goods of the country and not in silver or gold.[44] The French vessels were obviously becoming increasingly important as sources of the supplies of cod. A fixed price on codfish, sardines, and whale oil was held responsible for the non-arrival of twenty ships and for creating a danger of ships already in the harbour of Pasage going to France, and a petition dated San Sebastian, November 12, 1627, asked for their removal.[45]

In the period from 1620 to 1628 an attempt was suggested on a large scale to revive the Newfoundland fishery in Cantabria and especially in the Basque provinces of Guipuzcoa and Biscay. A large company with monopoly powers was proposed similar to the four companies in operation in the East Indies, the West Indies, the North, and the Levant.[46] The plan included participation to the extent of 100,000 ducats on the part of His Majesty limited to 5 per cent for three years but with the right to a proportionate share in the profits after that period. After three years the company received a monopoly of the fishing trade with ability to fix prices. The company was to acquire a fleet of thirty vessels of 200 to 250 tons, either by building ships or by acquiring through hire or purchase. Wholesalers in Castile were forbidden to trade in whale oil or codfish unless they had subscribed at least 1,000 ducats. It was planned that the charter should exist for nine years and that it should have its head office at Bilbao and San Sebastian alternately for periods of three years, the first choice being determined by lot. Although the plan was submitted to the provinces of Biscay and Guipuzcoa and to the four towns for consideration, it apparently went the way of all monopolies in the fishing industry. That industry never provided fertile soil for the growth of companies.

A heavy blow to the Newfoundland fishery from Spain was given by the imposition of a salt tax. In 1631, Guipuzcoa claimed that losses of men killed in the navy and the scarcity of salt had caused severe suffering in the province during the past four years. Freedom of trade in salt had been the life blood of the provinces. In that year for the first time people failed to go to Newfoundland because of the lack of salt. Salt meat and cured fish were expensive. The French in the province of Labort gained from Spanish decline. They gathered up doubloons and pieces of eight and refused to take iron with the result that the iron works were closed. French fishermen prospered with a cheap supply of salt. For each carga of fish two and one half fanegas of salt were necessary and with salt costing two to five reals per

44*Ibid.*, no. 57 and no. 59.   45*Ibid.*, no. 60.   46*Ibid.*, no. 54.

fanega the Spanish fishery continued with difficulty and was limited to fresh fish. The inland trade in dried cod fell into the hands of England and France. Salt produced near La Rochelle, and used to supply Holland and England and sold at two reals per fanega, competed in devastating fashion with Spanish salt at twelve reals. It was pointed out that Sibiburo, situated two leagues from Spain, had increased in twenty years from thirty houses to five hundred houses and men were continually leaving Guipuzcoa because of the scarcity of provisions. Guipuzcoa argued[47] as before that the decline of shipping injured the navy, that one voyage to Newfoundland was of more value than four voyages elsewhere from the standpoint of training seamen, and that provisions would be more expensive for the fleet. In vain did she plead her old rights and privileges in the free entry of ships and in vain did she complain of the unfairness of the tax. The Newfoundland fishery declined and San Sebastian was decimated. In spite of a favourable decree of 1636 it was not until 1638 that a ship was sent to Newfoundland and this was followed by an addition in 1639. With the hope that five ships might go out in 1640 a reduction of the tax on fish from two reals to one real on each carga was granted on October 11, 1639.[48] In the same year fishing vessels along the coast of Cantabria were made exempt from the order commandeering ships and supplies and impressing men.[49] But the fifty ships of Spain referred to in the document as formerly engaged in the fishery[50] had been largely displaced by the French Basques and the English. The importance of the fishery as a supply for seamen, as a source of provisions for the poor, and as a basis of trade was no longer in evidence.

The decree of October 11, 1639, was confirmed in a decree of March 12, 1642.[51] The following year six ships, three of 300 tons, two of 250, and one of 150, sailed for Norway and Newfoundland for fish and whales.[52] But there was little evidence of a return to the hopes of a petition that the former prosperity of twenty large ships up to 600 tons and two thousand sailors sent from Guipuzcoa would be recovered.

[47]Las razones que se pueden alegar y poner en nombre de la provincia de Guipuzcoa para la defensa del nuevo impuesto de la sal y que se manda que Guipuzcoa sea comprendida en el son las siguientes. Coleccion Vargas Ponce, V, no. 35. See also Coleccion Vargas Ponce, V, no. 33 and no. 36. Copia de una en el archivo de la ciudad de San Sebastian en el legajo de Pesca bacallao y ballenas. Coleccion Vargas, III, no. 6.

[48]Coleccion Vargas Ponce, III, no. 65.

[49]Ibid., no. 64 and Oct. 15, 1644, no. 69.

[50]Ibid., no. 43.

[51]Ibid., no. 67.

[52]Adventencias para la yntroducion del Trato y Navegacion de la Provincia de Terranova y Norvega en las Puertos de Cantabria. Coleccion Vargas Ponce, III, no. 68.

The French Basques of Labort continued to carry out of the country 400,000 ducats of silver and the English to take their profits. Labort with its annual fleet of sixty ships and three thousand seamen had captured the Spanish market. The commandeering of ships and the impressment of sailors was held responsible for the decline. Salt continued at its high level, and since it was brought from Corsica and Andalusia, the dangers to continuity of supply were serious and the expense of long distance carriage was large; the seamen had declined in numbers and in skill. The small dry and relatively poor quality fish of the English had displaced the excellent fish of the banks caught by the Spanish. Shipping declined in the face of cheaper supplies of masts, tar, pitch, canvas, fishing tackle, cordage, and rigging of the French. A "memorial regarding the revival of the fishery to Norway and Newfoundland from Cantabria where it has very much declined" was suggestive of the change.

Guipuzcoa was continually faced with the dilemma of increasing her own fisheries and limiting her supplies, or increasing her supplies from foreign ports at the expense of the fishery. Her ancient rights to receive supplies in view of the sterility of the province were always in danger of encroachment but were always successfully maintained. In 1636 in spite of war conditions foreign vessels were allowed to bring in goods to Guipuzcoa. These rights were extended and strengthened in 1642 and in 1643. The seizure of goods of French vessels in May 1645 led to new protests. Codfish from Newfoundland had always assumed a doubtful position but Guipuzcoa had always contended successfully that this product was the most important of all for naval supplies and provisions. And again in 1645 the protests[53] against embargoes on French vessels from Newfoundland were successful. Codfish was included in the supplies and all vessels loaded with that commodity were allowed to come in free. Free trade was practically conceded between the peoples of Guipuzcoa and Labort. On the other hand a petition signed by seventeen citizens of San Sebastian in 1652 asked that codfish should be exempt from the tax of one real per carga and supported the argument with the usual statements regarding the importance of the fishery to the navy,[54] but apparently without effect. The fishery had declined too far and the obstacles to its develop-

[53]Cedula Real de Felipe IV para que no obstante su tiempo de guerra no se pusiese embargo a los Baxeles Bascos ó Labortanos que traxesen Bacalao de Terranoba, y en que interesaban los Guipuzcoanos, sin embargo del impedimento puesto de orden del capitan General de la Provincia de Guipuzcoa. Acompaña la representacion hecha sobre este asunto al Rey por la dicha Provincia. . . . Feb. 2, 1645. Coleccion Vargas Ponce, III, no. 70, and V, no. 44.

[54]Coleccion Vargas Ponce, V, no. 46.

ment were too serious for recovery to follow minor measures of this character. Indeed, with the shift of the fishery to Saint-Jean-de-Luz there is considerable evidence to show that capital followed labour and that residents of San Sebastian were engaged in supplying capital to masters of Saint-Jean-de-Luz. These loans[55] varied from 100 to 200 ducats at rates from 26 to 28 per cent and vested interests were created which favoured a continuation of the fishery from Saint-Jean-de-Luz and were opposed to measures which threatened its position.

The position of oil continued to create difficulties. This commodity could not be regarded as a foodstuff and a preference given to oil brought in by natives might continue to serve as a means of encouraging the fishery to Newfoundland and Norway. The Spanish Basques were able to continue the whale fishery in spite of the loss of the cod fishery. San Sebastian and Bilbao were both willing to insist on preference to native oil in opposition to oil brought from Labort.[56] A decree dated Madrid, November 15, 1644, and re-enacted March 22, 1649,[57] gave the native citizens of the provinces of Guipuzcoa and Biscay a preference in the sale of oil over that brought by the Basques from Labort.

The decline of the Spanish fishery is the reverse side of the opening of the Spanish market to the fisheries of France, England, and New England. It ushered in the trade which for centuries meant to England the development of Newfoundland, the continuation of a nursery for seamen, the consumption of British manufactured goods, and the means of draining Spanish specie. It is probably not too much to say that in the sixteenth and seventeenth centuries the cornerstone of the British Empire had been well and truly laid in Spanish trade. Protestant England's consumption of cod declined with the changing standard of living but Catholic Spain presented a steady and increasing market. The toast of Newfoundland fishermen, "To the Pope and

[55]See especially a list of loans, 1632, and references to the interests of San Sebastian outfitters in Saint-Jean-de-Luz and Sibiburo vessels in other documents, especially 1645. Memoria y Relacion del dinero que se a dado a Terranoba en diferentes navios este año de 1632 que nuestra señor les de buen viage. Coleccion Vargas Ponce, V, no. 38 and no. 41.

[56]Carta a la ciudad por Don Diego de Hino Josa Veedor del Almirantazzo de Bilbao Setiembre 3 de 1645 en respuesta a otra de dicha ciudad inserta aqui sobre que no debian admitiese en el señorio de Vizcaya las grasas de Bascos y Labortanos de que sa seguiria perjuicio a los armadores de navios con destino a Terranova y Norwega, Coleccion Vargas Ponce, III, no. 71.

[57]Real cedula original de Felipe IV dada en Madrid a 22 de Marzo de 1649, mandando que para formenta de la navegacion y comercio a Terranova sean preferidos los Guipuzcoanos y Vizcaynos a los Labortanos en la venta de Grasas, que traguen de aquel destino. Coleccion Vargas Ponce, III, no. 72.

ten shillings," is a toast in which all good citizens of the British Empire will join.

The change was of far-reaching importance to the New World. The development of trade favoured the dry-fishing industry. The Spanish were accustomed to taking the large fish from the banks and drying them on their return to Spain. Countries trading in fish to Spain were forced either to dry them in the New World or to dry them in their own countries before taking them to Spain. It became much more profitable to dry them in the New World and to return direct to Spain. The opening of the Spanish market was the prelude to the expansion of the dry-fishing industry not only on the part of England in Newfoundland but also on the part of France and New England. The opening of the gulf fishery, especially in Gaspé, was undoubtedly a result of the opening of the Spanish market. The growth of the gulf fishery was accompanied by the opening of the St. Lawrence and contributed to the beginning of the fur trade and the settlement of Canada. Moreover it led to the development of trade in New England. In 1616 Captain John Smith wrote a letter,[58] dated London, December 19, 1616, to the city of San Sebastian, offering to go with ships from Guipuzcoa to reconnoitre the fishing grounds and land described in his book. The larger fish of the Gulf of Maine favoured the development of New England and the sale of New England fish in Bilbao and other ports.

The task of appraising the importance of the factors leading to the decline of the Spanish fishery is more difficult than the task of describing the results of the decline. It may be suggested that the element of distance was a factor of ultimate importance and that Spain was unable to compete with countries located within a shorter distance from the banks. The growth and persistence of the neighbouring province of the French Basques seriously weaken that argument. It has been generally assumed that the decline of the Spanish navy after the Armada and increasing taxation were determining factors, but the evidence suggests that every effort was made to protect the rights of Guipuzcoa and of the fishery generally. Certainly the demands of the navy for ships and men, and taxes such as the salt tax, had serious consequences for the fishery but they do not appear to have been determining factors. They contributed to the decline rather than determined it. An important suggestion which is supported in the documents was the decline of shipping through the cutting off of the timber. On the other hand a prosperous fishery

58Original en el archivo de San Sebastian, Coleccion Vargas Ponce.

might have been built up on ships purchased from other countries just as Saint-Jean-de-Luz built up a fishery in Cape Breton a century later with ships purchased from New England. It has been suggested earlier in this paper that the technique of the Spanish fishery was confined to wet fishing on the banks. This fishery may in part explain the lack of settlement on the part of Spain in the New World as it explains in part the weak position of France and as dry fishing explains in part the strong position of England in the colonization of Newfoundland. But it does not serve as an adequate explanation of the marked decline of Spain as contrasted with France. It would be possible to argue that a salt tax was particularly serious for a type of fishery which demanded large quantities of that commodity, but this tax was imposed long after the fishery had started on its decline.

The decline of the fishery may have been a result of the cumulative effects of the factors described, but they appear rather as ripples on the surface than as factors determining the main current. The current runs deeper and stronger. Its trend is suggested in the constant recurrence of the struggles of Guipuzcoa to maintain its rights as to freedom of trade in provisions, and the success with which those struggles were prosecuted. The failure of attempts to check exports of specie and to increase exports of goods was significant. The persistence and increasing importance of the trade carried on by the French Basques and later by England and New England to the northern ports of Spain in Newfoundland cod as well as in provisions and supplies are outstanding factors in the period. It was apparent that powerful forces were tending toward an increase in trade which overwhelmed the relative advantages of Spain in the fishery. High prices of fish and other provisions and supplies had powerful attractions for France, England, and later New England. The effects of the importing of gold and silver from the New World to Spain, which have been all too conspicuous in the popular mind, following the buccaneering exploits of Drake and Hawkins, became important through the more peaceful channels of trade. The Newfoundland fishery proved persistent and effective in the transfer of specie to the countries of northern Europe. The importation of gold and silver by Spain raised the prices of commodities; and the relative advantages of the Spanish fishery as compared to the position of Spain as an importer of treasure led to her steady decline in importance in the fishery. With the turn of the century the fishery had become strongly entrenched in the northern countries and specie poured out of Spain in return for imports of dried cod. Even the "poor john" of England in Newfoundland was powerful enough with the assistance of specie to over-come the excellent fish of the Banks taken by the Spanish Basques. The nursery for seamen flourished, the navy was strengthened, the market for manufactures expanded in the fishery, cod was a commodity in continuous and steady demand, and it only remained for England to place her blessing on the whole by passing the navigation acts and elaborating the mercantile policy.

Finally we may refer to the work published recently by Professor E. J. Hamilton on records in the Spanish archives on the influence of American treasure on Spanish prices.[59] In the period from 1503 to 1660 an index number of general prices rose from 24.8 in 1503 to 47.5 in 1530 to 66.5 in 1552 to 101.7 in 1575 to 111.0 in 1601 to 114.2 in 1626 and to 129.1 in 1651. The rise in this period of the prices of codfish and white bread point directly to the influence of the importation of treasure from America to Spain, especially in the sixteenth century, on the decline of the Spanish fishery, the rise of the English fishery in Newfoundland, the penetration of the French to the Gulf of St. Lawrence[60] which led to the development of the St. Lawrence basin, and the establishment of New England. The establishment of settle-ment in Northern North America by England and France in the early years of the seventeenth century may be regarded as another of the far-reaching results of the importation of specie into Spain in the sixteenth century.

[59]Earl J. Hamilton, "American Treasure and Andalusian Prices 1503–1660: A Study in the Spanish Price Revolution," *Journal of Economic and Business History,* I (1928), 15 ff. See also Earl J. Hamilton, "Imports of American Gold and Silver into Spain 1503–1660," *Quarterly Journal of Economics,* XLIII (1929), 436–72, and Earl J. Hamilton, "Monetary Inflation in Castile 1598–1600," *Economic History,* II (1931), 177–211, and C. H. Haring, "American Gold and Silver Production in the First Half of the Sixteenth Century," *Quarterly Journal of Economics,* XXIX (1915), 433–79.

[60]For a discussion of the position of Spanish authority in North America in the sixteenth century in relation to the papal bulls, see P.-E. Renaud, *Les Origines économiques du Canada* (Mamers, 1928), pp. 195–215.

Transportation as a Factor in Canadian Economic History*

TRANSPORTATION has been of such basic importance to Canadian economic history that the title of this paper may appear redundant and inclusive. The paper is intended, however, as an attempt to consider the general position of transportation in Canada, with special relation to its peculiar characteristics and their relationships to Canadian development, rather than to present a brief survey of Canadian economic history.

The early development of North America was dependent on the evolution of ships adapted to crossing the Atlantic. Water transportation, which had been of first importance in the growth of European civilization, had improved to the extent that, by the beginning of the sixteenth century, long voyages could be undertaken across the north Atlantic.[1] These voyages were continued in relation to the acquisition of commodities for which a strong demand existed in Europe, and which were available in large quantities within short distances from the seaboard of the new countries. In the north Atlantic, cod was a commodity in the handling of which the advantages of water transportation were capitalized to the full. On the banks, ships from Europe caught and cured the fish in preparation for direct sale in the home market. Early in the seventeenth century, following the opening of the Spanish market and the new demand for dried cod, ships from England and France developed dry fishing in Newfoundland, the remote parts of the Gulf such as Gaspé, and the New England shore.

Mr. Biggar has shown the relationship between dry fishing and the fur trade.[2] Penetration to the interior brought Europeans in touch with the resources of the mainland. The continued overwhelming importance of water transportation for the development of the interior warrants a

*From Proceedings of the Canadian Political Science Association, 1931, pp. 166–84, and Problems of Staple Production in Canada (Ryerson, 1933), pp. 1–17.

[1]Vide S. A. Cudmore, History of the World's Commerce with Special Relation to Canada (Toronto, 1929).

[2]H. P. Biggar, Early Trading Companies of New France (Toronto, 1901); H. A. Innis, "The Rise and Fall of the Spanish Fishery in Newfoundland," Transactions of the Royal Society of Canada, third series, vol. XXV (1931), Section II, 51–70. [See this volume, p. 43.]

brief survey of the more important waterways and their characteristics. The course and volume of the waterways in the northeastern half of North America is largely determined by the geological background of the area. The Precambrian formation is in the form of an angle, with one side pointing toward the northeast, including northern Quebec and Labrador, and bounded on the north by Hudson Straits, and the other to the northwest and bounded by the western Arctic. Hudson Bay constitutes a large portion of the territory in the angle. The resistant character of the formation and its relatively level surface have been responsible for a network of lakes and rivers. Its youthful topography following the retreat of the ice sheets is shown in the number of rapids and obstructions to the tributaries and rivers. The major water courses flow roughly along the junction of the formation with later weaker formations, as in the St. Lawrence waterway which begins with the Great Lakes and flows northeast toward the Gulf, and the Mackenzie which flows northwest toward the Arctic. The St. Lawrence is fed from the north by important tributaries, such as the Saguenay, the St. Maurice, and the Ottawa, which are separated by low heights of land from rivers flowing to Hudson Bay. The main waterway[3] is broken by serious obstructions at Niagara and the St. Lawrence rapids above Montreal, and the tributaries have numerous rapids. The drainage basins to the south, the Mississippi, the Ohio, and the rivers of New York, are separated by comparatively low heights of land.

The commodity supplied by this vast stretch of northern Precambrian territory, and demanded by Europe, was fur. The sailing ships were restricted to the mouth of the St. Lawrence River, and the opening of trade on the river and its tributaries necessitated the use of pinnaces.[4] Tadoussac became the first terminus, but was displaced by Quebec after the French became more familiar with the river channel to that point. The relatively level stretch of water from Quebec to Montreal was adapted to the use of large boats, and with the improvement of the route the depot shifted from Tadoussac to Quebec, to Three Rivers, and thence to Montreal. In 1642 Montreal was established and the position of the French on this stretch of waterway consolidated. Beyond Montreal a third type of transport equipment —the canoe—became essential. The French were able to borrow directly from the equipment of the hunting Indians of the northern Precambrian area, and to adapt the transport unit, worked out by them,

[3]M. I. Newbigin, *Canada: The Great River, the Lands and the Men* (New York, 1926).
[4]Champlain in 1608 went from Tadoussac to Quebec in pinnaces.

to their needs. With this unit French and English succeeded in bringing practically the whole of northern North America under tribute
to the demands of the trade.

The canoe was adapted to the shorter Ottawa route to the upper
country rather than to the longer and more difficult upper St. Lawrence
and Great Lakes route. The trade of Georgian Bay, Green Bay on
Lake Michigan, and Lake Superior was developed from this route to
Montreal. Eventually La Vérendrye and his successors extended it
northwest to Lake Winnipeg and the Saskatchewan. The limitations
of the birch-bark canoe, even after its enlargement and adaptation by
the French, necessitated the establishment of depots for provisions
at convenient points. Its labour costs were heavy.

The upper St. Lawrence and Great Lakes route was never developed
as a satisfactory substitute by the French, and the difficulties of La
Salle with Great Lakes transportation in its initial development characterized its later history. The problems of organization of the route
were enhanced by the competition of the Dutch and English through
the Iroquois and the Mohawk route to Oswego prior to 1722, and
through direct trade after the establishment of Oswego in that year.
As a result of this competition, the St. Lawrence and Great Lakes
route involved a substantial drain on the trade. Posts were established
at Frontenac, Niagara, and Detroit as a means of checking English
competition, and the upkeep of these posts involved heavy expenses
for the colony. Eventually Toronto was added in 1749 as a further
check to Indian trade with the English. The shorter route to Oswego
and the use of large boats on the lake were factors which seriously
weakened the position of canoe transport on the Ottawa.

Only with the disappearance of the French after 1760 did it become
possible to combine satisfactorily the upper St. Lawrence–Great Lakes
route for boats and vessels with the canoe route on the Ottawa. The
lake boat became an ally to the canoe rather than an enemy. Heavy
goods were carried by the lakes, and light goods were taken up and
furs brought down by canoes. Cheaper supplies of provisions were
available at Detroit and Niagara, and were carried at lower costs up
the lakes to Grand Portage and later to Fort William. Niagara portage
was organized and a canal was built at Sault Ste Marie. With the
organization of Great Lakes transport it became possible to extend
the trade far beyond the limits reached by the French. The Northwest
Company succeeded in penetrating from Fort William to Lake
Winnipeg and the Saskatchewan, by Cumberland House and Frog
Portage to the Churchill, by Methye Portage to Athabaska, the Peace,

and the Mackenzie, and by the passes across the Rockies to the upper Fraser and the Columbia. Supply depots were organized on the Red River, on the Saskatchewan, and on the Peace.

The efficiency of the canoe in serving as a transport unit from Montreal along the edge of the Canadian shield almost to the Arctic was dependent in part on the efficient organization of water transport along the Ottawa to Montreal, and on the Great Lakes. In 1821 this elaborate system collapsed and the canoe ceased to be a basic factor in transport. The boat again became an important factor in contributing to its failure, but from the north or Hudson Bay and not from the south. Ocean transport, in addition to supremacy of the Bay with boats in inland transport, was overwhelmingly important.

Hudson Bay was developed as a trading area over fifty years later than the St. Lawrence basin, and its growth depended largely on experience acquired in the St. Lawrence. Radisson and Groseilliers saw the possibility of tapping the trade from the centre of the Precambrian angle rather than from the outer edges. Accordingly ships were despatched to the mouths of the rivers flowing into James Bay and into Hudson Bay, and after the formation of the Hudson's Bay Company in 1670 the trade of the drainage basin began to flow toward the north. Ships were unable to visit the posts at the foot of James Bay because of the shallow character of the bay, and smaller boats were used to collect fur and distribute goods from a central depot on Charlton Island.[5] On Hudson Bay ships were able to visit the mouths of the Nelson and the Churchill rivers. The tributaries of the Hudson Bay drainage basin flowing from the east and the south were similar to those on the opposite side of the height of land flowing toward the St. Lawrence. But the vast interior of the continent to the west poured its waters toward Hudson Bay and forced a main outlet across the Precambrian formation by the Nelson River. This outlet and its tributaries served as an entrance to the northwest from Hudson Bay. The advantages of the route were continually in evidence but were overcome temporarily by the canoe route under the French and under the English. With the use of the boat on this relatively short stretch the long line of the canoe route was cut in the centre, and after 1821 all goods for the West were taken in by York Factory, and the Fort William route was abandoned. For over half a century the York boat and Hudson Bay dominated the transport of western

5In 1932 as a result of construction of the railway to James Bay, the voyage conducted annually for over two and a half centuries through Hudson Straits to Charlton Island was abandoned.

Canada. Brigades were organized throughout the Hudson Bay drainage basin and across to the Churchill, the Athabaska, the Peace, and the Mackenzie rivers.

Water transportation facilitated the exploitation of furs throughout the Precambrian area and beyond, but the efficiency of technique determined the routes to be used. The ocean ship to Quebec, the large boats to Montreal, the *canot de maître* to Fort William, and the *canot du nord* to the interior, assisted in the later period by the vessels on the lakes, proved unable to withstand the competition from the ocean ship to Nelson and the York boat to the interior.

The comparative ease with which the transport unit was borrowed and adapted, or devised to meet the demands of the water routes, gave the waterways a position of dominant importance in the moulding of types of economic and political structure. Rapid exploitation of the available staple product over a wide area was inevitable. Undoubtedly the character of the water routes was of fundamental importance in shifting the attention of Canada to the production of staple raw materials. It became necessary to concentrate energy on the transport of raw materials over long distances. The result was that the Canadian economic structure had the peculiar characteristics of areas dependent on staples—especially weakness in other lines of development, dependence on highly industrialized areas for markets and for supplies of manufactured goods, and the dangers of fluctuations in the staple commodity. It had the effect, however, of giving changes of technique a position of strategic importance in fluctuations in economic activity. In one year transport to the west shifted from Montreal to Hudson Bay. The St. Lawrence basin flourished with the opening of trade to the west and languished when it was cut off. The legacy of the fur trade has been an organized transport over wide areas especially adapted for handling heavy manufactured goods going to the interior and for bringing out a light, valuable commodity. The heavy one-way traffic made the trade discouraging to settlement, and in turn made the trade a heavy drain on settlement. The main routes had been well organized to handle trade over vast areas.

The disappearance of fur from the St. Lawrence basin was accompanied by the rise of lumber as a staple export.[6] The economy built up in relation to fur and water transport was shifted to the second product available on a large scale chiefly from the Precambrian area. Lumber in contrast to fur was a heavy, bulky commodity

---

[6]*Vide* A. R. M. Lower, "Lumbering in Eastern Canada," doctoral thesis, Harvard University, 1929.

whether in the form of square timber, logs, deals, planks, or boards, and consequently its transport on a large scale was confined to the larger tributaries and the main St. Lawrence route. The Ottawa and upper St. Lawrence and Lake Ontario drained the most favourable areas for the growth of the large coniferous species, especially white pine. Rapid exploitation was limited to the softwoods which had a low specific gravity and could be floated down the rivers to Quebec. Lumber supplied its own method of conveyance, and the evolution of rafts suitable to running the rapids of the lower Ottawa in 1806, and the rapids of the St. Lawrence at a later date, and finally the introduction of slides for the upper Ottawa, solved the problem of technique. Square timber was floated down the lower St. Lawrence to be stored along the tidal beach at Quebec in preparation for loading on wooden ships for the protected markets of England.

The effects, on the economic development of the St. Lawrence basin, of dependence on lumber as a staple product, were the opposite of the effects of dependence on fur. Whereas fur involved a heavy incoming cargo, lumber favoured a large return cargo and consequently provided a stimulus to immigration and settlement. The coffin ships of the lumber trade made an important contribution to the movement of immigrants which became prominent after 1820. The trade created a demand for labour and for agricultural products. As in the case of fur it also created violent fluctuations in the economic activity of the colony, and its position as a raw material for construction made the St. Lawrence basin susceptible to an unusual extent to the effects of the business cycle.

The increase in settlement in Upper Canada after 1783 and the decline of the fur trade in 1821 raised serious problems for transportation above the Niagara Peninsula and on Lake Ontario. As early as 1801 a Kentucky boat with 350 barrels of flour was sent down the St. Lawrence rapids with success,[7] and boats were used to an increasing extent to overcome the drawbacks of the route. A satisfactory outlet was obtained for goods going down-stream, but up-stream traffic continued a serious problem.

The limitations of the St. Lawrence route were accentuated with the introduction of steam. The industrial revolution and its effects on transportation were destined to have a far-reaching influence on the economic history of Canada. Application of the new technique to a

[7]Milo M. Quaife, ed., *John Askin Papers*, II (Detroit, 1931), 343, also H. A. Innis and A. R. M. Lower, eds., *Select Documents in Canadian Economic History, 1783–1885* (Toronto, 1933), pp. 138ff.

transport system adapted to the handling of raw materials on the existing waterways accentuated the influence of the waterways on the later development. The steamship was adapted first to the stretch of river between Montreal and Quebec and continued in operation after 1809. It served as a complement to the lumber trade, and immigrants were taken up-stream from Quebec without the inconvenience of a long up-stream pull. The pressure from improved transportation to Montreal became evident in the increasing seriousness of the handi-caps of the St. Lawrence rapids and the Great Lakes. Steamship communication on Lake Ontario was limited by the rapids of the St. Lawrence. Under these handicaps the competition of the Erie Canal at Buffalo above Niagara, and of the Oswego route above the St. Lawrence rapids, became important. An attempt to draw traffic from the upper lakes to the St. Lawrence River was made in the building of the Welland Canal, with eight-foot depth, completed in 1833. This improvement made increasingly necessary the improvement of the final link of the St. Lawrence rapids to Montreal. Eventually pressure from Upper Canada resulting from the handicap of high costs on the up-stream traffic of manufactured goods contributed in part to the Rebellion of 1837, to the Durham *Report*, to the Act of Union, and to a determined effort to build the St. Lawrence canals. These canals were completed to nine feet in the forties, and lake steamers were able to go down regularly to Montreal after 1848.

It is important to emphasize at this point the relationship between the beginnings of the industrial revolution as seen in the application of steam to the St. Lawrence route, first from Quebec to Montreal, and later on the upper lakes, and the consequent pressure which led to the building of canals. These developments involved essential de-pendence on the government as seen in the Act of Union and the energetic canal policy of the first ten years. The Welland Canal was begun as a private enterprise, but inadequate supplies of cheap capital necessitated purchase by the government.[8] The relation be-tween governmental activity and water transportation became an im-portant factor in later developments.

The completion of the St. Lawrence route, and the stimulus to settlement, industry, and trade which it occasioned, intensified other limitations of the route. Moreover the delay in opening the route was responsible for rapid depreciation through obsolescence. Attempts

[8]The Lachine Canal was also begun as a private enterprise. *Vide* J. L. McDougall, "The Welland Canal to 1841," master's thesis, University of Toronto, 1923.

to improve the St. Lawrence and compete with the Erie Canal, and to attract the export trade of the Middle West, were defeated by the construction of American railways.[9] The problem of offsetting the handicaps of the route by land transport began at an early date. In 1727 complaints were made that contrary winds were a serious cause of delay on the journey between Montreal and Quebec, and by 1736 a road had been built along the north shore. Stage roads became necessary above Montreal and along the north shore of Lake Ontario to Toronto and west to Dundas and western Upper Canada. The numerous ports along Lake Ontario became termini for roads to the back country.

This form of land transport, however, was far from adequate to meet the demands of trade and industry. Consequently the Grand Trunk was completed from Sarnia to Montreal in 1858. The old road from Toronto to Georgian Bay was abandoned with the completion of the Northern Railway from Toronto to Collingwood in 1854. Chicago and Lake Michigan traffic was captured by this route, and traffic was developed on Lake Superior by the Sault Ste Marie Canal, completed in 1855. Finally the handicap of closed seasons for navigation on the lower St. Lawrence disappeared with the completion of a short line through the Eastern Townships to Portland (1853), and of the Victoria Bridge (1859). By 1860 the St. Lawrence had been amply supplemented by a network of railways. After 1863 the trials of the Allan line on the St. Lawrence route in the fifties were overcome and the ocean steamship became an increasingly powerful factor in the development of the route.[10] Unfortunately the location of the Grand Trunk as a line supplementary to the St. Lawrence route left it exposed to competition from that route and it was brought to the verge of bankruptcy in 1857. The overwhelming importance of water transport was shown in the route followed by the Grand Trunk in tapping traffic areas built up on the St. Lawrence. The completion of these early railways marked the beginning of the amphibian stage of transport history.

The cost of improving the St. Lawrence route in terms of canals and railways brought new problems to the government. These problems with their solution were clearly presented by Alexander T. Galt in his reply to the Sheffield manufacturers in 1859:

[9]D. A. MacGibbon, *Railway Rates and the Canadian Railway Commission* (Boston, 1917).
[10]William Smith, *History of the British Post Office in British North America, 1639–1870* (Cambridge, 1920), chaps. xvii–xviii.

Dependence could hardly be placed upon a revival of trade to restore the revenue to its former point: but this would afford no means of meeting the future railway and municipal payments; and parliament had to choose between a continued system of borrowing to meet deficiencies or an increase of taxation to such amount as might, with economy of administration in every branch of the public service, or a revival of trade, restore the equilibrium of income and expenditure. It is true that another course was open, and that was to exact the terms upon which the railway advances were made; and to leave the holders of the municipal bonds to collect their interest, under the strict letter of the law. By these steps Canada would certainly have relieved herself from the pressure of increased taxation, and might have escaped the reproaches of those who blame the increase of her custom's duties. But it would have been at the expense of the English capitalists and legislation; and it would have been but poor consolation for them to know, that, through their loss, Canada was able to admit British goods at 15 instead of 20 per cent.

He elaborated this statement three years later in a report on the Reciprocity Treaty with the United States:[11]

The undersigned commences with two propositions which will not be denied: first that the consumer, under all circumstances, pays the entire cost of the article he uses; and secondly, that his ability to buy depends upon the net results to him of his labor after its product has gone into consumption in any form. Assuming these points as necessarily conceded, it is evident that in a new unsettled country, such as Canada was, and to a certain extent, still is, without roads, without canals, without railroads, with an uncertain, long and perilous communication with Great Britain, the cost of British goods at the early settlement of the country was enhanced by the doubtful credit of its merchants, high ocean freight, high insurance, heavy charges for lighterage, and finally after the goods reached Canada, by the enormous charges consequent on a trade conducted in the most primitive way, by the most primitive conveyances, and subject to the profits demanded by the numerous parties through whose hands it passed before it reached the ultimate consumer. Equally were the still more bulky articles produced and forwarded in payment for goods, subject to similar deduction. Consequently not very many years ago, the settler in Upper Canada, and in many parts of Lower Canada, paid the maximum for his goods and obtained the minimum for his produce.

It has been remarked that legitimate protection, which home manufacturers may enjoy, is that afforded by the cost of bringing foreign goods into competition. It must therefore be admitted that under the circumstances in which Canada was then placed, this legitimate protection was necessarily very large, and that British goods were at a very great disadvantage. In very many cases it may, with perfect truth, be stated that

[11]Report of the Minister of Finance on the Reciprocity Treaty with the United States, *Sessional Papers of the Legislative Assembly of the Province of Canada,* 1862, no. 23.

the cost of the goods imported was enhanced to the consumer one hundred per cent., and equally that he only obtained one-half the ultimate price, or much less, of his produce in England. At the time to which reference is made, the duty on British goods, generally, was two and a half per cent., but the price to the consumer was raised enormously by the causes referred to, and his means of purchase in an equally important degree diminished. Now, under these circumstances, it cannot admit of a doubt, that if by an increase of five per cent. on the duty, a reduction of ten per cent. on the other charges were produced, the benefit would accrue equally to the British manufacturer and to the consumer, and the indirect but legitimate protection to the home manufacturer would be diminished; the consumer would pay five per cent. more to the Government but ten percent. less to the merchant and forwarder. In this illustration lies the whole explanation of the Canadian Customs. The government has increased the duties for the purpose of enabling them to meet the interest on the public works necessary to reduce all the various charges upon the imports and exports of the country. Light-houses have been built, the St. Lawrence has been deepened, and the canals constructed, to reduce the cost of inland navigation to a minimum. Railways have been assisted to give speed, safety, and permanency to trade interrupted by the severity of winter. All these improvements have been undertaken with the twofold object of diminishing the cost to the consumer of what he imports, and of increasing the *net* result of the labor of the country when finally realized in Great Britain. . . .

Finance Department,   (Signed) A. T. Galt,
  Quebec, 17th March, 1862.   Minister of Finance

Fiscal policy was therefore directly linked to problems of transportation, and it is scarcely necessary to add that the link has been a permanent one.

Fiscal policy became involved not only in the improvement of transportation by providing funds according to Galt's explanation but also in developing manufactures, trade, and traffic. The development of industry contributed in turn to the growth of centres of large population and to an increase in traffic, a decrease in deficits, and a lighter burden for the government. The demands of transportation improvements were reflected directly and indirectly in fiscal policy. The fixed charges involved, especially in canals and the improvement of water transportation and in railways, led to a demand for new markets in the East and in the West. Expansion eastward and westward involved Confederation. The debates of the period suggest that the Intercolonial was not commercially feasible and that it was undertaken as a political measure, but it is difficult to conceive of its construction without reference to the demands for new markets. In any case, the results were evident. An excellent line was built at heavy initial cost, as is the custom with government undertakings, heavy interest charges followed, the line was operated at a loss, and goods were carried at unremunerative rates from the larger industrial centre to the Maritimes. The industrial area of central Canada strengthened its position with cheap water transport and access to the coal of the United States and Nova Scotia, and new markets were found in the Maritimes.

Sir Edward Watkin of the Grand Trunk regarded expansion to the West as the solution of its difficulties.[12] The interest of Sir Hugh Allan in the early plans for expansion westward, which occasioned the Pacific Scandal, is significant of the continued importance attached to the development of traffic to the West in relation to the St. Lawrence route. The opening of the Intercolonial in 1876 gave the Allan line a Canadian winter port at Halifax, and the deepening of the St. Lawrence ship channel from seventeen and a half feet in 1860 to twenty-two feet in 1878 and to twenty-seven and a half feet in 1887 completed an efficient ocean steamship connection to Montreal in summer and to Halifax in winter. The immediate effects were evident in such divergent results as the rapid growth of the live-stock industry in central Canada, the rapid decline of the wooden sailing vessel, the displacement of Quebec by Montreal, and the substitution of square timber by sawn lumber.

But of more striking importance was the demand for more rapid expansion westward to open markets for improved transport. From the standpoint of fiscal policy the outlay of capital in these improvements of transportation in canals and railroads contributed to the difficulties of the Mackenzie Administration and its free-trade policy in the depression of the seventies. The slow development of transportation to the West which followed from this policy was finally speeded up with the National Policy, which provided a guarantee of earnings on traffic carried within Canadian territory in case of success in keeping out goods and protecting the manufacturer, and a guarantee of revenue in case of failure to keep out goods with which to pay the deficit due to loss of traffic. The double-barrelled effectiveness of the policy was enhanced by recovery from the depression and the energetic construction of the Canadian Pacific Railway. Subsidies in money and in land and further protection of east-west traffic by the monopoly clause hastened the early completion of the line in 1885. It is only necessary to refer briefly to such additional developments as the establishment of the Pacific Ocean Services and the improvement of

[12]Sir E. W. Watkin, *Canada and the States* (London, 1887).

the line by the short line to Saint John in 1890 and the construction of the Crow's Nest Pass Railway after 1897.

The depression of the nineties was in part responsible for the delay in expected results, but the final expansion after 1900 was undoubtedly dependent on the deepening of the Sault Ste Marie Canal to nineteen feet in 1895, of the Welland Canal to fourteen feet in 1887, of the St. Lawrence canals to the same depth by 1901, and the St. Lawrence ship channel to thirty feet by 1906. The efficient transport system built up around the St. Lawrence basin for the handling of wheat hastened the industrial development of eastern Canada, including the iron and steel industry of the Maritimes, and contributed to the development of minerals, lumber, and fish in British Columbia. Eastern Canada lost her position as an exporter of dairy products to England and became a producer largely for rapidly increasing urban population in the home market. Improved transportation, followed by the opening of the West, was responsible for the period of marked prosperity from 1900 to 1914.

An important result of the dependence of staple products on transportation has been the suddenness of the changes which followed. The St. Lawrence canals were not available until the last lock had been built, and then the whole route was opened. Again the rapidity of construction of the railway from Skagway to Whitehorse revolutionized the placer mining of the Yukon. These sudden and unpredictable results were particularly important in the rapid accumulation of revenue from the tariff after 1900 and in the unexpected profitableness of Canadian Pacific Railway operations. These developments contributed in turn to the construction of two other transcontinental lines, the Canadian Northern Railway by guaranteed government bonds, and the Grand Trunk Pacific by the construction of the National Transcontinental Railway. The results included bankruptcy, the Drayton-Acworth report of 1917, and the Canadian National Railways and its problems.

The railway network has spread beyond the St. Lawrence basin but no one can deny the pull of the Great Lakes in the failure of wheat to move over the National Transcontinental Railway to Quebec. Canada has become to an increasing extent amphibian, but is still powerfully affected by the St. Lawrence basin. Nevertheless there are signs that the immense physical plant involved in transcontinental railways is beginning to have effects similar to those of the Northwest Company at the peak of its activities. The decline in importance of virgin natural resources has tended, with the railways as with the Northwest Company, to favour independent lines of growth. The Hudson Bay Railway, the opening of the Panama Canal, and the growth of trade through Vancouver to the Orient parallel the independent development on the Pacific coast and the supremacy of the Hudson Bay route in the fur trade. Even with the support of the industrial revolution there are signs in the growth of regionalism that the second unity of Canada is beginning to drift in the direction of the first and that the control of the St. Lawrence waterway is slightly but definitely on the ebb. The increasing strength of the provinces in contrast to the Dominion parallels the increasing importance of railroads and the staples dependent on railroads—minerals, pulp, and paper. The seasonal fluctuations which characterize dependence on water transport tend to become less important with the continuous operation of industries linked to the railroads. The revolution which has followed the use of the gasoline engine as seen in the automobile, the truck, the tractor, the aeroplane, and the motor boat, and the opening of the north, appears to point in the same direction. We have been able to change the winter to the open season, and with electricity the sources of early difficulties to transportation have been converted into sources of power. All these tendencies point to an emergence from the amphibian to the land stage.

It is difficult to summarize the importance of transportation as a factor in Canadian economic history. We can suggest, however, the overwhelming significance of the waterways and especially of the St. Lawrence. Cheap water transportation favoured the rapid exploitation of staples and dependence on more highly industrialized countries for finished products. It favoured the position of Canada as an exporter of staples to more highly industrialized areas in terms of fur, lumber, and finally wheat, pulp and paper, and minerals. The St. Lawrence was important in the establishment of British power in Canada by its possibilities from a naval and military point of view, but even more from the standpoint of providing a basis for the economic growth of the Empire in the export of staple raw materials and the import of manufactured goods. We cannot in this paper describe the economic effects of dependence on these staple products other than to indicate the drain which they made in transportation costs on the energy of the community. We can suggest that each in its turn had its peculiar type of development and that each left its stamp on Canadian economic history. We can suggest that changes in technique, improvements in the waterways and in types of boats were responsible for rather violent fluctuations in economic development through the dependence on staple raw materials. It is scarcely necessary to describe the effects of dependence on water transportation on problems of finance involved in heavy expenditures which led ultimately to subsidies and government ownership. Water transportation and dependence on staples have been responsible for a variety of heavy overhead costs. Dependence on staple products and the difficulties of the waterway probably delayed improvement of transportation on the one hand and hastened it on the other by permitting the borrowing of mature technique from the United States. Railroads built at a later stage of development were completed more rapidly and the Canadian Pacific Railway was able to draw heavily on American experience in its early stage of development. Moreover, depreciation through obsolescence in American transportation hastened Canadian development, and steamboats, captains, and pilots, displaced on the Mississippi by railroads, moved up to the Red River, and the Saskatchewan, and the Fraser, as they did in turn in Canada from the Saskatchewan and the Fraser to the Mackenzie and the Yukon. The arrival of the first steamboat down the Red River to Winnipeg is surely the most dramatic event in Canadian economic history.

We have traced the evolution of transport in the fur trade, which reached its height in the expansion from the St. Lawrence following the development of vessels on the Great Lakes in combination with canoes on the rivers. This transport system disappeared with competition from the York boat from Hudson Bay. The disappearance of the fur trade from the St. Lawrence was followed by the rise of the lumber trade. Lumber tended to emphasize the efficiency of down-stream traffic on the large rivers, whereas fur tended to emphasize the efficiency of up-stream traffic on smaller rivers. The growth of settlement which accompanied the development of the lumber trade led to a demand for efficient up-stream transport. This demand became more effective with the introduction of steamboats on the St. Lawrence from Quebec to Montreal, and on Lake Ontario and the upper lakes, especially after the completion of the Welland Canal. Pressure from Upper Canada for improved up-stream traffic led to the completion of the St. Lawrence canals by 1850.

The St. Lawrence route, as improved by canals, was further strengthened by the completion of the Grand Trunk Railway and its connections with the seaboard in the following decade. These developments were in turn responsible for the completion of the Intercolonial to Halifax in 1876, and the deepening of the St. Lawrence to

Montreal to twenty-two feet in 1878, and for the construction of the Canadian Pacific Railway completed in 1885. Finally the deepening of the Sault Ste Marie, the Welland, and the St. Lawrence canals, and the St. Lawrence ship channel paved the way for the opening of the West, the export of wheat, and the addition of two transcontinental railways.

Again, we have suggested the relationship between the importance of the St. Lawrence waterway and Canadian fiscal policy. The Act of Union was a prerequisite to the financial support adequate to completion of the St. Lawrence canals, and in turn Confederation was essential to the financial support necessary to round out the policy inaugurated in canals and supplementary railways, by further improvements and extensions to the east with the Intercolonial Railway and to the west with the Canadian Pacific Railway. The policy necessary to provide financial support was outlined by Galt, and whether or not his explanation was one of rationalization after the fact, or of original theoretical analysis, reliance on the customs was undoubtedly the only solution. In the main this policy provided the basis for the elaboration under the National Policy of 1878. According to Galt's argument, the payment of duties actually reduced protection in so far as they were employed in reducing the cost of transportation on imports and exports. But the growing importance of railways, after the construction of the Intercolonial Railway, favoured the addition of the protection argument as a means of increasing traffic, especially in manufactured products. The National Policy was designed not only to increase revenue from customs from the standpoint of the waterways but also to increase revenue from traffic from the standpoint of railways. The increasing importance of railways has tended to emphasize the position of protection rather than revenue.

We can trace in direct descent from the introduction of steam on the St. Lawrence waterways, the Act of Union, the completion of the St. Lawrence canals, the Grand Trunk, Galt's statement, Confederation, the Intercolonial, the National Policy, the Canadian Pacific Railway, improved St. Lawrence canals, the new transcontinentals, and the drift toward protection. The overwhelming importance of the St. Lawrence waterways[13] has emphasized the production and export of

[13]The proposed improvement of the St. Lawrence waterways has not been given adequate consideration from the standpoint of the position of the St. Lawrence in the economic development of Canada. The valuable work done by antagonists and proponents of the scheme in terms of neatly calculated estimates has in the main tended to leave out of account the historical background and various incalculable items. This paper cannot undertake a detailed analysis but

raw materials, and in the case of wheat the extraordinary effects of a protective tariff during a period of expansion contributed to the construction of two new transcontinentals, and to the emergence of the Canadian National Railways. The problem of the railways is essentially one of traffic to enable them to increase earnings without excessive cost to the producers of exports. The problem of protection is therefore that of increasing the traffic of manufactured goods and thereby increasing earnings, with the result that railroad costs may be decreased to the producers of raw materials to an amount equal to or more than the rise in the price of manufactured goods as a result of protection. Dependence on the application of mature technique, especially in transport, to virgin natural resources must steadily recede in importance as a basis for the tariff. It will become increasingly difficult to wield the tariff as the crude but effective weapon by which we have been able to obtain a share of our natural resources.

---

it does suggest that the tremendous investments of capital built up around the St. Lawrence system in terms of ships, canals, terminal facilities, harbours, and railroads, from the standpoint of the export of wheat from the West will suffer materially from drains in other directions. Improvement of the St. Lawrence will contribute toward reducing the overhead costs of these tremendous investments. The strains of the political and economic structure built up largely in relation to the St. Lawrence would be lessened accordingly.

Government Ownership and the Canadian Scene

(AN ECONOMIC INTERPRETATION OF THE APPEARANCE OF ECONOMISTS AT POLITICAL SUMMER SCHOOLS)*

THE appearance of an economist at the summer school of a political party may even at this late date give rise to some comment.[1] I can assure you that it is not yet a result of the retreat of academic freedom to these bodies. The pronouncements of the economist have so deteriorated in importance during the past few years that he has become the contempt even of the politicians, and no politician will treat with contempt any group which commands a vote. Nor can the economist be held free of responsibility for his present low status in the community. He has assumed that he can compete with demagogues and his assumption has proved to be palpably wrong, except to those economists who have become demagogues themselves in the competitive process. His excuse is understandable during a period of depression, if not during a period of prosperity—something should be done to relieve human misery and his knowledge should be applied to bring about alleviation—but the results are nevertheless unfortunate. Democracy will defeat the economist at every turn at its own game.

By this time I hope you will realize that I am under no illusions in appearing before this gathering. On the other hand, I hope that my appearance here may suggest that I am not entirely pessimistic as to the ultimate solution. I do not expect to exert any influence on your views on any question of public policy, and I do not expect that many of you will understand any economic exposition which may be advanced in this paper. I am sufficiently humble in the face of the extreme complexity of my subject to know, first, that I am not competent to understand the problems much less to propose solutions; and, second, that I am not confident that I can propose and explain

*From *Canadian Problems: As Seen by Twenty Outstanding Men of Canada* (Toronto, Oxford University Press, 1933, pp. 69–90).

[1]It will be obvious to economists that the point of view of this paper has been strongly influenced by the writings of Professor F. H. Knight and by a speech of Professor Stephen Leacock given before an inaugural meeting of the Canadian Political Science Association.

solutions to you which I do not understand myself. This will be done for you by other "economists." But let me warn you that any exposition by an economist which explains the problems and their solutions with perfect clarity is certainly wrong. Economics is an extremely difficult biological subject not discussed or understood except by groups of preferably three trained economists.

Having said this perhaps I should explain my presence here. I came here partly because I was asked and therefore presumably because of some belief that any contribution I might make would be useful, but rather because I take it as symptomatic that a powerful political party at present in office is at least willing to consider possible contributions of an economist. Economists have been asked and are being asked to investigate particular problems by governmental authorities, but so far as I am aware they have never been asked to take part in political discussion. It may be that their possibilities as demagogues are being gradually appreciated in political circles, or it may be that the politicians still feel that they are not entirely beneath contempt particularly if they are cloaked with the university prestige which surrounds the academic economist. My belief that the invitation was genuine was based on broad historical grounds. The politician has realized finally that the place of an economist in political life should be discussed, and it is with reference to this problem that I propose to develop this paper.

The question as to the place of the economist has not arisen prior to this depression chiefly because no other depression has been so serious and because other depressions have been solved successfully by politicians. The immediate problem has arisen partly because of the methods used by politicians to overcome previous depressions, but in the main Canadian politicians have used over a long period and in crude fashion the devices recommended by economists of the present day. A brief review of depressions ranging from 1835 to 1857, 1873, 1893, and 1921 illustrate a striking uniformity in Canadian political methods in overcoming depressions. The depression of 1835 was followed by the Rebellion of 1837 and by the recommendation under the Durham *Report* that the provinces of Upper and Lower Canada should be united in order to provide the necessary financial arrangements for large-scale public works involved in the St. Lawrence canals. During the forties the canals were built but construction was not adequate to offset the effects of the repeal of the Corn Laws and the depression of that decade. Further efforts were necessary and substantial support was given to the construction of the Grand Trunk

Railway. The depression of 1857 illustrated the problems involved in this method of attack. Outlays of the government for the improvement of transportation involved heavy fixed charges during a period in which returns from revenue declined rapidly. The method and its effects were inevitable. The key position of the St. Lawrence necessitated dependence on government support and accentuated emphasis on staple products such as wheat and lumber. As a result fixed charges essential to improvement of transportation contrasted sharply with the wide fluctuations of returns and in turn of revenue from staple products. The severity of the problem of government finance involved solutions of a diverse character ranging from the issue of provincial notes—inflation by the printing machine if you will—an increase of the tariff which involved the beginnings of protection and the end of reciprocity, a search for a wider base for the increased debt which ended in Confederation, and attempts to build additional public works which ended in the construction of the Intercolonial Railway. But again the depression of 1873 brought fresh troubles in terms of government deficits arising from the same phenomenon of outlays by the government to improve transportation, and the consequent heavy fixed charges supported by staples exposed to sharp fluctuations characteristic of the business cycle. The solution ran in similar terms —a rise of tariff marking the beginning of the National Policy, and arrangements for the construction of public works, in this case the Canadian Pacific Railway. The depression of the nineties brought a continuation of the problems and similar solutions—in this case a strong policy of immigration and construction of two new transcontinental railways, the Canadian Northern and the Grand Trunk Pacific. The difficulties of the war and the post-war period involved the most marked increase in debt and in turn bankruptcy of the railroads, amalgamation, and the appearance of the Canadian National Railways. In turn the time-honoured methods of recovery were invoked and railway construction increased on an unprecedented scale during the period of boom in the twenties. The results have followed according to form in the depression.

From the standpoint of strict accuracy the development has not been as simple as has been outlined but the broad outlines stand out with sufficient clarity to enable one to write this paper without any serious twinge of scientific conscience. In the main the solutions adopted by the politicians were successful. At least two important considerations contributed to their success: (1) each expansion of capital imports, particularly as directed to improvement of transportation, has tapped fresh natural resources; or (2), it has involved reductions in cost of transportation of marked advantage to the competitive position of raw materials. Railway rates and the tariff, failing the possibility of charging canal tolls, have served in rough fashion as methods by which the improvements were financed.

It is crucial to our discussion that the two important considerations are destined to play a very much less important role in future development.[2] Fresh natural resources have become much less conspicuous and cannot be expected to support a major expansion in the importation of capital. The tariff can no longer serve as a crude instrument designed to obtain a share of new resources and must take a less important place in governmental revenues. On the other hand improvements of transportation, with the possible exception of the St. Lawrence waterways, no longer offer a way of escape. The importance of government ownership and its consequent rigidity of fixed charges tend to make further improvements of transportation difficult. In the first place returns on further investment of capital in transportation improvements have become much more dubious, and in the second place transportation improvements may involve serious depreciation through obsolescence which involves an additional burden to the government. The competition of motor transportation, for example, has added to costs of operating the Canadian National Railways. The Panama Canal and the Hudson Bay Railway will tend to have similar effects. The St. Lawrence waterways may increase the burden of fixed charges to the government directly by cost of construction and indirectly through competition with the Canadian National Railways. Our past policies have been policies based on expansion. We are no longer able to rely on public works as a method of recovery from the depression and that we have relied on this policy has left us with a legacy of large government debts and heavy fixed costs which bear down with great pressure particularly during a period of low yield and low prices of staple products, especially wheat. The difficulties of this situation explain the attention given to the economist. We are obliged to adopt more refined methods than have been necessary in previous depressions and to set up more delicate machinery. Political parties must draw to an increasing extent on the economic intelligence which is at hand. Economic planning which characterized an era of expansion becomes inadequate and inefficient and serious for an era in which expansion ceases to play an important role.

[2]See H. A. Innis, *Problems of Staple Production in Canada* (Toronto, 1933), for a general survey; also appendix 1.

It is fortunate that in Canada we have become accustomed over a long period to economic planning and without committing myself to the policies of any party it is only fair to point out the important part played by the party at present in power. It is possible that this tradition may be responsible for the steps which have already been taken toward the introduction of more adequate machinery. From the Board of Railway Commissioners and the Canadian National Railways we have been able to proceed by a logical step to the recent Railway Commission and the subsequent legislation. Tariff legislation will become more efficient with more adequate studies carried out under the Tariff Board. It is altogether probable that a central bank will be recommended to overcome the limitations of machinery set up under the Finance Act. Other types of machinery such as the Combines Investigation Act will suggest themselves to anyone caring to reflect on the whole subject.

Our brief survey of the history of economic planning in Canada points clearly to the dangers of inadequate planning. The rigidity of government debts which followed the construction of the St. Lawrence waterways in the forties becomes progressively more dangerous with the course of each business cycle and leads inevitably by such devious paths as additional government support to government ownership and in the case of the railways to the present arrangement. And this is not the end. Failure to maintain an even balance between the two railways will lead to further maladjustment[3] and probably to larger government debts and to greater rigidity.

If in the case of transportation it has eventually been found impossible to operate one part on a planned basis and another part on a basis of private enterprise, it will be obvious that one cannot introduce planning for railways and leave unrestrained private enterprise in other activities. Planning leads inevitably to more planning. In an economy based on raw materials and exposed to violent fluctuations the extension of planning introduces a serious dilemma. With the basic importance of capital equipment in Canada we are forced to emphasize the drive of private initiative and the necessity of commanding the energy and enthusiasm of our population and particularly our younger men. Even with improved transportation and communication a vast area with diverse densities of population cannot be developed economically without reliance on all the energy and skill and drive we can command. The development of an intense patriotic nationalism along the Russian lines to meet this problem would be undesirable if not inadequate. The problem was solved by the North-

³See appendix 2.

west Company by a co-partnership system on the basis of constant expansion, but constant expansion must be disregarded in any solution of the problem. The dilemma explains the necessity on the part of political parties of inviting the consideration of economists.

Interdependence in modern economic life necessitates the extension of planning once it has been started. Planning in any one direction introduces certain rigidities the impact of which is felt throughout the whole economy, and in a violently fluctuating economy tends to produce inequalities and to create maladjustments which have serious consequences for the regions or classes most directly exposed to effects of world competition—for example, western agriculture and in turn labour in urban areas as shown in unemployment. To avoid the unfortunate consequences of such maladjustments—and no one who has visited the West can fail to appreciate the suffering and misery involved—further planning becomes essential. And the process continues. It will be obvious that machinery should be introduced rapidly and widely for the purpose of adjusting the burdens. Such machinery must be introduced, however, only after the most careful consideration and each piece of legislation should provide the basis for the next piece of legislation. Obviously it must permit of the greatest possible flexibility.[4] Any large rapid extension of machinery with vague notions as to its character and effects would undoubtedly have serious consequences. But thorough study, careful integration, ample provisions for flexibility, and carefully adjusted relationships to existing machinery with a view to capitalizing available economic skill and intelligence should provide a base for a structure which can be gradually improved as experience is gained from its operations and effects.

The difficulties involved appear at times almost insuperable. An economist would find it extremely difficult to predict the effects of any proposed action assuming adequate control of disturbing factors, but with no control over labour movements or of capital movements the task becomes infinitely more difficult. Drastic checks on immigration and in turn on emigration are possible and their introduction would facilitate the work of the economist. Control over credit carried out under a proposed central bank could be made effective by extension to forms of credit other than commercial credit. Internal machinery involves, particularly for Canada with her dependence on foreign trade, the closest possible study of world trade. Canada must continue to play an increasingly prominent role in international developments and to contribute to the improvement of existing machinery. Nationalism provides the only sure basis for internationalism.

4See appendix 3.

The most serious difficulty which underlies to a large extent all other problems is the ineffectiveness of the economist in a democracy. Maladjustments and rigidities involve vested interests which are vocal in politics. The economist dare not begin to meet this situation. He can only concentrate on the causes of disturbance and prepare himself for the occasion in which the politician may dare to consult him. I have already suggested that my appearance at the summer school of a powerful political party which has played an important role in economic planning in Canada in the past is an indication of my faith that this party will continue to play an important role in economic planning in the future and that the economist will be accepted as increasingly necessary in meeting new and more acute difficulties. I have indicated the inevitability of planning in Canada—it remains for the economist, realizing his limitations, to render the best advice of which he is capable that the plans may not do more harm than good to the economic structure.

This paper is concerned wholly with the place of the economist in the programmes of a political party. It is intended to suggest the dangers of confusion of economics and politics. Political summer schools have their ultimate concern in the winning of elections and economists cannot make any contribution along those lines. Economists cannot compete with politicians. The specialized character of the subject makes public discussion prohibitive. While the economist is forced to assume an increasingly smaller role in public discussion the demands for his services in the state become increasingly great.

Government ownership in Canada has assumed a crucial position and has developed as a result of strong underlying forces with a drift toward economic planning. The dangers of economic planning have become acute and the necessity of further planning has created a demand for the work of economists. Government ownership and the tariff have been employed during the present depression to undertake tasks including protection, unemployment relief, control of exchange, production of revenue, and transportation charges. The burden has proved far too heavy. New machinery has already been provided and more will follow.

It may be that we are already on the upward swing of the business cycle and that we will be able to invoke to a minor extent the old remedies. In that event and with a successful Conservative or Liberal election you will probably not hear from economists until the next depression. I can only assure you we will be on hand with the same arguments but reinforced.

APPENDIX 1

The present economy of Canada is dominated by wheat. Expansion of production of this commodity has involved the improvement of navigation on the St. Lawrence and the Great Lakes, the building of railroads, the opening of ports in the Maritimes, on the St. Lawrence, on Hudson Bay, and on the Pacific, the construction of elevators, the growth of towns, and the development of a vast proportion of Canada's existing capital equipment. This expansion has had its effect directly in the emergence of the iron and steel industry in relation to the production of rails and railway supplies, of the lumber industry of eastern Canada and British Columbia to meet the demands of increasingly large urban centres in eastern Canada and in the Prairies, and of a great wealth of industries. Indirectly the railroads built to meet the demands of wheat have been responsible for the growth of the mining industry—the development of Sudbury on the Canadian Pacific main line, the opening of Cobalt, Porcupine, Kirkland Lake, and Noranda in territory tributary to the Temiskaming and Northern Ontario Railway, built to develop the clay belt of Northern Ontario and to link up with the National Transcontinental Railway, and expansion of the Kootenay in southern British Columbia.

The capital necessary to support this enormous investment was obtained to a large extent from Great Britain prior to the war and from the United States since the war. It involved credit instruments in the form of Canadian Pacific common stock and preferred stock and Canadian National bonds guaranteed by the government, provincial debentures, municipal debentures, mortgages on farms, corporate securities, stock and bonds, and other evidences of debt. Interest on these securities has been paid in the form of dividends on Canadian Pacific stock and other corporate stocks and interest on bonds of the Canadian National, the federal, provincial and municipal bodies, and corporate organizations as well as on farm mortgages. In addition deficits have been paid by security holders and, in the case of the Canadian National, by the government.

Interest on the various forms of securities has been paid and repayment of the securities has been accomplished chiefly through the sale of wheat in Great Britain; funds for these purposes have been collected as earnings on the railroads and on the operations of companies, as taxes in various forms levied by governments, and as payments on mortgages, and have been paid by security holders in case of deficits. The method of collection varied from direct payment through railroad rates on wheat and on imports involved in the production and transportation of wheat to the infinite variety of taxes including the tariff. In the case of the Canadian National Railways and capital invested in improvement of navigation the deficits and interest on capital have been paid chiefly through the tariff on imports.

The ability to make these payments depends therefore on the returns from the sale of wheat and flour in export markets. These returns are a result of various factors, such as the price of wheat and the size of the crop, which in turn is a result of yield and acreage. The price of wheat is determined by world factors, particularly production in competing areas and demand. Yield is a result in the main of climatic factors, and fluctuates violently. Acreage available for wheat is a result of competition for land for other agricultural products, of rotation systems, of settlement, and other factors. Expansion in production of wheat with constant price level or rising prices with constant production facilitate payments. Accessibility to new land has been largely responsible for an increase in production, and in turn for a lightening of the burden, unless it has been offset by the interest necessary to support new capital expenditures.

In an able analysis Dr. D. A. MacGibbon, Canadian Grain Commissioner, states, "I do not expect much increase. On the other hand, I see no ground for believing that average exports will fall below 200 million bushels for many years to come."[5] We cannot expect, therefore, that the burden of interest payments will be reduced materially through an expansion of wheat production. On the other hand, fluctuations in yield are inevitable and in turn fluctuations in price. Returns from wheat cannot be expected to increase naturally as a result of increased wheat production. It becomes increasingly necessary, therefore, to indicate the problems in relation to the burden of payments and to suggest possible solutions.

The depression has brought out sharply the character of the problems involved. Returns on wheat have been drastically reduced as a result of declining yields and prices. Earnings on the railroads have been reduced following decline in yield and decline in purchasing power in the West. In the case of the Canadian Pacific Railway it has been forced to reduce and later to pass dividends on common stock and has practically reached the position of a deficit in relation to the fixed charges on other securities. The Canadian National has been

---

[5]"The Future of the Canadian Export Trade in Wheat," *Contributions to Canadian Economics*, V, 1932 (University of Toronto Studies, History and Economics, 1932).

forced along with the Canadian Pacific to reduce expenses drastically and in spite of the reduction to show a large deficit primarily because of an inelastic financial structure in which the government is directly involved through guarantee of securities. In the one case the loss has been shifted in part to the holder of the Canadian Pacific securities and in the other to the general Canadian public, and in both cases part of the loss has been passed on to the employees. On securities outstanding in relation to navigation improvements such as canals and ports the loss is again carried by the Canadian public. These charges have been paid, in accordance with the general policy of the government, chiefly by returns from revenue from customs. The implication has been that transportation improvements reduced the costs of transport on imports and that the tariff should be imposed to force the importer to contribute to the cost of improvements.

Returns from the pulp and paper industry depend primarily on production and prices, which in turn are a result chiefly of the demands of the United States for advertising. These demands are notoriously the result of swings in the business cycle and returns will fluctuate as to price and production accordingly. Decline in price involves a decline in production in high-cost mills and concentration on relatively efficient low-cost mills. The burden of depression consequently falls on the employees of high-cost mills and on the security holders of capital invested in those mills. Towns built up around these mills decline in population, and depreciation through obsolescence is borne largely by investors and the people concerned. Fluctuations in production in relation to demand are limited to problems of supply. Following the boom of the past decade, further increase in paper-mill capacity cannot be expected. On the other hand, pulpwood supplied by settlers tends to become exhausted and costs of pulpwood to increase in terms of prices paid or of lower standard of living for the settler provided he has not been able to shift to established agriculture. Low-cost mills operating continuously tend to exhaust the more available supplies unless reforestation from the standpoint of sustained yield has been adequately supported. Assuming adequate reforestation policies in relation to low-cost mills able to operate at capacity during a period of depression, the burden of fluctuation is shifted to the marginal mills. The problems of reforestation, of labour, of investors, become more acute in direct ratio to the cost of operation of the mills. The basic importance of electric power to the newsprint industry and the importance of overhead charges in relation to the fixed type of capital equipment essential to development of electric power raise serious problems in the creation of alternative uses during periods of depression or off-peak periods for the newsprint industry as a whole. These problems are linked to those of labour and reforestation. Their solution in relation to a unified policy involves control over the resources of the provinces, probably including Newfoundland.

Problems of the lumber industry have been solved in part by emergence of the pulp and paper industry in relation to spruce. Demands for lumber in eastern Canada vary largely with the construction industry in Canada and in the United States. Capital and labour have become adjusted over a long period to wide fluctuations and the industry has been integrated in part with agriculture and other activities. Flexibility of organization facilitates the introduction of remedies which follow intensive surveys. In British Columbia prices and demands are more largely determined on the coast by foreign demands and in the interior by demands of the Prairies. Overhead costs on the coastal mill and the position of the industry from the standpoint of natural resources permits to some extent relatively continuous operations. The problem of mills advantageously located is similar to that of pulp and paper. Exhaustion of the accessible forests will place the industry in a weaker competitive position and protection from wide fluctuations will be linked in part to conservation measures.

The mineral industry from the standpoint of metallic minerals has been in some sense a by-product of wheat production. Railways built to produce and transport wheat were responsible for the discovery and development of minerals. The effects were evident in the impetus given by the development of mining in the Yukon and in the Kootenay to the development of agriculture. The Crow's Nest Pass Railway was directly linked by subsidy to a reduction of rates, but the relation is generally more obscure. Expansion of mining tends to reduce costs on unremunerative sections of railway but on the other hand the inevitable exhaustion brings an increase in cost. The development of Cobalt, Porcupine, Kirkland Lake, and Noranda provided a direct stimulus to agriculture and to the lowering of costs of transportation. Fortunately the decline of one camp, for example, Cobalt, has been offset by the rise of other camps, for example, Kirkland Lake, and the impermanence of previous metals, silver and gold, by the more permanent base metals. The inevitable shift to base metals accentuates the problem of competition from other countries and leads to a gradual weakening of our position as low-cost ore bodies are exhausted. Copper plants have already been forced to close down unless supported by exceptionally low costs of mining as at Flin Flon or by a heavy mixture of gold as at Noranda. The monopoly position of nickel places this industry on a more permanent basis. Asbestos on the other hand has felt the effects of foreign competition. The advantages of minerals as a by-product of agriculture and their position as a support during periods of depression will tend to become less obvious with exhaustion, with the result that the effects of a fluctuation in wheat economy will become more pronounced. Lead and zinc mining, for example, as at Trail, has become an important supplement to wheat production through the supply of fertilizer. The possibilities of integration in the use of by-products through the development of research may tend to offset the effects of decline. Electric power and development subsidiary to mining may be shifted to alternative uses. Non-metallic minerals vary in relation to the demands of the foreign and domestic markets. Gypsum, brick, and building materials are directly affected by the construction industries. Coal mining in the Maritimes is related to increasing costs and increasing development of industry, limited, of course, by the competition of electric power from the projected St. Lawrence waterways and to attempts to encourage and enlarge the domestic market by tariffs and bounties and again the St. Lawrence waterways.

APPENDIX 2

It is a strange comment that finance should present the most serious aspect of the railway problem and yet remain the subject about which almost the least work has been done. Periodic crises lead to the establishment of Royal Commissions, and the results are in the form of panic literature rather than exhaustive studies of the field as a whole. Nevertheless, the recommendations of Royal Commissions indicate decided trends, especially when considered over a long period. It has become fairly obvious that transportation must be considered as a unit, and that navigation cannot be isolated from rail transportation nor the Canadian Pacific and private enterprise from the Canadian National and government ownership.

The transportation problem began with the construction of canals and improvements of the St. Lawrence waterways. Railways were built as supplements to the canals to overcome the hardships of slow transportation and closed seasons of navigation. Transportation was dependent, from the beginning, on government support. The Grand Trunk operated under private enterprise was given strong support by the government; the canals and the Intercolonial and P.E.I. railways were constructed by the government. From the beginning, returns on capital invested were met by earnings on traffic in the case of railways and to a certain extent in the case of canals by collection of tolls. It was obvious, however, that these means were inadequate, with the result that the tariff was imposed to meet the deficits. The tariff was regarded as a secondary toll or rate on traffic.

The overwhelming importance of water transportation in relation to the St. Lawrence contributed to an emphasis on the production and export of staples, as shown in the dominance at various stages of fur and lumber, and, with the improvement of transportation by canals and railways, of wheat and agricultural products. Emphasis was on raw materials which were subject to wide fluctuations in returns as a result of prices and yields. Consequently, while on the one hand returns on capital invested by the government in canals and by the government and private enterprise in railways were inflexible as far as the government was concerned and relatively inflexible (in so far as securities were in the form of bonds rather than stocks) as far as private enterprise was concerned, earnings were subject to wide fluctuations since returns from customs fluctuated with imports, which were directly affected by exports. Returns from freight rates and tolls fluctuated similarly.

During periods of depression, government finance was exposed to serious deficits as a result of the importance of staples and of the tariff. Private enterprise in railways was exposed to losses from the same source. On the other hand, the tariff was more flexible than rates, and during a period of depression increases were made as a result of government deficits, and of attempts of manufacturers to secure protection from manufactured products dumped by more highly industrialized countries. Increase in the tariff and attempts to stimulate imports of capital by further transportation improvements, coinciding with the prosperity phase of the business cycle, brought a temporary solution to the problem of deficits. Completion of the Intercolonial Railway by the government in 1876, the National Policy of 1878, and the plan to construct the Canadian Pacific Railway were factors overcoming the difficulties of the seventies. The part played by the government in the construction and deepening of the canals and in the construction of the Intercolonial Railway, and the problems of fixed charges during a period of depression, accentuated the importance attached to construction under private enterprise. The tariff tended to impose too heavy a burden on the staple industries. Private enterprise provided for greater flexibility without the danger of fixed charges and deficits during the depression stage. The determined attempts to enlist the interests of private capitalists for construction of the Canadian Pacific Railway, and the generous support in land, money, and railways made possible avoidance of inflexible drains on the government and provided a flexible financial structure for private enterprise.

Inflexibility of the tariff downwards contributed to the difficulties during the period of prosperity which began with the discovery of gold in the Klondike in 1896, the opening of the Kootenay by the Crow's Nest Pass Railway and the lowering of railway rates on settlers' effects and grain which accompanied the same development, completion of the St. Lawrence waterways to fourteen-foot draught, the opening of the West and its accompanying increase in immigration of labour and importation of capital. Expansion made possible a marked increase in dividends to Canadian Pacific shareholders and a marked increase in surplus from the tariff, which provided support for government construction of the Transcontinental Railway from Moncton to Winnipeg and for construction of the Canadian Northern and the Grand Trunk under private enterprise with governmental assistance. With the war, the elasticity of private enterprise was not in evidence and the Canadian Northern, the Grand Trunk Pacific, and Grand Trunk came into the hands of the government. Attempts to locate a scapegoat for the present railroad problem have led to charges that the Laurier Administration was responsible in not forcing an amalgamation of the Canadian Northern and the Grand Trunk Pacific[6] and that the Borden Administration should have refused assistance to the Canadian Northern Railway at the onset of the war. It is important to emphasize that expansion of credit in the period from 1900 to 1914 facilitated expansion of railroads with government assistance and under private enterprise by the Canadian Pacific Railway. In the war and the post-war period further expansion of credit, which followed the enormous speculative boom of the United States, led to marked expansion on the part of the Canadian Pacific and Canadian National Railways. Again attempts to locate a scapegoat have been in evidence.

The problem of government finance has become acute with the depression, partly because natural resources have not shown adequate resilience. Expansion of credit has crystallized with government ownership into heavy fixed charges during a period of depression. Moreover,

6"The Canadian National Railway System," letter addressed to the Rt. Hon. Arthur Meighen, Prime Minister of Canada, by Sir Joseph Flavelle, Bart., Aug. 12, 1921, p. 3.

the loss of traffic has been responsible for operating deficits which have accumulated with fixed charges. Private enterprise, representing the alternative of elasticity, has been forced to give evidence of elasticity by passing dividends. Government finance, in so far as it was related to lands and railroads, was dependent on earnings and on continued application of the tariff. Elimination of the elasticity feature, as shown in the disappearance of C.P.R. dividends, tends to accentuate the burden of government finance. The formation of the arbitration board centres directly on the problem of solving the inelastic factors, and renders more urgent an analysis of the position of the tariff and of government finance generally. The efficacy of the tariff from the standpoint of waterways and railways varies in part with imports, and in turn with exports and accordingly with earnings dependent on railway rates and traffic. Deficits on the railway and on canals are directly linked to returns from the tariff. The more complicated phases of the problem arise from the marked expansion incidental to rapid exploitation of virgin natural resources, accentuated by the prosperity phases of the business cycle. The tariff, by remaining at a high level, or by an increase, may lead to a substantial increase in revenue without affecting relatively the position of the burden, but if the increase in revenue is followed by an increased expenditure on the part of the government, and by new flotations of capital, the fixed charges increase rapidly. Increasing surpluses are thus devoted more and more to the payment of interest charges on capital when they should be devoted to an increasing extent to capital. As a result, during periods of depression, fixed charges on capital invested during the boom period become a serious burden. The burden may be borne without serious difficulty, provided the chief exports continue in a strong competitive position in relation to other exporting areas. On the other hand, falling prices and exploitation of virgin natural resources may seriously accentuate the burden. The tariff tends to become inadequate as a result, and it may, by virtue of protective features, add to the burden. The impasse which develops under these conditions, and which has been evident in this depression, can be met in part by further improvements in transportation, such as the St. Lawrence waterway, which will lower costs of transportation and strengthen the position of Canada as a wheat producer. The difficulties are, of course, obvious but not insuperable. It is a temporary solution and serves to emphasize the importance of making the tariff a more flexible and scientific instrument. During a period of prosperity the tariff should be raised to act as a brake and to provide for surpluses not only to meet the short-run railway operating deficits of Canadian transportation, but also the interest and depreciation of capital. If railroad rates are lowered at the beginning of a period of prosperity tariff rates should be raised accordingly. A scientific application of the tariff offers at least a partial solution to the dilemma which arises from fluctuations in a country dependent on staples, especially wheat, and in turn on government ownership and fixed charges. Lowering the tariff during the period of a depression[7] and raising the tariff[8] during a period of prosperity might do much to alleviate the problems of a staple-producing area.

The disappearance of elasticity in railroad finance which follows the passing of dividends on common stock in the Canadian Pacific Railway and the emergence of the arbitral board involve considerations of fresh standards for rate adjustment. It is no longer feasible to regard 7 per cent dividends on common stock of the Canadian Pacific Railway as a measuring rod for railway rates and it may no longer be feasible to regard the financially healthy state of the Canadian Pacific Railway as a guide. This arrangement implied that rates providing satisfactory returns for the Canadian Pacific did not necessarily provide satisfactory returns for the government railways. Earnings from these rates were necessarily supplemented by support from the government to make up deficits either in terms of deficits on operation or of interest on capital. Assuming that the arbitral board maintains an even balance between the two railroads and avoids encroachment of the Canadian Pacific on the Canadian National or of the Canadian National on the Canadian Pacific, rates must be adjusted in relation to the total capital structure of the railways rather than to the capital structure of the line dominated by private enterprise. It becomes possible and essential that the burden of railroad finance be adjusted more closely to the relative ability of supporting areas. Assuming relative stability in the production of raw materials as a result of exhaustion of natural resources the tariff must assume to an increasing extent the position of a toll, as Galt originally planned, and should approximate the deficit on transportation finance. Consequently the tariff and railway rates, but particularly the former, must be linked in more direct fashion to the problem of returns on investment, whether in terms of government ownership or private enterprise. The tariff may serve to operate as a

[7]We tend to put the Liberal party in power for periods of prosperity and the Conservative party for periods of depression and thereby to put the wrong party in power at the extremes of the business cycle.

[8]Tariff is used in a broad sense and might be extended even to the point of an export tax.

new base, in the place of dividends on Canadian Pacific stock, by which deficits on the Canadian National and on canals should approximate returns from the tariff, and railway rates should provide in addition earnings on the Canadian National adequate to provide returns on Canadian Pacific securities.

Aside from the problem of meeting deficits on transportation, the public debt of Canada (provincial, municipal, and federal) remains of serious proportions. The transportation problem has accentuated the difficulties and has forced consideration of fiscal and monetary policy. Fiscal difficulties and inelasticity of structure have steadily driven toward a realignment of monetary policy. Commercial credit in a young country subject to wide fluctuations has been subject to systematic protection by banking policy and banking legislation. Governmental credit and corporate credit have suffered as a result of their relatively weaker position in the credit structure. Continued expansion of government credit in terms of continued deficits and increasing rigidity have become imperative factors in the appointment of a Royal Commission on banking and in the recommendation and establishment of new machinery designed to eliminate strains and so introduce unity, strength, and flexibility.

APPENDIX 3

The effect of the industrial revolution on Canadian development as shown in the expansion of wheat production, of mining—for example in Northern Ontario and British Columbia—and of the lumber and pulp and paper industry has been obvious, not only in each basic industry but also in subordinate industries. Integration between basic industries has hastened development—for example, the development of mining as a by-product of wheat production, and the expansion of lumbering in British Columbia in relation to the demands of agriculture on the Prairies. Slowing down of the rate of expansion through exhaustion of raw materials necessitates (1) the development of export markets in basic industries, and (2) closer integration between basic industries—such integration as is evident in the development of the fertilizer industry in relation to mining at Trail to assist agriculture in western Canada. This integration may be assisted materially by scientific research.

The development of subordinate industries in relation to basic industries has been evident primarily in areas of cheap power and cheap water transportation, as in Ontario and Quebec. The growth of industry in Ontario and Quebec has been evident in the urbanization of population, the revolution of agriculture in eastern Canada to meet the demands of an industrial population (winter dairying), and in the emergence of large cities such as Toronto and Montreal. The development of the Hydro-Electric Power Commission in Ontario and of large power corporations in Quebec, and the rise of diversified industry, have been chiefly a result of the demands of the basic industries. This industrial area is powerfully influenced by fluctuation in the basic industries as shown in wheat, pulp and paper, and mining. The position of gold mining during a period of depression has tended to serve as a cushion for the decline in certain staples.

The problem of subordinate industries, particularly as represented by eastern Canada, consists chiefly in the relative rigidity in the capital structure—for example, in government support to the Ontario Hydro-Electric Power Commission. The burden of this rigidity was not evident during a period of prosperity and during a period in which relatively low costs were possible as a result of government owner-ship, of practically virgin natural resources in terms of a large un-tapped source of power such as Niagara Falls, and of the application of mature technique. Moreover, the burden of the tariff on sources of power—for example, coal and the subsidy to coal mines in Cape Breton operating on an increasing cost basis—tends to accentuate the effects of rigidity. Support of the iron and steel industry has the same effect. In addition to the problem of government ownership, emphasis on inefficiently capitalized industries, that is, with emphasis on bonds and possibly over-capitalization, accentuates rigidity. The effect of this rigidity becomes serious with attempts to maintain prices of manu-factured products with or without attempts at combination. Such rigidity bears with great severity on the staple-producing region in the form of debts, high costs of production, and lower standards of living during a period of depression. Elasticity in private enterprise provides limited relief as shown in the passing of dividends. The burden is shifted in part to employees and becomes evident in a lower standard of living in the East as in the West. The tendency of gold mining to buoy up the industrial East may have the effect of increasing the rigidity in relation to the West in so far as it makes less necessary the urgent scaling down of debts.

The burden is divided unevenly in the East, industries subject to marked competition being forced to lower prices, as in the case of agriculture, more rapidly than industries which possess greater possi-bilities of monopoly. In the meantime, certain industries have the advantage of foreign markets for specialized commodities such as apples, potatoes, and fur, but the advantage has been offset in part by competition from other areas—for example, British Columbia as a result of the Panama Canal—by tariffs in the United States, by depreciated exchange in Great Britain, or by violent fluctuations in prices, such as have affected fur farming. The fishing industry has been linked to an increasing extent with the internal market as a result of the development of the fresh-fish industry and the severe competition which has affected dry fishing.

From this analysis it becomes obvious that the fluctuations of the Canadian economy which follow from its dependence on wheat demand the introduction of elastic machinery by which the burdens imposed may be adjusted with the greatest possible speed. Improvement of transportation for wheat with a view to lowering the cost of production, in the case of the St. Lawrence waterways or the Peace River outlet, may reduce the burden on western Canada and strengthen the competitive position of Canada among the wheat producers of the world. On the other hand, along with technological improvements, political institutions must be developed to solve adequately the problem of inequality of burden. Such institutions involve adequate control in a federal centre, in order that mechanisms may be devised which will check the effects of rigidity and provide relief from the problems of a fluctuating economy. Such mechanism involves safeguards to labour in industry and agriculture.

Interrelations between the Fur Trade of
Canada and the United States*

IT is no easy task to survey the interrelations between the significant
and continuous fur trade development characterized by the Canadian trade and that phase of the fur trade in which, to quote Chittenden, "the events have been so diverse, and have borne so little
relation to each other, that the task of making a connected narrative
has been well-nigh impossible" and "lacking in . . . deep national
significance."[1] It is possible that such a survey may throw light on the
complex problems of the American trade. Although the excellent
monographs on the American fur trade, such as those by Kellogg,
Stevens, and Chittenden, provide substantial footing for a broader
interpretation of the movements of the American trade and throw
important light on Canadian development, it is scarcely necessary to
emphasize the extent of the work yet to be done in both the Canadian
and the American fields before an adequate interpretation is possible.

The beginnings of the fur trade in North America corresponded
roughly with the marked rise in prices in Spain which followed the
importation of treasure from North America and led to the opening
of the Spanish market, the development of the fishing industry,
especially dried fish, and the opening up of the Gulf of St. Lawrence,
particularly Gaspé, and the progress of settlement in New England.[2]
The accessibility of the St. Lawrence to the forest areas of the Precambrian shield of the northern half of North America led to the
rapid growth of trade with the hunting Indians, to the expulsion of
the agricultural Indians from the St. Lawrence Valley, and to the
beginnings of strife between the Iroquois and the Algonquins and
French.

*From Mississippi Valley Historical Review, XX (1933), 321–32.
[1]Hiram M. Chittenden, The American Fur Trade of the Far West (New York,
1902), I, ix, xi. "The complexity of its problems is such as almost to defy unified
treatment." Wayne E. Stevens, The North West Fur Trade, 1763–1800 (Urbana,
Ill., 1928), pp. 13.
[2]Harold A. Innis, "The Rise and Fall of the Spanish Fishery in Newfoundland,"
Transactions of the Royal Society of Canada, third series, vol. XXV (1931),
Section II, 51–70. [See this volume, p. 43.]

In the United States as in Canada the geographic background had a profound influence on the evolution of the fur trade. The short rivers of the Appalachian drainage basin and especially of New England, and the position of fur as a commodity which commanded an immediate sale and large returns in the European market, were factors contributing to the rapid destruction of fur-bearing animals following expansion of the fishing industry and the growth of settlement along the New England shore. Profits from the fur trade contributed directly to the growth of industries which displaced it. Organization of the trade was consequently not elaborate and the shift to new activities was made without serious handicaps from vested interests. The character of fur trade development in New England was symbolic of the United States.[3]

The key to this development from the Atlantic coast was the Hudson River which tapped a wide area and by a narrow height of land reached the interior of the St. Lawrence drainage basin by the Richelieu River and, what was of more significance, by Oswego on Lake Ontario. The Dutch by the Hudson route came in contact with the Iroquois, agricultural Indians at war with the French and the hunting Indians, with the result that trade advanced through middlemen to the interior in competition with the St. Lawrence. The competitive struggle involved destruction of the Hurons in 1648–9 and substantial control of the fur trade in the interior by the Dutch[4] and the Iroquois. The relatively weak position of the Dutch trading organization on the Hudson restricted by the location of the Iroquois, the increasing strength of English trade based on the growth of settlement in New England and the expansion of the fishing industry and trade between England, Newfoundland, New England, and the West Indies, and the aggressiveness of the English in attacks on Dutch trade as shown in the Navigation Acts of the fifties and sixties, led to the disappearance of the Dutch from the Hudson in 1664. The limitations imposed on the Dutch trading organization by the Iroquois and the displacement of the Dutch by the English precluded the development of a vigorous trading organization on the banks of the Hudson River.

The disturbance which accompanied the capture of New York by the English in 1664 and the aggressiveness of the French after 1663, following the difficulties attendant on the disappearance of the Hurons

[3]See F. X. Moloney, *The Fur Trade in New England, 1620–1676* (Cambridge, Mass., 1931), *passim*.
[4]See R. J. Parker, "The Iroquois and the Dutch Fur Trade, 1609–1664," master's thesis, University of California, 1930.

and the activity of the Iroquois, enabled the French to expand the trade to the interior by the Ottawa, first by attracting new Indians such as the Ottawas as middlemen and later by sending French traders to the north by the Ottawa and to the south, for example La Salle, by the upper St. Lawrence and the Great Lakes. By the end of the century France had achieved substantial control at the mouth of the Mississippi, on Hudson Bay, and in the interior, but success was destined to be of short duration. The success of the French in penetrating the interior and the relatively weak position of the Iroquois and the English hastened the development of trade through other routes to the interior and particularly to Hudson Bay. Gillam from New England and Radisson and Groseilliers from New France, combined with English capital, contributed to the establishment and growth of the Hudson's Bay Company, 1668–70. Moreover, expansion of the fishing industry and of trade in New England and the trade in slaves and sugar to the West Indies and the consequent improvement of British industry and trade were responsible for the retreat of the French from Nova Scotia and Hudson Bay in the Treaty of Utrecht.

The Treaty of Utrecht released English competition from the north and the south. Expansion of trade with the West Indies and of fishing and of shipbuilding in New England strengthened the position of the English from New York and made possible the development of a trading organization, the establishment of Oswego on Lake Ontario, and the sale of cheap West India rum and superior English cloths and kettles as an attraction to the Indians of the interior. This aggressive support encouraged the Iroquois in the expansion of activities to Detroit and to Lake Michigan and led, through the Fox wars, to the marked decline of French control over trade in the Great Lakes region. The decline of French control of the upper lakes from Montreal was offset in part by the expansion of control from New Orleans by the Mississippi.[5] On the other hand, penetration of the Iroquois and the English implied division of French control from New Orleans and Montreal. Withdrawal of the French from Hudson Bay and occupation of posts by the English led to competition in the interior by the numerous large rivers flowing to Hudson Bay. Pressure from the north and from the centre by English trade prompted expansion under La Vérendrye and his successors to the Northwest by way of Lake Superior.

[5]See N. M. Miller Surrey, *The Commerce of Louisiana during the French Régime, 1699–1763*, Columbia University Studies in History, Economics and Public Law, LXXI (New York, 1916).

The relatively low heights of land between the drainage basins pointing toward the Atlantic and the Arctic in North America, the character of fur as a commodity with light bulk and high value, the length of the main rivers and the difficulties of control from political centres at the mouth of the rivers, and the relative mobility of the Indian and the trader, facilitated the flow of trade between territories marginal to each drainage basin. Political influence was not adequate to check trade between the St. Lawrence and the Hudson, Hudson Bay, and the Mississippi. Traders such as Radisson and Groseilliers moved easily from one sphere of influence to the other. Nevertheless, in spite of this ease of movement in the interior, the drainage basin continued as an important geographical and trade unit; mastery over the main entrance to the drainage basin was therefore of vital importance.

Control from the Atlantic was based largely on the relative success of integration of trade and industry of the European empires. New England and Newfoundland exported cod[6] and other products to the West Indies and to Europe and received sugar, molasses, and rum from the West Indies, spices and other products from Spain and the Mediterranean, and manufactured products from England. Slaves were purchased with English manufactures and sold to the West Indies for the production of sugar and the consumption of cod. France, on the other hand, found it difficult to link her limited dry fishing from Cape Breton and the Gulf of St. Lawrence to the products of Canada and the French West Indies. The French West Indies became a support to New England rather than New France and to the English fur trade rather than the French. France had no New England, with its shipping, fishing, industry, and trade. The interpretation of the history of North America in terms of rum and brandy has not been written, but in the fur trade, rum represented the contribution of the West Indies to trade of the Old Empire, and brandy the emphasis on French vineyards and self-sufficiency. The trade of Great Britain in tropical products made it possible for Anthony Henday to write, in describing the causes of French success in the fur trade in the Northwest in 1754–5, "if they had Brazil tobacco, which they have not, [they] would entirely cut off our trade." The economic strength supported by this integration of industry and trade weakened the internal position of the French and contributed to the collapse of the French empire

[6]See Harold A. Innis, "An Introduction to the Economic History of the Maritimes," in *Canadian Historical Association Report*, 1931. [See this volume, p. 27.]

brought about by the naval and military victories at the entrance to the St. Lawrence, the results of which were embodied in the Treaty of Paris.

In the first decade after the withdrawal of the French, disturbances in the interior, especially Pontiac's war and the disruption of trading organization to France, were followed by the rapid expansion of the English organization from Albany and from Montreal to the interior. The commissariat organization of the army and existing French experience and technique assisted in the expansion of the fur trade. Supported by West Indies rum and British manufactures, and with the use of boats from Oswego on the Great Lakes, English traders expanded trade to the posts at Detroit and Michilimackinac. Competition, especially in the northern posts and at posts located in the Mississippi drainage basin by the French and Spanish from New Orleans, led to the breakdown of regulations restricting traders to the posts and to more rapid penetration to the interior after 1768. Recovery of trade[7] was the result of the combination of the West Indies rum, the position of Albany and lake boats, and the accessibility of the St. Lawrence to English manufactures and to the interior by canoes and the Ottawa route as well by the upper St. Lawrence. The geographic strategy of the St. Lawrence route as shown in the French régime became increasingly evident with expansion of trade to the interior. Canoes and the Ottawa route were important in the relatively rapid transport of furs to Montreal and England.

Expansion of the internal trade from Albany and Montreal was accompanied by an expansion of trade in the English colonies. This expansion was met by a closer check following the application of Great Britain's colonial policy and particularly with pressure from the vested interests created in British legislation by the sugar planters of the West Indies. The Molasses Act of 1733, the diplomatic compromise[8] resulting in the retention of Guadaloupe by France and the taking over of Canada by England, and the Sugar Act of 1764, accentuated the difficulties of the English colonies in meeting the increased demands for sugar, molasses, and rum for the expanding fur trade by prohibiting the acquisition of supplies from the French West Indies. External difficulties contributed to internal difficulties, as shown in the extension of the control of the St. Lawrence by extending the boun-

[7]See Marjory G. Jackson, "The Beginning of British Trade at Michilimackinac," *Minnesota History*, XI (1930), 231–70; also W. S. Wallace, "The Pedlars from Quebec," *Canadian Historical Review*, XIII (1932), 387–402.

[8]See Frank W. Pitman, *The Development of the British West Indies, 1700–1763* (New Haven, 1917).

daries of the province of Quebec under the Quebec Act in 1774, and were followed by the disturbances of the American Revolution. As a result of these disturbances traders moved from Albany to Montreal,[9] and with supplies of manufactured goods from England and of rum from the West Indies[10] the control of trade from the St. Lawrence to the interior became practically a monopoly. English traders continued to penetrate to the interior and particularly to the Northwest. Again and in part as a result of hostilities they crowded to the far Northwest and in 1778 Pond penetrated to the Athabaska region and opened the trade to the Mackenzie River drainage basin.

The result of these developments was shown in the emergence of the Northwest Company, the first organization to operate on a continental scale in North America. Large-scale organizations characterized the Canadian trade and their strength was registered directly in the activities of the weaker organizations of the American trade. This organization was a combination or partnership which brought together aggressive individualistic traders, trained in the school of American commercialism and in the clan and family organization of Scotland. It combined navigation on the Great Lakes and on the Ottawa, the organization of food supplies in meeting the demands of the heavy transportation costs to distant posts in the interior, the support of cheap British manufactures and West India rum, and an effective trading organization in relation first to Albany and later to Montreal, with remarkable success. The completion of an important agreement in the history of the Northwest Company in 1783, the date of the Treaty of Versailles, was probably more than a coincidence, but the trade to the northwest and to the southwest continued to be supported from Montreal. Expansion to the northwest was accompanied by expansion to the southwest. In the face of competition from Spanish and French from New Orleans, British traders were strongly entrenched in the upper Mississippi valley. The problems of the southwest were accentuated by more rapid decline of the fur trade and eventually by the recovery of the American trade and the withdrawal of Montreal traders from the western posts following the Jay Treaty. This retreat led to the migration of traders to the north and to the intense competition between the New Northwest Company or the XY Company which culminated in the amalgamation of 1804. The enlargement of the Northwest Company necessitated expansion to new

[9]See R. H. Fleming, "Phyn, Ellice and Company of Schenectady," in *Contributions to Canadian Economics*, IV, 1932 (University of Toronto Studies, History and Economics, 1932), 7–39.

[10]G. S. Graham, *British Policy and Canada, 1774–1791* (London, 1930), chap. VI.

territory and Simon Fraser and David Thompson moved into the Pacific coast drainage basin.

The difficulties of the American trade during the period of hostilities which attended a lack of cheap manufactured goods and the entrenchment of Montreal in the trade in American territory, during and after the hostilities, precluded rapid recovery from Albany. Limited development in the interior was offset by the expansion of external trade. The break-down of British control in the American Revolution enabled New England vessels to extend their trade to the Pacific. The voyages of Captain Cook along the Pacific coast attracted traders from England and New England. Expansion of the Northwest Company to the Mackenzie River and the discovery of Cook's Inlet stimulated interest in possibilities of a final discovery of the northwest passage[11] and led to the expeditions of Mackenzie down the Mackenzie River in 1789 and to the Pacific in 1793. Prospects of this route were communicated through the Northwest Company to New England[12] and further encouraged New England vessels to participate in Pacific and oriental trade. The failure of the northern passage guaranteed more substantial control in the face of English monopoly of the East India Company and the South Sea Company on the Pacific. New England shipping expanded rapidly in the exploitation of the sea otter trade of the Pacific coast.[13] Exhaustion of the maritime fur trade on the Pacific coast was accompanied by the gradual recovery of the internal fur trade and the spread of settlement to the Ohio and the Mississippi. In the recovery of the fur trade John Jacob Astor played an important role through his success in re-establishing the position of the Albany and New York route, through his ability to develop the European and English markets, and through his reliance on the experience and organization of the trade from Montreal. The example of the Northwest Company as the first large-scale continental organization in North America stimulated Astor in the development of a similar organization in the United States.[14] Relying on officers and men trained in the Northwest Company and realizing the

[11]Harold A. Innis, "Peter Pond and the Influence of Captain James Cook on Exploration in the Interior of North America," *Transactions of the Royal Society of Canada*, third series, vol. XXII (1928), Section II, pp. 131–41.

[12]See Alexander Henry to William Edgar, Sept. 1, 1785, in Harold A. Innis, *Peter Pond, Fur Trader and Adventurer* (Toronto, 1930), pp. 129ff.; also Samuel E. Morison, *The Maritime History of Massachusetts, 1783–1860* (Boston, 1921), chap. IV.

[13]F. W. Howay, "An Outline Sketch of the Maritime Fur Trade," in *Canadian Historical Association Report*, 1932, pp. 5–14.

[14]Kenneth W. Porter, *John Jacob Astor, Business Man* (Cambridge, Mass., 1931).

importance of moving inland following the exhaustion of the sea otter on the Pacific coast, he attempted to link up the internal trade to the Pacific. His failure was partly the result, as suggested above, of the entrenched position of the Northwest Company and of the effects of pressure on the Company in the Great Lakes area leading to their expansion on the Pacific. Astor's defeat on the Pacific facilitated concentration on the Great Lakes trade and enabled him to build up the American Fur Company. The ground had been prepared for his activities in the gradual withdrawal of the British traders after the Jay Treaty and the establishment of the factory system by the government of the United States in 1795–6.[15] The Louisiana Purchase and the development of the Missouri trade, the emergence of the American Fur Company, the War of 1812, and the Act of 1815 prohibiting British trade in American territory and presumably passed at Astor's instigation, were factors steadily improving the position of the American traders.[16]

Increasing strength of the Hudson's Bay Company, particularly after the War of 1812, and withdrawal of Canadian traders from American territory contributed to the difficulties of the Northwest Company from Montreal and hastened the amalgamation of 1821 and the emergence of supremacy of the Hudson Bay route. American trade after 1815, in a sense, squeezed the two large Canadian companies into one unit. Decline of the St. Lawrence route to the Northwest and its practical disappearance after 1821 released labour for the expansion of the American trade. In a letter dated April 1817, Ramsay Crooks wrote: "It will still be good policy to admit freely & without the least restraint the Canadian Boatmen, these people are indispensable to the successful prosecution of the trade, their places cannot be supplied by Americans who are for the most part . . . too independent to submit quietly to a proper controul, and who can gain any where a subsistence much superior to a man of the interior."[17] Amalgamation released not only labour but men trained in the rigorous school of intense competition in the decade from 1810 to 1820. Kenneth Mackenzie became a powerful support to the aggressiveness and expansion of the American Fur Company in the Missouri trade. Amalgamation

[15]See Edgar B. Wesley, "The Government Factory System among the Indians, 1795–1822," *Journal of Economic and Business History*, IV, pt. 2 (1932), 487–511.

[16]Edgar B. Wesley, "Some Official Aspects of the Fur Trade in the Northwest, 1815–1825," *North Dakota Historical Quarterly*, VI (1932), 201–9.

[17]Cited by Grace L. Nute, *The Voyageur* (New York, 1931), pp. 203–4, 279n., and chap. viii, *passim*.

of the Northwest Company and the Hudson's Bay Company, the rise of the American Fur Company, and the disappearance of the government factory system were closely interrelated.

In the period after 1821 the close control and centralization of the Hudson's Bay Company in northwestern Canada provided a substantial check to American expansion. Neutrality between the American and Canadian companies was shown in agreements for handling trade in competitive territory along the border.[18] Increased settlement weakened the position of company control and led to the development of the small private trader and trading organization. In eastern Canada American traders purchased furs at various centres throughout the country.[19] The introduction of the steamboat on the Missouri and the Mississippi improved the position of the small trader and led to the development of trade from Minneapolis and St. Paul by the Red River to territory of the Hudson's Bay Company.[20] Finally the steamboat to Red River hastened the decline of Hudson's Bay Company monopoly and the sale of Hudson's Bay Company territory to Canada. The growth of settlement in the Columbia River region was followed by the retreat of the Hudson's Bay Company after the settlement of the Oregon boundary dispute in 1846. This change was hastened by the emergence of trading organizations in London designed to handle the furs of large numbers of private traders. The firm of Lampson's[21] became an important competitor of the Hudson's Bay Company and eventually a working agreement was arranged through Sir Curtis Miranda Lampson who reached the highly influential position of deputy governor of the Hudson's Bay Company (1863–71). In this

[18]See letters in Porter, *Astor*, II, 1198, 1203; also agreements of 1833 and 1840 regarding competition in Rainy Lake, Winnipeg, and Red River districts, in E. H. Oliver, ed., *The Canadian North-West, Its Early Development and Legislative Records*, Canadian Archives Publications, no. 9 (Ottawa, 1915), II, 716, 805–6. On the other hand concentration accentuated severity of competition in the mountain region and was followed by systematic destruction of fur-bearing animals. John McLean, *Notes of a Twenty-Five Years' Service in the Hudson's Bay Territory* (London, 1849), II, 262–3.

[19]See the description of fur sales at Haliburton with buyers from New York, Boston, Toronto, Quebec, and Peterborough, in G. S. Thompson, *Up to Date or the Life of a Lumberman* (n. p. [1895?]), p. 18. On the activities of an agent selling furs to New York see *History of the County of Middlesex* (Toronto, 1889), p. 713.

[20]W. J. Petersen, "Steamboating in the Upper Mississippi Fur Trade," *Minnesota History*, XIII (1932), 221–43. Also Fred A. Bill, "Steamboating on the Red River of the North," *North Dakota Historical Quarterly*, II (1928), 100–19.

[21]On the relations of Lampson with the American Fur Company see Grace L. Nute, "The Papers of the American Fur Company," *American Historical Review*, XXXII (1926), 527.

crucial period the Hudson's Bay Company lost control to Grand Trunk interests in 1863 and finally to Canada with the sale of Rupert's Land in 1869. On the other hand the position of the field service of the company, in other words of the wintering partners, led to a struggle headed by Donald Smith in which control of the fur trade was regained. It would carry this paper too far afield to trace the influence of Donald Smith (Lord Strathcona) in the construction of the Canadian Pacific Railway. It is sufficient to note that improvement in transportation facilitated competition, and American and Canadian traders have steadily continued to press on the last reserves of the monopoly of the Hudson's Bay Company. American whalers have become traders and have been followed by traders along the route through Bering Sea to the western Arctic. American traders, particularly during the war under the Lamson Hubbard Company of Boston, made a determined drive on the position of the Hudson's Bay Company but without eventual success. The American market assumed new importance in the post-war period and supported new competition. Finally it has been charged[22] that, during the speculative boom which centred about the New York market, American finance contributed to the expansion of the Hudson's Bay Company and to its present difficulties. In Canada the boom was accompanied by the construction of railway lines to Churchill and to Moosonee on Hudson Bay.

The fur trade of the North American continent was an index of wide movements. It persisted in space and time with greatest continuity in the forested areas of the Precambrian formation and in relation to the support of a highly industrialized area and a metropolitan market. Throughout the history of the continent the territory restricted in diversity of product and dependent on a staple commodity steadily drifted into the control of a metropolitan market dependent on cheap year-round water transportation. Cod from Newfoundland, beaver from Canada, and sugar from the West Indies depended on commercial and industrial England. In the face of this drift Spain, Holland, and France disappeared from North America, and because of this drift the United States emerged as a separate entity.

The fur trade of the United States gradually evolved as independent of British control. New England shipping exploited the accessible territory of British Columbia. Rise of settlement was followed by decline of the fur trade and the shift in the trade route from St. Lawrence to Hudson Bay was followed, as has been shown, by a

[22]*The Reflections of Inkyo on the Great Company* (London, 1931), *passim.*

migration of labour and skill to the American West. In the United States the divided character of the upper reaches of the Mississippi drainage basin, particularly in the Missouri[23] and the Mississippi, the cultural traits of the Indians especially on the plains, the difficulty of obtaining cheap supplies of manufactured products, the following up of settlement on arable land, the importance of coarse furs and hides as in the case of the buffalo and the rapidity of their exploitation, were factors responsible for a development along a different line than was characteristic of the Canadian trade. Lack of continuity, Indian wars, the control exercised by one man or one family as in the case of the Astors, characterized the American rather than the Canadian trade. The American Fur Company deserves thorough investigation as an institution representing the fur trade at its peak in the United States.

The interrelations of theories of development in the United States and Canada have been influenced by studies of the fur trade. The importance of settlement gave the fur trade of the United States an essentially frontier aspect and strengthened the position of Turner's thesis.[24] In Canada the fur trade assumed a permanent and not a transient phase. It is significant that during the past year (1932), the Hudson's Bay Company boat made no visit to the depot at Charlton Island in James Bay for the first time in over two and a half centuries.

[23]Isaac Lippincott, A Century and a Half of Fur Trade at St. Louis, in Washington University Studies, III (St. Louis, 1915–16), series 4, pt. ii, 205–42.

[24]Frederick J. Turner, The Character and Influence of the Indian Trade in Wisconsin, in Johns Hopkins University Studies in Historical and Political Science, IX (Baltimore, 1891), series 9, pts. xi–xii; Wilson P. Shortridge, The Transition of a Typical Frontier (Menasha, Minn., 1922).

An Introduction to the Economic History of
Ontario from Outpost to Empire*

IN view of the important work on various phases of the subject considered in this paper it may seem presumptuous that one should use
the title selected. On the other hand it is the plan of the paper to
emphasize the essential unity of the subject and the underlying factors
responsible for peculiar types of development, and it is perhaps not
too much to say that from this standpoint the title might more accur-
ately be "An introduction to an introduction to the economic history
of Ontario." It is scarcely necessary to emphasize the enormous gaps
in our knowledge of the economic history of Ontario. We have almost
no thorough survey of any of our industries and we have no adequate
history of agriculture. Extension of the subject is possible with increasing stress on the part of the archives, museums, and libraries, on
economic material. The most serious weakness, however, is the lack of
appreciation of the relative value of economic material or the lack of
attention on the part of economists to the evolutionary character of
economic institutions. Economics and history have suffered immeasura-
bly from this neglect.[1] These considerations are the justification and
the danger of this paper.

An understanding of the main features of the geographic background of the province is essential to an appreciation of the main
trends of economic development. Geological history is a prerequisite
to the study of later history. The ice age left its stamp on the history
of Ontario and of Canada. Retreating ice sheets contributed to the
formation of large bodies of water. Lake Agassiz (now dwindled to
Lake Manitoba), Lake Algonquin (now the upper lakes), and Lake
Iroquois (now Lake Ontario), all with the northern outlets by Hudson
Bay and St. Lawrence River dammed by the ice, poured through
southern outlets following respectively the Red River, the Mississippi,

*From *Papers and Records of the Ontario Historical Society*, XXX (1934),
111–23.
[1]H. A. Innis, "The Teaching of Economic History in Canada," *Contributions to
Canadian Economics*, II, 1929 (University of Toronto Studies, History and
Economics, 1930) 52–68. [See this volume, p. 3.]

and the Hudson. Lake Algonquin flowed into the Mississipi, and then into Lake Iroquois, alternately by Niagara Falls and the Trent valley.[2] The final retreat of the ice sheet opened the outlet of the St. Lawrence following Logan's fault line along the southeastern edge of the Precambrian formation. These shifting outlets have had a profound influence on economic development since trade like water has tended to flow at different periods through the same outlets but finally has tended to settle down to the St. Lawrence. Soil was again largely the result of the ice age. Earth was scraped from the Precambrian area, carried down and deposited in what is now Southern Ontario, or was held in Lake Ojibway by the retreating ice sheet, further north, to be deposited as the clay belt. The geologically recent emergence of the topography has been responsible for the broken character of the waterways especially in the Precambrian area, and in the serious obstructions evident in the rapids of the main outlet, the upper St. Lawrence. The existence of large bodies of water in the Great Lakes tempered the climate and occasioned long autumns and late springs.

Flora reflected the influence of soil and climate. Migration of species following the retreating ice sheet and the geographic background have been responsible for distinct zones, first the Carolinian zone in territory south of a line from Toronto to Windsor, and including such species as the hickories, oaks, chestnut, and walnut;[3] second, the hardwood forest zone extending north to a line roughly from Anticosti to the head of Lake Winnipeg, or the northern limits of white and red pine, and including these conifers in addition to basswood, maple, ash, elm, birch, and beech; and third, the sub-arctic forest, extending north of the second zone to the boundaries of the province, which includes the black and white spruce, Banksian pine, poplar, larch, and balsam. Fauna was determined in part by thermal lines and by flora. Fur-bearing animals flourished in the hardwood forest and sub-arctic forest zones.

The culture of the Indians indicated more broadly the effects of the geographic background. The agricultural tribes of the eastern woodlands, the Hurons north of Lake Ontario, the Tobaccos in western Ontario, and the Neutrals north of Lake Erie, occupied the agricultural regions of Southern Ontario; and the migratory tribes of the eastern woodlands, the Algonquins on the Ottawa, the Ojibway north of Lake

[2]A. P. Coleman and W. A. Parks, *Elementary Geology* (London, 1930), pp. 354ff.

[3]See a brief survey of flora, *Canada Yearbook*, 1922–3, pp. 25–43, and of fauna, *ibid.*, 1921, pp. 82–7.

Superior, and the Crees south of Hudson and James bays, occupied the Precambrian forested areas and depended primarily on hunting.[4]

Recorded history begins with the appearance of Europeans in this setting. The importance of cheap water transportation to Quebec and Montreal accentuated dependence on staple products[5] and led to the development of trade in furs with the hunting Indians. Exploration and trade led to penetration of the northerly forested Precambrian regions by the numerous tributaries of the St. Lawrence by the use of facilities such as canoes provided by these Indians. The territory which has become the province of Ontario begins roughly at the point on the St. Lawrence above which the river was practically inaccessible. It is significant that this area was approached by a tributary which later became its western boundary. Champlain went up the Ottawa, crossed the portage to French River, and came down to Georgian Bay. The discovery of Lake Ontario was made from the north by Brulé on the Humber and by Champlain on the Trent system. Champlain might have descended the upper St. Lawrence before he ascended it.

Trade expanded to the north and was extended in the first half of the seventeenth century chiefly by the agricultural Indians marginal to the hunting regions, especially the Hurons in the vicinity of Lake Simcoe (Huronia). An alternative approach to Southern Ontario was available by the old outlet of Lake Iroquois to the Hudson River. In competition, the Dutch, and later the English (1664), obtained furs from this region through the Iroquois. The struggle waged between the Iroquois and the Hurons was a prelude to the struggle between New York and Montreal, which dominated the economic history of Ontario. The Iroquois, with a strong agricultural economy as a base, trapped and traded along the north shore of Lake Ontario and carried war to the point of destruction among the Hurons, the Neutrals, and the Tobaccos.

To oppose this development, the French were obliged to take a more direct interest in trade to the interior. Radisson and Groseilliers were among the forerunners of traders who endeavoured to re-establish the trade broken by Iroquois incursions, and who built up the trade carried on first by Ottawa middlemen and later by *coureurs de bois*. Finally a direct attempt to check the Iroquois and the New York route was made by a journey up the difficult St. Lawrence rapids by La Salle

---

[4]See D. Jenness, *The Indians of Canada* (Ottawa, 1932), chaps. XVIII, XIX.

[5]H. A. Innis, "Transportation as a Factor in Canadian Economic History," *Proceedings of the Canadian Political Science Association*, 1931 [see this volume, p. 62], also *Problems of Staple Production in Canada* (Toronto, 1933).

and the establishment of Fort Frontenac in 1673. Boats were built on Lake Ontario in 1677, and in 1679 the *Griffon* was launched on the Niagara River above the Falls and navigated the upper lakes, and a post was established at Niagara. A line of defence was slowly built up by the St. Lawrence, particularly with the energetic measures of Frontenac.

The Iroquois wars, which were revived after 1684, the massacre of Lachine (1689), and constant smuggling to the English were indications of the difficulties involved. Lahontan, an expert in military affairs, however disputed may be the merits of his work as an explorer, wrote on November 2, 1684:

In time of war I take it [Fort Frontenac] to be indefensible; for the cataracts and currents of the river are such, that fifty Iroquois may there stop five hundred French, without any other arms but stones. Do but consider, Sir, that for twenty leagues together the river is so rapid, that we dare not set the canoe four paces off the shoar; besides Canada, being nothing but a forrest, as I intimated above, tis impossible to travel there without falling every foot into ambuscades, especially upon the banks of this river, which are lined with thick woods, that render 'em inaccessible. None but the savage can skip from rock to rock, and scour thro' the thickets, as if 'twere an open field. If we were capable of such adventures, we might march five or six hundred men by land to guard the canows that carry the provisions; but at the same time 'tis to be considered, that before they arriv'd at the fort, they would consume more provisions than the canows can carry; not to mention that the Iroquois would still out-number em.[6]

Development of forts along the lakes as a means of checking New York trade was accompanied by measures to check encroachment of trade from the north.[7] In revolt at the restraint imposed on traders penetrating to the interior Radisson and Groseilliers deserted to the English and the Hudson's Bay Company, under their direction, established posts at the mouths of rivers flowing into James Bay. Competition from this direction was followed by the establishment of posts north of Lake Superior, designed to prevent Indians going to the Bay, and by the capture of English posts. To the north and to the south, Ontario was being hammered by French policy into a fortified unit, guaranteeing control for the lower St. Lawrence.

In the half century following the Treaty of Utrecht (1713) the struggle became more intense and led to the fall of New France. The establishment of a post on Lake Ontario at Oswego by the English

[6]See Baron de Lahontan, *New Voyages to North-America* (Chicago, 1905), I, 66ff.

[7]H. A. Innis, *The Fur Trade in Canada* (New Haven, 1931), pp. 41ff.

and the growth of the rum trade as a result of increased trade between the English colonies and the West Indies created serious problems. A strong post was built at Niagara in 1726 and this post as well as Fort Frontenac were subsidized as King's posts. In 1750 Fort Rouillé was rebuilt to prevent trade by the Toronto portage. The difficulties of transportation on the upper St. Lawrence continued and as late as 1736 the late arrival of the King's vessels made it impossible to forward from Kingston to Niagara goods from France.[8] On the north, return of posts on Hudson's Bay to the English under the terms of the Treaty of Utrecht necessitated renewed activity in the construction of posts in the interior. To check English trade at Port Nelson, La Vérendrye and his successors pushed exploration and the fur trade to Lake Winnipeg and the Saskatchewan. In spite of these aggressive advances, or possibly because of them, France proved unequal to the task. The English in the final campaign broke the southern line of fortifications by the capture of Fort Frontenac. Temporarily the New York route prevailed.[9]

After the downfall of New France, English traders from Albany and New York pushed into the newly opened territory. Boats were used to transport goods along the south shore of Lake Ontario to Niagara and in turn to Michilimackinac and the interior. The New York–Great Lakes route became an effective competitor. On the other hand the advantages of the Ottawa route and of Montreal as a depot of skilled labour and technique continued to be of first importance.

With the beginning of hostilities in the American Revolution, traders were forced to abandon the New York route and to move to Montreal.[10] Nevertheless the expansion of boat navigation on the Great Lakes in relation to the Albany route made possible a combination of the advantages of the St. Lawrence and the Ottawa routes. The canoe on the Ottawa and the boats and vessels in the Great Lakes combined to support a marked expansion of trade to the interior. At the close of the American Revolution the upper St. Lawrence had become for the first time a vital link in the development of the interior in relation to the lower St. Lawrence. The system of lake navigation[11]

[8]H. A. Innis, ed., *Select Documents in Canadian Economic History, 1497–1783* (Toronto, 1929), p. 400.

[9]See M. I. Newbigin, *Canada* (New York, 1926), chap. XIII.

[10]See R. H. Fleming, "Phyn, Ellice and Company of Schenectady," *Contributions to Canadian Economics*, IV, 1932.

[11]See E. A. Cruikshank, "Notes on the History of Shipbuilding and Navigation on Lake Ontario to September, 1816." *Papers and Records of the Ontario Historical Society*, XXIII (1926), 33–44; also G. A. Cuthbertson, *Freshwater* (Toronto, 1931).

built up from Albany and the development of boats on the upper St. Lawrence under the French were combined and improved in relation to Montreal. The agricultural beginnings at posts developed under the French régime on the Great Lakes, for example at Detroit, served as a base for the expansion of navigation and settlement under the English and especially after 1783.

With the improvement of navigation on the upper St. Lawrence fertile land along the north shore of Lake Ontario and in the Niagara district was opened to settlement. Moreover, population in the form of disbanded regiments, the United Empire Loyalists,[12] and settlers moving westward from the English colonies was available to settle new territory. That a large proportion of this population was in opposition to the colonies which had broken from British control was a favourable consideration from the standpoint of military consolidation of the outlying territory. In this sense Haldimand deserved the title of his biographer, "the founder of Ontario." The new settlemnts, especially at Niagara, provided a stronger agricultural base for the Northwest Company. With the decline of the fur trade in the United States after Jay's Treaty (1794), traders moved to the Northwest and larger supplies of provisions and more adequate transport facilities were necessary to support the extended trade. By the end of the century goods were taken up the St. Lawrence, across the Niagara portage, and even by Yonge St.

The emergence of a new community and the necessity for its protection were evident in the Constitutional Act in 1791 and in the energetic activities of Simcoe in the planning of roads and in reinforcing the new province against possible aggression from the United States.[13] The capital was moved, roads were planned, and the general military strength of the colony was placed in a position which successfully withstood the aggressions of the United States in the War of 1812.

As a result of increasing population, larger quantities of goods were taken up the St. Lawrence and the continued incentive to land speculators hastened immigration. Population advanced beyond the importing stage and in 1790 Campbell[14] noted that 6,000 bushels of wheat

[12]See W. S. Wallace, The United Empire Loyalists (Toronto, 1914), chap. x, and Jean M. McIlwraith, Sir Frederick Haldimand (Toronto, 1926) chap. xiii.

[13]William Smith, Political Leaders of Upper Canada (Toronto, 1931); E. A. Cruikshank, ed., The Correspondence of Lieut. Governor John Graves Simcoe (Toronto, 1923–31); W. R. Riddell, The Life of John Graves Simcoe (Toronto, 1926).

[14]P. Campbell, Travels in the Interior Inhabited Parts of North America (Edinburgh, 1793).

were bought at Kingston. In 1800 Elias Smith, the founder of Port Hope, was engaged in selling flour in Toronto and in Montreal.[15] By the turn of the century the problem of transportation on the St. Lawrence became serious and larger boats were introduced.[16]

The beginnings of settlement and of exports of wheat and flour coincided with the development of the timber trade. Square timber was floated first down the St. Lawrence, and about 1806 Philemon Wright succeeded in taking rafts down the Ottawa to Quebec. The American Revolution, the French Revolution, and the Napoleonic Wars provided a powerful stimulus to the energetic development of settlement and of the timber trade. The importance of naval supplies and the decline of European and United States sources of supply led to emphasis on the British North American colonies. Following the substantial preference of 1808, the timber trade increased with marked rapidity, and with the more aggressive attitude toward settlement after the War of 1812 immigration provided a source of labour for the industry. Settlement of Upper Canada, preference on colonial timber, and the interrelations by which emigration was supported by the timber ships and in turn agriculture and new supplies of labour supported the timber trade, were closely linked to imperial policy.[17] Decline of the fur trade to Montreal after the amalgamation of the Northwest Company and the Hudson's Bay Company in 1821 and concentration on the York boat and the Hudson Bay route to the Northwest necessitated increased emphasis on other commodities. New settlements such as the Talbot settlement, the Selkirk settlement, and the settlement which followed migration of Selkirk settlers from the

[15]Letter Book, Baker Memorial library. See list of flour shipments in 1801. C. E. Cartwright, *Life and Letters of the Late Hon. Richard Cartwright* (Toronto, 1876), p. 82.

[16]A boat, probably a Durham boat (invented about 1750) was introduced between Chippawa and Fort Erie in 1799, which with six men carried 100 barrels and displaced the batteaux which with five Canadians carried only 20 to 24. H. A. Innis and A. R. M. Lower, eds., *Select Documents in Canadian Economic History, 1783–1885* (Toronto, 1933), pp. 138–9. Writing at Queenstown on June 15, 1801, to John Askin, Robert Nichol stated, "Mr. Clark . . . is building a Kentucky boat at the former place [Kingston] in which he intends going to Quebec with 350 barrels of our flour. It will (I imagine) be the first boat of the kind that ever descended the Saint Lawrence, and interests all the mercantile people of this part of the country very much. . . . The quantity of flour going down this year from the district of Niagara is immense, say upon a moderate calculation five thousand barrels, which for the first year is really very great." Mr. Clarke made the trip from Kingston to Montreal in this boat in ten days with 340 barrels of flour. Milo M. Quaife, ed., *The John Askin Papers*, II (Detroit, 1931), 343, 353, also *Life and Letters of the Late Hon. Richard Cartwright*.

[17]See A. R. M. Lower, "Lumbering in Eastern Canada," doctoral thesis, Harvard University, 1929, chap. IV.

Northwest[18] as a result of the aggressiveness of the Northwest Company, and larger numbers of immigrants[19] after the War of 1812 gave Upper Canada an additional labour supply for the expansion of trade in timber, wheat, and flour.

Imperial policy and its influence reached its peak and started on its decline in the period 1820 to 1850. The Rideau Canal, with its supporting canals on the Ottawa, was built by the Imperial government and completed for navigation in 1832–3. After a slight reduction in 1821 the preference on colonial timber continued at a high level to 1843. The corn laws followed a similar trend.[20] The decline was a result of far-reaching changes which were traceable ultimately to the sweep of the later stages of the industrial revolution. Labour displaced by machinery was available for emigration and weavers moved to the district of Bathurst. Emigrants, assisted and unassisted, moved in every increasing numbers to the New World.[21] Under the auspices of the Canada Company, and of the British North American Land Company, capital was mobilized respectively for settlement on land in the Huron Tract in western Ontario and in the Eastern Townships.

The Welland Canal (1829) gave access to the upper lakes and provided for movement of population to western Ontario and for the growth of the Talbot settlement and of Goderich on Lake Huron. Roads were extended from Hamilton, Dundas, and Ancaster westward and from Toronto northward to meet the demands of new areas. In 1815 the first steamship, the *Frontenac*, was launched on Lake Ontario and in 1818 the *Walk-in-the-Water* was launched on Lake Erie. Access to the seaboard was provided on the upper lakes by the Erie Canal, completed in 1826. On the Ottawa the first steamboat, the *Union*, was built in 1882.[22]

The timber trade emphasized the basic importance of large rivers and strengthened the position of the St. Lawrence and the Ottawa. Timber could not be handled by New York and as a consequence the St. Lawrence became essentially a monopoly route. Laurentia[23] or the

[18]C. Martin, *Lord Selkirk's Work in Canada* (Oxford, 1916).

[19]Total immigrants to 1815 were estimated at 5,000. In 1816, 1,250 arrived, in 1817, 6,800, in 1818, 8,400, and in 1819, 12,800. See A. R. M. Lower, "Immigration and Settlement in Canada, 1812–1820," *Canadian Historical Review*, III (1922), 37–47; also H. I. Cowan, *British Emigration to British North America, 1783–1837* (University of Toronto Studies, History and Economics, IV, no. 2, 1928), chap. IV.

[20]A. Brady, *William Huskisson and Liberal Reform* (Oxford, 1928).

[21]H. I. Cowan, *British Emigration*, chap. X.

[22]See H. R. Morgan, "Steam Navigation on the Ottawa River," *Papers and Records of the Ontario Historical Society*, XXIII (1926), 370–83.

[23]See A. R. M. Lower, "The Trade in Square Timber," *Contributions to Canadian Economics*, VI, 1933.

St. Lawrence drainage basin, which coincided roughly with the white and red pine areas, was the basis of the timber trade and in turn was linked to settlement and to trade by the lower St. Lawrence to Great Britain. Decline in importance of the timber trade followed exhaustion of the larger trees in the more accessible areas, the diminishing demand which accompanied increased competition in Great Britain from European sources, and the relatively minor importance of timber with the achievement of industrial maturity. Settlers had increased beyond the point necessary to meet the demands of the timber trade for provisions and supplies, if not for labour, and the demands of western settlers,[24] while the population of Great Britain demanded flour and wheat rather than timber.

Increase in population, the introduction of steam navigation on the upper lakes, increase in the production and export of wheat, the powerful influence of the commercial interests of Montreal,[25] and the serious effects of the depression of 1835, which contributed to the distress culminating in the Rebellion of 1837, created problems which were solved by the recommendations of Durham's *Report*, the consummation of Union of the two Canadas in 1840, and the building of the St. Lawrence canals. By the end of the first decade after Union, a nine-foot channel had been completed and steamships were able to go down to Montreal and return. These steamships were linked with the newly opened route for steamships below Montreal.

The rapid increase in the importance of agricultural produce and especially wheat precipitated the problem of the upper St. Lawrence. Steamships, canals, and wheat involved the financial support of the state. Wheat, unlike lumber, was faced with competition from New York and in turn involved railways as supplemental to water transportation. Portage railways across the Niagara Peninsula and from Toronto to Collingwood, and even the Grand Trunk, were developed in co-ordination with water transportation. Steam navigation and railways hastened immigration, with the result that, by the end of the decade 1850 to 1860, the available, more desirable land was exhausted.[26] Population began to pour through to the western states.

The decline of wooden sailing vessels and of the market for timber

[24]The demands of new settlers in the West was regarded as one of the causes of the difficulties of the Welland Canal. See J. L. McDougall, "The Welland Canal to 1841," master's thesis, University of Toronto, 1923. In the depression of 1837, 400 vessels loaded with produce were sent to Chicago.

[25]See D. G. Creighton, "The Commercial Class in Canadian Politics, 1792–1840," *Proceedings of the Canadian Political Science Association*, V (1933), 43–58.

[26]H. A. Innis, *Problems of Staple Production*, chap. II.

from Great Britain, the rise of Montreal as a rival to Quebec, and the coming of the iron steamship and the railway coincided with the depletion of forests in the eastern states, the growth of cities, and the migration of sawmills to the Ottawa and the district north of Lake Ontario. Water power and steam power made their impact on the lumbering industry. The reciprocity treaty, the Civil War in the United States, and the shift from square timber to deals for the British market hastened the growth of lumber mills. The trend was accentuated in turn by the decline in the number of small trees.

The rise in importance of wheat and agricultural products, and the emergence of steamships, canals, and railways coincided with and implied responsible government and the establishment of new devices for finance. The upper St. Lawrence waterways, which had needed government support by means of subsidized posts in the fur trade of the French régime and by an aggressive imperial policy in the timber trade in the English régime, now demanded, under a wheat economy, continued support. Capital investment on a large scale necessitated more direct responsibility and supervision and more adequate methods of finance. The Act of Union and responsible government provided the solution; and these in turn were involved in the problem of government guarantees and the tariff as means of acquiring revenue. The problems of the clergy reserves, of seigniorial tenure, of immigration and colonization roads, of railways and canals, and of money, credit finance, and trade, were attacked directly and vigorously. The imperial nursery continued and became more efficient with the decline of commercialism and the rise of capitalism. Eventually the difficulties of finance which followed dependence on raw materials, particularly on wheat, and the accumulation and rigidity of fixed charges which accompanied government support to railways and canals, provided a powerful driving force toward Confederation and the creation of a new institution to carry the burden of debt of the united province.

Exhaustion of the more fertile land areas, problems of continued cropping of wheat, improved transportation and navigation, and abrogation of the reciprocity treaty led to the development of the dairy industry in the sixties,[27] and of the live-stock trade in the late seventies. Specialized agriculture was facilitated, and the varied geographic background supported the production and export of barley, fruit, dairy products, and live-stock. Minerals were discovered and exploited in the

---

[27]"Cows numerous as swarm of bees/Are milked in Oxford to make cheese." James McIntyre the Cheese poet. W. A. Deacon, *The Four Jameses* (Ottawa, 1927), p. 68.

agricultural area, for example, petroleum and its successor, salt. The railways hastened urbanization and in turn directly and indirectly the growth of industries and increased the demands for iron and raw materials. Trade and finance flourished in the new metropolitan areas of Hamilton and Toronto. Ontario began to develop its own nucleus of metropolitan growth independent of that of the province of Quebec. The success of the struggle of Senator McMaster and the Canadian Bank of Commerce with E. H. King and the Bank of Montreal in the first banking legislation of the new Dominion was an indication of maturity. The aggressiveness of the new area was in direct descent from the aggressiveness with which imperial policy had supported the development of Upper Canada.

The problem of Confederation was that of linking together relatively isolated areas and of providing a new base for the support of the debt lifted from the shoulders of the provinces. The Intercolonial to the Maritimes (1876) and the railway from St. Paul to Winnipeg (1878) corresponded roughly with the depression and the National Policy. The tariff was extended to provide revenue to support new capital investment and to guarantee control over new areas. Increase of population, the disappearance of free land, decline in wheat production, and fluctuations in the lumber industry released settlers for migration to new lands made available in the West. The economy of agricultural Ontario based largely on wheat was available to support expansion to the Prairie Provinces of western Canada. (Completion of the Canadian Pacific railway in 1885 repaired the breach in control over the Northwest which followed the amalgamation in 1821 and enabled an area which had become diversified from a wheat base in relation to the effects of improved transportation to Great Britain to become in turn a support for the expansion of wheat production in the West.) In some sense the Prairie Provinces paralleled in their development that of Ontario; and the difficult stretch of the railroad from Fort William to Winnipeg had its counterpart in the rapids of the upper St. Lawrence. Continued competition from the New York route and the difficulties of Montreal and the St. Lawrence necessitated further efforts in the improvement of navigation below Montreal and the deepening of the upper St. Lawrence canals to fourteen feet.

The improvement of the Montreal route by the end of the century provided the base for rapid expansion in the production and export of wheat in western Canada. The turn of the century brought a violent development with the exploitation of placer gold in the Yukon (1896) and the opening of the Kootenay region following construction of the Crow's Nest Pass railway. As a result of these developments and of free land, population poured into western Canada from the United States, Great Britain, Europe, and the older provinces. Immigrants from the old settlements of Ontario were replaced by immigrants from Great Britain. The demands of western Canada had immediate effects on the industries of eastern Canada. The agricultural implement industry[28] and the iron and steel industry[29] illustrated the effects of western demands. The financial nucleus of Toronto supported, through the Canadian Bank of Commerce and other institutions, and such men as Mackenzie and Mann, the construction of a rival road to that of Montreal, in the Canadian Pacific Railway. The ambitions of the Dominion and of the Grand Trunk were realized in the National Transcontinental. Increased urbanization[30] was the result, and in turn eastern agriculture shifted from an export to a domestic industry. Exports of dairy products and of live-stock declined steadily in the first decade of the century. Production of butter and cheese for export was displaced by the production of milk for domestic consumption. Winter dairying expanded rapidly. The apple industry declined from the standpoint of exports but increased from the standpoint of consumption in Ontario and western Canada. Lumbering was stimulated by the demands of the construction industries. The embargo on exports of logs in 1898 hastened the growth of mills along the north shore of Georgian Bay.

The effects of the increase in wheat production were accentuated by other developments. The railroad to western Canada necessitated penetration of the vast Precambrian area and led to the discovery and development of the copper nickel mines at Sudbury. It provided a base at North Bay for the construction of a railway supported by Toronto and government auspices to open the clay belt to settlement. The Temiskaming and Northern Ontario Railway led to the discovery of silver at Cobalt, and in turn of gold at Porcupine and Kirkland Lake, and of copper at Noranda (Quebec). Settlement in the clay belt and the spruce forests of the area north of the hardwood zone supported pulp and paper mills at Iroquois Falls, Kapuskasing, and Smooth Rock Falls. The decline in importance of pine in the region north of Georgian Bay and the embargo on the export of pulpwood from Crown lands hastened the growth of mills at Sturgeon Falls, Espanola, and Sault Ste Marie and in the vicinity of Fort William. With the mining industry and the pulp and paper industry, towns came into existence, agriculture was encouraged and the hydro-electric

[28]Massey Harris—an Historical Sketch, 1847–1920 (Toronto, 1920).
[29]W. J. Donald, The Canadian Iron and Steel Industry (Boston, 1915).
[30]S. A. Cudmore, Rural Depopulation in Southern Ontario (Toronto, 1912).

power development advanced with amazing rapidity. Extension of the Temiskaming and Northern Ontario Railway to Moosonee was followed by the development at Abitibi Canyon and the opening of the new north of Northern Ontario facing on Hudson Bay.

The advance of industrialism which followed the opening of the West and of New Ontario was accomplished by the activity of the state and of private enterprise. The rapidity of development, the long tradition of state support dating to the French régime and linked to the problem of the upper St. Lawrence waterways, and the relatively late development of metropolitan areas as contrasted with Montreal were factors responsible for the part of the government in the formation of the Ontario Hydro-Electric Power Commission and of the Temiskaming and Northern Ontario Railway. The peculiarities of the economy of Ontario are deep rooted and vitally related to her position as an outpost of the lower St. Lawrence.

The war period stimulated industrial growth and the post-war period was dominated by the enormous speculative boom of the United States and by the later stages of the industrial revolution based on gasoline. Road construction, automobile factories, and the tourist trade, with hotel construction and the decline of prohibition, were a phase of this revolution. Again the state assumed a role of direct importance in financing roads.

From this tentative outline we may venture to suggest the general underlying factors of the economic history of Ontario. The difficulties of the upper St. Lawrence and the importance of fur as a staple of trade with the hunting Indians of the northern forested Precambrian area were responsible for the development of the Ottawa River as an eastern boundary, and as a canoe route to the interior. Competition from New York compelled the state to support ventures to the interior by the upper Great Lakes in the form of subsidized forts. The effectiveness of this competition was evident in its contribution to the breakdown of French control and in the consolidation against New York in the combined effects of the activities of the British government, the importance of British manufactures to the fur trade, and the combination of canoe and lake navigation by the Ottawa and the St. Lawrence. Moreover, it eventually forced the fur trade to the Northwest and contributed to the final adjustment of the boundary from Grand Portage along the main route of the trade.[31] Competition from the

---

[31]H. A. Innis, "Interrelations between the Fur Trade of Canada and the United States," *Mississippi Valley Historical Review*, XX (1933), 321–32. [See this volume, p. 97.]

Hudson's Bay Company through Hudson Bay and its tributary rivers finally broke the control of the St. Lawrence drainage basin to the interior. By 1821 the supremacy of Hudson Bay had indicated roughly the northwestern boundary of Ontario.

The determined efforts of the British government to maintain control over the upper lakes[32] were followed by the development of lumbering and agriculture. The St. Lawrence and the Ottawa became ideal routes for the export of square timber. The problem of control was temporarily solved. Timber and an effective imperial policy involved settlement and in turn the shift to wheat. The difficulties of the upper St. Lawrence and of the Niagara River again became acute since wheat and an agricultural population demanded cheap transportation for imports. Competition from New York by Lake Ontario and by the Erie Canal again accentuated the demands for state support which implied the Act of Union, the building of canals, and the addition of railways. From this background emerged the problem of fixed charges for transportation improvements, the tariff for revenue and for protection, the demand for larger capital imports, Confederation, and the Intercolonial and the Canadian Pacific railways. The problems of the state in overcoming the difficulties of the St. Lawrence were met by the activities of the state in building and supporting a railway to western Canada.

Confederation provided for release and continued expansion in the upper St. Lawrence area. The Toronto-Hamilton metropolitan area assumed greater control with release from the out-grown clothes of Union. Ontario was determined to secure a substantial share of the trade from newly opened areas, and railways tapped the new transcontinental. She gained appreciably from the similarity of her economy to that of the newly opened West. Improved navigation in the form of deepened canals on the St. Lawrence system and shorter railway lines to seaboard hastened the expansion of the West and in turn of Ontario. Deepening of the St. Lawrence ship channel to thirty feet by 1906, and of the St. Lawrence canal to fourteen feet by 1901 brought to successful completion the long and determined struggle with New York. These improvements, the rise in prices which began with the turn of the century, the migration of mature technique from depleted resources in the United States to virgin resources in terms of wheat, minerals, pulp and paper, and the growing interdependence of these industries were factors supporting the phenomenal boom from 1900 to 1914. Railways brought to the expanding metropolitan area

[32]G. S. Graham, *British Policy and Canada, 1774–1791* (London, 1930).

of Toronto and Hamilton the results of expansion in minerals, pulp and paper, and hydro-electric power in Northern Ontario.

It is suggestive that the last new frontier was opened by the James Bay Railway in 1932. As a province, Ontario has gained enormously by the expansion of the Dominion and has been quick to press for advantage, and to undertake as government enterprises hydro-electric power and railways. The Temiskaming and Northern Ontario Railway, the Algoma Central, and other lines tapped directly the lines to Montreal and the East. The disadvantages which arose with the dominance of water transportation have been converted into advantages. Rapids and falls have become sources of hydro-electric power. Competition of the New York route has been converted to an advantage by the lower rates for Ontario compelled by competition and water routes. The new staples pulp, paper, and minerals have been linked to railways and the continental development of the United States. The tapping of fresh resources has brought problems of exhaustion and of conservation. Integration has already brought its problems, as shown in the establishment of the Ontario Research Foundation. We can already see the effects of competition in the pulp and paper industry. The uneven growth based on sudden improvements in transportation and in exploitation of natural resources will tend to be displaced by stability and increasing reliance on diversification. Ontario combined the development of furs, minerals, pulp and paper and lumbering, hydro-electric power and agriculture in Northern Ontario with the development of wheat in the West. In turn industrialism and agriculture in the south gained from the expansion and from the possibilities of integration. The diversity of her geographic background has provided for specialized production, cheap power, and low costs of transportation, and the results have been evident in an efficient, balanced, and relatively elastic economy.

The emergence of Ontario to maturity has brought problems for the province as well as for the Dominion. The elasticity of the economy of Ontario has been based on a wealth of developed natural resources and has been obtained in part through inelastic developments[33] which bear with undue weight on less favoured areas of the Dominion. The strength of Ontario may emphasize the weakness of the federation. An empire has its obligations as well as its opportunities.

[33]See D. A. MacGibbon, *Railway Rates and the Canadian Railway Commission* (Boston, 1917).

The Canadian Economy and the Depression*

THE papers in this volume are concerned with the immediate problems of the depression in Canada, but they are also intended to suggest the importance of problems peculiar to the secular trend which have accentuated the decline characteristic of the business cycle. The type of expansion which has characterized this century, namely, railroad construction and the opening of the West, the installation of hydro-electric power and pulp and paper plants, the development of mines and the construction of roads and hotels which have accompanied the increasing use of motor transport, will very materially decline. While the readjustment in economic life which this decline implies is taking place, the markets for our products have been narrowed partly as a result of competition from similar activity in other countries. The effects have been evident in the extension of defences such as are involved in economic nationalism which has intensified the depression. We are faced with the far-reaching results of the technological drift of modern industrialism. The success of measures designed to solve the problems of the depression is necessarily determined by their relation to problems of the secular trend. An analysis of the factors peculiar to a long-run development is essential to an understanding of immediate difficulties.

The trend of industrialism has strengthened the trend of nationalism. Industrialism based on coal and iron and on year-round water transportation implied a world dominated by the Atlantic basin and by areas with ample reserves of these basic commodities. Population density in the coal-producing regions assumed transportation and finance for the movement of raw materials inward and of manufactured products outward. Areas with access to cheap, year-round water transportation became dominant as termini of ocean routes and of land routes and were supported by nuclei of economic activity developed in smaller metropolitan centres. These centres have gradually emerged to a position of relative financial independence and metropolitan stature.

The twentieth century and especially the post-war period has wit-

*From *The Canadian Economy and Its Problems*, ed. H. A. Innis and A. F. W. Plumptre (Canadian Institute of International Affairs, 1934), pp. 3–24.

nessed an expansion of new areas, beyond the territory dominated by cheap water transportation and abundant supplies of coal, to territory in which hydro-electric power and oil have played an important role. Oil and electric power have contributed to the flexibility and expansion of metropolitan centres based on coal and to the widening of the whole base to areas formerly handicapped by a lack of cheap supply of that commodity[1]—for example the opening of the Pacific, or Russia and northern Canada. The last regions of expansion have been staked.

The marked realignment of the post-war period was in large part a result of the contributions to mechanistic improvement of the war period, of the application of new sources of power to transportation, for example the aeroplane, and of a major technological transport improvement, the Panama Canal. The expansion of mining and of wheat production and the Ottawa agreements may be cited as results of interest to Canada. The Hochkapitalismus of Sombart, reached immediately before the war and based on coal and coke and iron and steel, was rounded out in the post-war period by oil, hydro-electric power, and the new industrial metals.

Hydro-electric power development implies a geographic background

[1]"The pre-war development of extreme specialization has been not merely arrested but even reversed. . . . pre-war production was based upon steam power and the use of steam gave the coal-bearing regions of the world so great an advantage that the benefits of geographic concentration were obvious and of extreme importance. Post-war production has been based largely, and to a rapidly increasing extent, upon oil and electricity which favour a wider distribution of industry not only within a country but also between different countries. Natural advantages tend to diminish in respect of a large group of industries: differences in real costs tend to be reduced. For this reason the penalty suffered from the pursuit of a policy of economic nationalism is not so severe as of old." J. H. Jones, "A Policy for Sterling," *Lloyds Bank Monthly Review*, Feb. 1934. "Over an increasingly wide range of industrial products and perhaps of agricultural products also, I become doubtful whether the economic cost of national self-sufficiency is great enough to outweigh the other advantages of gradually bringing the producer and the consumer within the ambit of the same national economic and financial organization. . . . As wealth increases, both primary and manufactured products play a smaller relative part in the national economy compared with houses, personal services and local amenities which are not the subject of international exchange; with the result that a moderate increase in the real cost of the former consequent on greater national self-sufficiency may cease to be of serious consequence when weighed in the balance against advantages of a different kind." J. M. Keynes, "National Self-Sufficiency," *New Statesman and Nation*, VI (July 8, 1933), 36–7. See also the *Yale Review*, XXII (summer 1933), 755–69, and E. A. Robinson in the *New Statesman and Nation*, VI (July 22, 1933), 102, pointing out that the size of the national market has increased so greatly that for some products no considerable economy would be likely to be obtained from adding foreign markets and further increasing the scale of production. The trend has been toward exhaustion of economies of specialization; see also a criticism of N. Kaldor, *New Statesman and Nation*, VI (Aug. 5, 1933), 158.

of adequate rainfall and uneven topography and a region relatively inaccessible to coal in which its competitive advantage is enhanced. Regions formerly under a decided handicap from the standpoint of industrialism as dependent on coal become endowed with decided advantages. Power sites involve enormous initial investments of capital, in many cases requiring support of the state. The significance of overhead costs necessitates expansion of power consumption to capacity and in turn the development and encouragement of exploitation of natural resources in the growth of basic industries, such as mining and pulp and paper, and of more highly integrated industries.

Whereas hydro-electric power development is strongly characterized by regionalism and tends to be concentrated in a few areas, oil is essentially a basis of mobility, since it is widely available and provides its own means of transport. Its impact has been primarily on transportation and distribution. Areas with emphasis on labour rather than on supplies of coal and iron have succeeded, as in the case of Japan in the production of textiles, in expanding the range of markets. Production of raw materials dependent on cheap supplies of power has increased materially; wheat, for example, as it has been influenced by the tractor, the truck, and mechanization generally. In conjunction with the Panama Canal, oil burning vessels have increased the range of markets for Pacific countries and introduced disturbances of far-reaching proportions.

New sources of power strengthened tendencies emerging from the war. Emphasis on the iron and steel industries and on the wide range of industries linked to war demands brought fresh impetus to post-war industrialism. The peace consolidated industrialism's gains from the war. New nations were carved out and industries which had grown up during the war were supported by nationalism and tariff barriers. Competition from highly industrialized areas with industries stimulated by the war was checked in areas more recently industrialized. Nationalist sentiment and organization, developed during the war, provided support for tariffs to protect new industries. In turn, competition from more recently industrialized areas based on hydro-electric power and the pressure of overhead costs, and on oil, on improved technique, and on less exhausted natural resources was followed by tariffs imposed by highly industrialized regions to protect older industries based on coal and iron, more exhausted natural resources, less tractable labour, and plant affected by depreciation through obsolescence, and to stimulate new industries based on new sources of power, as in Great Britain. Nationalism becomes cumulatively more intense. Migration of improved technique and the shift from primary production to secondary production have been hastened by expanding purchasing power and a wider range of markets in the large number of new industrial areas. Increased mobility through transportation facilities, particularly evident in the completion of road systems in the last decade, and the advantages of new plant and equipment working on lower-cost raw materials contributed to the movement in these areas.

The pressure of industrialism based on new sources of power has been most striking in continental regions and large political organizations. Freedom of trade, diversified resources, mature industrial equipment (including the Panama Canal), enormous supplies of capital and skilled labour contributed to the expansion of the United States in the boom of the twenties. Centralized political control, and in turn concentration on the development of natural resources through application of mature capital equipment and skilled labour imported from highly industrialized countries culminating in five-year plans in the second large continental region, Russia, combined with expansion in the United States to give capitalism a final strong upward swing which collapsed in 1929. State activity in Europe supported restoration of the devastated areas; and credit organization characteristic of the boom in the United States contributed to reconstruction of the capital equipment of Europe following inflation. The marked expansion of credit and of capital equipment in the twenties assumed the efficiency of private enterprise and the support of weaker economic and political organizations, to mention only the guarantees by the Canadian government of borrowings of the Canadian National Railways, and loans to Australia, South American republics, and to Russia. The pressure of continental industrialism during a period of expansion was followed by resistance on the part of more recently industrialized areas in the form of protection to infant industries. Moreover, the importance of state support for capital borrowings strengthened this trend, through reliance on tariffs as a source of revenue to meet interest on loans. United States tariffs accentuated this trend by making it difficult to export goods in payment. More recently industrialized areas, more dependent on production and export of raw materials, have been subjected to the effects of the more rapid decline in prices of raw materials and have found it more difficult to meet the burden of fixed charges of capital borrowed during the boom period. They have been subjected, as a result of extensive state intervention, to heavy fixed charges, partly through more rapid decline of prices of raw material, and partly through depreciation from obsolescence which accompanied the introduction of new sources of power. In Canada motor competition in areas with heavy traffic density and competition of the Panama Canal have been partly responsible for larger railway deficits to be borne by the government. Nationalism fostered by the war and the boom period became more intense as a result of depression. Dumping from more highly industrialized countries presents serious problems to industries of recent growth in weaker industrial regions, particularly in the form of unemployment, and is followed by increased tariffs and anti-dumping legislation. The National Policy of 1878 in Canada followed the long period of depression in the seventies, and the present Canadian tariff belongs to the present depression. Relative lack of governmental machinery in weaker industrial regions tends to throw increased burdens on customs administration, which becomes in turn a means of controlling exchange, of relieving unemployment, of producing revenue, and of maintaining railway rates. Difficulties become evident in internal rigidities and unequal spreading of the burden. Prices of raw materials for export, exposed to world competition, crush the primary producer between declining returns and relatively stable costs in terms of prices of manufactured products, of interest on debts, and of railway rates.

Within national boundaries the effects of these strains have been evident in the increasing strength of metropolitan centres. New sources of power and increasing industrialism have been responsible for increasing urbanization and increasing dominance of the city. Democratic institutions accentuate the influence of urban population and metropolitan centres and, in turn, mechanization strengthens the position of centralized control. Improved communication such as the press and the radio, improved transportation, and the development of modern architecture (for example, the skyscraper) tend to stress similarities of language and ideas. Expansion of the pulp and paper industry has supported intensive advertising and revolutions in marketing essential to the demands of the city. It has coincided with the decline of editorials and of freedom of speech, and the emergence of headlines and the modern newspaper with its demands for excitement, including wars and peace, to appeal to a large range of lower mental types. The coincidence with the advent of radio of dictatorship in Russia, Germany, Italy, Great Britain, the United States, or Canada is not accidental. Mechanization, moreover, implies more effective utilization of physical force. Machine guns are effective keys to the city. Metropolitan centres have continued to play increasingly important roles in the war, the peace, and the post-war period. The peace set its seal on the ambitions of older European metropolitan centres in the break-up of large political units. New nations brought into existence by the Treaty of Versailles reflected the demands of Prague and other centres in opposition to Vienna. Further realignments in the postwar period have continued in the increasing control of metropolitan centres, the weakening of competitors, and the decline or disappearance of powers of subsidiary units such as the state or the province in Germany, Italy, the United States, and Canada.

Nourished in a friendly fashion by the state, the metropolitan region, without any formal sort of constitution and until recently without plan, has grown to be a potential rival of the state. Born of a mixture of physical and economical convenience it promises to take on a measure of cultural unity. Under the guidance of business men of large calibre, it is likely in America to develop a policy that leads at once to the conservation of regional interests and the advancement of general social welfare. Rooted as it is in the facts of nature rather than in political expediency, it promises to have vitality and endurance.[2]

Metropolitan centres in recently industrialized regions which are still important producers of raw materials are strengthened in part by new sources of power[3] and lower prices of raw materials, in contrast with metropolitan centres in highly industrialized regions which have been weakened by higher prices of raw materials incidental to protection and economic self-sufficiency, and particularly in relation to wheat. The trend of modern industrialism has been toward the more recently industrialized regions with new sources of power, and less exhausted natural resources, but this trend has been strengthened by cumulative forces in economic nationalism. The results have been evident in the increasing disparity between standards of living of urban and rural populations—a disparity accentuated by the increasing strength of established metropolitan centres as opposed to more recently developed centres. The political strength of metropolitan areas implies support of the depressed classes in unemployment relief and the forging of political weapons to operate more effectively to advance metropolitan demands. Recent legislation in the United States tends to reflect the interests of large manufacturers through its emphasis on price fixing arrangements, in spite of determined efforts to relieve agriculture and the exposed industries. The struggle between miner and peasant which has characterized the industrial revolution becomes progressively more intense. Relief through the application of science

[2]N. S. B. Gras, "Regionalism and Nationalism," *Foreign Affairs*, VII (April 1929), 466. The problem of government following metropolitan expansion has become acute—the conflict with suburban areas, for example.

[3]See R. D. McKenzie, *The Metropolitan Community* (New York, 1933), with reference to the effects of motor transportation.

and closer integration holds little promise, since scientific advance has been particularly important in the production of raw materials. Pressure of technological innovations, particularly in large political units with free trade, a large market, and adequate resources, tends to be restricted with the growth of nationalism to internal development and in turn leads to the development of internal resistances which take the form of regionalism. Internal pressure again supports attempts to restrict imports of goods from lower-cost producing regions and reinforces the demand for higher tariff barriers. The results have been evident in the growth of regionalism in the United States, in the recent legislation of British Columbia and Alberta, in the unrest of the Maritimes, and in threats of secession in Western Australia. Failure to accept the St. Lawrence waterway may be interpreted in part as a reflection of the increasing strength of New York and of Chicago as metropolitan areas and of the increasing difficulty of political organizations in breaking the grip of rigidities characteristic of rail transport.

The development of rigidities has strengthened the growth of nationalism and in turn regionalism. Large political organizations adapted to periods of expansion become inefficient with the decline in importance of virgin natural resources, and metropolitan areas become increasingly significant. The position of the state in the more recently industrialized areas, especially in relation to guarantees of loans to transportation, implies ability to rely on general taxing power rather than direct returns and involves a lower interest rate, but this is offset by larger capital outlay than is involved by reliance on private enterprise. Guaranteed fixed interest rates on large capital outlay create serious rigidities in an economy which is dependent on raw materials subject to wide fluctuations in price and yield. Governmental guarantees imply an intensification of nationalism on the part of the borrower and the lender. The post-war business cycle has been enormously influenced by the rigidities which have emerged with nationalism.[4] Rigidities of labour costs in Great Britain and Australia have paralleled rigidities of capital charges, railway rates, and interest levels in Canada. The importance of fixed capital equipment characteristic of modern industrialism, particularly in recently industrialized continental countries with emphasis on transportation, on hydro-electric power, and on the expansion of metropolitan centres, has emphasized the increasing significance of overhead costs. Heavy fixed charges and overhead costs, particularly in continental countries, were responsible for policies favouring marked increase in the production of raw materials. These

4See W. A. Mackintosh, "Gold and the Decline of Prices," *Papers and Proceedings of the Canadian Political Science Association*, III (1931), 88–110.

policies became more effective with the addition of motor power, notably in the production of wheat[5] and of minerals. The impact of overhead costs in increased production of raw materials and declining prices has coincided with the extension of fixed charges. Increased specialization in production of raw materials and decline of self-sufficiency involved further extension of a monetary economy and additional burdens with the depression. The low price of raw materials necessitated additional support of the state in relief measures and in market control in various forms. Within the political units involved, metropolitan areas have gained with lower prices of raw materials and have been forced less quickly to adjust prices of finished products, particularly with the coincident existence of demand from raw-material-producing regions—e.g., the gold mining areas of Northern Ontario—which have gained in importance as a result of the depression.[6] Prices of foodstuffs (wheat) have been held down further by the spread of nationalism in more highly industrialized regions and the trend toward self-sufficiency. As a result of the importance of overhead costs, in its effects on inelastic supply and especially joint supply, the price level has become an uncertain and far from delicate indicator in adjusting supply and demand. The state has been concerned either with attempts, as in Canada, to restrict production and to maintain railway rates, interest levels, and other indications of rigidity in order to avoid the vicious circle of inflation on the ground of attracting capital, or with attempts, as in Australia, to reduce interest rates and to eliminate rigidities rather than to restrict production. Canada, with inadequate, badly co-ordinated machinery, stands on the one hand in danger of being burned at the stake of natural resources and on the other hand of being boiled in the oil of unrestricted competition. It is only necessary to mention the writings of J. M. Clark and the pronounced swing of economic theory to problems of monopoly rather than competition in order to note the reflection of recent trends in economic development.

The implications of the increasing importance of overhead costs are significant to capital and to labour. Increasing intervention of the state may involve a marked improvement in efficiency and offset in part the stifling effects of rigidities. The pronounced swing from gold and the shift to a commodity basis for the value of the monetary unit is

[5]See J. F. Booth, "Some Economic Effects of Mechanization of Canadian Agriculture with Particular Reference to the Spring Wheat Area," *Proceedings of the World's Grain Exhibition and Conference* (Regina, 1933); A. Stewart, "The Economy of Machine Production in Agriculture," *Essays on Canadian Problems*, Royal Bank of Canada Essay Competition 1930–1, vol. IV (Montreal, 1931).

[6]E. A. Forsey, "Equality of Sacrifice," *Canadian Forum*, XIV (Nov. 1933).

evidence even of the possibility of weakening rigidities! But the difficulties which have necessitated these developments, as well as the developments themselves, tend to restrict capital movements. Extensive borrowings of recently industrialized countries for purposes of transportation, urbanization, and the war have entailed a long-term burden of fixed charges at a relatively high level and a marked increase in production of raw materials for export with consequent lower prices with which to meet heavy charges payable abroad. The effect of uncertain prices of raw materials has been evident in the freezing of short-term credit shown in the insistence of the banks on governmental guarantees for the handling of wheat and the decline of speculative activity. Governmental control weakens speculative interest in commodities and securities. Internal control and the shift on the part of new countries from capital importing to capital exporting regions or the marked decline of capital movements between countries imply increasing internal absorption of surplus capital and, with determined financial control, may be followed by lower interest rates. Increased taxation (sometimes disguised as inflation) which resulted from the war has wiped out capital reserves and the capital-supporting middle classes. The emergence of urban centres to metropolitan status assumes not only financial independence but, with the demands of modern democracy, the absorption of capital surplus in government services. Increasing complexity facilitates bureaucracy and dictatorship. Financial institutions such as insurance companies or investment trusts engaged as capital-distributing organizations tend to become more concerned with internal investments which promise greater security. Skill and technique are moved more easily than commodities. Henry Ford prefers to establish plants in other countries rather than export automobiles from the United States.

Population like capital has declined in mobility. Democracy, nationalism, and regionalism are involved in vicious circles which imply lowering of the standard of living, protection in unemployment relief, and restrictions on immigration. Restriction of immigration is followed by more rapid distribution of population within nations and in turn by the growth of metropolitan regions at the expense of regions producing goods for export. Increasing industrialization and urbanization mean higher standards of living for urban than for rural labour and inability to promote readjustments by back-to-the-land movements or immigration of agricultural labour from European countries. The effects are evident in areas formerly supporting substantial migration such as Italy, where the state has been active in developing industrialism to absorb population, and in areas such as Japan which has attempted to combine industrialism with population increase and an improved standard of living. In highly industrialized countries, restrictions on immigration and urbanization have been accompanied in the main by a decline in the birth rate. Lowering of the death rate and decline of the birth rate imply larger numbers of the population in advanced age levels and less flexibility. The war accentuated the contrast between upper and lower age limits and in the youth movements contributed to dictatorship.

The rapid strides of technological improvement, which accompanied the war and the use of new sources of power, have involved relative exhaustion of the last virgin natural resources. The disappearance of free land has coincided with the rise of nationalism.[7] The pressure of population on the land has been interpreted as a basic factor in the marked emigration of the last century and the discontent which has characterized the trend toward nationalism in older agricultural regions, such as Ireland, Russia, Germany, and other countries.[8] The rise in cost of production, especially of transportation, in the agriculture of new countries strengthens the position of agriculture in old countries. Consequently demands for more adequate domestic wheat supply become less difficult to meet and restricted imports impose less serious burdens on the general economy. Pressure of natural resources and sudden disturbances which accompanied new developments will tend to be less severe. The determining factors in recently industrialized countries have spent their force and flexibility has declined. The trust movement has solidified industrial development. Inventions are patented and placed in cold storage. The metal industries have been influenced to an increasing extent by the market for scrap and to a lesser extent by new ore production. The costs of protecting established industries based on more exhausted resources tend to decline. On the other hand, demand tends to become saturated and stable. We have begun the process of abandoning rather than constructing railways, of restricting rather than increasing wheat production, of closing down pulp and paper plants rather than opening them. We avoid saturation in the automobile industry by new models. We protect obsolescence in the iron and steel industry by substantial tariffs. The enormous impetus of the war to iron and steel industries and the relatively light demands of armaments following the peace treaty, and of railroads with the competition of motor transport, created a surplus of steel for the construction of skyscrapers, bridges,

7See C. R. Fay, "Adam Smith and the Doctrinal Defeat of the Mercantile System," *Quarterly Journal of Economics*, XLVIII (Feb. 1934), 304–16.
8Isaiah Bowman, *The New World* (London, 1929).

and motor cars. But the vital relationship of militarism to capitalism and to the modern state, which has become to a large extent a collector and distributor of funds for war purposes, persists. The depression closed these new outlets for iron and steel products and has led to a search for new possibilities which have been satisfied in part by minor wars, the manufacture of beverages following the repeal of prohibition, and the clearing of slums. Armaments and housing supported by the state appear at the moment the more promising outlets and these strengthen nationalism and metropolitan growth. Russia remains as a possible safety valve for capitalism. The enormous increase in the production of such raw materials as fish or wheat which followed the pressure of the iron and steel industries and new sources of power has so disorganized the price structure that it restricts the possibility of financial support to further expansion of iron and steel.

Continental areas with emphasis on capitalistic types of development in terms of heavy equipment, mass production, and overhead costs have, in mature metropolitan regions, witnessed the emergence of rigidities. Maritime areas such as Italy and Japan, which are characterized by increasing density of population without relief by emigration and with access to new sources of power, have concentrated on types of industrialism which stress the importance of labour—for example, the textile industry. Low prices of raw materials and accessibility to the wheat and wool of Australia, and to the products of the Atlantic basin by the Panama Canal, have supported strong competition from Japan with established textile industries in England and the United States. Retreat from the markets of Pacific areas by Atlantic basin industries accentuated competition between nations in this area and in turn increased protective duties, as in Canada. Continental areas characterized by rigidities tend to be exposed to competition from maritime regions characterized by flexibility.

In conclusion, we have reached the stage in which natural resources in the form of free land have relatively disappeared. In continental countries the importance of fixed capital, especially in transportation, and thus the importance of overhead costs, added to the importance of new sources of power (oil and hydro-electric), have involved a marked increase in the production of raw materials and a decline in price.[9] Cheap raw materials, new sources of power, and the opening of the Panama Canal have hastened the development of the Pacific and particularly the industrial growth of Japan. Competition from cheap raw materials involved depreciation through obsolescence on a

[9]M. T. Copeland, *Raw Material Prices and Business Conditions*, Harvard University Business Research Studies, no. 2 (Boston, 1933).

wide scale, particularly in established industrial regions based on coal. The rigidity of the credit structure in the coal regions and depreciation through obsolescence have necessitated the introduction of protection and in turn of the complex machinery of economic nationalism. We are faced with the problems of overhead cost on a vast scale, prices have become less satisfactory as indicators, and the solution depends on the introduction of economic intelligence which avoids monopoly and perfect competition—nationalism with intelligence —an intelligent dictator (e.g., civil service) preferred. Democracy in its attempt to force governments to meet the difficulties of an increasingly complex economic development has been met with the loss of leadership during the war and the rise of the youth movement, and has been forced to emphasize centralization of control and various forms of dictatorship.[10] Political duplicity has become an asset of first importance in democratic countries. The stakes are not the downfall of western civilization and the beginning of the new middle ages but a standard of living.

The implications of the struggle for Canada are serious.[11] Canada developed at the latest stages of modern industrialism and is among the first to feel the effects of the turn. The importance of the state, reliance on production of raw materials for export, particularly wheat, and the rigidities of continental development create serious problems of internal maladjustment as shown by quotas, bonuses, unemployment relief, the break-down of provincial-federal relations, and the like. The sheltered metropolitan areas tend to impose burdens on regions exposed to world fluctuations. These problems have already contributed to a marked extension of governmental machinery and governmental machinery involves more machinery. It would appear probable, as has been suggested, that areas producing a surplus of raw material may be forced to extend the two-price system by which world market price becomes a price of dumped goods and domestic prices are increased by protection.[12] The resulting disturbances can be prevented only by recourse to the new devices which have already made substantial advances. According to the wisdom with which they are designed, exchange controls, quotas, dumping legislation, empire agreements, and regional arrangements may endanger, or

[10]J. Coatman, "Economic Nationalism and International Relations," *Political Quarterly*, IV (Oct.-Dec. 1933), 561–74.
[11]See "Canadian Trade Policy in a World of Economic Nationalism," *Queen's Quarterly*, XLI (spring 1934), 81–98.
[12]See also C. Schrecker, "The Growth of Economic Nationalism and Its International Consequences," *International Affairs*, XIII (March-April 1934), 208–25.

offset the implications of the decline of, the most favoured nation clause, Elliotism, economic autarchy, and the new weapons which have grown up to take the place of war. "The new internationalism is upon us."[13] No country stands to gain or lose more than Canada. We may accept the losses incidental to economic nationalism as inevitable and beyond relief, or we may attempt to divert the drift of international development along lines which involve the least possible difficulty; but assuming the most favourable results from such a policy we are forced to consider the possibility of internal readjustment in the interests of a more efficient economy and of the relief of human misery. The dangers of introducing badly designed machinery in a country susceptible to the slightest ground-swell of international disturbance are as obvious as the necessity of introducing machinery correctly designed. The policy of economic nationalism which attempts to create a self-sufficient economy in order to obtain stability and security at the expense of the production of goods has grave consequences for an economy which rides on the crest of modern industrialism and has been concerned with the demands of an international market. Industrialism has provided an abundance of goods but not the first luxury of security.

We lack vital information on which to base prospective policies to meet this situation. The emphasis on speculative discussion as to the probable effects of certain proposals, the reliance on works dealing with the economies of countries other than Canada, for example Australia, and the absence of finality are indications of our weakness. The causes of the weak position of the social sciences in Canada are varied and numerous, but in part they are linked to the phenomenal expansion which has characterized Canadian development during this century and which has absorbed the energies of a small population. The effects have been evident in the "solutions" which have been proposed during the present depression and in the phenomena which are described as election campaigns. On the other hand a demand for a systematic and sympathetic understanding of Canadian problems has become increasingly urgent during the depression.

The outstanding characteristics of Canadian problems have been clearly outlined, but the details are relatively obscure and the obscurity makes prescription difficult. The importance of a relatively small group of raw materials and in particular of wheat in Canadian income is accentuated by dependence of these raw materials on enormous investments of capital which imply problems of overhead costs and of fixed charges. The pressure of overhead costs involved in transcontinental

13C. Foreman, *The New Internationalism* (New York, 1934).

railway lines and capital equipment essential to the handling of wheat[14] is evident in immigration policies, construction of branch lines as feeders, and intense competition between the railways. Additional capital equipment introduced as a result of overhead costs implies additional overhead costs and more intense competition. Finally, the costs of abandoning capital equipment, assuming the vicious circle of expansion to have exhausted itself, increase overhead costs. Meanwhile, in spite of a decline in price and particularly with a slight decline in price which accompanies speculative activity in a boom period, production of the raw material is increased with lower costs of transportation accompanying the enormous advantages of railroads[15] and particularly with the introduction of new sources of power such as gasoline. The economics of overhead costs introduces a serious disturbing factor in the automatic adjustments incidental to changes in price. The results are evident in a sharp decline in prices during a period of depression, in the accumulation of debts, in the passing of dividends by the Canadian Pacific Railway, in Canadian National deficits, in election turnovers, in relief measures, in letters to editors, in a marked reduction in standards of living, and in a slow readjustment such as is involved in the migration of population, the production of hogs and livestock, empire agreements, and wheat agreements. The effects are far reaching. It might be expected that a decline in the price of wheat would involve reduced costs of living in the urban industrial centres so far as bread is concerned but again overhead costs and fixed charges are implied in the enormous capital investment peculiar to the flour milling[16] and bread baking industries and in the emergence of monopoly control, with the result that the price of bread has declined very slightly during the depression. In competitive industries overhead costs stimulate production whereas in industries with monopoly possibilities the drive is toward restriction and control. The vicious effects of overhead costs on production have been checked in part by industries that have evaded the Combines Investigation Act, with serious results for competitive industries such as farming which have been at a disadvantage, not to forget the pools.

The newsprint industry again implies enormous capital equipment

[14]Professor V. W. Bladen prefers the terms rents and quasi-rents in his article in emphasizing the specific and specialized character of Canadian equipment: "The Theory of Cost in an Economy Based on the Production of Staples: Canada and Wheat," *The Canadian Economy and Its Problems.*

[15]See W. A. Mackintosh; *Prairie Settlement: The Geographical Setting* (Toronto, 1934); p. 56.

[16]A. C. Oakhurst, "The Staff of Life Supports the Millers," *Canadian Forum,* XIV (June 1933).

in mills and power plants, heavy fixed charges, and serious problems
of overhead costs. A vast range of accessible raw materials in spruce
forests and available power sites, an immediate large market, ample
financial resources, and government policy with embargoes on exports
of pulpwood from Crown lands caused rapid expansion in the production of newsprint. The heavy initial outlay and important overhead
costs necessitated continuous operation in spite of a decline in price
and during the depression involved further attempts to increase production and a further decline in price. The results have been evident
in bankruptcy and receiverships, financial amalgamations, abandoned
mills and towns with wholesale migration of labour and futile attempts
to check the downward spiral by price agreements. But whereas in the
case of agriculture the impact tended to fall with greatest severity on
the farmer, in the pulp and paper industry it tended to fall on the
security holder.

The mineral industry, with particular reference to gold and the base
metals, copper, lead, zinc, and nickel, is characterized similarly by
heavy capital equipment and large overhead costs. Relatively low
costs of production with freshly opened ore bodies and improved
methods of extraction contribute to the general effects of overhead
costs in maintaining production in spite of a decline in prices. In the
production of gold, low prices of supplies characteristic of the depression have been responsible for marked expansion of activity. The
effects have been evident in the closing down of weak marginal mines,
reduction of earnings, and the weakening of the position of capital and
labour, but the character of ore reserves has served as a cushion to
prevent the more drastic effects shown in wheat production and newsprint.

Minerals and newsprint are affected not only directly by overhead
costs but also indirectly through the overwhelming importance of
hydro-electric power. A conspicuous determining factor as to the
extent and character of power sites is the geographic background. The
relative scarcity of suitable power sites and the extremely heavy initial
cost of installation result in a powerful thrust toward utilization to
capacity of power production on the part of predominant consumers
such as the mining and newsprint industries. The character of price
arrangements which favour the large consumers, and long-term contracts for power indicate the type of pressure applied.

The problem of overhead costs incidental to the production of
staple products has been rendered more acute by the cyclical trend.
Plants of the most recent design, installed during the boom period,
came into production during the depression. The Welland Canal, the

Hudson Bay Railway, the Abitibi Canyon power project, and smelters at Noranda and Flin Flon illustrate the general development.[17] Mining activity at Bear Lake has expanded throughout the depression. Moreover, the rapidity and unpredictability of development on a continental scale has seriously reduced the value of the price mechanism as an effective means of adjusting supply to demand.

The basic position of overhead costs in the production of a small group of important staple commodities has involved the Canadian economy in a nose dive during the depression which has cut income in half. Each staple has its own peculiar developments and its peculiar relations with other staples. The gold mining industry, for example, has gained from the low price of raw materials and has tended to serve as a cushion by contributions to railroad earnings and increasing demand for supplies. The effects of the depression are determined in part by the character of competition from other producing areas. More effectively organized economies become stronger competitors and can be met in part by similar effective organization which implies an elimination of inequities and an adjustment of the burden in relation to the whole economy and the staple industries of the economy. Under conditions of production which involve highly specialized equipment such as railways, canals, and elevators for handling wheat, or newsprint mills, mining equipment, and hydro-electric plants, output to capacity represents the most efficient basis. With mature development, capacity is based largely on relatively inelastic limiting geographic factors such as power sites, ore bodies, or areas of land with a suitable climate. The effectiveness of the drive of overhead costs toward that point in competition with other areas will imply concentration on the most effective unit within each basic industry and in turn very serious losses to less effective units in terms of owners of farms or pulp and paper mills, or of farmers, capitalists, and labourers. Attempts to avoid the consequent maladjustment have been evident in the newsprint industry, the wheat pools and wheat agreements, the arbitration board of the railroads, amalgamation of banks, and evasion of the Combines Act. The peculiar character of the Canadian economy with its emphasis on overhead costs has been largely responsible for a persistent trend toward unity. Success has been haphazard and combinations in one field have caused increased severity of competition in others. The essential problem in the Canadian economy is to introduce limits to the vicious spiral. Mitigation of severe costs to

[17]See H. A. Innis, "Economic Recovery in Canada in 1933," *Commerce Journal,* Feb. 1934 (mimeograph; publication of the Commerce Club of the University of Toronto).

exposed groups by enhancing the burden of sheltered groups and reduction of the burden to the whole economy to a minimum are among the tasks involved.

The difficulties of bringing the economy out of a nose dive are very great. Panic generally prevails and the most courageous pilots with no experience with such disasters can do little more than apply nostrums used in other economies and possibly do more harm than good. Royal commissions, investigating committees, and the persistent search for scapegoats break out in a burning rash on the body politic. The political quack is ever alert to capitalize public fears.

It will be apparent that no single remedy can be recommended. Adjustment by arbitration or the scaling down of debts, which has already gone far, the application of direct control over individual industries, and monetary policy have been discussed and their limitations suggested. Dependence on exports and on capital borrowed abroad implies a widely fluctuating income beyond control of domestic policies. Exports are sold in competition with products produced under similar conditions of overhead costs on a world market. Important costs of production such as transportation are beyond control because of competition with the United States. The Canadian railway rate structure is based, as a result of geographic competition, on the American rate structure. Proximity to the United States places a severe handicap on control of capital movements. The character of our development results in rigidities such as those governing ownership. Assuming these limitations it is obvious that mechanism designed to remove inequities must be flexible and capable of rapid adjustment in response to economic changes in the United States and Great Britain and in other parts of the world. Such flexibility assumes a strong and unified control over income and expenditure. It assumes an appreciation of the economy of Canada as a whole sufficiently strong to support unified control. These considerations limit the importance of any single institution such as a central bank or a loan council. Controls of wages, agricultural returns, corporation finance, monetary policy, and public finance[18] must be linked together to provide an equitable adjustment of burdens.

The effects of reliance on a single method of control have been evident during the depression in the dominance of the tariff as a means of providing unemployment relief, protection, and control of exchange. The results have been evident in the innumerable devices

[18]See "A Submission on Dominion-Provincial Relations and the Fiscal Disabilities of Nova Scotia within the Canadian Federation," Royal Commission of Economic Enquiry (Nova Scotia), 1934.

which it has been necessary to introduce as a means of stopping leaks. Reliance on monetary policy would have had similar results. Extensive manipulation of monetary policy is particularly dangerous under conditions which involve large overhead costs and has the effect of pouring oil on fire. The close alignment of our competitive price structure with the United States (e.g., railway rates) would imply disturbances throughout the economy. We have built up in Canada in competition with the United States a delicately balanced economy which has more than once crashed through ill-designed machinery. Devices must be used with a view to creating the least possible disturbance and must involve important supplementary controls. Taxation machinery is most obvious and most important in achieving redistribution of income but difficulties of development necessitate emphasis on measures which are preventative and which will contribute toward equality of income.

The depression has illustrated the inevitable introduction of more elaborate machinery. The constitutional problem threatens to become a barrier of major difficulty and revision of the British North America Act an urgent task. Failing the introduction of more responsive machinery we are left with the alternative of the cumulative difficulties of the present depression with disaster breeding disaster. We need more information designed to throw light on specific problems and in turn to reinforce the demand for co-ordination of controls in more effective fashion than can be achieved under the cabinet system.

The specific character of the Canadian economy demands specific types of control. General remedial measures applied to the economy as a whole are limited because of the varying characteristics of basic elements of the economy. Measures suited to the improvement of conditions in western agriculture will tend to be advantageous to Canada as a whole but the effect of those measures on other staple products such as newsprint and minerals must be taken into account. Adequate control implies adaptation not only to the demands of the economy as a whole but also to the specific interests of each of a small group of basic commodities. The methods adopted to check the effects of overhead costs or to bring industry out of the nose dive of a depression will vary with conditions in each industry. Those who object to proposals for control must present the case for an economy responsible for the present unfortunate conditions. They will find the farmer, the labourer, and the capitalist difficult to convince. On the other hand the state of the social sciences will not support the arguments of those who favour the introduction of strait jackets.

Unused Capacity as a Factor in Canadian Economic History*

THE significance of navigation in the economic development of a region penetrated by the St. Lawrence to the south and by Hudson Bay to the north has been evident in concentration on production of raw materials for consumption in the highly industrialized area of Europe,[1] and in problems which have arisen with intense specialization, such as unused capacity in terms of vessel space as a result of inability to secure a balanced two-way cargo. The green fishery as conducted from French ports on the banks and along the coast required heavy outbound cargoes of salt to balance return cargoes of fish, but the dry fishery, which became important with the development of Spanish trade at the beginning of the seventeenth century, required smaller quantities of salt and equipment on the outgoing voyage and made necessary the carrying of ballast.[2] The English dry fishery in Newfoundland involved a further lack of balance in that crews necessary to carry on the industry were larger than those necessary to man the vessels, and, because of the seasonal fluctuations and agricultural limitations of that area, men were carried back at the end of the season. Sale of fish in the markets of Spain and the Mediterranean necessitated the dispatch of vessels to England with the men necessary to carry on the fishery, and additional larger vessels (sack ships) with cargoes of fish to market. The addition of sack ships lowered the cost of provisions and facilitated the beginnings of a settlement in which men remained over the winter. Consequently, competition between sack ships and fishing ships for cargoes of fish and for profitable return cargoes of salt, tropical products, and specie from Spain and the Mediterranean to England, contributed to the long severe struggle which dominated the history of Newfoundland and placed severe restrictions on the introduction of political institutions. New England, with a winter fishery and a favourable area for the development of

*From *Canadian Journal of Economics and Political Science*, II (1936), 1–15; reprinted in *Political Economy in the Modern State* (Ryerson, 1946), pp. 201–17.
    [1]See H. A. Innis, *Problems of Staple Production in Canada* (Toronto, 1933), chap. II.
    [2]Numerous regulations were enacted against the dumping of ballast in the harbours of Newfoundland.

agriculture, lumbering, and shipbuilding, offered possibilities of year-round operation. Settlers rather than ballast, therefore, were brought to New England. Expansion of settlement contributed to more effective exploitation of the fishery, shipbuilding, and trade and to the decline of control of fishing ships from England. Numerous small New England vessels extended the fishery to the banks and the shores of Nova Scotia, participated in the coastal trade to Newfoundland in spring and summer, and carried products to the West Indies to exchange for sugar and molasses in winter when these products came on the market and there was freedom from hurricanes. Relative absence of unused capacity in New England shipping meant low costs and contributed to rapid economic development which facilitated control over Nova Scotia after its loss to France in the Treaty of Utrecht in 1713. The expansion of New England involved a continued drain of labour from Newfoundland and weakened the position of settlement in that area.

The concern of French fishing ships with the home market and the green fishery led to a late development of the dry fishery in more distant areas not occupied by the English, such as Gaspé. An unbalanced cargo facilitated the addition of trading goods on the outward voyage for development of trade on the St. Lawrence in furs, which with small bulk and high value added little to the cargo of the home voyage. The importance of the Precambrian formation, and its limitations as to agricultural development, accentuated dependence on the fishing industry in the Maritime regions and on the fur trade in the area drained by the St. Lawrence. Severe competition of fishing ships for the fur trade made monopoly control impossible in the Maritimes and inevitable in the restricted areas of the St. Lawrence. Monopoly control in the fur trade and an unbalanced cargo were accompanied by attempts to reduce outbound cargo from Europe, to restrict settlement, and to increase return cargo by expansion of the fur trade. Similar effects were evident in the trade of the Dutch to New Amsterdam and up the Hudson and by the Iroquois to the Richelieu and to Lake Ontario. Competition between two routes characterized by long ocean voyages and unbalanced cargoes caused serious losses which culminated in the destruction of the villages of Huron middlemen north of Lake Simcoe. Severe losses in the fur trade, which accompanied monopoly under private enterprise, accentuated restriction of settlement. Intense competition between drainage basins necessitated direct control on the part of the French government in 1663 and active promotion of immigration and settlement and successful war against the Iroquois.

Groseilliers and Radisson attempted to avoid the difficulties of the St. Lawrence by developing trade through Hudson Bay, but they were discouraged by the French who were opposed to the additional costs of maintaining control over two routes.[3] They turned to the English who founded the Hudson's Bay Company. To meet competitive attacks from this alternative route, the French ruthlessly checked that Company's activities prior to 1713. Not only was possible competition checked in the north, but efforts continued to extend the St. Lawrence trade by the construction of military posts at Fort Frontenac, Niagara, and Detroit to prevent competition from the English, successors to the Dutch after 1664 to the south. The success of these efforts was followed by rapid increase in the number of lower grade southern furs brought on the market, a rapid decline in price, and attempts to increase prices by valorization schemes, which failed, particularly because of declining consumption caused by the lowering of the quality of materials used in the manufacture of beaver hats. The results accompanying the activities of the government in strengthening the position of the St. Lawrence by heavy military expenditures were evident in the development of inflation and in the loss of Hudson Bay and Nova Scotia in the Treaty of Utrecht. The persistent effects of unused capacity were evident under private enterprise in restriction of settlement and the necessity of governmental intervention. The consequent increased settlement in turn necessitated expansion of the fur trade to the interior. Inability to control the rate of expansion was particularly serious with a luxury product.

The Hudson's Bay Company, handicapped by limitations of agriculture in Hudson Bay, was similarly compelled to restrict a heavy outbound cargo, and to limit population, with the result that it was in a weak position to resist inroads from the French. The difficulties of combating the smuggling of a light, highly valuable commodity such as fur necessitated a highly centralized organization similar to that attempted by the Spanish in the handling of precious metals. (Possibilities of smuggling in the St. Lawrence checked efforts at centralization such as matured in the Hudson's Bay Company.) The problem of restricted population was eventually solved in part by governmental intervention in the form of military and naval campaigns, the success of which led to the reoccupation of Hudson Bay in the Treaty of Utrecht.

The penetration of the French to the interior and increasing dependence on the fur trade accentuated the weakness of agriculture in

[3]See G. L. Nute, *Cæsars of the Wilderness* (New York, 1943).

the St. Lawrence, with its limitations of soil, climate, and technique, to the extent that New France was not even self-sufficient and was unable to provide support to the fishing regions, particularly of Cape Breton after 1713, or to the French West Indies, or to compete with lumber and fish from New England and agricultural products—especially flour—from New York and Philadelphia. Moreover, the long closed season of the St. Lawrence restricted the possibilities of developing a satisfactory trade to the West Indies. The hurricane season coincided with the open season of the St. Lawrence and the sugar season with the closed season. Inability to link up the St. Lawrence with the fishing industry and the West Indies weakened the French Empire, in contrast with the economic integration of settlement in New England and expansion of the fishing industry and trade to the West Indies and Newfoundland which strengthened the English Empire. Expansion of the fur trade and the fishing industry in New France weakened the French, while integrated development increased the strength of the regions under British control on the Atlantic. After 1713, New England advanced to the fishing regions in the vicinity of Canso and extended trade to Newfoundland and the West Indies. Expanding trade involved exports to, and imports from, the foreign West Indies in spite of such legislation as the Molasses Act of 1733. From the south, New York, with cheap supplies of rum from the West Indies, began to compete more effectively in the interior with the French transatlantic, St. Lawrence trade with its dependence on brandy. To the north, the Hudson's Bay Company re-established its position on Hudson Bay, although the problem of unbalanced cargo continued; settlement was restricted and exploration and penetration to the interior were limited. Indians were encouraged to bring their furs down to Hudson Bay. Continued competition from the north and the south necessitated continued extension westward of the French fur trade of the St. Lawrence. La Vérendrye and his successors took advantage of the weakness of the Hudson's Bay Company on Hudson Bay by pushing trade to the Saskatchewan and making visits of the Indians to Hudson Bay unnecessary; but increasing costs of transportation weakened the position of the French Empire and contributed to its collapse. Renewed efforts to increase control over the fur trade by expansion westward, and over the fishing industry by fortification of Louisburg in Cape Breton, were again defeated and followed by the collapse of the French Empire in 1763.

That collapse facilitated the expansion of British colonial trade, as shown in the penetration of Albany traders to the St. Lawrence and to the upper lakes, but the problem of unbalanced cargo in the European Atlantic trade in furs by the St. Lawrence route remained, and with it the necessity for westward expansion. The divergence between the New York and the St. Lawrence trade was recognized in regulations permitting extension of trade beyond the posts in 1768, and in the Quebec Act of 1774, which attempted, by a boundary line down the Ohio, to re-establish control by Montreal over territory occupied by the French. Penetration to the northwest followed lines worked out by the French. On the Atlantic, expansion of integrated colonial trade increased the tension incidental to the restriction of West Indies trade through enforcements of the Sugar Act. Pressure in the interior and on the Atlantic contributed to the Revolution.

After the Revolution, England was scarcely more successful than the French had been in developing an empire based on the St. Lawrence, the Maritimes, and the West Indies. The West Indies lost their influential position for Great Britain, and although Britain paid heavy penalties to build up the Maritimes as a substitute for the American colonies, they were unable to provide adequate supplies of foodstuffs for their own needs. The fur trade of the St. Lawrence continued as a drain on agriculture in that area. Fur traders continued to solve their problems by expansion to the Saskatchewan, the Churchill, the Mackenzie, and the rivers draining to the Pacific. Reorganization in the formation of the Northwest Company, support of West Indies rum, use of vessels on the Great Lakes, and organization of food supply in the interior with reliance on pemmican and the potato, contributed to the achievement. The Hudson's Bay Company, with its persistent problem of unbalanced cargo to Hudson Bay, was again weakened by expansion from the St. Lawrence and was compelled to make determined efforts to overcome its handicaps and penetrate to the interior, in part by reorganization, and in part by settlement in the Red River district under Lord Selkirk as a means of reducing costs of imported provisions and supplies. The inevitable severe competition between rival organizations—on the one hand from the St. Lawrence with expansion to new territory with unexploited resources as a means of mitigating the increasing cost of transportation, and on the other from Hudson Bay with the necessity of penetration to the interior to meet traders from the St. Lawrence—was followed by outbreaks of hostilities and amalgamation in 1821. Continued expansion from the St. Lawrence and the increasingly difficult problem of an unbalanced cargo, accentuated not only by distance but also by the necessity of travelling up-stream with heavy outbound cargo, eventually weakened the Northwest Company as they had the French. The significance of unbalanced cargoes was evident in the intensity of competition, in the rapid extension westward from the St. Lawrence, in restriction in Hudson Bay, and in the clash which brought amalgamation.

The drain of the fur trade and its opposition to settlement in the St. Lawrence were ended temporarily in the French régime by the active intervention of government, and similarly in the English régime. Restricted settlement on the St. Lawrence, as a result of the characteristics of the fur trade, was overcome not only by active encouragement to migration of the Loyalists, particularly to Upper Canada, by military settlements, and by strong military support in the War of 1812, but also by determined efforts of Great Britain through an extremely high preference to build up the timber trade in order to offset the effects of dependence on European and American supplies during the Napoleonic Wars. The disappearance of the fur trade in the St. Lawrence was followed by exploitation of softwood (white pine) timber. As a bulky commodity with low specific gravity it could be floated down the long continental rivers, and with the manufacture of ships provided its own means of transportation to Great Britain. With a heavy return cargo and empty space on the outbound voyage, its effects were the reverse of the fur trade, and large numbers of settlers were brought out in preference to ballast. Rapid increase of settlement, particularly after 1820, was followed by rapid expansion of agriculture, especially in Upper Canada. Increased agricultural production, wheat and flour, in the newly settled regions of Upper Canada led to demands for construction of canals across the Niagara Peninsula and on the upper St. Lawrence. The difficulties of obtaining financial support for canal construction in newly settled regions, and increasing demands for cheaper transportation, contributed, together with the depression of the 1830's and the pronounced cyclical fluctuations of an economy largely dependent on the timber trade, to the outbreak of the Rebellion in 1837, Lord Durham's *Report*, the Act of Union, and creation of a financial structure capable of supporting rapid construction of canals. Concentration on the timber trade, with its unbalanced cargo and the indirect effect on increasing emigration and settlement, was followed by governmental intervention not only in the form of improvements of transportation but also of changes in land policy. The unwholesome conditions of immigration in dilapidated ships suited only to the timber trade, shown in outbreaks of cholera which spread through the continent, necessitated governmental regulation. The timber trade was encouraged by the development of settlement, as costs of transportation were lowered by securing immigrants for the outbound voyage, but as it expanded in these circumstances, the problems of settlement became more acute. The period of shifting from dependence on the timber trade to dependence on agriculture was essentially a period of difficulty.

After 1821 the fur trade as conducted from Hudson Bay continued to be involved in problems of unbalanced cargo, though they were less acute on account of settlement of Red River, more efficient transportation, and increasing possibilities of regulation. Continued expansion to new territory in the Yukon and Labrador was accompanied by attempts to lower costs by reducing the heavy incoming up-stream cargo. New England traders, restricted by the British Navigation Acts on the Atlantic, were free from the restraints of the East India Company on the Pacific, and could take advantage of the discoveries made by Captain Cook towards the prevention of scurvy during long voyages, and of the new resources of furs. On the other hand, Canadian traders, expelled from American territory after the Jay Treaty and the Embargo Act of 1807, pushed into the Pacific coast drainage basin and displaced Astor's establishment on the Columbia in the War of 1812. After amalgamation in 1821, the Western Department by virtue of its distance and its interest in the Pacific, tended to develop along lines independent of the Northern Department. Exhaustion of new territory for the fur trade accentuated economies of operation, particularly in transportation, and contributed to the development of settlement and agriculture, particularly on the Columbia and the Red River. Settlement eventually brought demands for new types of government, shown in the loss of Oregon and in the difficulties leading to the Riel Rebellion and the establishment of the province of Manitoba. The problem of unused capacity in the fur trade, and the necessity of reducing westbound up-stream movements of bulky provisions and supplies, resulted in constant expansion westward to the Pacific and the organization of settlement in relation to production of food supplies. In turn agriculture and settlement hastened the decline of the fur trade and provided abutments for the railway bridge. Monopoly in the fur trade receded and new trade routes emerged in which the Hudson's Bay Company deserted the Hudson Bay route and imported goods from the south.

In the Maritimes continuous efforts were made to develop an integrated economy similar to that of New England in a struggle for control over the fishery, trade, and shipping. Concentration of trade in Halifax was followed after the middle of the century, particularly with

148   ESSAYS IN CANADIAN ECONOMIC HISTORY

the advent of steamships, by attempts to overcome the handicaps of the fishing industry, evident in scattered ports, through government construction of short stretches of railway to the Gulf of St. Lawrence and the Bay of Fundy; and in Saint John by construction of a short stretch of railway to the Gulf of St. Lawrence. Competition of railways with shipping brought profound disturbances to an economy based on ships, and shifted interest from external to internal development. Decline of shipping and difficulties of the railways necessitated efforts to extend traffic to the interior by linking the railways to continental systems. An attempt was made to solve the problem of unused railway capacity by Confederation and construction of the Intercolonial Railway.[4]

On the St. Lawrence, the inadequacy of canals as a solution to the problems of agriculture in Upper Canada, the difficulty of securing traffic from the western states in competition with the Erie Canal, improved upper lakes steamboats, and railways, necessitated further governmental intervention in the form of substantial assistance to the Grand Trunk from Sarnia to Montreal and Portland, and later to Rivière du Loup to connect with the Intercolonial to Halifax. Private

[4]"It is to be hoped that the folly of expecting any large results from local and isolated railways is already fully demonstrated to both Nova Scotia and New Brunswick, and that it has now become a first consideration with them to direct their attention to the means by which both may be relieved from the consequences of a large debt incurred for works not only unproductive of any directly remunerative results but also unattended by any substantial advantage to our trade or commercial importance. The conviction must have forced itself upon the public mind that we must extricate ourselves from these difficulties by obtaining connection with the railways of Canada and the United States by one or other of the routes proposed. Much has already been done towards achieving that result." (From a speech by Sir Charles Tupper at Saint John, 1860, quoted in Sir Charles Tupper, Recollections of Sixty Years in Canada, Toronto, 1914, pp. 34–5.) "There is a little over a hundred miles of railway in the province but owing to some cause which is unintelligible to an outsider and many less important reasons, which are easily understood, this undertaking has burdened the province with a heavy debt and consequently heavy taxation while it has irritated politicians, and been a cause of deferring . . . perhaps for ever . . . many important acts of local legislation. The primary error, undoubtedly, was the making it a government work, instead of leaving it to a company. Heavy sums raised at six per cent. on provincial debentures make sad havoc with revenue of the country. And the next great error . . . patent to all . . . is the custom too prevalent in our colonies under the system of representative government, of changing every official, however petty, at every change of government." (F. Duncan, Our Garrisons in the West, London, 1864, p. 100.) "Provincial isolation and a blundering neglect to make railways which individually are burdens but would become as a grand whole a source of revenue and profit, are among the features at present most apparent on our British American Railway system. . . . It is well said, by one of their own journals 'We cannot afford to bear the burden of our present incomplete road.' " (Ibid., p. 280.)

enterprise with government support was able to build the short line to the American seaboard, but government ownership was essential to link up Maritime railways with the Grand Trunk by the Intercolonial and to supplement water transportation to Montreal during the summer season. As the Act of Union was a financial prerequisite to the St. Lawrence canals, so Confederation was a financial prerequisite to the Intercolonial. A more balanced cargo, which was available in New York and American ports, pulled Atlantic steamships—for example, the Cunard line—from Canadian ports. In spite of attempts to increase traffic by construction of through lines, the problems of unused capacity became more serious. Construction of a railway to the Pacific offered possibilities of relief.

On the Pacific coast the sudden economic expansion precipitated by the gold rush in the late fifties and early sixties was followed by rapid decline and serious financial difficulties accompanying heavy interest charges on the debt incurred in construction of roads to the interior.[5] Construction of a transcontinental railway as a condition on which British Columbia joined Confederation was expected to solve problems of debt in relation to existing transportation facilities in British Columbia and in the St. Lawrence. Substantial governmental support necessitated construction of a road through Canadian territory north of Lake Superior and precluded participation by the Grand Trunk Railway, insistent on building up traffic for its main line to the western states.[6]

The anxiety of the government to solve the problems of public finance, which followed the severe depression of the seventies, by development of traffic for existing transportation facilities enabled Montreal financiers, who had gained materially from the first line from Minneapolis to Winnipeg and from reversal of the flow of traffic from Hudson Bay on the north to the south, to obtain the contract for construction of the Canadian Pacific Railway. Rapid construction of the main line in the prairie regions, adoption of a southern route in spite of recommendations of Sandford Fleming in favour of the northern route, encouragement of immigrants, acquisition of feeders in the industrialized St. Lawrence region, completion of the line to a winter port at Saint John, and extension of ocean services were part of a policy incidental to the overwhelming importance of developing traffic on a transcontinental line. "It was the Oriental traffic that helped

[5]"Although sentiment in Vancouver Island on the whole was unfavourable to Confederation, the entire mainland including Cariboo, then an important factor, was practically a unit in its favour" (Sir Charles Tupper, Recollections, p. 126).
[6]Ibid., p. 140.

to save the Canadian Pacific from the disaster which sunk a hundred and fifty-six American railroads in the depression of 1893–95 and might well have overwhelmed a new railway through Canada depending for its existence on local business."[7] Oriental traffic during the depression was supplemented by economic expansion of British Columbia, particularly in the construction of the Crow's Nest Pass line, in the mines of the Kootenay region, in lumbering, in fishing, and in the gold rush to the Klondike. The tariff designed in the National Policy to support east-west traffic and the monopoly clause (cancelled 1888) supported the policy of following a southern route across the prairies to check competition from American roads for long-haul traffic.

Determined efforts to maintain control over traffic were accompanied by rapid increase in profits at the turn of the century, and release of contractors after completion of the main line led to the construction of a second main line from Winnipeg northwest to the Yellowhead Pass, with government support from the provinces in protest against the burden of monopoly from a transcontinental line supported by a federal government. Control by the Canadian Northern of a line carrying traffic from the prairies to the head of the lakes necessitated extension westward to Vancouver and eastward from the head of the lakes to the St. Lawrence. In eastern Canada the Grand Trunk was compelled by encroachment from the Canadian Pacific to secure control of local traffic by amalgamation with the Great Western, and to search for means of supplementing through-line traffic. Protection encouraged transcontinental lines and weakened the position of the Grand Trunk main line to the United States. Montreal became the apex of an angle of which one side—the main line of the C.P.R.—extended to British Columbia and the other—the main line of the Grand Trunk—to Sarnia and Chicago. Development of traffic on these lines, deepening of the upper St. Lawrence canals to 14 feet and of the St. Lawrence Ship Channel to twenty-five feet early in the century, and extension of wireless, enabled Montreal to compete more effectively with New York for grain and for ships. Inability to link up the Intercolonial as a government undertaking with railways under private enterprise which were anxious to take the shortest cut to seaboard, decline of Quebec as contrasted with the rise of Montreal, attempts to tap the clay belt extending westward to Winnipeg in order to provide for possible expansion in northern Quebec and in northern Ontario, and increasing revenue from the tariff led to the construction of the National Transcontinental Railway from Winnipeg to Quebec

[7]J. M. Gibbon, *Steel of Empire* (Toronto, 1935), p. 336.

and its extension to Maritime ports. The more distant Grand Trunk Pacific line, extending from Winnipeg, as the terminus of the National Transcontinental, to Prince Rupert, appeared as a possibility of developing through long-haul traffic to the Orient, British Columbia, and western Canada, and as a further means of checking the effects of monopoly from the Canadian Pacific under the National Policy. Attempts to link the Grand Trunk in the East and the Canadian Northern in the West were destined to defeat through the insistence of private enterprise in the Canadian Northern on a line to the Great Lakes and industrial areas of the St. Lawrence, and of the federal government in the National Transcontinental on a line opening new territory and recapturing lost ground for the Intercolonial and the Maritimes.

The enormous outlay of capital in canals and transcontinental railways accentuated problems of unused capacity, particularly because of the basic importance of the production and export of wheat from the prairie regions. Construction of elevators and of branch lines on a vast scale in the wheat-producing regions necessitated double tracking of lines to the head of the lakes and additions of lines from Georgian Bay ports to Montreal. Seasonal navigation implied rapid movement of grain and a pronounced peak load of east-bound traffic. Empty cars were distributed over a long period to points throughout the West in preparation for the harvest rush. Seasonal navigation on the lower St. Lawrence facilitated storage of wheat in Buffalo elevators for shipment to New York.

The secular trend of expanding wheat production shown in long-run peak-load problems of transportation was accompanied by short-run problems of annual fluctuations of crop, and affected government policy. The tendency of costs incidental to peak-load operation, made more rigid by competitive rates with American lines and the importance of government debt, to fall on regions exposed to world competition in prices of wheat, has involved the struggle for control over elevators, lower rates, the co-operative movement, the Hudson Bay Railway, and shipment via Vancouver and the Panama Canal. Finally, the recent depression and sustained drought led to governmental support of wheat prices and establishment of a wheat board.

The burdens were less conspicuous during the period of rapid expansion from the middle nineties to the beginning of the war on account of increased immigration, branch- and main-line construction, expansion of wheat production, and the development of mining in the Cordilleran region, especially the Kootenay and the Klondike. Rapid increase in capital equipment in western Canada was accompanied by expansion of the industrial areas of the St. Lawrence and of the Maritimes. Provincial government support of hydro-electric power in Ontario to utilize the enormous water powers of Niagara accompanied support by bonuses of the iron and steel industry of the Maritimes and the St. Lawrence for the production of coal, railway cars, rails, and machinery. Similarly, rapid increase of population in the west involved provincial government support in the construction of telephone lines and extension of other social services. Decline in rate of expansion in western Canada brought a sharp decline in the demand for railway cars, rails, and other types of capital equipment, with particularly serious effects for more distant regions such as the Maritimes, and in turn necessitated increased government support in subventions.

The acute difficulties of new transcontinental railways in competition with an established line before traffic had been developed, and the freezing of capital markets with the outbreak of the Great War, led to the appointment of the Drayton-Acworth Commission and formation of the Canadian National Railways to include lines built by private enterprise—namely the Grand Trunk, and its subsidiary, the Grand Trunk Pacific, and the Canadian Northern—and by government—the Intercolonial and the National Transcontinental. These lines were merged, and determined efforts were made to build up long-haul traffic by steamship lines, hotels, and branch lines. The Canadian Pacific, in an attempt to maintain control and to extend traffic, engaged in construction of branch lines, hotels, steamships, and extension of external activities. The upward swing of the business cycle favoured extension of capital equipment by both organizations. The necessity of competing for long-haul traffic in mature economic areas with which private enterprise had been particularly concerned, accentuated the problem of lines built by the government. These lines were essentially developmental and, being undertaken by the government with ample supplies of credit, were built with heavy initial outlays of capital. Consequently, light traffic, as a result of competition from lines built under private enterprise and privately owned and of their essentially developmental character, involved heavy unit costs of operation and maintenance, which were accentuated by heavy sunk costs of construction. Expansion of mining and of the pulp and paper industry, and settlement in northern Ontario and northern Quebec, were of first importance in reducing costs and meeting the deficit of the Canadian National Railways and in offsetting the effects of competition within the Canadian National System with lines to Chicago, to the northwest, and from the northwest to Quebec and the Maritimes.

The effects of the depression on the Canadian Pacific and the Canadian National have been evident in the passing of dividends and in the extent of Canadian National deficits. The Canadian Pacific has been relatively barred from further participation in expansion and has even been seriously affected by decline in the southern drought areas, but, on the other hand, its entrenched position has served as a powerful bulwark and it has continued to develop external traffic through its steamship lines. The Canadian National has been restricted by competition from the Canadian Pacific and by financial stringency. A more aggressive developmental policy in new territory would ease its difficulties.

The basic importance of transportation in the economic history of Canada has been responsible for the profound effects of unused capacity. The restrictive effect on settlement of an unbalanced cargo from Europe, and of up-stream traffic for heavy goods in the fur trade, resulted in governmental intervention on an extensive scale and collapse in the French régime. On the other hand, the expansive effect of an unbalanced cargo in the timber trade, which followed governmental intervention in the form of high preferences and military settlements to overcome the restrictive influences of the fur trade, brought expansion of agriculture and the necessity of further government intervention to solve the problems of improved transportation.

The significance of water transportation in the export of fur and timber involved emphasis on commercial credit. In the fur trade governmental support to military and naval ventures brought problems of government finance and led to inflation. The severity of fluctuations in the timber trade brought disastrous losses to interests concerned. Production and export of wheat necessitated railways and canals and the introduction of long-term credit through corporate and government finance. Fixed interest charges accompanying extensive government support, and insufficient revenue, necessitated further governmental intervention with Confederation, and extension to the Maritimes and the Pacific. Government intervention took the form of ownership and operation of the Intercolonial to the Maritimes and strong support to private enterprise westward to the Pacific. The expansion westward from the St. Lawrence which was typical of the fur trade was also essential to agriculture. The necessities of a transcontinental railway system were evident in the policies of the federal government—for example in tariff and immigration policy—and of the Canadian Pacific Railway; but they implied the development of competing lines to offset the effects of monopoly control, supported by the provinces of the prairie region and the metropolitan centres of Toronto, Quebec, and Halifax, and the emergence of control through the Board of Railway Commissioners, and of statutory rates such as the Crow's Nest Pass Rate Agreement and more recently British Columbia rate adjustment and the Maritime Freight Rates Act. The Hudson Bay Railway was a conspicuous illustration of the continued necessity for, and significance of, governmental intervention in relation to the problems of monopoly in western Canada. Ostensibly intended to provide relief from the problem of monopoly, it has been regarded as creating additional burdens of debt. Capital equipment essential to the production and export of wheat, in the form of a transcontinental railway, brought acute problems in non-competitive areas, which were temporarily solved, with the assistance of an upward swing of the business cycle and favourable prices of wheat, by further additions of capital equipment in two transcontinental railways. Decline in the rate of expansion, and the depression, emphasized the weight of overhead costs in relation to extensive capital equipment, and the heavy fixed charges involved in government ownership were evident in rigidities of railway rates and interest charges. These factors contributed to a decline in standards of living in the exposed areas and in turn to a reduction in demands for manufactured products from central Canada, to industrial unemployment, to numerous disparities and destructive eddies in the current of economic life—described in the evidence before the Royal Commission on Price Spreads—and to governmental intervention on a vast scale, ranging from the spate of federal legislation of the session 1935 to the cancelling of power contracts by the provincial government of Ontario. Dependence of the Prairie Provinces on wheat, and the tariff, are factors accentuating the burden on western Canada and are not offset by lower costs through competition for westbound traffic in manufactured products from eastern Canada. The sharp decline in prices of raw material, especially wheat, and low returns on bulk movements of grain and additional competition from motor transport in the competitive St. Lawrence region compel the railways to search for more remunerative westbound traffic of manufactured products in the face of declining purchasing power in the wheat area. More exposed regions with rigidities of freight rates and interest charges and shrinking income through drought and falling prices, and without an integrated balanced economic structure, have been more seriously affected by political disturbance, as evident in the movement for social credit in Alberta. The inadequacy of methods of control, increasing unit costs with shrinkage of volume and plant built for peak-load operations, and limited possibilities of further expansion, have necessitated substantial federal support of the Prairie Provinces in a wide variety of relief measures during the depression, and have brought forth protests from the Maritimes and British Columbia in favour of readjustment of federal-provincial relations.[8]

Problems of unused capacity have had the effect of quickening and accentuating the long-run general trends of economic development and have necessitated govermental intervention as a steadying or remedial factor. In the main, problems have been solved by aggressive developmental measures but limitations have been apparent in the present depression. Governmental intervention as a means of solving problems during a period of expansion creates problems to be solved by new types of government intervention during a depression. Lower tariffs bring relief, particularly to the regions more distant from the St. Lawrence and probably throughout the entire economy, but they do not solve the problems of reducing the violence of the swings incidental to the significance of unused capacity.

The long-run period of depression of the latter part of the last century was accompanied by continued determined efforts to enable the St. Lawrence to compete with New York, and the long-run period of prosperity of a third of a century which followed was marked by the success of those efforts and by further efforts to swing the Canadian economy further to the north to support Quebec and the Maritimes. The failure of those efforts, shown in an enormous debt and heavy deficits, has been accompanied by a retreat. Heavy outlay incidental to government construction and ownership of the railways designed to support the lower St. Lawrence and Maritime regions have accompanied lower rates incidental to water competition and statutory intervention. Narrowing of the range of the economy dependent on the St. Lawrence as a result of the development of a competitive region on the Pacific coast, largely as a consequence of the Panama Canal, has complicated the problem. Drastic revision of debts, ranging from the passing dividends on the C.P.R. to agricultural debt adjustment operations, has been inevitable. Transfers to more exposed regions have been gradually developed, but much remains to be done before the implications of unused capacity are understood.

[8]See "A Note on Problems of Readjustment in Canada," *Journal of Political Economy*, Dec. 1935, for a discussion of the implications of W. A. Mackintosh's *Economic Problems of the Prairie Provinces* (Toronto, 1935).

An Introduction to Canadian
Economic Studies*

THE St. Lawrence River represents a significant division of the North American continent bounding as it does the vast stretch of Precambrian formation on its north and the later less resistant formations on the south. The geological formations, climate, flora, and fauna of the north cross over to the south, those of the south cross over to the north, and the basic division disappears toward the west. The diversified mature economic development supported by the geographic background of the south has been of profound significance to the character of northern economic development in the minor areas of similar geographical structure in the east, and of even greater significance in the west. Its influence has been indirect as expansion has proceeded toward the west and increasingly direct in later stages of development in the east.

The significance of the economic development of the United States to Canada has been indirect because of the dominance of the Precambrian formation and the St. Lawrence, which necessitated concentration on the fishing industry in the maritime regions and on the fur trade in the interior in the production of exports for European markets. The fur trade followed the waterways along the edge of the Precambrian formation and eventually extended to the Pacific coast. The geographic unity built up on the fur trade,[1] which approximated the present boundaries of the Dominion, collapsed with exhaustion of furs and increasing costs of transportation in 1821. It was followed on the St. Lawrence by exploitation of the white pine in exports of square timber to Great Britain, and agricultural development in the narrow fertile regions to the south of the Precambrian formation in exports of wheat and, later, products of the dairying and live-stock industries. As the Precambrian formation with expansion of the fur trade was a basis for Canadian unity, and with exhaustion of furs, a cause of its collapse, so it delayed re-establishment of unity by support-

*From J. A. Ruddick et al., The Dairy Industry in Canada, ed. H. A. Innis (Ryerson, 1937), pp. v–xxvi.
[1]See H. A. Innis, The Fur Trade in Canada (New Haven, 1930); A History of the Canadian Pacific Railway (London, 1923).

156

ing the monopoly of the Hudson Bay route and turning immigration to the fertile plains of the western states. Occupation of the prairie region of the United States and of the placer mining regions of the Pacific coast finally supported construction of the Canadian Pacific Railway and re-established unity. Overhead costs incidental to railway construction across the Precambrian formation were a powerful factor hastening expansion of wheat production northward from the United States. American technique supported the rapid expansion of Canada in the economic development of British Columbia and the Prairie Provinces during the early years of the present century. As the Precambrian formation delayed development prior to construction of the Canadian Pacific Railway, it hastened development after construction. The long depression which preceded the turn of the century trained a population in American agriculture, and the marked boom which followed was accentuated by the adoption of American experience. The effects were evident in the rapid increase in exports of wheat to Great Britain, rapid industrialization of the St. Lawrence region, and the retreat of its agricultural products from the markets of Great Britain. As the influence of the metropolitan demands of Great Britain was extended in the more remote areas, the influence of the metropolitan demands of the United States was increased in less remote areas. The St. Lawrence region turned to the mining and pulp and paper industries for exports to the United States. The Canadian economy has been faced with problems of adjustment in relation to these varied demands.

Penetration of the continent by the St. Lawrence facilitated development of trade from Europe in staple products[2] beginning with the fur trade and continuing with the timber trade, and, after 1850 and construction of railways, with live-stock products and wheat. The fur trade, with heavy up-stream cargo from Europe and light down-stream cargo in return, restricted settlement, but steady expansion westward necessitated agricultural development supported by the United States in Ontario, the Red River, and the Columbia. The timber trade, with heavy down-stream cargo to Europe and light return cargo, hastened immigration and settlement from Great Britain. Expansion in the United States and exhaustion of the forests adjacent to the Atlantic seaboard began to turn trade in lumber from the St. Lawrence to the south. Wheat production moved steadily westward,

[2]See H. A. Innis, *Problems of Staple Production in Canada* (Toronto, 1933), and "Unused Capacity as a Factor in Canadian Economic History," *Canadian Journal of Economics and Political Science*, II (1936). [See this volume, p. 141.]

including Ontario in its sweep and eventually reached western Canada. The dairying and live-stock industries in relation to the demands of Great Britain spread from New York to Ontario, following the diminution of wheat production, but declined as a basis for exports as wheat production increased in the West and the domestic market expanded in the East.

Extension of the European economy to North America involved exploitation of the fishing grounds of the North Atlantic by the divided political units of Europe. The elastic, diversified organization of an island such as Great Britain supported the colonial occupation of an extensive coast line, varying in geographic characteristics from Newfoundland to New England and the southern seaboard states. The relatively inelastic, self-contained organization of France was concerned with the exploitation of the banks and shore fisheries from Nova Scotia to Labrador. The expansion of shipping, the fishing industry,[3] and trade in New England in relation to Newfoundland on the north and the southern colonies and the British West Indies on the south gradually narrowed the influence of France by retreat first from Nova Scotia in 1713 and then from the northern half of North America in 1763. But even the political capacities of Great Britain proved unequal to the strain, and the southern colonies withdrew.

The legacy of European divisiveness persisted in the interior as on the Atlantic. France advanced from the fishing industry in the Gulf of St. Lawrence to the fur trade of the St. Lawrence and the Precambrian formation.[4] The extension of trade by the relatively accessible Ottawa River to the interior involved competition in the less accessible upper St. Lawrence and the lakes, first with the Dutch, and later with the English (1664) through the Iroquois from New York.[5] Pressure from Hudson Bay (1668) and from New York was accompanied by attempts to fortify the St. Lawrence, first in the lower river and later in the upper river and the Great Lakes, and to drive the English out of Hudson Bay. The retreat from Nova Scotia and from Hudson Bay after the Treaty of Utrecht was followed by more determined efforts at defence on the Great Lakes and at Louisburg, and by penetration westward under La Vérendrye, and by the Mississippi from the south. These activities failed to check encroachment by the English from New York on the Great Lakes and from Hudson Bay and pressure from concentrated areas on the north and the south brought collapse to an

[3]R. F. Grant, *The Canadian Atlantic Fishery* (Toronto, 1934), pp. vii–xxi.
[4]Innis, *Fur Trade in Canada.*
[5]H. A. Innis, "An Introduction to the Economic History of Ontario," *Papers and Records of the Ontario Historical Society*, XXX (1934), 111–23. [See this volume, p. 108.]

extended line of development in the interior. With that collapse the English were quick to occupy the Gulf of St. Lawrence and the river and to extend their control of the Great Lakes region. Anglo-American traders, supported by West Indian rum, pushed from Albany to the Great Lakes, the Mississippi, Lake Superior, and the Northwest and moved to Montreal to prosecute the trade via the Ottawa.

The clash between expanding economic regions was accentuated by the withdrawal of the French. Increasing restriction, imposed by Great Britain after the fear of the French was removed in North America, was followed by continued control by Great Britain over the St. Lawrence and the Precambrian area, with its exports of raw material to a metropolitan market and its imports of manufactured products, and its accessibility to the British navy. The region defended by France was now defended by Great Britain.

The intrusion of trade from New York by Albany to the debatable area tributary to the upper St. Lawrence, shown in the use of boats on the Great Lakes and the development of shipping, and the exclusion of Canadians from American territory, supported an extension of the fur trade built up and grafted on the French structure beyond the limits occupied by the French on the Saskatchewan, to the Mackenzie and to the Pacific coast.[6] The migration of the United Empire Loyalists to the same debatable area of Upper Canada brought agricultural production and support to an expanding fur trade. From a source of weakness in the French régime, the region tributary to the upper St. Lawrence became a source of strength in the English régime.

Migration from New England to Nova Scotia after 1713, hastened by restriction due to French occupation in the interior, continued after 1763 and, with the United Empire Loyalists, after 1783. As in the St. Lawrence, American technique in the fishing industry and in agriculture (in the latter industry grafted on the technique of the French, evident in the diked lands of the Bay of Fundy), supported a trading organization which became competitive with New England. As expansion of New England involved conflict with England, expansion in Nova Scotia was supported by England. American trade was limited by the tariff and by exclusion of New England from trade with the British West Indies and, after the War of 1812 and the Convention of 1818, from fishing in British waters.

With the War of 1812 control of Great Britain was established in

[6]H. A. Innis, "Interrelations between the Fur Trade of Canada and the United States," *Mississippi Valley Historical Review*, XX (1933). [See this volume, p. 97.] R. H. Fleming, "Phyn, Ellice and Company of Schenectady," *Contributions to Canadian Economics*, IV, 1932 (University of Toronto Studies, History and Economics, 1932).

the fur trade across northern North America to the Columbia, and in the upper St. Lawrence, and the Maritimes. It was strengthened, particularly in New Brunswick and in the St. Lawrence, by substantial preferences granted to develop the timber trade to offset the loss of Baltic supplies during the Napoleonic Wars,[7] by the establishment of soldier settlements, by assistance to emigration, and by construction of the Rideau Canal. It was strengthened in western Canada by amalgamation of the Northwest Company and the Hudson's Bay Company, the disappearance of the long and difficult route from the St. Lawrence, concentration on the short route from Hudson Bay, and development of the Pacific coast region. And it was strengthened in Nova Scotia by relaxation of the colonial system through the work of Huskisson in the Colonial Trade Acts.

After the Napoleonic Wars, immigration to Upper Canada, supported by the timber trade and by the westward movement of population from the United States, was followed in turn by expansion of the timber trade and increasing agricultural production, part of which was available in the early period to meet the demands of incoming settlers, and in the later period for export. American technique of agriculture introduced by the United Empire Loyalists was extended by later immigration. Increase in exports brought problems for limited transportation facilities. The completion of the Erie Canal in 1825 provided an outlet to New York for the regions tributary to the upper lakes and hastened the demand for improvement of the St. Lawrence canals, met in part by construction of the Welland. The increasing importance of steamboats on the lakes accentuated the difficulties of the upper St. Lawrence. Increasing difficulties in securing the necessary financial support for carrying out the gigantic task of constructing the St. Lawrence canals were evident in the Rebellion of 1837, Lord Durham's *Report*, and the Act of Union of 1840. By 1850, with construction of the canals, steamboats were able to proceed down the river to Montreal and return.

The opening of the British West Indies to New England in 1830 and the expansion of the New England mackerel fishery led to more aggressive efforts in Nova Scotia to check New England encroachment in British inshore waters, by means of tariffs, the Hovering Act of 1834, and a narrower interpretation and more vigorous enforcement of rights granted by the Convention of 1818. The *Royal William* was

---

[7]See A. R. M. Lower, "The Trade in Square Timber," *Contributions to Canadian Economics*, VI (1933), and R. J. Albion, *Forests and Sea Power* (Cambridge, Mass., 1926).

expected to increase trade with the St. Lawrence and to reduce dependence on the United States. In spite of these efforts, continued expansion in the United States and effective use of the tariff, especially on Canadian fish, attracted Nova Scotia labour and skill. Donald McKay[8] achieved fame as a shipbuilder in New England, and Samuel Cunard, a native of Halifax, became a founder of the steamship line concerned chiefly with American trade.

The effects of gradual reduction of preferences under the colonial system (culminating in the repeal of the Corn Laws and the Navigation Acts in the forties) were offset in part by lower costs of transportation, incidental to the completion of the St. Lawrence canals, and by the Reciprocity Treaty of 1854. The addition of the Grand Trunk Railway to supplement the St. Lawrence canals, by providing more rapid service and an outlet at Portland on the Atlantic seaboard during the winter season, was designed under the Reciprocity Treaty to extend control of the St. Lawrence route over traffic from the western states. The significance of relative freedom of trade between Great Britain, Canada, and the United States[9] was possibly less, however, in the effective competition of the St. Lawrence with New York in relation to the British market than in the increase in exports in relation to the American market. The tremendous drain on the Canadian economy involved in a shift from the timber trade, which capitalized the advantages of the St. Lawrence in water transportation and wooden ships, to the introduction of steamships and railways, shown in a rising public debt and the competition of New York, enhanced the importance of the American market. Lumbermen such as Eddy, Booth, Bronson, and Perley came, chiefly from Vermont, into the Ottawa valley and built sawmills on important power sites for the production of lumber for the eastern states. On the other hand, the effects of improved agricultural machinery in the United States,[10] particularly during the period of labour scarcity in the Civil War, were evident in the St. Lawrence region in the increased production of wheat which followed the high prices incidental to the Crimean War. In the Maritimes, reciprocity and the Civil War were ac-

[8]F. W. Wallace, Wooden Ships and Iron Men (Toronto, n.d.), pp. 331ff.

[9]See S. A. Saunders, "The Reciprocity Treaty of 1854: A Regional Study, "Canadian Journal of Economics and Political Science, II (1936), 41–53, and "The Maritime Provinces and the Reciprocity Treaty," Dalhousie Review, XIV (1934).

[10]H. A. Innis and A. R. M. Lower, eds., Select Documents in Canadian Economic History, 1783–1885 (Toronto, 1933), pp. 541ff.; F. Landon, "Some Effects of the American Civil War on Canadian Agriculture," Agricultural History, VII (1933).

companied by retreat of the New England fishing industry and expansion of the Nova Scotia industry and by demands for coal and agricultural products. Similarity of institutions, race, language, and geographic background facilitated the spread of skill and technique peculiar to the economic development of the United States[11] to Ontario and the Maritimes. Canadians enlisted in the armies of the United States and Americans migrated to Canada. The Civil War brought internal strains on the financial structure of the United States and served to accentuate the tilt of the North American economy toward Canada. Industries migrated to Canada in relation to the markets of the United States and Great Britain.

The Civil War was followed by expansion of industrialism, evident in the iron and steel industry and in the construction of railways, increased public debts, demands for revenue and protection, and the abrogation of the Reciprocity Treaty in 1866. In the St. Lawrence, as in the United States, problems of debt incidental to the construction of canals and support of the railways, and the depression of 1857, strengthened demands for protection. The philosophy of William Carey and his support of protection was adopted and expounded by Isaac Buchanan. Increasingly effective competition from railways in the United States and the imposition of tariffs intensified the transportation problem and necessitated improvements, particularly in the navigation of the lower St. Lawrence, and the search for solutions which culminated in Confederation, extension of the Intercolonial to the Maritimes, higher tariffs, and plans for construction of the Canadian Pacific Railway to British Columbia. In the Maritimes problems of debt incidental to the construction of railways[12] coincided with the loss of markets for coal and fish in the abrogation of the Reciprocity Treaty, and enhanced the possibility of Confederation, both as a solution of the railway and the debt problem, and as a means of compelling the United States to open her markets for fish, shown in the success of the Washington Treaty, and of providing a market for coal in the St. Lawrence.

In the Red River settlement and on the Columbia, after the amalgamation in the fur trade in 1821, live-stock were brought in from the United States to reduce the heavy one-way traffic of the trade from England. The problem of overhead costs peculiar to dependence on the fur trade continued to involve dependence on American technique

----

[11]See C. W. Wright, "American Nationalism: An Economic Interpretation," *Facts and Factors in Economic History* (Cambridge, Mass., 1932), pp. 357–80.
[12]See Innis, *Problems of Staple Production*, pp. 17–23.

in agriculture. The nucleus of settlement in the Columbia became the centre of attraction to American immigrants, and in the Oregon boundary dispute in 1846 the Hudson's Bay Company was forced to retreat. The spread of placer mining north from California led to the gold rush on the Fraser River in the late fifties and to the Cariboo in the sixties. Rapid decline in gold mining contributed to the problem of debts, incurred for improvement of transportation, and necessitated dependence on the development of other industries. In Red River, trade increased with the United States, and the route via York Factory and Hudson Bay was abandoned. Steamboats, displaced on the Mississippi, moved to the Red River and, as the railway followed, to the Saskatchewan and eventually to the Mackenzie. British Columbia was admitted to Confederation under an agreement requiring construction of a transcontinental railway within ten years and Rupert's Land was purchased from the Hudson's Bay Company.

The opening of the western states with the Homestead Act of 1862 and the construction of American railways, over against the previous occupation of the more fertile land of the St. Lawrence region and the continued control of northwestern Canada by the Hudson's Bay Company under the protection of the Precambrian formation, were factors responsible for the migration of Canadians to the western states in the sixties and seventies.[13] Plans to construct the Canadian Pacific Railway were thwarted by competition of American railways for capital and labour.[14] The interest of Jay Cooke and Company in construction of the Northern Pacific and of Hugh Allan in the Canadian Pacific brought collapse of the latter project in the Pacific Scandal. The Grand Trunk, formerly concerned with the possibilities of the Canadian Pacific, became absorbed with the expanding traffic of the middle western states. Its gauge was changed to the American standard. Determined efforts to stem the tide toward the United States involved construction by the Mackenzie Administration of the Canadian Pacific as a government undertaking along lines similar to the construction of the Intercolonial and the canals, and strong support to private enterprise by the succeeding Macdonald Administration. Canadian and Hudson's Bay Company interests concerned with western expansion in the United States, represented by J. J. Hill, R. B. Angus, G. Stephen, and D. A. Smith, proceeded from the construction of American roads and acquisition of land, to link up with

13O. D. Skelton, *General Economic History of the Dominion, 1867–1912* (Toronto, 1913).
14Innis, *A History of the Canadian Pacific Railway.*

the government railway from Winnipeg to the American boundary in 1878, and to secure the charter of the Canadian Pacific Railway. The opposition of the Grand Trunk in the London market made dependence on European and New York capital necessary. A "National Policy" designed to check imports of American goods dumped into the Canadian market during the depression of the seventies, to increase traffic over the Intercolonial to the Maritimes, to increase consumption of Nova Scotia coal, and to complete the construction of the Canadian Pacific Railway, was initiated in 1878. The Honourable Charles Tupper, Minister of Railways and Canals, pressed energetically for rapid construction of the railway to strengthen Confederation and to offset the effects of opposition in the Maritimes. The importance of American experience and technique was evident in the character of the charter, with its emphasis on private enterprise and grants of land and money,[15] in the use of American steel in the railway, in construction by American contractors, and in the energetic direction of Van Horne. Competition for immigrants and traffic necessitated adoption of the American survey system and homestead regulations.[16] Rapid occupation of the Prairie Provinces followed the development of methods of producing, handling, marketing, and manufacturing spring wheat in the United States,[17] while ranching extended from the United States to the foothills of Alberta.

As the fur trade in its extension from the St. Lawrence to the Pacific was supported by the transfer of American agriculture to Ontario, and from Hudson Bay by the transfer of agriculture to the Red River and the Columbia, so the Canadian Pacific Railway was dependent in its inception on the migration of gold seekers from California to British Columbia, and in its construction on the migration of skill and technique from the United States.[18]

The necessity of rapid development of traffic to support a transcontinental railway structure was evident in the location of the main line near the American border and in the abandonment of the Saskatchewan route and the Yellowhead Pass for the Kicking Horse Pass. The exclusion of American lines by a southern location and by con-

[15]The Grand Trunk had set a precedent based on English experience, but the Canadian Pacific Railway contract had notable differences based on American example.

[16]H. M. Morrison, "The Background of Free Land Homestead Law of 1872," Canadian Historical Association Report, 1935, pp. 58–66.

[17]Innis, Problems of Staple Production, pp. 90ff.

[18]Van Horne conceded that the English system of financing railways was "as far superior to the American as the English system of working is inferior to the American." W. Vaughan, Sir William Van Horne (Toronto, 1926), p. 235.

struction of the line north of Lake Superior compelled J. J. Hill to resign from the directorate and to concentrate on construction of the Great Northern near the Canadian border to exclude Canadian lines. Van Horne, the American, pursued a policy in the development of Canada which involved restriction of J. J. Hill, the Canadian, to the development of the United States.[19] The Crow's Nest Pass line was built to the Kootenay country, the Trail smelter was acquired, and tariffs were imposed to compel a retreat of the Great Northern from this territory and to strengthen the position of the Canadian Pacific Railway. A steamship line to the Orient was added, and lines were acquired to Chicago. In eastern Canada the system was rounded out by acquisition of lines in Ontario and Quebec, by construction of a short line across Maine to Saint John, New Brunswick, and by development of an Atlantic steamship service. The effectiveness of Canadian Pacific competition was evident in the amalgamation of the Great Western and the Grand Trunk and in the appointment of an American general manager, Charles M. Hays, in 1896. The aggressiveness of the Canadian Pacific Railway was evident not only in extension of lines, but also directly and indirectly in the development of natural resources. Van Horne was concerned with the organization of a salt company at Windsor, the establishment of the Laurentide Pulp and Paper Company at Grand Mère, control over the Grand Falls power site in New Brunswick, and, with the co-operation of the Whitney interests in Boston, the development of the coal mines of Cape Breton by the Dominion Coal Company.[20]

In the upper St. Lawrence region, abrogation of reciprocity, improvement of the St. Lawrence, and expansion of exports based on technique imported from the United States accentuated trade with Great Britain and supported economic development adequate to the construction of a transcontinental railway. The migration of farmers to the United States, coinciding with the disappearance of unoccupied fertile land in Ontario and increasing difficulties of raising wheat because of exhausted soil, was followed by the spread of the cheese-making industry from New York, by its rapid expansion, and by the growth of a live-stock industry. Improvement of navigation on the St. Lawrence, and restrictions on imports of live cattle to Great Britain from the United States, led to a marked increase in exports of live-

[19]Hill commented on Van Horne's decision to build the Lake Superior section by saying, "I'll get even with him if I have to go to hell for it and shovel coal," and Van Horne complained of Hill's threat of invasion by saying, "Well, if he does, I'll tear the guts out of his road." *Ibid.*, p. 248.

[20]*Ibid.*, chap. XXI.

stock from Canada in the late seventies. In the lower St. Lawrence a background of French tradition and more direct accessibility to the European markets provided a less suitable environment for American technique.

The migration of technique from the United States was followed by the migration of institutions, especially during the long period of the depression which followed the American Civil War. The Grange movement invaded Canada in 1872 and the Dominion Grange was organized in 1874.[21] The Patrons of Industry appeared in 1887. Branches of American unions had appeared in various trades in the fifties and sixties but the Knights of Labor which came in 1881 exercised the widest influence. It declined rapidly in the closing years of the century with the coming of the American Federation of Labor with its strong emphasis on craft unions.

The migration of technique and institutions from the United States involved competition in the American market and led to attempts to resist imports from Canada. A bitter controversy followed abrogation of the Washington Treaty and feelings of hostility were not softened by the grave injustice attributed to the McKinley tariff during the sharp depression of the nineties. The consequent difficulties of industries which had formerly exported to the United States, for example the disappearance of barley raising in specialized areas, supported the attempt to build up trade with Great Britain by preferential tariffs. The province of Ontario imposed an embargo (1898) on the export of logs cut on Crown lands. Difficulties in exporting Nova Scotia coal to the United States, tariffs on American coal, and expanding markets in western Canada increased the demand for cheap power in Ontario and hastened the development of the Ontario Hydro-Electric Power Commission. Moreover, they led to the payment of bounties on iron and steel and the development of an iron and steel industry in Nova Scotia and in Ontario at Hamilton and Sault Ste Marie.

With the turn of the century the long period of strain which accompanied the decline of the timber trade and the use of canals, steamships, and railways came to an end with the rapid development of long-haul traffic incidental to expansion on the Pacific coast and the opening of the West. In the continual struggle with New York, Montreal at last came into her own and American wheat began to pass through that port. Long and sustained depression was followed by the boom after 1900. The tide which had run against the St. Lawrence, necessitating constant pouring of funds to its support

[21]L. A. Wood, *A History of Farmers' Movements in Canada* (Toronto, 1924).

through waterways and railways, together with the increasing difficulties with overhead costs and the increasing fixed charges, now began to run with it and its greater volume of traffic lowered its overhead costs so that earnings increased in cumulative fashion. The migration of technique from the United States proceeded along blazed trails with cumulative intensity. The northward spread of placer mining on the Pacific coast was followed by the discovery of gold on the Yukon and the economic cyclone of the Klondike gold rush. Population and capital poured in from the United States and ushered Canada into what was heralded as her century. The migration of population from the United States to the Yukon was paralleled by the migration of population to the Prairie Provinces. The disappearance of free land in the United States by the end of the century, a rise in the price of wheat, completion of the St. Lawrence canals to fourteen feet and deepening of the St. Lawrence ship channel to twenty-five feet, lowering of rates under the Crow's Nest Pass agreement, and an aggressive campaign for settlers from the United States were followed by a pronounced movement of experienced farmers, with capital and capital equipment, to the unoccupied areas of Saskatchewan and Alberta. Grain firms followed the settlers from Minneapolis to Winnipeg with the expansion of the Winnipeg grain exchange. American capital and technique seized on the advantages of a potential expanding market and branch plants were established in Canada in increasing numbers.

The hostilities of the late nineteenth century intensified, and were intensified by, the optimism of the twentieth century. The feverish intensity with which Seattle and San Francisco competed with Vancouver and Victoria, with which the Great Northern and other American lines competed with the Canadian Pacific, provoked the bitterness of the controversy over the Alaska boundary dispute. The high-handed insistence of President Theodore Roosevelt on adjustment in favour of the United States was a powerful factor in the antagonism of the Honourable Clifford Sifton and the defeat of the reciprocity treaty.[22]

The rapid expansion of wheat production in western Canada had far-reaching repercussions on the railways. The Grand Trunk, with

[22]J. W. Dafoe, *Clifford Sifton in Relation to His Times* (Toronto, 1931). "Of all the restrictive or exclusive legislation on the statute books of both countries from the early navigation and trade laws down to the child labor law there is no instance in which Canada had been the aggressor. They have all been of United States design and have arisen from United States initiative, while the Canadian laws have been in self-defense or retaliation," *Pulp and Paper Magazine*, Sept. 1905.

C. M. Hays as general manager, attempted to gain a share not only of the traffic in wheat but also of the more remunerative westbound traffic in manufactured products. A continuation of tariffs and expanding revenues supported the government in an arrangement to build the National Transcontinental from Winnipeg to Quebec and Moncton to link up with a subsidized line built by the Grand Trunk Pacific from Winnipeg to Prince Rupert. The vast area of agricultural land left unoccupied by the southern location of the Canadian Pacific Railway, together with the low gradient of the Yellowhead Pass, attracted the interest of an aggressive and experienced group of railway builders in Mackenzie and Mann, who constructed a third Canadian transcontinental, the Canadian Northern Railway.

Eastern Canada developed not only in relation to western expansion, but also in relation to local natural resources of mines and forests. The international character of capital and technique in the mining industry was illustrated in the development of nickel mining and smelting at Sudbury. The mature development of refining in the United States facilitated competition with the refining industry of Great Britain, and International Nickel became an important rival of the Mond Nickel Company. Mining interests were attracted in turn to the rich discoveries of silver at Cobalt and shipments were made to American smelters. American technique, notably in the flotation process, supported American control at Cobalt and Porcupine (the Dome Mine) and later at Kirkland Lake and, in turn, the increasing dominance of Canadian control as Canadian engineers trained in the mining camps of the United States returned to Canada.

Exhaustion of supplies of pulpwood in the United States was accompanied by increase in imports from Canada. Embargoes on pulpwood cut from Crown lands in Ontario and a concession policy attracted American capital and led to the construction of plants; but it was not until reciprocity as regards newsprint (1911)[23] and removal of duties on newsprint (1913) and imposition of an embargo on pulpwood from Crown lands in Quebec and New Brunswick, that plants were established on a large scale. The conservation movement in the United States was followed by the establishment of the Conservation Commission in Canada.

With the defeat of the reciprocity treaty through the opposition of manufacturing, transportation, and financial interests, the migration of American industry and the establishment of branch plants con-

[23]C. Southworth, "The American-Canadian Newsprint Paper Industry and the Tariff," *Journal of Political Economy*, Oct. 1922, pp. 681–97.

tinued at an accelerated pace.[24] Governmental policy was increasingly concerned with measures designed to hasten the migration of American industry to Canada, not only in relation to the Canadian market, but also in relation to imperial markets made accessible by preferences and agreements.

Labour organization continued to follow skill and capital. In British Columbia the Western Federation of Miners began activity in the Kootenay in 1895 and the Industrial Workers of the World appeared in 1906. The American Federation of Labor increased its strength throughout the pre-war period. The United Mine Workers began to organize Nova Scotia miners in 1908.

The war and post-war periods were marked by increasing co-operation between Canada and the United States. Industrialism advanced in relation to war demands[25] and contributions of American technique were numerous.[26] The World War precipitated the railway problem because of the inability to borrow in European markets. The government assumed control of the Canadian Northern, the Grand Trunk Pacific, and the Grand Trunk and merged them with the Intercolonial Railway. Sir Henry Thornton, with railway experience in the United States and Great Britain, was placed in charge of the Canadian National Railways and proceeded to weld the various units into a unified whole. The Baltimore and Ohio plan of union management[27] was adapted to the labour problems of the Canadian National. The emergence of the United States as a creditor nation after the war and the speculative boom of the late twenties supported rapid expansion of railways and facilities such as hotels. The increasing importance of motor transportation was evident in the expansion of branch plants of American manufacturers of automobiles, notably General Motors and Ford; in the expansion of the Imperial Oil and other companies; in the construction of roads supported by funds borrowed by provinces, municipalities, and the Dominion; and in the repeal of prohibition. In the mining industry the speculative movement of the United States supported extensive exploration through the use of the aeroplane, the development of numerous properties, and

[24]H. Marshall, F. A. Southard, and K. W. Taylor, *Canadian-American Industry* (New Haven, 1936).

[25]A. Shortt, *Early Economic Effects of the European War upon Canada* (New York, 1918).

[26]For example, the solution of the complex problem of handling zinc ore in the Kootenay. The nickel refining industry was developed at Port Colborne.

[27]L. A. Wood, *Union Management Cooperation in the Railroads* (New Haven, 1931).

the completion of smelting plants at Flin Flon and Noranda based on American capital and technique. In the pulp and paper industry the increasing importance of exports from Canada to the United States was evidenced by the marked increase in capacity largely supported by American capital and subject to American control. The mining and pulp and paper industries necessitated the development of hydro-electric power and of industries based on it—to mention only the Duke-Price power interests and the Aluminum Company of Canada plant at Arvida. In the fishing industry the expanding market and declining natural resources of the United States continued to support migration of capital and technique to Canada. Exhaustion of the lobster fishery on the coasts of Maine in the eighties was followed by the establishment of American plants in Canada. A tariff was imposed by Canada on American fish to support a subsidized transportation service and encourage the consumption of fresh fish in the St. Lawrence region. Demands for capital in the fresh fish industry and development of the American market were followed by American control of the largest organization in Nova Scotia, the Maritime National Fish Company, in 1929. In agriculture the increasing importance of the American firm of Borden was conspicuous. The penetration of American capital and control in the basic industries during the speculative boom of the twenties was followed by further migration to Canada of branch plants during the depression under the shelter of the high tariff of 1930 and the extension of imperial markets.[28]

In the fields of labour and agriculture penetration persisted. The United Mine Workers succeeded in occupying the Nova Scotia field in 1917. The American Federation of Labor continued in its strong position. The One Big Union and the Winnipeg Strike followed demands for industrial unionism. The Grange movement bore fruit in the influential position of Henry Wise Wood, a native of the United States, in Alberta and western Canada, in the emergence of a farmers' government in Alberta, Manitoba, and Ontario and of farmers' representatives in Ottawa, and in the influence of Sapiro and Brouillette in the wheat pool movement. The St. Francis Xavier co-operative movement traced its origin to Wisconsin.

The success of Montreal in competing for transcontinental traffic with New York was diminished by the effects of the Panama Canal. A decline in importance of wheat was accompanied by increasing

[28]The Ford plant at Windsor sells largely to New Zealand for export and thereby lowers the peak load costs of Canada by working in the off-peak winter season for the southern hemisphere market. Ford Motor Company, *Statement to Tariff Board*, Oct. 1935.

regionalism and increasing interdependence with the United States, as shown in the pulp and paper and mineral industries. The increasing extent of American influence has involved problems of international adjustment and the development of diplomatic machinery. The International Joint Commission was created in 1901 to settle disputes affecting the international boundary. The Behring Sea dispute was settled in 1893, and the North Atlantic coast fisheries arbitration in 1910 settled problems of definition in the terms of the convention of 1818. The Migratory Birds Convention was signed in 1916 and the North American Council of Fishery Investigations established in 1921. The halibut treaty of 1923, the first to be signed by Canada without the intervention of Great Britain, was designed as a conservation measure in the Pacific. The establishment of a Canadian legation in Washington provided a permanent channel for the discussion of problems of mutual interest. The reciprocity agreement of 1936 may be regarded as an important step in recognition of the increasingly vital character of Canadian-American economic relationships. The spirit of mutual antagonism which has supported a long series of retaliatory measures has become intolerable to the interests of both regions. During a period of expansion in the development of the natural resources of a continent, tariffs were significant as means of directing economic activity; but with a relative decline in the rate of expansion, trade restrictions involve economic loss as well as psychological disturbances. Mature technique migrates more slowly and ceases to act as a sufficiently powerful neutralizer to the influence of tariffs.

Decline in rate of expansion and increasing interdependence between Canada and the United States have necessitated increasingly rapid adjustments of governmental and industrial policy in Canada to that of the United States. The immigration quota of the United States was followed by restriction on immigration in Canada. Wage schedules adopted by organized labour, notably in the railways and the pulp and paper industries in the United States, are extended to Canada. Railway rates are closely adjusted to American rates. American tariffs, as in the case of dairy products, compel similar measures in Canada. The tourist trade demands similar accommodations in both countries, and the decline in prohibition in Canada to capitalize the American tourist trade contributed to its disappearance in the United States. Moreover, the increasing importance of the United States in Canadian economic development enhances difficulties of adjustment in trade with Great Britain.

The thrust of the Precambrian formation across the St. Lawrence above Montreal turned the fur trade up the Ottawa to the interior and facilitated penetration of the Great Lakes region from New York. The migration of agricultural technique from the United States under the United Empire Loyalists to the Great Lakes region supported the extension of the fur trade under the English to the Pacific coast, and the development of the timber trade effectively linked the Great Lakes region to Great Britain. The handicaps to agriculture in the Great Lakes region were eventually overcome by construction of the St. Lawrence canals and the Grand Trunk Railway. The dairying and live-stock industries expanded rapidly with continued support from the United States. As the Precambrian formation delayed, and the canals and railways hastened the development of the Great Lakes region, so it delayed, and, after completion of the Canadian Pacific Railway and further deepening of the St. Lawrence hastened, the development of the prairie regions. Dependence on the United States was even more conspicuous in the case of wheat in western Canada than in the case of the dairying and live-stock industries of Ontario. The increasing importance of overhead costs with extension westward, and more mature industrialism, accentuated the influence of the United States on Canada as producer of exports to Great Britain. The effects of relative decline in rate of expansion in western Canada as a result of migration of labour, skill, and capital equipment from the United States have been accompanied by competition from other wheat-producing regions and by the problems of the depression. The influence of the United States has been evident in accentuating the swings of Canadian economic development which followed westward expansion and the production of exports to Great Britain. As the indirect influence of the United States increased with expansion westward in relation to Great Britain, the direct influence increased in eastern Canada in the pulp and paper and mining industries.

The economic history of North America[29] is an index of the character of metropolitan growth.[30] The outward sweep of the control of France was evident in the extension of the fur trade by the St. Lawrence to the interior, but it succumbed to the control of Great Britain, which in turn broke into the two regions—the relatively inaccessible continental region which became politically independent, and the accessible region by the St. Lawrence which remained tributary to Great Britain. As the fur trade moved toward the northwest and became more

[29]J. W. Dafoe, *Canada, an American Nation* (New York, 1935).
[30]N. S. B. Gras, *An Introduction to Economic History* (New York, 1922), chaps. v, vi.

accessible to Hudson Bay, the timber trade emerged on the St. Lawrence in relation to the demands of Great Britain. The more compact type of economic development of the southern continental area proceeded along lines of greater self-sufficiency and diversification. Expansion and shift in the production and export of staple products was supported in the northern area by contributions from the United States. Concentration on staples involved exhaustion of resources, increasing costs of transportation, and shifts to new staples more adapted to regions relatively inaccessible to water transportation. Production of wheat in the United States moved westward with improved transportation. It became established in Canada with improvement of the St. Lawrence—a development coincident with the decline of the square timber trade and the extension of metropolitan demands in the United States, during the reciprocity treaty, which led to the increase of the sawn lumber industry. The disappearance of free land, the exhaustion of the wheat-growing regions, the movement westward of the wheat belt, and improved transportation, all led to a shift from wheat exports to live-stock and dairy products. This continued westward movement was followed by the production of wheat in the Prairie Provinces, primarily for the British market. The increasing importance of the metropolitan demands of the United States became evident in the mining industry, the pulp and paper industry, and more recently the fishing industry. It was evident not only in increasing exports to the United States, but also in the growth of industry in relation to exports to regions outside North America. The establishment of branch plants was fostered by governmental policy in tariffs and extension of imperial preferences.

The impact of European metropolitan influence through the St. Lawrence on a region dominated by the Precambrian formation was accentuated by the possibility of borrowing from a region less directly influenced by Europe and with technique characteristic of American metropolitan development. The significance of the St. Lawrence was shown in the more rapid development of staples in relation to the demands of Great Britain when supported by the United States, and the rapid transfer from the United States to Canada of industries concerned with the European market. The expansion of the metropolitan areas of the United States and decline of the white pine involved a shift from the production of square timber for Great Britain to lumber and pulp and paper dependent on spruce and the development of the St. Lawrence as a part of the American metropolitan territory. The essentially centralized character of Canadian development, the emphasis on staples, the significance of overhead costs and unused capacity, and dependence on the St. Lawrence hastened the migration of technique from the United States. The tariff was a powerful weapon on the part of Canada, necessitating the migration of American capital equipment. American technique was seized and transformed into the demands of the Canadian structure in relation to the European market.

The implications of the cumulative influence of the United States on Canadian economic development have been far reaching, while the financial structure of Canada has been profoundly influenced by the St. Lawrence and its relation to Great Britain. The Act of Union and Confederation were instruments through which Canada secured low interest rates and constructed the St. Lawrence canals, deepened the ship channel, built the Intercolonial Railway, and assisted materially in the construction of railways by private enterprise, notably the Grand Trunk and the Canadian Pacific Railway. With the turn of the century Canada built the National Transcontinental and assisted in the construction of the Canadian Northern and the Grand Trunk Pacific, and with the war assumed control of these lines to merge them in the Canadian National Railways. The policy of governmental intervention supported largely by British capital in the pre-war period continued in the speculative boom of the United States in the post-war period. The results were evident in a marked increase in federal debt. Provinces and municipalities constructed railways, roads and other public works with funds from the same source. As Canadian finance had been linked to New York, particularly with the telegraph and rapid communication, in the mechanism of short-term credit in the pre-war period, as shown in the investment of funds by Canadian banks in call loans, so it became increasingly dependent on that market for long-term credit in the post-war period.

With the depression, prices of basic exports to the United States (notably pulp and paper) declined sharply, as did prices of basic exports to Great Britain, especially wheat. It had been possible to have the best of two worlds; and it also proved possible to have the worst. The results have been evident in a wide range of governmental activities, including repudiation, and in violent political changes.

Now that American policy[31] has become of basic importance to

[31]Conciliation in points of view tends to become increasingly difficult with increasing American influence. American branch factories established under the protection of the Canadian tariff and the advantages of imperial preference have strong vested interests in Canadian nationalism and imperial connection. Nationalism and imperialism in Canada have become valuable American assets.

Canada and governmental activity has become more pronounced in the United States, would it be too much to ask that Americans consider the probable effects of measures, which appear to be their own concern as affecting only territory within their political boundaries, on regions which are scarcely less their own for being outside of their boundaries? Perhaps Americans may ask in turn that Canadians should appreciate their position and that in matters of domestic, imperial, and foreign policy should realize that their actions affect a continent as much as they affect themselves.

Labour in Canadian Economic History*

THE studies by Professor N. J. Ware of Wesleyan University and Professor H. A. Logan of the University of Western Ontario have been concerned with organized labour and with standards of living in similar industries in the United States and Canada chiefly in the highly industrialized St. Lawrence region. Organization of farmers and labour thrives on achievement and emerges in industries and regions providing a suitable environment for the formation of associations and during periods in which wages can be increased or maintained by pressure. They have necessarily been less concerned with industries and regions in which organization has been restricted and in which standards of living are on a lower level and subject to wider fluctuations. Studies of these standards are being published elsewhere.[1]

PROBLEMS OF DEFENCE AGAINST THE UNITED STATES

The European economy first touched North America in the development of the fishing industry in the maritime regions, an industry characterized by the mobility typical of sailing vessels. Fishing ships were quick to exploit the industry on the coasts of New England in the seventeenth century, and expansion in that area attracted labour on a large scale from the restricted industry of Newfoundland. The French settlements in the Bay of Fundy traded with New England rather than with France. Attempts to develop a sedentary fishery on Cape Breton after 1713 were defeated by an inevitable dependence on the English colonies for food and ships. Penetration to the interior by the St. Lawrence and extension of the fur trade involved competition from New York, and French traders carried furs to Albany. The establishment of forts at points along the Great Lakes designed to

*From Norman J. Ware and H. A. Logan, *Labor in Canadian-American Relations*, ed. H. A. Innis (Ryerson, 1937), pp. v–xxxi.
[1]See G. E. Britnell, "Saskatchewan, 1930–1935," *Canadian Journal of Economics and Political Science*, II (May 1936), 143–66. A series of studies on standards of living in western Canada, British Columbia, and the Maritimes has been planned under the auspices of the Institute of Pacific Affairs. See also a study of Winnipeg in 1915, *Board of Inquiry into Cost of Living in Canada Report* (Ottawa, 1915), II, 1018–19, and "Family Living Expenses in the Red River Valley of Manitoba," *Economic Annalist*, III (1933), 51–3. Throughout, the term, standards of living, is given the narrow meaning of standards of expenditure.

check trade to the English colonies, and extension to the Northwest to check trade to Hudson Bay, brought collapse because of burdens imposed on the colony, evident in the outbursts of inflation, and because of the barrier imposed against the English colonies in the interior, which contributed to the difficulties leading to the expulsion of the Acadians and the occupation of Nova Scotia. The retreat of the French Empire from North America was a reflection of the inability of France to maintain a standard of living comparable to that of the English colonies.

Resistance to the expansion of the New England colonies involved not only misery and hardships for the French population but also increasing organization. New France was an efficient armed camp and regimentation was reflected in policies of immigration, settlement, industry, and trade. Protestants were severely discouraged, lands were occupied in relation to strategic military sites, industry was regulated in the interests of mercantilism, and trade was supported by extensive fortifications. In Quebec the guild system was introduced, as in the case of the tanning industry;[2] and wages reflected the influence of government regulation, extensive government intervention in industry, and scarcity of skilled labour. In Cape Breton the share system continued in fishing ships from France, but wages were controlled in the interests of a sedentary fishery. Great Britain assumed control of a thoroughly disciplined population in the lower St. Lawrence: a foundation had been hammered out which was destined to support an increasingly powerful and coherent cultural group in North American history.

The conquest of New France and the consequent displacement of French by English government and of French trading organizations by Anglo-American merchants accentuated the importance of the Church as a factor providing continuity and a cohesive institution. It became the shield and sword of a race and language exposed to foreign domination. The French-Canadian population supplied the labour for Anglo-American enterprise in reconstruction of the fur trade. With the outbreak of the American Revolution and the closing of the Albany route demand for labour increased, and as early as 1778 governmental authority was invoked by employers to decide disputes.[3] The co-ordination of Great Lakes shipping with the Ottawa route, the efficiency of the Montreal route in relation to British manufactured

[2]See *Select Documents in Canadian Economic History, 1497–1783*, ed. H. A. Innis (Toronto, 1929), pp. 301–2, 393–4, 402, and *passim*.
[3]H. A. Innis, *The Fur Trade in Canada* (New Haven, 1930), p. 221.

goods, and the power of the British navy, together with a disciplined population, enabled Great Britain to succeed where France had failed, in maintaining control over the St. Lawrence when the thirteen colonies withdrew. Efficient business organization in the Northwest Company facilitated extension of the fur trade to the Mackenzie River and the Pacific, but not without indications of protests from French labour.[4] Wage contracts were drawn up in detail for men engaging with the Northwest Company and in 1789 each employee was required to pro- duce "a certificate from his curé." Encouraged by the hesitancy of magistrates in enforcing punishment for breaking contracts, voyageurs struck for higher wages at Rainy Lake in 1794 only to have the ring- leaders sent back to Montreal.[5] Competition with the Hudson's Bay Company and its shorter route by Hudson Bay, and a rigid discipline at its ports on the Bay, and later in the interior, involved a decline in standards of living for all concerned and the clash of organization in the massacre of Seven Oaks. After the amalgamation of 1821 Sir George Simpson "ruled with a rod of iron" in western Canada.

The Northwest Company was based not only on French labour but also on the expansion of agriculture by the United Empire Loyalists in Upper Canada. Following the outbreak of the American Revolution and the Treaty of Versailles in 1783 United Empire Loyalists were encouraged to occupy strategic military regions along the Great Lakes and in the Maritimes. On the principle "divide and rule," New Bruns- wick was organized as a separate province in 1784[6] and Upper Canada in 1791. They served as fortified outposts which guaranteed control over the French and resisted encroachment from the United States. Like New France in the wars with England, Upper Canada was a disciplined military community in the War of 1812 with the United States. Competition of Nova Scotia with New England after the Treaty of Versailles involved measures to check New England trade with the British West Indies, and insistence on the restrictions involved in the Convention of 1818 and on modifications of the colonial system. But privateering and smuggling were indications of the limitations of restrictive measures. The pressure on standards of living in Nova Scotia was accentuated by migration from areas with lower standards such as Newfoundland, during the disturbed years of the Napoleonic Wars. On the other hand, the United Empire Loyalists in New Bruns-

[4]G. L. Nute, The Voyageur (New York, 1931).
[5]Innis, Fur Trade in Canada, p. 245.
[6]See M. Gilroy, "The Partition of Nova Scotia, 1784," Canadian Historical Review, XIV (Dec. 1933), 375–92; also ibid., XVI (March 1935), 91–3, and J. B. Brebner, ibid., XV (March 1934), 57–9.

wick gained from the substantial preference given by Great Britain to colonial timber.

After 1821 British America was divided into compact units—western Canada dominated by the Hudson's Bay Company from Hudson Bay, Upper Canada by a strong official class supported by military organization, Lower Canada by the Church, Nova Scotia by Halifax mercantile interests, Prince Edward Island by landlords, and New Brunswick by Loyalist control.[7] The policy of defence implied in the military settlements, the construction of the Rideau Canal, and encouragement of immigration, particularly in Upper Canada, involved a centralization of control which contrasted sharply with the outlook of immigrants pouring into Canada after the Napoleonic Wars. Large numbers of settlers displaced by the industrial and agrarian revolution in Great Britain and fleeing from the intolerance of the period[8] were quick to resent the restrictions of centralized control evident in land policy, public finance, and transportation handicaps. Immigrants supported by the timber trade poured into areas unprepared to absorb them. Unfavourable contrasts with the expansion in the United States, and the development of the competitive route by the Erie Canal, supported the demands for reform which culminated in the outbreak of rebellion in 1837, Lord Durham's Report, the Act of Union, the achievement of responsible government, the construction of canals, and numerous reforms.[9] The demands of farmers for lower costs of transportation for exports and imports coincided with the demands of commercial interests in Montreal and Upper Canada.[10] In Lower Canada English commercial interests were opposed by the French. The Church protested against the exploitation of dispossessed Acadians employed by Channel Island firms which had become intrenched in the fishery on the Gaspé coast and in Cape Breton after the Treaty of Paris.[11] In both Lower and Upper Canada the problems of commercial interests were met by the Act of Union. In Nova Scotia the increasing importance of

[7]H. E. Conrad, "The Loyalist Experiment in New Brunswick," doctoral thesis, University of Toronto, 1934.

[8]See The Narrative of Gordon Sellar, Who Migrated to Canada in 1825 (Huntingdon, 1915), chap. III; also R. A. MacKay, "The Political Ideas of William Lyon Mackenzie," Canadian Journal of Economics and Political Science, III (Feb. 1937), 1–22.

[9]See H. M. Morrison, "The Principle of Free Grants in the Land Act of 1841," Canadian Historical Review, XIV (Dec. 1933), 392–408.

[10]D. G. Creighton, "The Commercial Class in Canadian Politics, 1792–1840," Proceedings of Canadian Political Science Association, 1933, pp. 43–58; and The Commercial Empire of the St. Lawrence (Toronto, 1937).

[11]F. de Saint Maurice, De Tribord à Babord (Montreal, 1877), p. 361.

commercial and agricultural interests contributed to the early development of responsible government. New Brunswick and Prince Edward Island followed. In western Canada the control of the Hudson's Bay Company clashed with settlement and increasing trade to the south. Adam Thom, who had stoutly resisted the French in Lower Canada, continued to pursue his role in the employ of the Hudson's Bay Company. Concessions to freedom of trade in 1849 were followed by increasing difficulty with French Canadians. On the Pacific coast, the settlement of the Oregon boundary dispute compelled the Hudson's Bay Company to retreat from Fort Vancouver on the Columbia River to Victoria. The movement toward responsible government was a corollary to the movement toward abolition of the colonial system in Great Britain. It was hastened by the aggressive development of newspapers under such leaders as Mackenzie and Howe, by the cohesiveness of the clan, strengthened by military organization, which continued among Scottish immigrants,[12] and by the solidarity of religious groups.[13]

The weakening of centralized control, through the Colonial Office, from Great Britain tended to strengthen rather than weaken opposition to the United States in the units involved. In Nova Scotia the Hovering Act of 1836 followed the admission of the United States to the West Indies trade in 1833. Indeed, the restraining hand of Great Britain was imposed to keep the zeal of Nova Scotia from causing international disturbance. In 1854 an attempt was made in both the Canadas and the Maritimes to capitalize the increasing division in the United States by securing entry to the American market through the Reciprocity Treaty. Increase in the tariff in 1858 in the Canadas, the problems of debt which followed the depression in the late fifties, difficulties with the United States during the Civil War, and the victory of the north were factors contributing to abrogation of the treaty by the United States in 1866. Survival of the Union in the United States increased the necessity of union in British North America.[14]

The stress of organization which characterized the separate provinces in their resistance to the United States continued in these areas and was reinforced by the formation of a federal government including first the four provinces and later extending to the Pacific. The St. Lawrence area again divided into separate cultural groups in Ontario

[12]W. S. Wallace, "Some Notes on Fraser's Highlanders," *Canadian Historical Review*, XVIII (June 1937).

[13]See C. B. Sissons, *Egerton Ryerson* (Toronto, 1937).

[14]See C. Martin, "The United States and Canadian Nationality," *Canadian Historical Review*, XVIII (March 1937), 1–11.

and Quebec. The Intercolonial was built as a government undertaking with Imperial support to provide a military railway between the Maritimes and the St. Lawrence. Tariffs were imposed to increase the consumption of Nova Scotia coal and interprovincial trade. Confederation was extended to include Manitoba and British Columbia on the basis of railway construction. The Hudson's Bay Company, faced with increasing competition from the United States to the south following steady improvement of transportation facilities, finally abandoned the Hudson Bay route. In 1859 a report on insubordination of freighters at York Factory stated that "The Red River freighters had agreed among themselves to make the company pay a much higher freight, in which they were disappointed in seeing it taken out of their hand via St. Paul's and I doubt not in a short time will rue the day of their abuse to the Company."[15] Displacements of labour by a change of routes and the introduction of steamboats contributed to the unrest, marked by the Riel Rebellion, which accomplished the sale of Rupert's Land to Canada by the Hudson's Bay Company. The death of Thomas Scott in the Rebellion of 1870 accentuated the bitterness in Ontario which led to the execution of Louis Riel in 1885. The division between French and English in Quebec and Ontario was deepened and extended to Manitoba.[16] With the retreat of the Hudson's Bay Company to Victoria, and the gold rush to the Fraser River and its tributaries in the late fifties, Crown colonies were established in Vancouver Island and the mainland, and they were united and brought under Confederation. Rigid opposition to American encroachment, evident in regions adjacent to the United States, particularly in Nova Scotia, New Brunswick, Ontario, Manitoba, and British Columbia, was consolidated, particularly through the influence of such individuals as Tupper and Macdonald, in the route of the Canadian Pacific Railway on Canadian territory close to the American boundary in western Canada and British Columbia, especially with the construction of the Crow's Nest Pass line. The line of defence was supported by the monopoly clause, substantial government support in land and cash, the tariff, and government ownership of the Intercolonial Railway.

RESISTANCE TO THE BURDENS OF DEFENCE

The burden of defence measures prior to and after Confederation changed with the stage of economic development in Great Britain, Canada, and the United States and was evident in the movement of

[15]Innis, Fur Trade in Canada, p. 230.
[16]G. F. G. Stanley, The Birth of Western Canada: A History of the Riel Rebellion (London, 1936).

population and of goods. Competition for labour in the United States and the movement of population from Canada set up a vicious circle in which the resistance and burden of organization opposed to the United States increased as population emigrated from Canada. On the one hand rebellion broke out in the thirties, and on the other hand extensive public works in canals and railways became inevitable. As an example, as a refuge for rebels, and as a source of technical innovations, the United States exerted a modifying influence in the earlier period, an influence accentuating later economic trends.

In the period dominated by commercial activity and water transportation preceding 1850 farmers merged their protests in opposition to centralized control or they migrated to the United States. Even the French habitants offered resistance to the demands of the government in the French régime. "Although the common people in Canada have not the docility of the French peasant, they are quite willing to do what is asked of them if the project always suits their taste. They consider that the governors and intendants come and go but that they will only disappear with the disappearance of the country."[17] Their refusal to obey the government was evident in their insistence on raising horses rather than cattle. In the French régime "They [the French] say among themselves Lesse enrager les merchands pour trouver en bon prix."[18] Papineau became the centre of activity in support of the interests of the farmers while Mackenzie was supported by the farmers of Ontario. In Nova Scotia agricultural societies were promoted by John Young to reduce dependence on agricultural products from the United States;[19] but agriculture was limited by the demands of the fishing industry and the lumbering industry. Fishermen from Nova Scotia joined the mackerel fleet of the United States and labour continued to move from Newfoundland to Nova Scotia and from Nova Scotia to New England. Labour and agriculture, concerned more directly with the timber trade in New Brunswick and on the St. Lawrence, were affected by the wide fluctuations of the industry arising from the business cycle, imperial preferences, and exhaustion of resources. They accepted sharp fluctuations in the standard of living or migrated.

[17]*Select Documents in Canadian Economic History, 1497–1783,* ed. Innis, p. 35.
[18]*Ibid.,* p. 525. "1 Jan, 1773. Mr. Stuart arrived here a few days ago; seems dissatisfied with his progress, as he expected a great deal, not only from the rum and dry goods but from the influence of his brother in law who married the priest's niece, and if it were possible that his mother and sister were married to the priests themselves would not hinder the inhabitants to buy cheap and sell dear." *Ibid.,* p. 526.
[19]John Young, *The Letters of Agricola* (Halifax, 1922).

The organization of skilled labour was limited by the character of urban and industrial growth. A printers' union was formed in Quebec City in 1827, in Toronto in 1832, and in Montreal and Hamilton in 1833. Journeyman carpenters organized in Montreal in 1833, and stone cutters, coopers, and shipwrights were represented by unions by 1850. A tailors' riot broke out in Montreal in 1830 and shoe-making had an organization by the middle of the century. William Lyon Mackenzie wrote that "Dutcher's foundry-men and Armstrong's axe-makers all . . . could be depended on" in the outbreak in 1837.[20]

Construction of railways and canals was followed by rapid growth of settlement, and by an increase in the number of small towns and in the size of urban centres. The development of the live-stock industry and of exports of agricultural products was accompanied by a decline of a relatively self-sufficient economy and the rise of small domestic industries such as flour and grist milling, lumber milling, woollen mills, boot and shoe and harness plants, wagon and cart making, agricultural implements, and blacksmith shops. Construction of railways and shipbuilding brought demands for labour in the St. Lawrence and the Maritimes. The depression which followed the prosperity of the early fifties was marked by an aggressive agitation among farmers led by the Honourable George Brown and the Toronto Globe.[21]

While increased tariffs and the rise of industrial towns, marked by the shift from wood, water, and sail to iron and coal, brought protests from agriculturalists, they encouraged the expansion of the factory system and the rise of organized labour. In 1851, as a result of the increase in the number of vessels and the demand for labour in Montreal, "the labourers now dictate to the trade in what manner the vessels shall be discharged and loaded and during what hours the work shall be continued—On several occasions of late the captains and crews of American vessels have been grossly maltreated in addition to having been compelled to pay for the work in the expensive manner insisted on by the labourers."[22] They resisted the introduction of horses. In 1852 the journeymen tailors in Toronto organized to

[20]C. Lindsey, The Life and Times of W. L. Mackenzie (Toronto, 1862), II, 55.
[21]See F. H. Underhill, "Some Aspects of Upper Canadian Radical Opinion in the Decade before Confederation," Canadian Historical Association Report, 1927, pp. 46–61; also G. W. Brown, "The Grit Party and the Great Reform Convention of 1859," Canadian Historical Review, XVI (Sept. 1935), 245–65. On the decline of rural population and industries, see C. Shott, Landnahme und Kolonisation in Canada (Kiel, 1936), pp. 245ff and 274ff.
[22]Select Documents in Canadian Economic History, 1783–1885, ed. H. A. Innis, and A. R. M. Lower (Toronto, 1933), p. 453.

resist the introduction of the Singer Sewing Machine. The prosperity of 1854 led to a successful strike by the printers in the same city. British technique and capital involved in the construction of railways were accompanied by labour organization. The English Amalgamated Society of Engineers was introduced in 1854 and the Amalgamated Society of Carpenters and Joiners followed.

The impact of machine industry on labour in the United States was felt in Canada, particularly during the period of the Reciprocity Treaty and the Civil War. The end of the Civil War and abrogation of the Reciprocity Treaty were accompanied by the migration of skilled labour and establishment of additional international unions. In 1861 the International Iron Moulders Union entered Canada and in 1865 the International Cigar Makers Union established a branch at Montreal. It was followed by the International Journeymen Coopers' Association and the International Typographical Society. The Brotherhood of Locomotive Engineers established branches in 1864 and the Brotherhood of Railway Conductors in 1868. In the iron and nail works in Montreal in 1866 "the greatest proportion of the skilled labor comes from the United States, the workmen there being accustomed to the peculiar tempering of the steel required for our cold climate."[23] At the same time it was claimed that "our American friends would find plenty of excellent openings for skilled workmen" in the boot and shoe industry.[24] The Knights of St. Crispin, which began in the shoemaking industry in Milwaukee in 1867, spread rapidly into Massachusetts and into Canada where it had seventeen unions in 1870.

The organization of unions provided a basis for the formation of city assemblies (in Toronto in 1871, and in Ottawa and Hamilton shortly afterward) and for the spread of labour movements from the United States and Great Britain. In the spring of 1872 the Typographical Union led a concerted demand for a nine-hour day in Toronto,[25] which capitalized the hostility of the Honourable George Brown and the Toronto *Globe* by securing the passage in the federal house by the Conservatives under Sir John A. Macdonald of an Act based on British legislation in 1871 legalizing unions. The success was followed by further activity, with British precedent in the British Trades Union Congress of 1858, and with American precedent in the National Labor Union, which resulted in the formation of the Canadian Labour Union in 1873.

23*Ibid.*, p. 598.   24*Ibid.*, p. 612.
25B. Ratz, "United Front in Toronto—1872," *New Frontier*, 1936.

FARMER AND LABOUR ORGANIZATIONS IN THE LONG DEPRESSION

The success of labour organization in the early seventies was paralleled by the rapid spread of farmers' organizations from the United States. The depression was marked by collapse of the labour movement and rapid spread of the farmers' movement. The Patrons of Husbandry[26] spread from Vermont to the Eastern Townships in Quebec and Ontario in 1872–3, to the Maritimes in 1875, and to Manitoba in 1876. The movement in Canada became independent of the United States with the formation of the Dominion Grange (1875), which increased to a peak in 1878. While opposed to intervention in politics, it supported the National Policy in a tariff on agricultural products from the United States.

The stimulus to industry which followed the completion of the Intercolonial Railway, and the increase of tariffs and of railway construction under the National Policy, coincided with recovery in the early eighties. The depression "caused the entry into the Dominión of large numbers of the mechanic class" from the United States.[27] At Hamilton in 1878 "the demand for cotton operatives has been largely in excess of the supply and in some instances this class of hands has been imported from the mills in New England by our mill owners owing to the increased capacity of the mills and the demand for this class of goods."[28] The increasing importance of machine industry and its impact on Canada[29] involved support not only to craft unions but also to the organization of unskilled labour. In 1881, under the leadership of the International Typographical Union, the Toronto Trades and Labor Council was organized and was followed by similar organizations in other centres. In the same year the Knights of Labor swept across the boundary from the United States and district assemblies were formed at various centres in Ontario and Quebec. It was conspicuously successful in penetrating the province of Quebec, which had scarcely been influenced by the earlier development of international unions, and reached its peak in the late eighties. The Trades

[26]See L. A. Wood, *A History of Farmers' Movements in Canada* (Toronto, 1924), *passim*; also S. J. Buck, *The Grange Movement* (Cambridge, Mass., 1913) and H. Michell, *The Grange in Canada* (Kingston, 1914).

[27]*Select Documents in Canadian Economic History, 1783–1885*, ed. Innis and Lower, p. 622.

[28]*Ibid.*, p. 611.

[29]*Ibid.*, pp. 619ff; also *Report of the Royal Commission on the Relations of Labor and Capital in Canada* (Ottawa, 1889), E. Young, *Labor in Europe and America* (Washington, 1875), and H. B. Ames, *Incomes, Wages and Rents in Montreal* (U.S. Dept. of Labor Bulletin, 1898), pp. 39–51.

and Labor Congress of Canada was organized in Toronto in 1886 to include representatives from both international unions and the Knights of Labor. The completion of the Canadian Pacific Railway was followed by industrial development in Manitoba and British Columbia and by representation from these areas in 1895. The Maritime Provinces sent delegates in 1901. Increasing specialization in industry was evident in the formation in Toronto of the Federated Council of Building Trades in 1886, the Allied Printing Trades Council in 1895, and the Federated Metal Trades Council in 1901. In the United States and Canada the Knights of Labor declined and the increasing strength of international unions in the American Federation of Labor finally brought the expulsion from the Trades and Labor Congress in 1902 of twenty-three unions, in part representing the Knights of Labor and chiefly from Quebec. These unions formed the Canadian Federation of Labour which in turn expelled the Knights of Labor in 1908.

As labour organizations became entrenched following the growth of industrialism, the farmers' movement declined in the long depression of the eighties and nineties and shifted from a position favourable to the tariff to one of opposition. The Patrons of Industry started in Michigan. With the enthusiasm of the populist movement it swept across the border, entered Canada in 1889, was incorporated in Ontario in 1890, and became independent of the United States in 1891. The short-lived Manitoba and Northwest Farmers Protective Association (1883–86) and the Farmers Alliance (1890–2) paved the way for the establishment of branches in western Canada. It spread to Quebec and the Maritimes and reached a peak with the election of seventeen members in Ontario in 1894. Defeat in the federal election of 1896 brought collapse of the movement.

FARMER AND LABOUR ORGANIZATIONS AND THE OPENING OF THE WEST

With the turn of the century improved transportation, disappearance of free land in the United States, higher prices, a marked increase in immigration, and the opening of the West brought a rapid advance of industrialism in the St. Lawrence region. Increasing industrialism was accompanied by concentration on export staples such as wheat in western Canada, and minerals, lumber, and fish in British Columbia and the Maritimes. Labour and farmers' organizations reflected the character of industrial growth. The Maritimes had felt the full impact of industrialism in the decline of shipbuilding, the disappearance of industries through competition from the St. Lawrence region, and the shift to concentration on coal and iron.[30] Coal miners in Nova Scotia were organized in the Provincial Workmen's Association in 1879 and, following the development of the iron and steel industry, it became aggressive in strikes in 1904 and later years. It affiliated with the Canadian Federation of Labour, but the inevitable weak support facilitated the entry of the United Mine Workers in 1908 and amalgamation with that organization in 1917.

In British Columbia the high rate of wages, which characterized the gold rush, attracted Oriental labour[31] with low standards of living, and involved constant friction. A strike at the Wellington colliery in 1883 and other labour difficulties were followed by an extended investigation and by legislation which became increasingly restrictive to Oriental immigration. The extension of metal mining from the western states to the Kootenay was followed by migration of organized labour. The Western Federation of Miners entered the Rossland district in 1895 and, with the completion of the Crow's Nest Pass Railway and the opening of the coal mines in the Crow's Nest region, extended its range by the formation of District Union Number 7 in 1902. It severed affiliation with the American Federation of Labor in 1898 and joined the American Labor Union. The aggressiveness of industrial unionism under the American Labor Union in British Columbia and Alberta was evident in the formation of the United Brotherhood of Railway Employees, in the withdrawal of the Vancouver Trades Council from the Trades and Labor Congress in 1902, and in numerous strikes. The difficulties led to the appointment of a Royal Commission by the Dominion government, which recommended that foreign radical unions and foreign leadership of strikes should be declared illegal and that investigation of trade disputes and arbitration in "public service industries" be compulsory.[32] Continued difficulties in Alberta coal mines in 1906 led to the Industrial Disputes Investigation Act in 1907.[33] Radical unionism had declined and the United Mine Workers had displaced the Western Federation in the Crow's Nest coal region in

[30]See E. A. Forsey, *Economic and Social Aspects of the Nova Scotia Coal Industry* (Toronto, 1928); *Report of the Royal Commission, Provincial Economic Inquiry* (Halifax, 1934); *The Maritime Provinces, 1867–1934* (Dominion Bureau of Statistics, Ottawa).

[31]See Cheng Tien-Fang, *Oriental Immigration in Canada* (Shanghai, 1931); P. C. Campbell, *Chinese Coolie Immigration in the British Empire* (London, 1923); *Report of the Royal Commission on Chinese Immigration* (Ottawa, 1885); W. L. M. King, *Industry and Humanity* (Toronto, 1918).

[32]*Report of Royal Commission on Labor Disturbances in British Columbia* (1903).

[33]See B. Selekman, *Postponing Strikes* (New York, 1923).

1903. A working arrangement was reached between the two organizations in 1908 and the Western Federation joined the American Federation of Labor in 1910. The United Mine Workers extended control over Vancouver Island mines in 1911, but disappeared in 1915. The Western Federation of Miners supported the Industrial Workers of the World in 1906 and a strike developed on the Grand Trunk Pacific Railway in 1912.[34]

Labour organizations with English-American traditions were unable to penetrate French Quebec effectively. The Knights of Labor disappeared, the Canadian Federation of Labour held its position with difficulty, and the Trades and Labour Congress was restricted. Migration of French-Canadian labour, particularly to the shoemaking and textile centres of New England, facilitated the spread of labour organization from the United States, but insistence of the Church on compliance with the encyclical *Rerum Novarum* (1891) necessitated independent growth. Language and religion were effective bulwarks against English-American unions. Catholic unions[35] spread persistently in the early part of the century and particularly during the war and post-war period. In 1912 the Féderation Ouvrière de Chicoutimi was formed, in 1915 the Western Federation was displaced in Thetford Mines, in 1918 the National Central Trades Council was formed in Quebec City, and in 1922 the Federation of Catholic Workers was organized.

The divergence of cultural and regional factors accentuated by the character of the spread of industrialism in Canada affected farmers' organizations as well as labour organizations. In Ontario the shift from wheat to the live-stock and dairy industries, and from the export to the domestic market during the prosperous period after 1900 involved severe strains on the farmers' movement. The Farmers' Association of Ontario was formed in 1902 but amalgamated with the Grange in 1907. The increasing importance of an expanding urban market weakened the opposition of farmers to protective tariffs. The Reciprocity Treaty of 1911 obtained slight support in the rural areas of industrial Ontario.

In western Canada, on the other hand, the dominance of the Cana-

[34]See E. W. Bradwin, *The Bunkhouse Man* (New York, 1928), and J. B. Bickersteth, *The Land of Open Doors* (Toronto, n.d.), for a description of labour conditions in railway construction. See also *Report on Immigration of Italian Laborers to Montreal and Alleged Fraudulent Practices of Employment Agencies* (1905).

[35]See A. B. Latham, *The Catholic and National Labor Unions of Canada* (Toronto, 1930); also A. S. Lortie, "Compositeur Typographe de Québec [1903]," *Les Ouvriers de Deux Mondes*, 1908, pp. 61–132.

dian Pacific Railway, rapid expansion, and dependence on exports of wheat implied efforts on the part of the farmers to combat high railway rates, elevator and marketing charges, and tariffs. The Territorial Grain Growers' Association was formed in 1902, and was divided with the formation of the provinces into the Saskatchewan Grain Growers' Association and the Farmers' Association of Alberta in 1905, the Manitoba Grain Growers' Association being formed in 1903. The migration of American farmers of the western states to western Canada was followed by the penetration of American organizations. The American Society of Equity penetrated Alberta in 1905 and was amalgamated with the Farmers' Association in the United Farmers of Alberta in 1908. An interprovincial council was formed in 1907. Opposition to the Winnipeg grain exchange was responsible for the emergence of the Grain Growers' Grain Company in 1907. Attempts on the part of Alberta and Manitoba to support a scheme of government ownership of elevators led to the acquisition of Manitoba elevators in 1912 and of Alberta elevators in 1917 by the Grain Growers' Grain Company, which became the United Grain Growers. Saskatchewan built up an independent organization, the Saskatchewan Co-operative Elevator Company. Increasing opposition to the tariff led to the formation of the Canadian Council of Agriculture in 1910, which linked organizations in western Canada to the Grange in Ontario.

FARMERS' MOVEMENTS AND THE WAR

Rising prices during the pre-war period and the outbreak of the war supported a rapid expansion of farmers' organizations. The United Farmers Co-operative Company, formed in 1914, expanded rapidly in Ontario. The United Grain Growers and the Saskatchewan Co-operative Elevator Company flourished with high grain prices and the introduction of the Wheat Board. Political movements emerged from a background of financial success. The weakness of the Liberal party following the defeat of the Reciprocity Treaty, the establishment of the Union Government and the isolation of Laurier and the French population led to the emergence of Progressive groups in western Canada. Opposition to conscription was accompanied by opposition to high tariffs. The Canadian Council of Agriculture was reorganized with ample financial resources and the new National Policy formulated. With the end of the war farmers' governments succeeded in capturing control of the provinces on a wide scale. In Ontario the United Farmers of Ontario formed a government in 1919. In western Canada the influence of the Non-Partisan League spread to Saskatchewan and

Alberta. Mr. Henry Wise Wood advocated, with striking effect, group government with adequate representation of farmers, and the United Farmers of Alberta secured control in 1921. The United Farmers of Manitoba were elected to office in the following year. This success of the farmers' movement in the provincial field was accompanied by the election of sixty-five Progressive members in the federal field in 1921 (Prairie Provinces, thirty-nine; Ontario, twenty-four). But the anchorage of tradition held in the older provinces of Quebec and Nova Scotia, and the strength of the farmers' movement soon began to recede.[36] In Ontario the power of urban influence became evident in the divergent views of Premier Drury, who advocated a "broadening out" policy, and of Mr. J. J. Morrison, who insisted on the occupational basis, and in the collapse of the Government in 1924. The persistence of the influence of the Progressive movement continued and was shown in the inclusion of the Honourable Mr. Nixon in the Liberal cabinet in 1934. In Manitoba the Farmers' Government continued under Mr. Bracken, first by amalgamation with the Liberals and later by agreement with Social Credit; in Alberta the United Farmers were defeated by Mr. Aberhart in 1935; in Saskatchewan the dominance of wheat and the relative absence of metropolitan development implied basic dependence of party organization on agriculture, with the result that the provincial government continued under the control of Liberals until the election of 1929. The religious issue contributed to their defeat. The significance of group government as developed in Alberta was evident in the break-up of party organization and the necessity during a depression of choosing other alternatives such as that of Social Credit. Like the philosophy of group government, that of Social Credit has swept into Saskatchewan and Manitoba and the federal house. The increasing strength of the Conservatives contributed to a decline of Progressive representation in the federal house to twenty-four members in 1925. Alberta federal representation following the independent development of Alberta provincial politics became the nucleus of a more aggressive group (while Progressives from the remaining provinces became increasingly concerned with the broader policies of the old parties, particularly the Liberal), and suffered the fate of the provincial party, in the victory of Mr. Aberhart when Social Credit members were elected in 1935.

[36]See E. M. Reid, "Canadian Political Parties: A Study of the Economic and Racial Bases of Conservatism and Liberalism in 1930," *Contributions to Canadian Economics*, VI (University of Toronto Studies, History and Economics, 1933), 7–39.

Co-operative organizations reflected the influence of the war and post-war difficulties. The disappearance of the Wheat Board and a sharp decline in the price of wheat led to demands for the introduction of pooling methods. Owing to the aggressive interest of Mr. H. W. Wood and the dominance of the farmers' movement in Alberta politics, a pool was organized in Alberta in 1923. The enthusiasm of Mr. Aaron Sapiro, who had been conspicuously successful in the co-operative movement in California and elsewhere, was enlisted to support extension of pools to Saskatchewan and Manitoba. The strength of the old parties in Saskatchewan concentrated the influence of the pool movement and intensified its activities. The pool acquired the assets of the Saskatchewan Co-operative Elevator Company. In Manitoba the strength of private elevator companies and of the United Grain Growers limited the extent of pool activities. In Ontario and the older provinces agriculture became increasingly specialized, with the result that co-operation has developed along specialized lines. In Quebec the influence of cultural factors was in evidence in the formation of "Les Fermiers de Québec" in 1917 and the Catholic Farmers' Union in 1924, and in the success of credit unions.[37] In Nova Scotia the success of the co-operative movement[38] directed from St. Francis Xavier University has been strengthened by religious factors.

Similarly, specialization with increasingly complex problems has supported the formation of associations. In Ontario and Quebec the dairying and live-stock industries, fruit farming, and tobacco farming, and in the Maritimes potato and apple growing and fur farming, illustrate the general trend. Geographic limitations in British Columbia have strengthened organizations concerned with the marketing of dairy products and fruit. With these trends the importance of broad movements has declined. The dairying industry has tended to develop along protective lines in contrast with wheat and apples, which depend on the export market. The Canadian Council of Agriculture disappeared in 1924. The sharp decline in prices during the depression has accentuated the problem of marketing as seen in the introduction of the short-lived Natural Products Marketing Act and in the formation

[37]On the success of A. Desjardins, see H. Michell, *The Problems of Agricultural Credit in Canada* (Kingston, 1914); see also, an account of the self-sufficient character of rural life, M. Gauldrée-Boileau, "Payson de Saint-Irénée (Bas-Canada-Amérique-du-Nord), [1861–1862]," *Les Ouvriers des Deux Mondes*, V (1885), 51–108.

[38]For a description of co-operative stores in Nova Scotia see H. Michell, *The Cooperative Store in Canada* (Kingston, 1916).

of the Canadian Chamber of Agriculture in 1935, followed by provincial organizations in Manitoba in 1936 and Ontario in 1937. The Canadian Dairy Farmers' Federation[39] has become an important rival to the National Dairy Council.

THE WAR AND LABOUR ORGANIZATION

The effect of the war was as evident in the labour movement as in the farmers' movement. In western Canada protests arose against the more conservative policies of the Trades and Labor Congress dominated by the craft organizations of the industrial areas of the St. Lawrence. Agitation which centred about the Winnipeg strike contributed to the election of members to the provincial and federal governments. Labour organization reflected the unrest in the formation of the One Big Union in 1919, as an attempt to meet the problems of radical unionism. In 1927 it was merged with unions not affiliated with the Trades and Labour Congress or the American Federation of Labor, nor influenced as in the case with the Catholic unions by cultural factors, to form the All-Canadian Congress of Labour. The Canadian Federation of Labour served as a nucleus to which was added the Canadian Brotherhood of Railroad Employees, which had its origin among workmen of the Intercolonial Railway and was extended to include chiefly the industrial workers on Canadian railways not under the jurisdiction of Railway Brotherhoods affiliated with American unions. The depression imposed a severe strain on an organization including divergent groups, and in 1936 the Canadian Federation of Labour withdrew from the All-Canadian Congress. Industrial unionism became increasingly important during the depression, as shown in the growth of the Workers Unity League and in the extension of activities of the C.I.O. from the United States. The wave of industrial unionism with political implications which swept from the United States to British Columbia early in the century and led to the Royal Commission of 1903, was followed by the C.I.O., which at Oshawa met with the determined opposition of the provincial government of Ontario. The Industrial Disputes Investigation Act, which emerged from a background of strikes in Alberta and British Columbia, was declared *ultra vires* in 1923, and subsequent legislation of the same kind has not been introduced in the province of Ontario. Consequently the task of directing labour disputes has fallen more obviously on the shoulders of the provincial government.

[39]See J. A. Ruddick *et al.*, *The Dairy Industry in Canada* (Toronto, 1937), *passim.*

GENERAL RÉSUMÉ

The impact of American influence on farmer and labour movements in Canada has become increasingly direct with westward expansion. Competitive routes from the interior to the seaboard early necessitated constant efforts to secure adjustment in the St. Lawrence region which took the form of smuggling, in the French régime, and later of lower standards of living except in so far as the St. Lawrence permitted dependence on the highly efficient industrialized area of Great Britain, and offset the disadvantages of dependence on raw materials with wide fluctuations in yield and prices. The advantages were evident in the migration of traders from Albany to Montreal and in the extension of the Northwest Company. They were not evident in the difficult period after the Napoleonic Wars, when population was released with the inroads of industrialism in Great Britain, transported by returning empty timber ships, and settled in the virgin forest areas of Upper Canada, and when prices of lumber and wheat fluctuated in relation to imperial preferences, the business cycle, and changes in price and yield. The results were apparent in the outbreak of rebellion, and the difficulties were met by lowered costs of transportation as a result of the construction of railways and canals, and the reorganization of government following Lord Durham's *Report*. The attempt to capitalize the advantages of lower costs of transportation through the Reciprocity Treaty by extension of traffic to the western states were offset by a more rapid lowering of costs in the United States. The financial burden of transportation improvements and depreciation through obsolescence meant that an increase was needed in the tariff against goods from the United States and Great Britain; and the abrogation of reciprocity and the depression were followed by Confederation, and extension to the Maritimes and the Pacific coast by the Intercolonial and the Canadian Pacific railways. The effect of the burdens imposed by the tariff and transportation costs were evident during the depression in the last half of the century, in a realignment of agriculture in the St. Lawrence region toward dairy and live-stock industries facilitated by improved transportation to Great Britain and borrowing from the United States, in extensive migration to the United States, and in the spread of farmers' organizations from the United States. Expansion of industry and further reorganization of agriculture in the St. Lawrence increased after the opening of the West. The burden of the monopoly of the Hudson's Bay Company (which contributed to the Riel Rebellion) was followed by the burden of railway rates, tariffs, and marketing charges, leading to organized opposition from western farmers. Extensive migration from the United States, especially to Saskatchewan and Alberta, and heavier burdens which accompanied increasing costs incidental to distance from Montreal, contributed to the success of protest movements which spread from the grain-producing areas of the northwestern states. Alberta became a centre of disturbance which contributed to the success of the farmers' movement in the war and post-war periods. The burden of debt of the recent depression was again most vigorously resisted in Alberta. Opposition movements to the burdens of a northern transcontinental structure have developed persistently through the proximity and competitive influence of the United States. Protest movements have proved the centre of greatest stress to be the weakest point in the impact of American influence. In the East and the West the United States has exercised constant pressure in bringing the adjacent Canadian structure into line. Compensation to the Maritimes and to western Canada to meet the burdens of the tariff and railway rates has been compelled by American competition. While the contributions of American technique have helped to accentuate upward swings in the Canadian economy, contributions of American protest have hastened adjustments during the downward swings.

The wide swings of Canadian economic development, which have coincided with improvements of transportation on the upper St. Lawrence and across the Precambrian formation, have largely determined the character of American influence. Extension of the fur trade under the Northwest Company to the Pacific was supported by technique and personnel from the United States. The collapse of the fur trade and the problem of transportation on the upper St. Lawrence accentuated the importance of protests, built up on British radicalism and Jacksonian democracy, which led to the rebellion. The completion of the canals, the railways and Confederation increased the importance of technique and personnel from the United States. The long depression which followed brought protests in the form of dominance of Ontario politics by Liberals, attempts to secure reciprocity and agitation for commercial union which were offset by the National Policy, construction of canals and the Canadian Pacific Railway and the astute political activity and Scottish birth of Sir John A. Macdonald and his appeals to imperial connection. "A British subject I was born, a British subject I will die." The success of the Liberals was eventually built on a strong cultural group, such as the French Canadians under Laurier or the Scots under the two other Liberal Premiers of Canada of the Mackenzie clan.[40] The defeat of Laurier in 1911 was to prove again the limitations of possible attachments to American influence. The achievement of Dominion status and the growth of Canadian nationalism have facilitated agreements with the United States, but imperialistic sentiment remains a factor of major political and economic importance. Periods of depression accompanied by migration to the United States have been accompanied by a hardening of the central structure and appeal to imperialist sentiment, and this in turn has increased the importance of governmental intervention during periods of prosperity. Government ownership in Canada is based on a hard core of defence against the United States.

The necessity of deodorization in political protest movements has accentuated American influence on protest organizations eschewing politics. American influence in political movements has been indirect. So far as the present writer is aware, no one of American birth has ever become premier of a province. Whether Mr. H. W. Wood might have been premier of Alberta is a question for academic discussion, but it is sufficient to say that he did not, and that his influence was strengthened because he stressed organization rather than political movements. The success of the pools was accentuated by the insistence of Mr. Sapiro on the avoidance of politics. The results were evident in strengthening the position of the Liberal party in Saskatchewan and weakening the Farmers' party in Alberta. Farmer and labour organizations have become powerful factors with American support, partly because they have been compelled to avoid political activities. Political organizations in Canada have in turn become more sensitive to the pressure of organized groups. The success of these organizations has led to a counter movement in the United States—the Canadian pools stimulated the interest of American farmers in similar organizations.

Labour organizations have occupied a more strategic position

[40]It is an interesting speculation as to how far the inevitable choice of a vigorous English-speaking leader as a means of rebuilding the Liberal party after the war has been responsible for the withdrawal of Quebec and as to how far this necessitated increasing dependence on western Canada. The present Liberal Administration includes Mr. T. Crerar, Mr. J. Gardiner, Mr. W. L. Mackenzie King, and Mr. C. A. Dunning—the first three representing western constituencies and the latter a former premier of Saskatchewan. Mr. Crerar and Mr. Dunning, as former prominent members of the two large farmers' organizations, the United Grain Growers and the Saskatchewan Co-operative Elevator Company, indirectly reflect the influence of the pool movement in their withdrawal from the farmers' organizations. The success of the Liberals in Ontario contributed further to the decline of the Liberals in Quebec. Politically the two provinces have proved difficult to drive in double harness.

through their more direct relations to the more rigid price structure of industry sheltered by the tariff. The success of labour organizations accentuates the necessities of political movements of farmers. While the farmers' movements have taken political form supported by American influence, labour organization[41] has been more effectively supported by American development, with the result that political movements have been of minor importance. The success of the affiliations of the American Federation of Labor has been partly a result of the policy of non-political intervention of Mr. Gompers. Labour movements with political possibilities have been resisted vigorously in Canada, to cite British Columbia in the strikes of 1902 and the Oshawa strike of 1937, partly because the relations of labour in Canada and the United States have been immediate and direct. Financial support from the United States has been important in winning strikes,[42] and the necessity of such dependence compels Canadian labour to avoid political movements and concentrate on indirect influence.

The development of separate governments as nuclei of defence against the United States, the addition of Confederation as a means of concentrating defence measures, and the formation of new provinces in western Canada as a continuation of the "divide and rule" principle have provided the basis for provincial rights as protected under the British North America Act and developed under decisions of the Privy Council. The provinces have served as compartments tending to reduce the effects of American influence, and have tended not only to weaken the political influence of the United States in the growth of farmers' movements in the federal field, but also to accentuate it in isolated provinces. The influence of farmers' movements has been weakened further by the concentration of industrialism. The character of agriculture increases the difficulties of co-operation with western Canada. The character of industry is reflected in labour organizations which by virtue of age, tradition, language, similarity of development, and proximity to the United States are linked to American influence. Labour organizations in exposed areas in the Maritimes and in western Canada tend to diverge in policy from those in Ontario. They are not only necessarily more closely associated with the production of

[41]The Canadian Federation of Labour and the All-Canadian Congress are at once tributes to the importance of national influence and indications of the importance of the non-political activities of the Trades and Labour Congress.

[42]See H. S. Ephron, "A Study of the Internal Workings of the International Typographical Union during the Forty-four-Hour Strike," master's thesis, University of Toronto, 1924.

raw materials such as lumber, coal, and minerals and more closely concerned with industrial unionism, but also more closely associated with American influence because of the cultural factors involved in the province of Quebec and, in turn, in Ontario. Labour organizations reflect the regional and cultural background. The more strongly organized industrial region involves more rigid wages, particularly with increasing dependence on the United States. Since 1918 railway wages in Canada have paralleled closely railway wages in the United States.[43] Organized labour in the pulp and paper industry attempts to maintain wages on a par in Canada and the United States. American branch plants as in Ford and International Harvester extend labour policies developed in the United States to Canada.[44]

Rigidity in prices tends to be strengthened by increasing dependence on the United States in eastern Canada. Prices of pulp and paper and gold serve as illustrations of the increasing importance of the American market. As prices and wages tend to become more rigid the fluctuations in income from products such as wheat exported to the extra continental markets become more severe. Producers of staple exports subject to wide fluctuations are penalized by the increasing rigidities which accompany the increasing importance of the United States. Unorganized groups of labour in the industrial areas are squeezed between the depressed income of exporters of raw material and rigidity of prices, as the evidence of unemployment and sweated labour has shown.[45] Professor Logan has attempted to give greater

[43]G. M. Rountree, The Railway Worker (Toronto, 1936), pp. 57ff; the Baltimore and Ohio plan of management was adopted by the Canadian National Railways. See H. A. Stark, "Industrial Democracy in Canada," master's thesis, University of Toronto, 1928; L. A. Wood, Union Management Cooperation on the Railroads (New Haven, 1930).

[44]See Canadian–American Industry (New Haven, 1936), p. 206. For an account of labour policies in part influenced by the United States, see H. Michell, Profit Sharing and Producers' Co-operation in Canada (Toronto, 1918), and Report of the Royal Commission on Industrial Relations (Ottawa, 1919).

[45]See Report of Royal Commission on Price Spreads (Ottawa, 1935); also H. M. Cassidy and F. R. Scott, Labour Conditions in the Men's Clothing Industry (Toronto, 1935); H. A. Innis and A. F. W. Plumptre, The Canadian Economy and Its Problems (Toronto, 1934); and the Fessenden Report submitted to the Royal Commission on the Textile Industry (Ottawa, 1938). According to the latter, actual wages in American mills for weavers were Northern, $16.46; Southern, $14.78; and in Canadian mills a range from $11.21 to $15.37; for spinners, Northern, $14.55; Southern, $12.08, and a range from $9.11 to $17.56; for doffers, Northern, $16.20; Southern, $13.09, and a range from $5.30 to $9.11; for all operatives, Northern, $15.38; Southern, $12.98; Canadian, $11.62. On unemployment, see R. W. Murchie, W. H. Carter, F. J. Dixon, Seasonal Unemployment (Manitoba, 1928); H. M. Cassidy, Unemployment and Relief in Ontario, 1929–32 (Toronto, 1932); Rountree, The Railway Worker.

precision to the character of the burden of defence[46] against the United States, as shown in a lower standard of living which suggests an even greater disparity in less organized groups and less sheltered areas.

The importance of staple products in terms of fish, fur, lumber, and wheat for export to Europe implied extensive credit facilities, with wide fluctuations in price and yield, distance from the market, dependence on the share system, the truck system, intensive self-sufficiency, and marked fluctuations in the standards of living. The increase of industrial development and the growth of urban centres, the development of the mining and pulp and paper industries, and the tourist trade and consequent dependence on American capital have involved increasing efficiency and extension of the monetary structure. These developments have been accompanied by increasing flexibility and increasing mobility.[47] On the other hand the shift from commercial capitalism to industrial capitalism has been striking in a country dependent on transcontinental railways and canals, hydroelectric power development, mines and smelters, and roads, and has led to a later stage of state capitalism with the attendant rigidities of capital structure. The impact on Canada of the business cycle in the highly integrated industrial system of the United States varies directly with the importance of American capital and of the American market, and with the character of the industrial structure in Canada. In the mining and pulp and paper industries, distant from the more highly integrated industrial structure, standards of living are influenced directly by American prices and by the character of labour organization. Isolation increases the importance of capital control, as shown in company towns. Regions exporting products to Great Britain are subject to the more intense competition of world markets and the greater rigidities of transportation costs. The conflict between a price structure dominated by Great Britain and a price structure increasingly dominated by the continent has serious implications for the Canadian economy in the inequalities between groups and regions. The influence of the United States has been, in part, to increase the rigidities of wages. It has contributed to the solution of difficulties involved in the depressed regions but such contributions have been inevitably

[46]For a description of the defence in terms of attitudes see *Canada and Her Great Neighbor*, ed. H. F. Angus (Toronto, 1938).
[47]For an excellent account of the decline of barter and the spread of the wage system and its implications to mobility see J. Davidson, *The Bargain Theory of Wages* (New York, 1898).

limited in scope. The importance of these regions necessitates the elaborate machinery, peculiar to Canada, providing for compensation in railway rates, railway deficits, subsidies, and grants in aid. The tariff, immigration quotas, and other restrictions accentuate the significance of transfer devices.[48] The tourist trade, the pulp and paper industry, gold mining, and capital movements provide rough balances in which mobility increases in response to fluctuating exchange rates.

The machinery of adjustment has emerged from a background peculiar to Canada in her relations with Great Britain and the United States. The significance of cheap water transportation to the St. Lawrence system has been evident in the export of staple products to Europe.[49] The migration of technique from the United States has supported the trend toward specialization on staple products for Great Britain. Concentration on staple products has involved maturity of development which in turn has had repercussions on the United States. Astor attempted the adoption of Northwest Company organization and temporarily occupied the Columbia region. Marquis wheat spread through Canada to the United States. But on the whole the migration of technique has been from the United States and has been hastened by the absence of political attachments. Political organization in Canada has thrived on importation of technique from the United States through support of extensive capital improvements. Political support of capitalism characteristic of the production of staple exports has contrasted with the demands of the industrial areas of the United States for labour. The immobility of labour described by Adam Smith was not applicable to a frontier population habituated to migration.[50] The problem of political organization in Canada has been that of restricting emigration to the United States.

[48]See Commerce Journal Annual Review, Feb. 1936, pp. 24ff.
[49]The general argument has been developed in The Dairy Industry in Canada (Toronto, 1937), pp. v–xxvi. [See this volume, p. 156.]
[50]See L. Hémon, Maria Chapdelaine (Toronto, 1921).

Significant Factors in Canadian Economic Development[1]

WRITING at the end of a long period of rapid expansion in the English colonies and at a time when such expansion threatened imminent revolt, Adam Smith concluded that "Plenty of good land, and liberty to manage their own affairs their own way, seem to be the two great causes of the prosperity of all new colonies."[2] The second cause was elaborated at great length. The colonies of England conducted their governments upon a much less expensive plan and with a much less expensive ceremonial than those of France, Portugal, and Spain. The colonies of the latter countries had even more serious difficulties to contend with:

Such ceremonials are not only real taxes paid by the rich colonists upon those particular occasions, but they serve to introduce among them the habit of vanity and expence upon all other occasions. They are not only very grievous occasional taxes but they contribute to establish perpetual taxes of the same kind still more grievous; the ruinous taxes of private luxury and extravagance. In the colonies of all those three nations too, the ecclesiastical government is extremely oppressive. Tithes take place in all of them. . . . All of them besides are oppressed with a numerous race of mendicant friars, whose beggary being not only licensed, but consecrated by religion, is a most grievous tax upon the poor people, who are most carefully taught that it is a duty to give, and a very great sin to refuse them their charity.

[1]This paper was read before the economics section of the British Association for the Advancement of Science at Nottingham on September 11, 1937, and it follows in logical order: the chapter on "Transportation as a Factor in Canadian Economic History" in *Problems of Staple Production in Canada* (Toronto, 1933), pp. 1–17; "Unused Capacity as a Factor in Canadian Economic History," *Canadian Journal of Economics and Political Science*, II (Feb. 1936), 1–15; "Introduction to the Canadian Economic Studies" in *The Dairy Industry in Canada* (Toronto, 1937), pp. x–xxvi, and editor's introduction to *Labor in Canadian-American Relations* (Toronto, 1937), pp. v–xxxi. [See this volume pp. 62–77, 141–55, 156–75, 176–99.] It is intended as a complement to C. W. Wright, "American Nationalism: An Economic Interpretation" in *Facts and Factors in Economic History* (Cambridge, 1932), pp. 357–80. [It was published in the *Canadian Historical Review*, XVIII (Dec. 1937), 374–84.]

[2]Adam Smith, *An Inquiry into the Nature and Causes of the Wealth of Nations*, ed. Edwin Cannan (Modern Library, New York, 1937), p. 538. For a reference to the continued influence of the physiocrats and the interest in land as a basis of wealth see J. Bonar, *Malthus and His Work* (London, 1885), pp. 246–7.

Over and above all this, the clergy are, in all of them, the greatest engrossers of land.

Fourthly, in the disposal of their surplus produce, or of what is over and above their own consumption, the English colonies have been more favoured, and have been allowed a more extensive market, than those of any other European nations [pp. 541-2].

The first cause was linked to the second and was described more briefly: ". . . the engrossing of uncultivated land, though it has by no means been prevented altogether, has been more restrained in the English colonies than in any other" (p. 539). "The labour of the English colonists, therefore, being more employed in the improvement and cultivation of land, is likely to afford a greater and more valuable produce, than that of any of the other three nations, which, by the engrossing of land, is more or less diverted towards other employments" (p. 540). "The political institutions of the English colonies have been more favourable to the improvement and cultivation of this land, than those of any of the other three nations" (pp. 538-9), although good land was less abundant. "It has been the principal cause of the rapid progress of our American colonies towards wealth and greatness that almost their whole capitals have hitherto been employed in agriculture" (p. 347). "Agriculture is the proper business of all new colonies; a business which the cheapness of land renders more advantageous than any other" (p. 575). He knew that good land was not abundant in the English colonies and that agricultural technique was inefficient (p. 223) and yet he concluded: ". . . through the greater part of Europe the commerce and manufactures of cities, instead of being the effect, have been the cause and occasion of the improvement and cultivation of the country. This order, however, being contrary to the natural course of things, is necessarily both slow and uncertain. Compare the slow progress of those European countries of which the wealth depends very much upon their commerce and manufactures, with the rapid advances of our North American colonies, of which the wealth is founded altogether in agriculture" (p. 392).

One may venture to suggest that the two causes were closely interlocked, but that expansion in the North American colonies as in Europe was the "cause and occasion of the improvement and cultivation of the country." Adam Smith in his analysis of the division of labour and the extent of the market as determined by transportation, can be quoted in support of this suggestion: "In our North American colonies the plantations have constantly followed either the sea-coast or the banks of navigable rivers, and have scarce any where extended themselves to any considerable distance from both" (p. 19). "As by means of water-carriage a more extensive market is opened to every sort of industry than what land-carriage alone can afford it, so it is upon the sea-coast, and along the banks of navigable rivers, that industry of every kind naturally begins to subdivide and improve itself, and it is frequently not till a long time after that those improvements extend themselves to the inland parts of the country" (p. 18). The improvement of transportation facilitated the expansion of external and internal trade.

Good roads, canals, and navigable rivers, by diminishing the expence of carriage, put the remote parts of the country more nearly upon a level with those in the neighbourhood of the town. They are upon that account the greatest of all improvements. They encourage the cultivation of the remote, which must always be the most extensive circle of the country. They are advantageous to the town, by breaking down the monopoly of the country in its neighbourhood. They are advantageous even to that part of the country. Though they introduce some rival commodities into the old market, they open many new markets to its produce. Monopoly, besides, is a great enemy to good management, which can never be universally established but in consequence of that free and universal competition which forces everybody to have recourse to it for the sake of self-defence [p. 147].

Cheap water transportation from Europe to North America stimulated commerce and brought "improvement and cultivation of the country." The fishing industry capitalized to the full the advantages of water transportation. The discovery of the abundance of fish in the New World was followed by the expansion of the industry from Europe to meet the demands of countries predominantly Catholic and with a limited production of meat products. France prosecuted the industry in relation to her own demands. England was attracted to the Spanish market by the specie obtained from the New World, and occupied Newfoundland, and later New England, as a base for the production of dry fish for that market. The expansion of trade from France to Spain was followed by the occupation of Nova Scotia and the Gulf of St. Lawrence. As a result of contact with the hunting Indians of the interior by the St. Lawrence and its tributaries, the fur trade emerged to meet the demands of metropolitan Paris for luxuries and of the aborigines for European goods. Fur, being a commodity of small bulk and high value, supported a trade carried on over increasing distances to the interior. In the more tropical regions, Spain and Portugal were concerned with treasure, England and France with tobacco and later, in the West Indies, with sugar (pp. 156ff, 162ff).

The technique of production of these various commodities involved sharply differentiated economies. Slaves were taken by English ships from Africa to the West Indies, and supplies and provisions for the consumption of slaves and the production of sugar were carried by colonial ships from the north temperate colonies. New England became an active commercial region with its prosperity based on the fishing industry and shipping to Europe, the West Indies, and Newfoundland. France had an expanding fur trade which handicapped the production of agricultural products on the St. Lawrence and in turn accentuated dependence of the French West Indies and the French fishing industry on the English colonies. Attempts on the part of France to check dependence on the English colonies helped to make a vicious circle in which the costs of production were increased and the necessity of overcoming restrictions enhanced. England had the advantage of a relatively co-ordinated empire, but the principle of exporting staples to the home market was violated to an increasing extent, especially as a result of the expansion of New England. The British Empire competed with the French Empire on all fronts—in the West Indies, in Europe, and in North America through the Hudson's Bay Company by Hudson Bay and through New York by the Hudson River. Adam Smith explained the weakness of the French Empire as due to its organization rather than to the character of its trade. "Of all the expedients that can well be contrived to stunt the natural growth of a new colony, that of an exclusive company is undoubtedly the most effectual" (p. 542). "The French colony of Canada was, during the greater part of the last century [seventeenth], and some part of the present, under the government of an exclusive company. Under so unfavourable an administration its progress was necessarily very slow in comparison with that of other new colonies; but it became much more rapid when this company was dissolved after the fall of what is called the Mississippi scheme" (p. 538). Recent investigation has shown that government policy, supplemented by the principle of commercial monopoly, the seigniorial system, and the dominance of the Roman Catholic church, was moulded and designed to strengthen control over the fur trade and was successful in resisting encroachments of the English until the fall of New France.[3] The prosperity of the colony noted by Adam Smith coincided with the extension of the trade from the St. Lawrence to the Saskatchewan, and

[3]See W. B. Munro, *The Seigniorial System in Canada* (Cambridge, 1907); also A. G. Bailey, *The Conflict of European and Eastern Algonkian Cultures* (Saint John, 1937).

its collapse with the inability to compete with the British Empire. The resistance of the French contributed to the unity of the British Empire, and the collapse of the French Empire was followed by the collapse of the British Empire in North America. The first British Empire eventually failed to co-ordinate the aggressive commercialism of the colonies, especially New England, with the demands of Great Britain that the colonies be primarily staple-producing regions. The commercial organization of New England became competitive with that of Great Britain. After the American Revolution, with the elimination of New England, the second British Empire proved more efficient than the French Empire in co-ordinating the interests of staple-producing regions. The success of the second British Empire was dependent on commercial organization which increased the value of land.

The fur trade on the St. Lawrence was extended beyond the boundaries reached by the French and eventually to the Pacific, as a result of the more efficient industrial and commercial organization of Great Britain, of the migration of technique from the United States as illustrated in the effective development of navigation on the Great Lakes, and of the efficiency of the co-partnership of the Northwest Company. Increasing costs of transportation, due to the extension of the fur trade over greater distances, combined with Scottish clannishness and nepotism to defeat the Northwest Company and to lead to its amalgamation with the Hudson's Bay Company and to the abandonment of the St. Lawrence in favour of the shorter route by Hudson Bay.

In the fishing industry of the Maritime Provinces, as in the fur trade of the St. Lawrence, migration of technique from the United States combined with the extension of commercial organization from the Channel Islands[4] to enable Great Britain to occupy territory vacated by the French in the Gulf of St. Lawrence, Cape Breton, and Nova Scotia. Nova Scotia attempted to reoccupy the place vacated by New England in the trade of the first Empire with the West Indies. The increasingly aggressive commercialism of Nova Scotia succeeded in excluding the United States from the British West Indies, but such exclusion compelled the United States to support expansion of trade in the South American republics. With the growth of their independence, and enunciation of the Monroe Doctrine in 1822, substantial modifications in the British colonial system were demanded by Nova Scotia and secured in the Trade Acts of 1825.

The decline of Britain's supply of timber from the American colonies

4See J. B. Brebner, *The Neutral Yankees of Nova Scotia* (New York, 1937).

as a result of exhaustion and of the American Revolution, and from Europe as a result of the continental system, led to the adoption of substantial imperial preferences on timber from the colonies as a means of hastening the exploitation of the resources of the St. Lawrence and the rivers of New Brunswick. British timber merchants from the ports on the west coast of Great Britain, such as Liverpool and Glasgow, established branch houses in British North America and purchased ships and timber to meet the demands of industrialism in the rise of urban communities and the construction of railways.

The disappearance of the fur trade on the St. Lawrence in 1821 was followed by the rise of the timber trade. The fur trade had involved concentration of a French Catholic population at Montreal at the junction with the Ottawa as the route to the northwest, and on the lower St. Lawrence. The timber trade, on the other hand, hastened the coming of English-speaking immigrants, who crossed the Atlantic in empty timber ships returning to Canada. Many of them were unemployed, displaced by the effects of the industrial revolution on handicrafts and agriculture, and they were compelled to settle the unoccupied regions of the upper St. Lawrence. The military and political organization which had been developed in the upper and lower St. Lawrence valley in the last decades of the eighteenth century, with the purpose, especially under the United Empire Loyalists, of resisting encroachments from the south, now came into conflict with the aggressive commercialism of Montreal which emerged as a result of increasing exports of grain from the newly settled areas of the upper St. Lawrence. The demands of the new commercial class for lower costs of transportation by roads and canals for imports and exports involved a reorganization of the political structure, which followed as a result of the outbreak of revolt in 1837, Lord Durham's *Report*, and the Act of Union in 1840. The decline of the British preference on grain and timber and the increasing effectiveness of improved transportation from New York, especially by the Erie Canal, necessitated the union of the governments of Lower and Upper Canada to provide a financial base for a competitive transportation route by the St. Lawrence.[5] But in spite of the completion of the St. Lawrence canals, the chagrin at the loss of the preferences was marked by the annexationist manifesto and the burning of the parliament buildings in 1849.

In Nova Scotia the defeat of attempts to exclude the United States

[5]See D. G. Creighton, *The Commercial Empire of the St. Lawrence* (Toronto, 1937).

from the British West Indies in 1830 was followed by a policy of rigid exclusion of American trade by tariffs and of American ships from British waters by a narrow interpretation and strict enforcement of the Convention of 1818. The retaliatory policy in Nova Scotia against American tariffs, and the effort to obtain a large share of traffic from the western states for the St. Lawrence route in Canada, led to the Reciprocity Treaty of 1854[6] which admitted Canadian fish duty free and arranged for increasing traffic on the St. Lawrence. In Canada, the competition of the St. Lawrence with New York was strengthened by the construction of the Grand Trunk Railway to provide transportation from the western states to Portland.

The demands of industrial Britain for foodstuffs and the significance of capital equipment for the transportation of grain involved a shift from commercialism to capitalism, from dependence on short-term credit to dependence on long-term credit. The commercial class, supported by the mother country in the French and British empires and with their chief interests in the fur trade and the timber trade, tended now to be displaced by the capitalist class. The earlier appeals on the part of commercial groups for continuations of the preferences were replaced by the appeals of Hincks and Galt for capital support from the houses of Baring and others. The autonomous capitalist state replaced commercial colonialism. Adam Smith's arguments, which had contributed to the decline of the colonial system, were now used to support the claim for Canadian fiscal autonomy. In his pamphlet *Canada 1849 to 1859*,[7] Galt wrote that in 1849 "the only hope lay in the fact that the people had at last the management of their own affairs." They had the right to impose a tariff on British goods to secure revenue to meet the demands of British capitalists for interest on loans spent on public works to reduce costs of transportation. "As the expence of carriage . . . is very much reduced by means of such public works, the goods, notwithstanding the toll, come cheaper to the consumer than they could otherwise have done; their price not being so much raised by the toll, as it is lowered by the cheapness of the carriage," wrote Adam Smith (p. 683), and "It might very easily be shown that any increase of duty which has been placed on English goods is quite indemnified by the decreased cost at which our canals, railways and steamships enable them now to be delivered throughout the province," wrote Galt.

[6]See D. C. Masters, *The Reciprocity Treaty of 1854* (Toronto, 1937).
[7]London, 1860. The influence of Adam Smith on Canadian political thought is extensive as a sampling of newspaper editorials, letters to the editor, and the works of Howe and Mackenzie will indicate. He was quoted to suit their purposes.

The emergence of fiscal autonomy as a basis of support for large-scale improvements of transportation necessitated further readjustment in the political structure. The Grand Trunk Railway, controlled from London through British capital support, unfortunately illustrated Adam Smith's comments on joint stock companies and was hampered by government-supported competition in canals. The imposition of tariffs for revenue involved tariffs for protection and led to the abrogation of reciprocity in 1866 and in turn to demands for measures of defence against the United States. The interests of the government and private capital in increasing traffic and in reducing the burden of fixed charges demanded the extension of the Grand Trunk Railway by the Intercolonial to Nova Scotia, the extension westward to the Prairie Provinces and the Pacific coast, and the creation of a new credit structure in Confederation under the British North America Act. The provinces of Quebec and Ontario were restored and Nova Scotia and New Brunswick were added. Cultural areas with their special interests of language, religion, and political and economic organization were given assurance of permanence by the federation. The position of the provinces under the British North America Act is a recognition of the differences in cultural characteristics: of Nova Scotia based on the fishing industry, of New Brunswick on the timber trade, of Quebec on the fur trade and later on agriculture and the timber trade, and of Ontario on the timber trade and agriculture. On the other hand, the influence of the new capitalism, which was essential to the completion of improvements in transportation by railway and canal, left its stamp on the Dominion government. This distinction is evident when we examine the creation of the new provinces in the prairie regions and on the Pacific coast.

The demands of private capitalism as represented by the Grand Trunk diverged from those of state capitalism. The Grand Trunk[8] became concerned with the extension of its line to Chicago to tap the traffic of the western states. The federal government engaged itself in a programme of extension to the east, marked by the Washington Treaty which admitted Canadian fish to the United States duty free from 1871 to 1885, and by the completion of the Intercolonial Railway in 1876, and to the west by the strong support given to the construction of the Canadian Pacific Railway which was completed in 1885. The National Policy was designed in 1878 to secure revenue to pay deficits and to increase traffic to reduce deficits. Loss of population,

[8]See G. de T. Glazebrook, A History of Transportation in Canada (Toronto, 1938).

especially from Ontario to the United States, during the long depression from the seventies to the nineties, was finally checked by
continual efforts extending from the deepening of the St.
Lawrence canals to 14 feet to a programme of intensive propaganda to attract
immigrants from Europe and the United States. Competition from
New York was eventually offset by improvements of the St. Lawrence,
and by the boom which followed the turn of the century and which
was hastened by the occupation of the Prairie Provinces and the
development of mining in British Columbia and the Yukon and of
lumbering and fishing on the Pacific coast. Two additional transcontinental lines of railway were completed by 1914 with substantial
government support. With the outbreak of war, the transcontinental
railways constructed after 1900 were forced into bankruptcy and
acquired by the federal government.

Throughout the economic history of Canada, the dominance of
water transportation in the Maritime Provinces and the St. Lawrence
has accentuated dependence on Europe for manufactured products
and for markets of staple raw materials. The fur trade was followed
by the timber trade and agricultural products. Concentration on staple
commodities was accentuated by the migration of technique from the
United States. As the export trade in staples from the United States to
Great Britain declined in importance, the Canadian trade in staples
was encouraged. The fur trade was strengthened by American aggressiveness and technique, the timber trade shifted from New England
to New Brunswick and the St. Lawrence, the fishing industry migrated
from New England to Nova Scotia, agriculture, in the production of
wheat in Ontario and the Prairie Provinces and in dairying, benefited
from the contributions of the United States. The dependence of
Canada on Great Britain was accentuated by the United States indirectly and by British and Canadian policy directly. European markets
and European capital dominated Canadian economic development
through the background of water transportation.

In the post-war period and during the depression, the St. Lawrence
has contracted in influence as a transcontinental factor. The Panama
Canal attracted wheat from territory as far east as the western
boundary of Saskatchewan. The end of expansion in western Canada
for the export of wheat has come in sight, and regions which contributed to rapid expansion in Canada have, by virtue of sustained
drought, contributed to sharp depression. The iron and steel and coal
industries of Nova Scotia and the St. Lawrence, and industrialism
based on expansion in western Canada, have felt the effects of the

end of a long-run secular trend. Another element in the decline of the St. Lawrence has been the growing insecurity of Canadian trade in the European markets which has made American capital and American markets increasingly important. The mining and pulp and paper industries have emerged as a result of the increasing population and the declining resources of the United States. With changed conditions, the activities and powers of the provinces have assumed a new importance. For example, as a result of the automobile and tourist trade, roads have been built on a large scale by the provinces, while the Dominion government continues primarily to be concerned with railroads and transcontinental traffic.

The end of the period of expansion based on the St. Lawrence and trade with Great Britain coincided roughly with the achievement of dominion status which followed the Great War and which was marked by the Statute of Westminster. The end of the struggle for control over external policy has been followed by problems of internal policy; and the decline of the St. Lawrence as a factor contributing to the centralization of the Dominion has been accompanied by the increasing importance of regionalism evident in the growth of the powers of the provinces. The cultural features in terms of language, religion, metropolitan and political organizations based on the peculiarities of staple trades from various regions of Canada to Europe, which provided the basis of the provinces in the British North America Act, have hardened and been strengthened by the decline in the influence of the St. Lawrence as a centralizing factor in the Canadian system. The expansion of provincial powers, conspicuous in New Brunswick, Ontario, and Quebec, has been scarcely less evident in Manitoba, Alberta, and British Columbia. The decline in commercialism which accompanied the rise of free trade advocated by Adam Smith and his disciples, left a structure which moulded the growth of capitalism (sponsored by those who paid lip service to Adam Smith) and hastened the growth of protectionism. The extension of the American empire, the decline of its natural resources, and the emergence of metropolitan areas, supported capitalist expansion in Canada and reinforced the trend of regionalism. The pull to the north and south has tended to become stronger in contrast with the pull east and west. The British North America Act and later decisions of the Privy Council have strengthened the control of the provinces over natural resources such as minerals, hydro-electric power, and pulpwood on Crown lands, resources which have provided the basis for trade with the United States and for investment of American capital. The problem of transportation—itself made possible by Dominion support to the construction of transcontinental railways—and problems of drought and depression in western Canada, have compelled the appointment of a federal Royal Commission, which must run the race between the Charybdis of increasing provincial powers and the Scylla of railway amalgamation masquerading as national unity. The energy and genius of Adam Smith have been replaced by a multitude of counsel and it is significant that the Commission has been announced, with regional representation, to consider a revision of financial and taxing powers in a year in which the Anglo-Saxon population of Canada ceases to be a majority.

The Historical Development of the Dairy Industry in Canada*

I. EARLY HISTORY

DAIRYING as the basis for the development of an extensive trade has followed increasing specialization in the live-stock industry. Migration of European population to North America was successful in so far as it was accompanied by methods of producing foodstuffs demanded by this population, that is, by European agriculture with its emphasis on mixed farming—domesticated animals and cereals. The agricultural technique of the aborigines, and the geographic characteristics of the region to which European population migrated left their stamp in modifications of European technique.

In Acadia an abundance of natural hay in the intervales and diked lands of territory tributary to the Bay of Fundy gave cattle a position of first importance as a source of foodstuffs, though they were little used as draught animals since the production of cereals was limited. Mild winters lowered the cost of housing cattle and made it unnecessary to store large quantities of hay. But the raising of live-stock handicapped dairying. According to a document dated about 1686 the cows were small, the calves milked them, and the people were not able to make butter for themselves. As a result of the exposed character of the region through its proximity to the English settlement, cattle were captured or even killed to avoid capture by the English. After the Treaty of Utrecht this problem was less serious, and agriculture increased in importance. In 1715 Shebenectoc had stocks of black-and-white cattle, Minas 3,000 head and Annapolis 2,000. The demands of Louisburg as a centre of the French fishery and the ease with which cattle could be driven across the Isthmus of Chignecto for shipment, providing their own transportation, facilitated expansion of the industry in the upper basins of the Bay of Fundy. But the outbreak of war, the destruction of Louisburg, and the expulsion of the Acadians were followed by large-scale destruction of cattle in Acadia and in Prince

* From J. A. Ruddick *et al.*, *The Dairy Industry in Canada*, ed. H. A. Innis (Ryerson, 1937), pp. 1–11.

Edward Island.[1] The disturbed history of the maritime regions restricted agricultural development.

In New France the difficulty of clearing the land placed a high premium on the production of cereals for human consumption. Long winters, the cost of housing and of producing extensive hay crops, and the competition of cereals with hay for cleared land placed an emphasis on wheat and horses rather than hay and cattle. A combination of the production of cereals and live-stock necessitated construction of fences and buildings, and scarcity of labour and high wages restricted this development. In spite of constant attempts to check the increase in horses and to encourage cattle, officials were compelled to recognize the insistence of the habitants on the advantages of horses in the economy of New France. Horses were effective competitors for hay. In 1731 the scarcity of cattle necessitated regulations prohibiting killing for production of salt beef, except to supply vessels for Europe or Cape Breton. A limited domestic market, low prices in comparison with wheat, fluctuating harvests, the necessity of destroying cattle in bad years from which depletion of stock recovery was slow, and competition of the fur trade for labour, involved handicaps to the industry. Limited possibilities for the production of cattle for meat or for draught animals tended to restrict the industry to dairying. As early as 1728 a regulation prohibited the milking of cows in a common enclosure because of the ease with which farmers were able to milk their neighbours' animals. Butter was apparently the chief product and was in demand in the markets of the larger centres.

After the expulsion of the Acadians, settlers from New England brought to Nova Scotia their cattle and their technique of agriculture, adapted rather to uplands than to diked lands. With settlement of the uplands hay and grain were raised to support live-stock and extensive wooden barns for housing live-stock and feed were a part of the equipment. According to an account published in 1774 the cattle were small and the cows gave "small quantity of milk for they fetch them up early every evening to milk and let them fast till seven or eight o'clock in the next morning." Cows let out all night were said to give double the quantity of milk. The raising of oxen required milk, and calves were allowed to run with the cows. Scarcity of capital was evident in the practice of wealthy farmers, who rented cows to poor people at 20 shillings a year, or at 30 pounds of butter per cow and

---

[1]See D. C. Harvey, *The French Regime in Prince Edward Island* (New Haven, 1926), chap. xii. In 1753 Prince Edward Island had 823 oxen, 1,497 cattle, 1,651 pigs, 1,440 sheep, and 152 horses. Apparently the number of cattle had increased to 6,000 by 1757.

half the cheese. Milk was poured into bowls before cooling, with the result that it soured in six or eight hours; after standing forty-eight hours the cream was taken off and made into butter which was sold in Halifax market at eight pence a pound. Cheese was produced in small quantities, and as early as 1764 Nova Scotia exported six tons valued at £280.

The migration of settlers to Upper and Lower Canada as to the Maritimes before and after the Revolution was accompanied by the introduction of agricultural technique developed in the southern colonies. Cattle played a more important role than in New France as draught animals and in supplying meat. The hog was the basic source of fat for the fur trade and the lumber industry, although cattle were taken to the interior in vessels on the Great Lakes and on Hudson Bay to provide fresh meat for the winter season. A small number of cows provided milk and butter for local consumption on the farm or for sale in adjoining centres. Simcoe, in 1793, encouraged imports of cattle from the United States to make Upper Canada self-sufficient, but prior to the War of 1812 Canada imported butter and cheese from the United States.

The rise of the timber trade in New Brunswick and in Ontario and Quebec, as a result of substantial preferences in the British market during the Napoleonic Wars, created a demand for agricultural products. Pork, flour, beans, potatoes, hay, oats, and horses were supplied to the lumber camps. Prince Edward Island became famous for the horses and oats which were raised for New Brunswick camps. Hay was obtained from the diked lands of Nova Scotia and the intervales of New Brunswick. The influx of large numbers of immigrants in the twenties and thirties, particularly to the St. Lawrence region, involved concentration of energies on clearing the land. The demands of agriculture and the timber trade for oxen weakened the possibility of expansion of the dairy industry. It was estimated that in 1831 the provinces had horned cattle as follows: Canada (Ontario and Quebec), 540,000; New Brunswick, 64,000; Nova Scotia, 142,000; Prince Edward Island, 32,000. The port of Quebec exported 140,710 pounds of butter and 6,751 pounds of cheese to the maritime British American colonies in 1830.

Prior to 1850, or in the period in which the economic history of Canada was dominated by water transportation, agriculture, and in particular the dairy industry, was handicapped by the concentration of energies on the production of staple products. In the French régime agriculture on the St. Lawrence was handicapped by increasing attention to the fur trade, and in Acadia was encouraged by the demands of the fishing industry but was devastated by wars. After the Conquest, attempts to reinforce the strength of the outlying regions of Ontario and the Maritimes by settlement of regiments and encouragement of pre-loyalists and loyalists directly encouraged agriculture. The demands of the fur trade were limited chiefly to flour, maize, and pork, but after the amalgamation of the Northwest Company and the Hudson's Bay Company and the closing of the St. Lawrence route, duplicate posts were closed in the interior and surplus labour was moved to Red River Settlement and to the newly established headquarters of the Western Department at Fort Vancouver on the Columbia River. Droves of cattle were brought to Red River by enterprising Americans in the early 1820's but limitations of the market restricted development. In 1849 Red River Settlement had 2,097 oxen, 155 bulls, 2,147 cows and 1,615 calves. At Fort Vancouver on the Columbia, cattle were brought in from California, and expansion of the fur trade and agreements with Russia provided a market. On the Pacific Coast, in the Red River district, in Ontario, and in the Maritimes cattle had been obtained from the United States. The demands on agriculture in an area dependent on staples had been met by extension of the industry chiefly from the United States. Cattle, providing their own means of transportation, were imported with the prevailing agricultural technique.

After 1856 the development of steamships and railways widened the market for agricultural products and accentuated production of commodities easily transported to the growing industrial areas of Great Britain and of the United States, and, with a protective tariff after Confederation, to deficient areas of the Dominion. In the fifties wheat and flour were exported in increasing quantities to Great Britain. The Reciprocity Treaty, the Civil War in the United States, increasing demands of urban centres in Canada, increasing use of agricultural machinery from the United States, westward movement of wheat production in the United States, and problems of soil exhaustion incidental to continued cropping were factors contributing to the rapid development of the live-stock industry in the decade after 1855.[2] Shorthorn cattle were imported to meet local demands for beef and to support an expanding live-stock and dairy industry. The release of labour by agricultural machinery in areas with large families, and improvement of roads facilitating the handling of milk, contributed to the development of the dairy industry in areas—such as the districts near

[2]*Select Documents in Canadian Economic History 1783–1885*, ed. H. A. Innis and A. R. M. Lower (Toronto, 1933), pp. 524ff; on dairying, pp. 557ff.

Ingersoll, Stratford, and Belleville—with sufficient rainfall to provide abundance of pasture, hay, grain, and roots. The technique of cheese production in co-operative factories, matured in New York State in relation to the demands of Great Britain for protein foodstuffs, took root in these regions. The first cheese factory was introduced in 1864 and the numbers increased to 353 in 1871, 709 in 1881, and 1,565 in 1891, chiefly in Ontario. Agricultural technique in Quebec with its French traditions was less adaptable, although cheese factories increased from 25 in 1870 to over 200 in 1880. An American tariff of 20 per cent *ad valorem* on live cattle, following the abrogation of reciprocity, and duties on cheese and butter stimulated expansion of cheese production for export to Great Britain. The St. Lawrence basin shifted from an importing to an exporting position.

In areas less suited to dairying, beef cattle became important. A dairy industry based on dual-purpose cattle provided milk for cheese, and surplus live-stock which could be driven to grazing areas. Rapid development in exports of live-stock to Great Britain beginning about 1875 can be attributed to the improvement of steamship navigation and the advantages of the St. Lawrence with its cool climate and the long journey before reaching the open sea, and a British embargo on American cattle in 1878. Within a decade exports exceeded 50,000 head annually. The live-stock and dairy industries, with their demand for pasture and forage in winter, revolutionized agricultural rotations by emphasizing the production of roots, maize, grain, and hay rather than wheat. The limited areas suited to the growth of the cheese and live-stock industries, the widespread development of agriculture in relation to other staple exports such as timber, and dual-purpose breeds such as the Shorthorn, provided a basis for the butter industry. Growth of towns increased the demand for butter, while exports were restricted because of the character of the commodity, as a fat rather than a protein, and by problems of production, with lack of uniformity as a result of the domestic system of production. Agriculture in Quebec, with its French traditions and its difficulties in responding to the demands of American agricultural practice, provided a more fertile soil for the technique developed in Europe in relation to butter production. The study of European systems of dairying[3] was followed in the eighties by the introduction of the cream separator[4] and the develop-

---

[3]See S. M. Barré, "Report on the Manufacture of Butter in the Principal Dairy Farming Countries of Europe," *Quebec Sessional Papers*, 1880–1, no. 2.

[4]E. Bouchette, "Les Débuts d'une industrie et notre classe bourgeoise," *Royal Society of Canada Transactions*, 1912, Section I, pp. 143–57.

ment of creameries for the manufacture of butter. Butter production expanded, with governmental encouragement, in the cheese-producing areas during the winter season and during the summer in areas less suited to cheese production. An embargo on live cattle exports to Great Britain in the middle nineties and expansion of the ranching industry in western Canada[5] and the United States contributed to the increasing importance of the dairy industry. By the turn of the century the St. Lawrence region produced specialized dairy products, particularly cheese and butter for export to Great Britain. Quebec was producing annually nearly twenty-four million pounds of butter and nearly eighty-one million pounds of cheese, and Ontario over seven and a half million pounds of creamery butter and nearly one hundred and thirty-two million pounds of cheese.

In the Maritimes, with abundant supplies of hay, the live-stock trade responded to the demands of Great Britain, but the demands of lumber camps and of other industries continued to mould the character of their agriculture. In the Prairie Provinces the advantages of wheat production restricted the dairy industry. On the Pacific coast the gold rushes of the fifties and sixties were followed by the movement of herds of cattle from the United States to supply the mining camps; and the development of industries, such as mining and lumbering after completion of the transcontinental railway, with the protection of high costs of transportation, led to the development of agriculture and dairying, particularly in the relatively easily cleared land of the Fraser delta region.

II. TWENTIETH CENTURY TRENDS

The turn of the century introduced a period of major expansion most significant to the dairy industry. Increase in gold production owing to the Yukon gold rush and the Rand contributed to a rise in prices which favoured importation of capital on a large scale for the opening of the Prairie Provinces. As the technique of agricultural production matured; as railway construction proceeded in the United States, and spread under similar conditions to Canada; as labour from the United States and from Europe poured into Canada with the disappearance of free land in the United States; as costs of transportation declined with marked improvements of railways and canals; and as the urbanization of Europe proceeded, wheat production in western Canada increased rapidly. Similarly, the new mining camps

[5]See R. W. Murchie, *Agricultural Progress on the Prairie Frontier* (Toronto, 1936), chap. v.

in the Klondike, the Kootenay, and Northern Ontario created demands for foodstuffs. The demand for iron and steel and railway supplies was one of the causes of the rise of the iron and steel and coal industries of Nova Scotia and of the rapid industrialization of the St. Lawrence.

The retreat of dairying from export markets as a result of concentration on wheat hastened the expansion of the industry in the Antipodes. Production of beef in the Argentine narrowed the possibilities of its production in New Zealand and brought about the increased importance of the dairy industry. Refrigeration enabled the Argentine, Australia, and New Zealand to compete in meat and dairy products. As Canadian exports to Great Britain had increased with the decline of exports from the United States, so they declined with the increase of exports from the Antipodes.

Increasing urban population, improved transportation, increased recognition of the food value of fluid milk, and more effective sanitary regulation[6] were responsible for a rapid expansion of the domestic market and for a rapid increase in the fluid milk trade. The rapid increase in the industrial population, including population engaged in the production of wheat, was followed by an increased demand for butter, condensed milk, and similar products, and in turn by a sharp decline in the production and export of cheese, and in the export of butter. Areas more accessible to the Antipodes, such as British Columbia, imported butter by the middle of the first decade of this century. The effects were evident in the decline of cheese factories and the increasing importance of creameries and condensed milk factories. The handicap of long winter seasons tended to increase the importance of abundant pasturage in the summer season and to limit forage for the winter season. Grain and by-products of dairying facilitated the raising of hogs in the off-peak season. But a revolution in agriculture incidental to winter dairying was caused by the demand for milk and for cream throughout the year, and by the increasing overhead of rising land values. Improved methods of feeding and increased emphasis on dairy breeds, particularly the Holstein, were accompanied by greater attention to crops suited to winter dairying. Corn became increasingly important and silos were built for winter feeding.[7] Corn tended to displace grain and roots, and with

[6]"Report of the Milk Commission Appointed to Enquire into the Production, Care and Distribution of Milk, 1909," *Ontario Sessional Papers*, 1910, no. 55.

[7]With inadequate supplies of winter feed through scarcity of grass in virgin forests, cattle were raised with difficulty. Natural grass limited to an occasional beaver meadow and its inadequate support necessitated dependence on twigs

the decline of cheese production and its by-products, hog raising declined. The expansion of grain production in western Canada provided cheaper supplies of feed in competition with grain produced in dairy regions. The live-stock industry was unable to compete with dairying and calves, other than those necessary for the maintenance of herds with an average milking life of five years, met a demand which was for veal rather than for beef.

These general developments were characteristic of the St. Lawrence, the Maritimes, western Canada, and British Columbia. In the Maritimes molasses tended to be displaced by butter, and creamery butter encroached on the cheese industry and on dairy butter production. In western Canada the rise of urban centres, and the demands of industrial development of British Columbia in mining, fishing, and lumbering, led to the emergence of dairying, particularly in regions less suited, because of distance and geographic background, to wheat production, as in parts of Alberta. The Calgary-Edmonton district became important as a dairy region through the direct and indirect (i.e., the tariff) support of the government and the demands of Kootenay mines.[8] In British Columbia limited agricultural areas accessible to urban centres involved concentration on the fluid milk trade in the Fraser valley.

In the war and the post-war period hydro-electric power development, expansion of the mining and the pulp and paper industries, the tourist trade, and construction of hotels stimulated demand for dairy products, and the increase in the use of automobiles and trucks, and construction of roads, contributed to the increase in supply. The importance of capital equipment, with more efficient creameries and larger-scale operations incidental to the wider range of the motor truck, with the development of condensed milk plants, and with the

---

and brush in winter. As larger areas were brought under cultivation straw became available and eventually hay. The growing of roots and mangels contributed enormously to the solution of the problem of winter feeding. "Corn stover" or corn without the ears was fed to cattle and the ears to horses and hogs. Ensilage provided a more adequate diet and overcame the labour difficulty incidental to the growing of roots on a large scale. The "horse tooth" (dent) corn was introduced about 1870. The seed at first was of slow-maturing varieties, and was usually sown broadcast, with the result that the crop had very little feeding value. With improved and earlier maturing varieties, the practice of planting in hills or rows was followed, and corn as a fodder crop came into more favour, although cutting by hand, shocking it in the field, and hauling to the stables as needed during the winter, involved much heavy and disagreeable labour. With the introduction of the silo in the eighties and later of a satisfactory corn harvester, the corn crop came into its own, and silage has since been the sheet anchor of the dairy farmer, especially in Ontario.

[8]H. A. Innis, *Settlement and the Mining Frontier* (Toronto, 1936), pp. 306ff.

use of pasteurization processes for fluid milk, brought a change in the character of organization from small units (which featured the cheese, and to a less extent, the creamery industries), to the corporate type of enterprise. Again, maturity of organization in relation to the industries of the United States was followed by rapid extension to Canada of control by American capital and by the increasing rigidity of capital structure. Co-operative enterprise maintained a strong hold in concentrated areas such as the Fraser valley.

These trends were accentuated by exclusion by increased tariffs of dairy products from the United States. Exports of raw material in the form of milk and cream from dairy regions adjacent to the densely populated areas of the United States were checked at a period when competition from New Zealand and Australia had increased. At the same time, decline in consumption in urban areas in the depression brought about a marked reduction in prices.

The penetration of the dairy industry from the United States to portions of Canada (less conspicuous in Quebec) facilitated the rapid acquisition of matured technique from that area, and rapid expansion of the industry in relation to the demands after 1900. Breeds of cattle, methods of production of dairy products from dehorning to the Babcock Test, improvement in corn, and agricultural technique generally, have been powerfully influenced by the American background.

Industrialization in the United States tended to reduce exports of dairy products to Great Britain, and to facilitate the development of exports from Canada to Great Britain. Rapid expansion in Canada accompanied the completion and construction of transcontinental railroads and increased production of wheat, lumber, pulp and paper, minerals, and fish, which was in turn to a large extent a result of the application of technique matured in the United States. This rapid expansion materially reduced exports of dairy products to Great Britain and revolutionized the dairy industry to meet the demands of the domestic market. Marked decline in the rate of expansion, the depression, increasing self-sufficiency in England, increasing exports from the Antipodes, and United States tariffs, have brought a decline in price which is only partly offset by lower costs of feed incidental to the sharp reduction in prices of wheat and other grains. Having powerfully contributed to the expansion of the dairy industry, the United States has prohibited entry to her markets by the tariff. Such prohibition may relieve the American dairy producer of a slight necessity to contract, but at the expense of the American consumer in his consumption of the important products of animal husbandry, and of the Canadian producer of dairy products.

Transportation in the Canadian Economy*

THE study of transportation in tracing routes of travel, and in appraising the work of the engineer in overcoming obstacles and lessening distance, is an approach to its study as a fundamental part of the national economy. The integration of national life depends on problems of distribution and of marketing, and these largely determine the direction of international policy. Nowhere are these elemental truths more clearly seen than in the economy of northern North America. There is the oceanic relationship with the mother countries in Europe, and there are not only the two national economies of Canada and the United States of America, but also varied local systems on each side of the border. An historical survey will show how deeply these elements have affected the political as well as the economic development of the communities that have wrested these areas from the wilderness and erected their similar but variant forms of social life.

Expansion of trade from Europe to North America assumed the existence of vessels of sufficient size to cross the Atlantic Ocean, and knowledge of prevailing winds and ocean currents at various seasons. Vessels from the ports of Europe carried on the fishing industry along the coast of Newfoundland and adjacent territory in the early part of the sixteenth century, and on the banks, along the shores of Nova Scotia, and in the Gulf of St. Lawrence and the Gulf of Maine later in the same century and in the seventeenth century. To England the fishing industry provided a supply of food for consumption by the crews of fishing vessels, and also for the home market, including ships in the navy and those going below the line, and for export to Spain and the Mediterranean. France, with a large Catholic population, was less concerned with export trade and with the dry fishing industry in the New World.

In the late sixteenth and early seventeenth century, the fishing industry and the shipping of Europe, and particularly of England, responded to the effects of imports of specie into Spain from the New World. English settlements emerged in Newfoundland and New England, and French settlements in Nova Scotia and at Gaspé in

*From G. P. de T. Glazebrook, A History of Transportation in Canada (Ryerson, 1938), pp. vii–xxi.

the Gulf of St. Lawrence. The rise of settlements in New England and the growth of trade and shipping stimulated expansion of the continental colonies and of sugar production in the West Indies. Small vessels suited to the fishing industry and the coastal trade were built on a large scale. Improved methods in the manufacture and handling of vessels, increase in numbers of aggressive traders, and the growth of settlements facilitated England's capture of New York from the Dutch in 1664, of Nova Scotia from the French in 1710, and of Cape Breton and Canada in 1763.

The importance of the home market in France encouraged the growth of the fur trade which followed contact with the Indians of the St. Lawrence. The short season, the high value and low bulk of furs, the centralizing influence of a large river, and the use of canoes and boats which characterized the St. Lawrence and the Mississippi accentuated the importance of the large ocean-going vessels. These large rivers drained the energies of France to the interior of the continent and tended to divide rather than unite her Empire. Moreover, large vessels from the St. Lawrence which supported canoes to the interior were unable to compete with English vessels going direct to the mouths of the rivers flowing into Hudson Bay. Shipbuilding on the St. Lawrence was limited[1] and shipping was handicapped by closed seasons,[2] long distances, limited facilities, and dependence on staple products, particularly in the fur trade with its heavy one-way upstream cargo.

With the collapse of the French Empire, vessels from England and the colonies swarmed up the St. Lawrence; and the route up the Hudson to Albany and Oswego, which had been developed during the French régime, became a basis for expansion to the territory vacated by the French. Anglo-American traders began to resort to Montreal. By using boats they succeeded in mastering Great Lakes navigation more effectively than the French, and made it a support to the Ottawa canoe route and a basis for re-establishment of the connections (confirmed by the Quebec Act), with the Ohio and the Mississippi. Restriction of access to the interior by the British government was resented by the coastal colonies even more than restriction by the French. This obstruction, combined with the increasing burdens of the English colonial system on external trade, led to the collapse of the British Empire following the withdrawal of opposition from the

[1]*Select Documents in Canadian Economic History, 1497–1783,* ed. H. A. Innis (Toronto, 1929), pp. 385 *et seq.*

[2]Ships were unable to arrive in some cases early enough to forward supplies to the upper lakes in the same season. See *ibid.,* pp. 399 *et seq.*

French. Sir Joshua Child's predictions were fulfilled: "New England," he had written, "is the most prejudicial to this kingdom because of all the American plantations, His Majesty has none so apt for building of shipping as New England, none comparably so qualified for the breeding of seamen not only by reason of the national industry of that people but principally by reason of their cod and mackerel fisheries, and in my poor opinion, there is nothing more prejudicial and in prospect more dangerous to any mother country than the increase of shipping in her colonies, plantations, or provinces."[3] The effectiveness of colonial shipping broke the chains of the British commercial system directly and indirectly. Control over raw materials for shipbuilding, such as masts,[4] contributed to the defeat of the British in the struggle for independence.

The second British Empire gradually retreated from the Mississippi to the St. Lawrence, driven back by the population which poured across the Alleghanies. In contrast to the fur trade, which involved taking heavy manufactured goods up the Mississippi, settlements around the headwaters sent heavy goods down the river. The failure of Americans to gain control over the St. Lawrence in the War of 1812 was offset by the increasing importance of the steamboat on the Mississippi. The Canadian fur trade withdrew northward, especially after the Jay Treaty, and pushed on to the Saskatchewan and the Athabaska and eventually to the Pacific. Competition from Hudson Bay with the advantage of shorter distances and the use of boats on the rivers was followed, in 1821, by the disappearance of the fur trade from the St. Lawrence.

The effects of the disappearance of the fur trade were alleviated by the rise of the square timber trade. This was sharply restricted to the drainage basins whereas the fur trade overcame these boundaries by the canoe and the portage. British preferences during the Napoleonic Wars and afterward fostered the timber trade on the long rivers of New Brunswick and on the tributaries of the St. Lawrence. Cheap English shipping after the war and abundance of white pine which could be floated long distances down-stream meant bulky cargoes for Great Britain and provided cheap reciprocal transportation for settlers coming to Canada.

Competition for the traffic of the upper Mississippi valley from

[3]Quoted in R. F. Grant, *The Canadian Atlantic Fishery* (Toronto, 1934), pp. xii-xiii.
[4]See the interesting thesis advanced in R. G. Albion, *Forests and Sea Power* (Cambridge, Mass., 1926).

Montreal and from New Orleans led to the construction of the Erie Canal from New York to Buffalo on the upper lakes, with a branch to Oswego on Lake Ontario. To avoid the St. Lawrence rapids and to strengthen colonial policy and military control on the St. Lawrence, Great Britain constructed the Rideau Canal. Construction of the Welland Canal was intended to offset competition on the upper lakes. The Union of Upper and Lower Canada provided a broader financial base for construction of canals on the upper St. Lawrence and for improvement of the Welland. Improvements on the St. Lawrence were offset, however, by a decline in the colonial system involving decreased preferences on wheat and timber and by the passing of bonding laws in the United States which facilitated shipments from New York to Upper Canada. The losses, real or imaginary, were in part responsible for the annexationist manifesto of 1849 and for the attempts to secure reciprocity with the United States. The completion of the canals on the St. Lawrence was followed by a period of truce from the competitive wars of transport rates and tariffs, brought about by the Reciprocity Treaty of 1854–66. Controversies over the fishing industry in Nova Scotia were also given a respite.

The inability of the French and British empires to maintain a balance within their own boundaries had been made evident, especially after 1713, by smuggling in Cape Breton, in the West Indies, and at Oswego on Lake Ontario, and it affected the readjustment of boundaries by the Treaty of Paris. The colonial system of Great Britain was extended to territory captured from the French;[5] but, unable to maintain a balance between the diverse interests of different regions, it broke down in turn. It was consequently adjusted to oppose the United States, especially in the Maritimes, the West Indies, and the St. Lawrence. After the War of 1812 and under the Convention of 1818 the United States was excluded from the British coastal fishery. Barred from these areas, more American shipping went to South America and to the Pacific coast. American traders staked out a claim to the Oregon. The aggressiveness of the United States contributed to the breakdown of the British colonial system in the Trade Acts of the twenties, in the concession of admission to the West Indies trade in 1830, and in the abolition of the Corn Laws in 1846 and of the Navigation Acts in 1849. Equilibrium was established by the ending of the colonial system; and the Reciprocity Treaty permitted relative freedom of trade between British North America and the United

[5]See D. G. Creighton, *The Commercial Empire of the St. Lawrence* (Toronto, 1937).

States, access of Americans to the St. Lawrence, and admission of American fishing vessels into Canadian waters and of Canadian fish into the American market.

The truce was gradually broken down by continued improvements in transportation. An increase in the size of vessels on the upper lakes made it impossible for them to proceed to Lake Ontario by the Welland Canal. In 1853 New York was connected with Chicago by a railway along the south shore of Lake Erie, and in 1855 by the Great Western through Southern Ontario. To offset the effects of this competition Canada supported an energetic programme of railway construction. Year-round open ports, such as Boston and Portland, competing with New York, joined with Montreal to build connecting lines to Montreal and in the early fifties the Grand Trunk Railway was extended westward to Toronto (1856) and Sarnia (1859) and eastward by the Victoria Bridge to Rivière du Loup (1860). A tariff was imposed in 1858 to secure revenue to support the outlay on improvements of transportation and to build up traffic.

The Civil War was evidence of disturbances to equilibrium between the North and the South, and its outcome established the dominance of the North, and stimulated resistance from Canada. The significance of the debt incurred for the construction of canals and railways by the Canadian political structure which had been built up on the Act of Union necessitated dependence on Great Britain for capital support, and, in its turn, for a general policy of development. The financial difficulties of the government and of the Grand Trunk Railway, and an inability to compete with American lines to the seaboard led imperial-minded capitalists like Sir Edward Watkin to propose an extension eastward to Canadian Atlantic ports and westward to the Pacific. In 1863 control of the Hudson's Bay Company was acquired by his group and plans were laid for construction of a railway through its territory to British Columbia. The Reciprocity Treaty was abrogated in 1866, and Confederation, with the construction of the Intercolonial between Canada and the Maritime Provinces as a *sine qua non*, became a reality in 1867. The Intercolonial was completed to Rivière du Loup in 1876.

The discovery of gold in California in 1848 and in other regions of the Pacific coast, including British Columbia in the late fifties and the early sixties, was followed by migration of population on a large scale. The construction of railways was begun from the Mississippi, and the Union Pacific was completed in 1869. Steamships were introduced along the Pacific coast and crossed the Pacific to Australia.

With the Suez Canal completed in the same year, Great Britain had alternative routes to the East, although one was partly on American territory. The Northern Pacific was planned to run from the American seaboard through Canada to Sault Ste Marie and the Pacific, under direction of Sir Hugh Allan in Montreal and Jay Cooke in Chicago. But the stubborn resistance of Toronto interests, and of the Grand Trunk, to American participation, and the crash of 1873, which precipitated the Pacific Scandal, brought an end to the project.[6] The Northern Pacific was completed under American control from Duluth to Puget Sound in 1883. The Grand Trunk, with its lines from Sarnia and Detroit to the seaboard, became increasingly concerned with the possibilities of the expanding traffic of the Mississippi valley and extended its lines to Chicago in 1880–1. In its increasing interest in traffic from the western states its hostility to alternative lines from western Canada to the Atlantic seaboard was enhanced. It refused to co-operate with either the Northern Pacific project via Sault Ste Marie or with the Canadian government in its determination to build a line around the north shore of Lake Superior in Canadian territory. After the addition of British Columbia to Confederation under an agreement to build a railway to the Pacific, and the difficulties with the Grand Trunk, the Canadian government started to build the line. Finally, an agreement was drawn up with the Canadian Pacific Railway Company, which was forced to depend on capital centres other than London and which consequently secured large-scale support in lands, cash, and a completed railway from the federal government. In 1885 a railway was constructed north of Lake Superior and across the prairies, close to the United States boundary, to Vancouver, providing an alternative all-British route to the Far East and a competitive Canadian line for important long-haul Pacific traffic.

The determination to build north of Lake Superior led to the resignation of J. J. Hill from the Canadian Pacific directorate and to the extension by him of the Great Northern to the coast, following a route between the boundary and the Northern Pacific (1893). As a result of competition for long-haul traffic, the Canadian Pacific acquired the Duluth, South Shore and Atlantic to Duluth, and the Minneapolis, St. Paul and Sault Ste Marie to the Twin Cities in 1890, and to the main line of the C.P.R. via Portal in 1893. It built, with government

[6]See H. A. Innis, *A History of the Canadian Pacific Railway* (London, 1923), pp. 79 *et seq*. Excellent maps on the transport routes should be consulted not only in Glazebrook, *History of Transportation*, but also in W. J. Wilgus, *The Railway Interrelations of the United States and Canada* (New Haven, 1937).

support, a line through the Crow's Nest Pass, obtained control of the Trail smelter,[7] and, with the assistance of the tariff, largely excluded American competition. The Canadian tariff was designed, along with other measures (including the monopoly clause, which excluded railways south of its main line in the prairies), to check competition from American railways and to compel the prairie and Pacific coast regions to purchase goods manufactured in eastern Canada rather than the eastern states. With the gold discoveries in the Yukon, and renewed severe competition between the Canadian Pacific and American lines[8] and between Seattle and Vancouver and Victoria, the tariff was used to throw trade toward eastern Canadian manufacturers. Similarly a customs post on Herschell Island[9] checked the exploitation of the Canadian Western Arctic by American traders to the north of Alaska.

The extension of the Canadian Pacific to the more densely populated industrial areas of eastern Canada brought competition with the Grand Trunk, and led to its amalgamation with the Great Western Railway. The growth of remunerative traffic to western Canada after the turn of the century led the Grand Trunk to assume an aggressive policy with plans to extend its line from Chicago to Winnipeg. Again the tariff and the refusal of the Canadian government to support a line through American territory compelled it to agree to co-operate in the construction of the National Transcontinental Railway from Quebec to Winnipeg in the west and to Moncton in the east, and to build, under a subsidiary, the Grand Trunk Pacific, a line from Winnipeg to Prince Rupert. The result was a transcontinental line from Moncton to Prince Rupert with no close connections with the parent system and ill adapted as a direct entry to Western Canada.

The federal government, however, secured a line suited to the development of northern Quebec and northern Ontario and intended as a means of exporting grain through Quebec or Maritime ports. After the Reciprocity Treaty, the construction of railways, and the introduction of steamships, wooden shipping in the Maritimes had declined sharply from its peak in 1874. The devastating effect on the economic life of the Maritimes of the shift from wood, wind, and water to coal and iron necessitated government support, with tariffs designed to increase the consumption of Cape Breton coal, railways across the Strait of Canso through Cape Breton to Sydney, bounties on iron and steel, and the extension of the National Transcontinental to Moncton.

[7]See H. A. Innis, Settlement and the Mining Frontier (Toronto, 1936).
[8]See Innis, A History of the Canadian Pacific Railway, pp. 206–7.
[9]See H. H. Bodfish, Chasing the Bowhead (Cambridge, Mass., 1936).

The Grand Trunk Pacific and the National Transcontinental as a through transcontinental from Moncton to Quebec, Winnipeg, and Prince Rupert via the Yellowhead Pass tapped the vast area in the clay belt and the prairies north of the southern location of the Canadian Pacific Railway.

The protest of settlers in western Canada against monopoly control of the Canadian Pacific Railway had been capitalized at an earlier date by the acquisition of a charter by Mackenzie and Mann for the construction of a line from Winnipeg to Hudson Bay. This line was extended as the Canadian Northern, with federal and provincial support, to tap the more promising traffic regions of the northern area; and it eventually reached Edmonton and Vancouver in the west, and Port Arthur, Toronto, and Montreal in the east. Whereas the Canadian Pacific was concerned primarily with Montreal, and the Grand Trunk Pacific with Quebec and Maritime ports, the Canadian Northern provided the most direct line from western Canada to Toronto and offset the competitive position of Montreal and the effects of the Grand Trunk's strategic blockade of a direct entrance to Toronto by the Canadian Pacific. (The latter secured a direct line to Toronto in 1908 but Montreal was its headquarters and terminus.)

The inability of the federal government to provide grants of land as a result of previous grants to the Canadian Pacific Railway compelled the Grand Trunk Pacific and the Canadian Northern to depend on cash grants and on funds provided through the guaranteed bonds of the Dominion and the provinces. Government support, access to the London market, and the boom which characterized the period from 1900 to 1914 financed the enormous increase in Canadian railway mileage. The outbreak of the war and the closing of the London market brought serious problems to lines without established traffic areas. During the war and the post-war period the Grand Trunk, the Grand Trunk Pacific, the National Transcontinental, the Canadian Northern, and the Intercolonial were amalgamated under government control under the name of the Canadian National Railways. The diverse parts of the system were combined and strengthened to compete with the Canadian Pacific Railway and the American transcontinental lines. The Grand Trunk main line to Chicago became an effective competitor for seaboard traffic and an important contributor to earnings through its access to an intensive industrial, and densely populated, area. The linking of the Canadian Northern with the National Transcontinental at Long Lac provided effective competition to Winnipeg. The extension of branch lines from the Grand Trunk

Pacific and the Canadian Northern brought marked increase in traffic in western Canada, and lower grades by the Yellowhead Pass to Vancouver were an advantage in the growth of traffic following the opening of the Panama Canal.

Increased competition in the dense traffic areas accentuated demands for efficient operation. Wheat from western Canada moved over the established routes, especially with improved Great Lakes shipping, to New York and Montreal, and efforts to stimulate shipments by alternative routes such as the National Transcontinental to Quebec and Maritime ports were largely unsuccessful. Consequently, demands for compensation arose from areas penalized by intensive competition and loss of traffic. The Maritime Freight Rates Act of 1927 introduced lower rates from the Maritimes. Areas with sharply fluctuating income, such as the prairies, secured lower rates in the renewal and extension of the Crow's Nest Pass rates agreement. The opening of the Panama Canal was followed by vigorous competition for traffic from the prairies to British Columbia ports and by the lowering of rates. Demands for increased earnings on the one hand, and for regional compensation on the other, were the basis for conflicting statements of efficient operation and of extravagance regarding the Canadian National Railways.

The significance of the St. Lawrence in the history of Canadian transportation is in striking contrast to the development of coastal transportation in the United States, accompanied by numerous approaches from the Atlantic to the interior. Control from Europe was effective on the St. Lawrence and ineffective in the United States. Cheap water transportation in the St. Lawrence economy accentuated dependence on export of staples to Europe, the specialization of technique in relation to these commodities, and support from government intervention. The canoe was borrowed from the hunting Indians of the Canadian shield and adapted to expansion in the northern half of North America. The square timber trade involved the use of cribs on the Ottawa, of rafts on the St. Lawrence to Quebec, and of cheaply built wooden ships to Great Britain. Seasonal navigation, which was a handicap to the St. Lawrence, was an advantage to the United States. Wooden sailing vessels turned from the Quebec timber in summer to the cotton trade of the southern states in winter, just as the later steamship changes its terminus from Montreal and Quebec to American ports. Dependence on Europe in the French and British régimes necessitated government assistance in the form of posts at strategic points on the Great Lakes and of active hostilities against competition from the south and north. The restrictions which the fur trade put on settlers required active intervention by the French government to support such widely varying activities as the construction of roads in New France and the conducting of naval wars in Hudson Bay.

When the British assumed control, they maintained an effective colonial system on the lower and upper St. Lawrence and overcame the St. Lawrence rapids, first by the construction of the Rideau Canal and later by tangible support in the form of guarantees of funds for the construction of the St. Lawrence canals. Trunk roads were planned and built in Upper Canada under Imperial direction and support. Following the gold rush in British Columbia, roads were built under the supervision of the Royal Engineers to supplement the rivers. The need for funds on a large scale to overcome obstacles of a major character such as the St. Lawrence rapids and Niagara Falls hastened the demand for domestic control over taxation and expenditures which was the essence of responsible government. The Act of Union, the construction and deepening of canals, the support of the Grand Trunk Railway, Confederation, the construction of the International, the National Policy, and the support of the Canadian Pacific, the Grand Trunk Pacific, the National Transcontinental, and the Canadian Northern were results of the necessity of checking competition from the United States, and of overcoming the seasonal handicaps of the St. Lawrence and the handicaps incidental to the Precambrian formation and the Rocky Mountains. To build canals and improve the St. Lawrence system, and to build railways to the Maritimes and across the Precambrian formation north of Lake Superior to British Columbia from Montreal, Quebec, and Toronto necessitated reorganization of the political structure, grants in land and cash, and the tariff, particularly the National Policy and imperial preferences.

Dependence on the Canadian political structure and on support from Great Britain to carry out these vast projects involved rigidity of finances without benefit of bankruptcy (the Grand Trunk arbitration award notwithstanding), and government ownership. Implications of control from Great Britain were evident in the payment of dividends on the Grand Trunk under conditions in which they were not warranted, in its consequent difficulties, and in the necessity of appealing to the government for support, of extending its line to Chicago, and of precluding it from participation in expansion to western Canada until after the turn of the century and in the face of the entrenched position of the Canadian Pacific. In the early sixties, before it felt the pull of the western states, it attempted to hasten construction to the Pacific by securing control of the Hudson's Bay Company, and in the seventies, after it felt the pull, to delay construction. The delay was accompanied by steady improvement of transportation west of the Mississippi; it was followed by the rush to completion of the Canadian Pacific in the early eighties and by its consolidation by the turn of the century. Payment of large dividends by the Canadian Pacific Railway after the turn of the century, on the other hand, hastened the construction of additional transcontinental lines. Difficulties of control from Great Britain, intensified by the geographic background as shown in the importance of rail and water competition in eastern Canada,[10] were evident in financial deficits in the operation of the canals, the Grand Trunk, including the Grand Trunk Pacific and the National Transcontinental, and the Intercolonial. These difficulties were further enhanced by the occupation of strategic territory, geographical and political, by the Canadian Pacific.

Control from Great Britain was strengthened throughout by migration of technique from the United States.[11] Retardation through control by Great Britain was followed by acceleration through support from the United States. Boats suited to the waterways of the United States were adopted by the Northwest Company on the Great Lakes and by the forwarders from Montreal on the St. Lawrence and supported the expanding trade of Upper Canada and the Northwest. Equipment displaced by new inventions in the United States migrated to less developed areas and to Canada. The Red River cart was displaced by the steamboat from St. Paul to Red River and in turn from Red River to the Saskatchewan and Edmonton. The railway displaced the steamboat on river after river. The Canadian Pacific was directed and built in western Canada by men trained in railway construction and operation in the prairies of the United States, and later railway construction borrowed much from American experience. The acceleration of development in Canada through contributions from the United States accentuated dependence on British capital and the increase of public debt.

During the war and post-war period imports of capital funds have accompanied imports of American technique from the United States

---

[10]See D. A. MacGibbon, *Railway Rates and the Canadian Railway Commission* (Boston, 1917).

[11]See J. A. Ruddick *et al.*, *The Dairy Industry in Canada*, ed. H. A. Innis (Toronto, 1937), pp. v–xxvi. [See this volume, p. 156.]

in response to the demands of government ownership in the Canadian National Railways and of the expansion of new forms of transportation. The automobile was first imported, and then built by American firms in Canadian territory for the domestic and imperial market. Federal, provincial and municipal governments have been concerned with extensive road construction for domestic demands and tourist travel. To the rigidities of finance peculiar to control from London have been added those involved by New York. The rigidities of finance incidental to government activity in the ownership of railways and roads involved encroachment on the elasticity of finance characteristic of the Canadian Pacific Railway. The elasticity incidental to government support in its construction and operation has declined with government support in the construction and operation of the Canadian National Railways. The results have been evident in the appointment and recommendations of the Duff Commission and the legislation which followed it, and in the Royal Commission on Dominion-Provincial Relations.

Rigidities of finance have an important effect on traffic movements between Canada and the United States. The influence of competition and regulation by the Interstate Commerce Commission and the Board of Railway Commissioners respectively on railway rates in the United States and Canada are offset by varying tariffs between the two countries, by disturbances of exchange rates, and by statutory transportation rates, all of which directly influence, and are directly influenced by, financial rigidities. Rigidity of finance in Canada in her relations with the United States and Great Britain enhances adverse exchange rates. The application by either country of higher tariffs, including dumping duties and the use of the cost-of-production principle, checks the influence of the flow of goods as an equilibrating measure and accentuates the importance of the tourist trade and of more intangible items in the balance of trade. They tend to injure railway traffic between Canada and the United States and to encourage automobile transport in Canada. The decline in the influence of the flow of goods on exchange rates is not offset and may be made greater by increasing flexibility in other items during a depression in a country largely dependent on exports to world markets. The significance to Canadian railways of a restricted flow of goods between Canada and the United States would be more serious to the basic Montreal-Chicago route of the Canadian National than to its transcontinental portions, or to the Canadian Pacific Railway, in spite of its extensive United States connections.

The problem of debt not only involves exceedingly complex short-run problems of adjustment between Canada and the United States, but it restricts the powers of the governments of North America in regard to long-run problems of development. It strengthens the powers of the provinces and weakens the treaty-making power of the Dominion. The St. Lawrence waterway is sacrificed on the altar of impotent constitutions. The position of the Senate as the graveyard of American treaties is paralleled by the position of the provinces in Canada.

Economic Trends in Canadian-American Relations*

THE general argument of this paper is to the effect that American policies are destined to affect the policies of Canada, and the policies of North America as a whole, to an increasing extent, and that it is to the interest of all concerned that the probable effects of American policies on Canada should be considered before they are finally formulated.

It is significant that I should be asked by an American committee of arrangement to prepare a paper of a popular character on economic trends in Canadian-American relations. A Canadian committee would, I hope, have been less certain about economic trends and would certainly have implied that political trends were included. I propose to follow the usual procedure by disregarding the title of the paper and presenting a compromise between the Canadian and American point of view, by adopting the Canadian approach or by attempting to indicate the background between the two points of view. We are in danger, particularly in the maritime regions, of taking for granted a common point of view, since it is from these regions that similarities have spread throughout the continent. The emphasis on regionalism which characterizes a long coastline has been sharpened on the Atlantic coast by the growth of the fishing industry dependent on the sea and by the development of trade in commodities produced from regions with a wide range of climate and geology. As has been pointed out elsewhere,[1] it is not an accident that four sovereign bodies are represented in the Atlantic fishing regions, Newfoundland, France, Canada, and the United States, and it is not an accident that the particularism of New England and the Maritimes, of Massachusetts and Nova Scotia, has been indelibly stamped in the character of the federal constitutions of Canada and the United States. Sir John A. Macdonald attempted to avoid the difficulties of the American Constitution, which became evident in the Civil War, by emphasizing

*An address delivered at the Conference on Educational Problems in Canadian-American Relations, at the University of Maine, Orono, Me., June 21–3, 1938.
[1]See R. F. Grant, *The Canadian Atlantic Fishery* (Toronto, 1934), p. vii.

federal power but the position of Nova Scotia limited federal power in the constitution and in its later development.

But we are being carried into the whirlpool of common points of view. The particularism of the maritimes was reflected not only in the constitutions of the United States and Canada but also in the sharp differentiation between the United States and Canada, and to that we must turn our attention. Separatist Nova Scotia and New England accentuated differences between the northern and the southern parts of the continent. The emergence of two nations in North America reflected the profound influence of geological structure and topography, with a large number of short rivers along the southern part of the Atlantic seaboard, a long river, the St. Lawrence, along the southern edge of the Precambrian formation to the heart of the continent, and a vast bay to the north. Penetration from Europe along the southern part of the Atlantic seaboard was slow and consolidated, by the St. Lawrence rapid and far-flung, and by Hudson Bay reluctant. Increase in population, trade, and industry in the English Atlantic colonies brought conflict with French control over the St. Lawrence and defeat of the French, and a sharp break with English control in the American Revolution and the emergence of the United States. In the final break Nova Scotia and the St. Lawrence remained under English control. The economy built up by the St. Lawrence reflected the continuous political influence of Europe, in contrast with the southern Atlantic coast. The export of staple products of the St. Lawrence to an increasingly industrialized Europe involved defence of a long thin line of settlement. The fur trade shifted to the short route by Hudson Bay and the timber trade responded to the urban demands of Great Britain and the definite encouragement of imperial preferences.

Emigration was stimulated by various devices. Capital equipment in canals and railways was designed to strengthen the St. Lawrence and to check the influence of routes to New York and other United States ports. The Grand Trunk was followed by the Intercolonial to the east and the Canadian Pacific to the west. The tariff was increased to strengthen the position of transportation facilities concentrating on the St. Lawrence. With this development, wheat succeeded lumber as a staple export by the St. Lawrence to Europe.

The structure of the Canadian economy was an extension of the European or British economy, with a consequent increase in efficiency guaranteed by cheap water transport, imperial preferences, and the opening of new resources. It was handicapped by the extent of government intervention, the rigidity of government indebtedness, railway rates and tariffs, and dependence on a commodity subject to wide fluctuations in yield and price. Increase in urban population in the United States was accompanied by a decline in exports of staple products to Europe and by the shift of this trade to Canada. In turn exports from Canada have been forced to retreat in the face of competition from other parts of the Empire as well as from Argentina, Denmark, and Holland. Rapidity of expansion in Canada and concentration on staple products, such as wheat, have accentuated rigidities imposed by competition from other wheat producing areas. In the face of this competition Canada has retreated behind tariffs and concentrated on other forms of production. Precluded by tariffs from exporting to the United States, Canada has imposed tariffs and secured empire preferences and agreements compelling the establishment of branch factories from the United States. Urbanization of the United States has meant not only the retreat of exports to Europe, the shift to Canada, retreat of Canada, and the development of exports of manufactured products, but also the pull of raw materials and finished products in which depletion of American resources has been conspicuous, such as pulp and paper, or of which Americans have deprived themselves by changes in the constitution, such as liquors, or of which they feel they have special need in cases of emergency, such as gold.

Canada is facing to an increasing extent the effects of contrast between two systems. An old system linked her to Europe by a geographic background dominated by the St. Lawrence and provided for the efficiency of specialization under free trade. The character of defence was apparent in the constitutional set-up of the federal system —a tariff along the international boundary and a series of compartments in the provinces built up on control over natural resources and designed to save the ship through the closing of bulkheads, as evident in the recent Saskatchewan elections. As the burden increases, the strain on the bulkheads increases. The costs of defence and of supporting those who hide behind it, as in the case of protected industries, become too heavy. The character of the defence is evident not only in the tariff but also in the development of government ownership, as in the case of hydro-electric power in Ontario and the Canadian Broadcasting Corporation, in the Canadian railway problem, the talk of nationalism, and bursts of oratory about the long undefended international boundary line, the long period of peace, and the work of the International Joint Commission. These are witnesses to the efficiency of defence as much as to the continuation of peace. The new system links Canada to the United States and is evident in the increasing importance of exports from Canada to the United States, such as pulp and minerals, and in the rapid spread of inventions from the United States to Canada and the consequent decline in efficiency of defence. The radio crosses boundaries which stopped the press.

The conflict between the two systems has cumulative effects. Nationalism becomes more intense. The influence of the radio is canalized through the Canadian Broadcasting Corporation and interest in national culture is intensified. The intensification of nationalism increases the burden of tariffs and fixed charges, precipitates regionalism, and enhances the importance of the provinces. Particularism leads to decline in national loyalties and to increase in imperial loyalties. The instability of the Canadian political and economic structure offsets the effects of rigidities and reflects the conflict between European and the American systems. It increases the weakness of Canada as a political unit in relation to Europe.

The burden of defence in Canada is made more severe by the character of the conflict between the two systems. The economic structure in relation to Great Britain and Europe implied an east-west haul on a transcontinental scale of raw materials for export and of manufactured products chiefly within Canada. The highly industrialized and urbanized character of Great Britain and its demand for foodstuffs, particularly from western Canada, necessitated railways, elevators, canals, ports, and steamships. The Panama Canal, and Churchill to a slight extent, have encroached on the St. Lawrence system but the effects have been offset by the increasing demands of the United States for pulp and paper and minerals and, indirectly, hydro-electric power. The stage of industrial development and the proximity of the United States create a demand for bulky cheap commodities of a non-agricultural character from non-agricultural regions. The contrast between western Canada and its relations with Europe, and eastern Canada and its relations with the United States, involves strains between the Dominion, concerned with federal problems of transportation, and, on the one hand the provinces in the West, coinciding in their interests with the federal government, and on the other hand the provinces in the East, opposed to the federal government through the background of tradition and the possibility of depending on their own resources for export to both the United States and Great Britain. These strains accentuate Canadian instability and the strengthening of imperial rather than national loyalties.

The nuisance value of Canada in Anglo-American relations, as a subject of investigation, has been neglected because of the importance attached by after-dinner speakers to the long "undefended" boundary line. It was Great Britain and the United States that had the "will to peace," and Canada cannot escape the accusation of playing the role of the small boy anxious to stick pins in either when there was something to be gained by it. We had muddied the waters, and the sentiment expressed by a typical Britisher is too generally applicable. He said, "Now I know why Americans and Englishmen are not too friendly. You think we are like these damn Canadians."[4] It was inevitable in an adolescent colony that Great Britain should find it necessary to step in, on various occasions, and call a halt to Canadian pin-pricking lest it should endanger Anglo-American relations.

A few examples must suffice. Nova Scotia badgered Great Britain into restricting American trade to the West Indies until 1830. She began with the Hovering Act of 1834, a policy of exclusion of the United States from British waters, which in 1840 compelled Great Britain to restrain her. She became such a nuisance with her protective system that reciprocity was welcomed as a relief. Canada was not less difficult. She fought for preferences on timber and on wheat, and when they were cut off, the disgruntled element stuck a vigorous pin in Great Britain in the annexationist manifesto of 1849. Here, too, reciprocity was welcomed. With the end of reciprocity, Nova Scotia compelled Canada and Great Britain to adopt a vigorous policy of exclusion, which led to the Washington Treaty as a way of escape. With the end of the Washington Treaty, Canada again became offensive and pursued vindictiveness to the point of preventing a treaty between the United States and Newfoundland. In Ontario export taxes were levied on lumber going to the United States, and in retaliation against American tariffs an embargo on lumber cut on Crown lands was introduced in 1898. Canada spurned the rising tariffs of the United States and introduced imperial preferences in 1896. We played our cards with effect and secured the free entrance of newsprint in the reciprocity arrangements of 1911 and the tariff of 1913. But largely because of our annoyance with Great Britain and the United States over the settlement of the Alaska boundary dispute, we refused in a very striking fashion the reciprocity treaty as a whole.[5] In spite of friendships arising from the war, we were annoyed with the Fordney-McCumber tariff and we countered the Hawley-Smoot tariffs with the Ottawa agreements. It is scarcely necessary for this paper to elaborate

[4]W. R. Curtin, *Yukon Voyage* (Caldwell, 1938), pp. 249–50.
[5]J. W. Dafoe, *Clifford Sifton in Relation to His Times* (Toronto, 1931).

on Canadian tactics. The politician is quick to seize upon the possibility of capitalizing hostility to either the United States or Great Britain, and Canadian nationalism flourishes under these conditions, but it is nationalism in the interest of the short run rather than the long run. It is only with maturity that Canada can be expected to play a role in which pin-pricking ceases to be a policy, in which we will cease fishing in troubled waters, and in which we will take advantage of the "will to peace" between Canada and the United States.

The weakening of nationalism, the strengthening of regionalism, and the stress on imperialism leaves Canada as the weak link in the North American structure—the Achilles heel to North American isolation. Outbreak of war in Europe involving Great Britain involves Canada and in turn, sooner or later, the United States. We turn, therefore, to the problem of possible contributions of the United States which might strengthen Canadian unity, render the voice of Canada more effective in the League of Nations and in the British Commonwealth of Nations, and enable her to take a stronger stand in the interests of world peace.

The Siamese twin relationship between Canada and the United States—a very small twin and a very large one, to be exact—is evident not only in the exports from Canada and the United States but also in the establishment of branch plants in Canada, important wage levels, for example in railway labour, competitive railway rates, movement of liquid capital, ownership of government securities, and the temporary migration of tourists, to mention significant relationships. The exchange rate between the Canadian dollar and the American dollar does not depart from par for any great length of time and then chiefly as a result of the importance of fluctuations in returns from agriculture in terms of price and yield.

It is scarcely necessary to stress the obvious significance of American economic policies to Canada and to point out the existence of an American empire without the desire to assume responsibilities which go with imperialism. This is not to say that any implicit statement as to responsibilities by the United States would not be regarded with hostility by Canada, that Canadians prefer to look upon vagaries of American policy as acts of God and Mr. Roosevelt over which they have no control, and that the United States would not resent any suggestion that Canada should plead for consideration of the effects of an American policy on her. But it is to suggest that the United States in her own interests must consider particularly the effects of any policy on Canada, which is without benefit of political representation. Lest I

should become involved in any breach of hospitality on these subjects, may I plead the indulgence of such courtesies as these conferences
make available. The emergence of governmental control on a large
scale in the United States, evident in tariffs and monetary policy,
makes the question increasingly acute. Whether the United States
agrees or not, its monetary and tariff policies are largely the monetary
and tariff policies of the North American continent, including Canada.
It is not surprising that devices should have been developed to prevent changes of too drastic a character. The Canadian legation at
Washington has become a more efficient clearance channel. An exhaustive discussion of treaty possibilities and the work of such bodies
as the International Joint Commission enable both countries to obtain
an appreciation of the implications of policy in one country to that of
the other. American branch plants in Canada ensure representation
of the American point of view in Canada and possibly the Canadian
point of view in the United States. Areas such as Detroit and the
border cities register immediately the effects of changes of policy.
These devices are defective because of lack of information, and because of the narrowness of interest in which it may be advantageous
for branch plants to support a high Canadian tariff against the United
States or for American interests to prevent measures which may lead
to conservation of resources, as in the British Columbia salmon fishery.

The tariff is a crucial point of conflict because it reflects the interests
of definite industries and is part of a background of traditional policy.
The American tariff is designed to check imports of goods produced
by groups in control of strategic voting power, which because of the
demands of increasing industrialism in the United States are threatened
by competition from imports. The application of the cost of production
principle was particularly adapted to defend this group. Agricultural
products were protected in the United States partly through the
efforts of organized interests and partly as a means of relief to rural
areas and at the expense of urban areas. While these products from
Canada are excluded, the monetary policy of the United States, and
in turn of Canada, prevents their export from Canada to Europe.
Canada can compete with difficulty with the Argentine, Australia, New
Zealand, Holland, and Denmark, and, failing attempts to secure preferences in the markets of Great Britain, as a defence measure is forced
to engage in protection for the dairy industry and to accept low prices
for such exports as wheat. In Canada as in the United States the voting
strength of the agricultural industry, particularly of the highly organized dairy industry, is sufficient to support measures of retaliation in

the form of higher tariffs and preferences to Great Britain. These high tariffs encourage the establishment of American branch factories—for example, automobiles—and increase the costs of Canadian agriculture. Lower prices for agricultural products exported to Europe and higher costs for manufactured goods precipitate the difficulties of Canadian agriculture and the strains of debt which have necessitated the appointment of the Royal Commission on Dominion-Provincial Relations and have led to the outbreak of provincialism.

Monetary policy, as has been suggested, cannot be confined to the United States and is particularly important to Canada. It immediately affects the production of gold and influences the prosperity of the St. Lawrence region, notably Ontario. The sharp difference in its effects on the regions of Canada accentuates the importance of regionalism and the difficulties of federation in Canada.

This paper was labelled "Economic Trends," and it may be expected with the more rapid growth of population in the United States and the continued decline of natural resources that Canada will become increasingly dependent on the United States and that the problem will become more, rather than less acute. All that can be asked is that consideration should be given to the implications of policy on a next-door neighbour. We can hope that closer co-operation between the United States and Great Britain automatically solves numerous problems of disequilibrium in Canada, but we can also hope that some curb may be placed on the influence of powerfully organized groups and that democratic government may function more effectively. There are certain strategic points which can be carefully watched but they are strategic because they are difficult to control.

I can best sum up the argument by an extract from A. A. Milne's *Winnie the Pooh* (pp. 117–18), with which I hope all of you are familiar.

"I think," said Christopher Robin, "that we ought to eat all our Provisions now, so that we shan't have so much to carry."

"Eat all our what?" said Pooh.

"All that we've brought," said Piglet, getting to work.

"That's a good idea," said Pooh, and he got to work too.

"Have you all got something?" asked Christopher Robin, with his mouth full.

"All except me," said Eeyore. "As usual." He looked round at them in his melancholy way. "I suppose none of you are sitting on a thistle by any chance?"

"I believe I am," said Pooh. "Ow!" He got up, and looked behind him. "Yes, I was. I thought so."

"Thank you, Pooh. If you've quite finished with it." He moved across to Pooh's place, and began to eat.

"It don't do them any Good, you know, sitting on them," he went on, as he looked up munching. "Takes all the Life out of them. Remember that another time, all of you. A little Consideration, a little Thought for Others, makes all the difference."

The Lumber Trade in Canada*

L UMBER followed fur as a staple for export from the interior of
the North American continent to Europe. It was adapted like fur
to the cheap water transportation of the St. Lawrence but was in
striking contrast in weight, bulk, and value. The fur trade extended
with comparative ease across heights of land from the St. Lawrence
to Hudson Bay and the Mackenzie River and Pacific coast drainage
basins, whereas the timber was restricted to areas with accessible
resources through ease of navigation down the St. Lawrence tributaries
and the St. Lawrence itself.

As a result of its characteristics the timber trade developed at a
comparatively late stage in Canadian economic history[1] and under
the impetus of substantial preferences,[2] as a vital support to the naval
strength of Great Britain. As a bulky commodity it involved the
return of large numbers of empty ships[3] seeking for cargoes of goods,[4]
or for immigrants. A heavy unbalanced trade was a source of constant
disturbance. Supported by British preferences, however, the timber
trade gained momentum, and its strength was evident in the bitter
struggle against the abolition of preferences and, after their disappear-

*From A. R. M. Lower et al., The North American Assault on the Canadian
Forest (Ryerson, 1938), pp. vii–xvii.

[1] The Hudson's Bay Company attempted but never succeeded in developing the
timber trade. See G. de T. Glazebrook, ed., The Hargrave Correspondence,
1821–1843 (Toronto, 1938). These attempts were made at Timiskaming in 1840-1
(p. 340) and on the Saguenay in 1841-2 (p. 375).

[2] See A. R. M. Lower, article on Lumbering in the Encyclopedia of Canada,
and "The Trade in Square Timber," Contributions to Canadian Economics, VI
(University of Toronto Studies, History and Economics, 1933).

[3] See H. A. Innis, Problems of Staple Production in Canada (Toronto, 1933),
pp. 6–7, and The Fur Trade in Canada (New Haven, 1930), pp. 397–401; also
"Unused Capacity as a Factor in Canadian Economic History," Canadian Journal
of Economics and Political Science, II (Feb. 1936). [See this volume, p. 141.]

[4] Salt was an important element in the return cargo to New Brunswick and to
Canada. The timber trade of New Brunswick gave Saint John a cheap supply of
salt and led Nova Scotia to bonus salt imports to prevent fishermen leaving for
New Brunswick. The Goderich salt industry complained of markets flooded by
salt brought out in ballast in timber ships. H. A. Innis and A. R. M. Lower, eds.
Select Documents in Canadian Economic History, 1783–1885 (Toronto, 1933),
p. 574. Timber ships released during the closed season of the St. Lawrence took
cotton from the southern states.

ance, in the welcome which was given to the Reciprocity Treaty. The marked increase in immigration and settlement involved repercussions such as appeared in the crisis of 1837, smuggling, the movement of population to the United States,[5] the increased construction of canals and railways, and Confederation.

On the Atlantic coast expansion of trade in the United States and, in turn, of industry and the growth of metropolitan centres created demands for lumber which rapidly exhausted the relatively limited resources of the small drainage basins. These demands then began to reach across the low height of land to the timber resources of drainage-basin areas of tributaries of the St. Lawrence, by the construction of canals and later of railways. They fluctuated with the varying demands for lumber by the building industry, and its sensitiveness to the business cycle.[6] Professor Lower has traced the development of American trade in the boom of the late forties. The channels of trade were more sharply cut with improved canals and railways, and the activity built up under the British preferences burst into the United States. The disappearance of preferential duties released all British restrictions on the flow to the southward, while the bonding legislation and the Reciprocity Treaty opened the gates still more widely. The proximity of the American market and the costs of transportation by canal and railway led to the movement of the manufacturing plant toward the source of raw material. The value of the product was increased by the sawmill. Whereas Canada exported square timber to Great Britain, she exported lumber to the United States. The demands of the United States reached the stage in which raw materials were diverted from Europe. White pine as an easily workable construction material responded first to the demands of metropolitan expansion.

Lumber occupied a frontier position in Canadian-American relations. The influence of the United States tended to increase directly with the increasing distance to the interior; but even in areas dominated by the English market where the huge trees suited to square timber were cut off for overseas shipment, the smaller trees suited to the production of saw logs were available for the manufacture of lumber for the American trade. With the opening of the Middle West, Chicago began to draw on the drainage basins facing the upper lakes. Railways cutting across the Ontario peninsula tapped the drainage basins flowing into Lake Huron and pulled timber to Great Britain

[5]R. S. Longley, "Emigration and the Crisis of 1837 in Upper Canada," *Canadian Historical Review*, XVII (March 1936), 29–40.
[6]See W. C. Mitchell, *Business Cycles* (Berkeley, 1913), pp. 104–9.

and lumber to New York. Steam power, along with the sawmill and the railway, mitigated the influence of the down-stream pull of the drainage basin. The site was dependent on access to large quantities of logs such as was provided by the smaller lakes and tributary drainage basins. Small mills were built along the railway and provided both a market for logs sold by farmers and settlers and a source of profit for the local sawmill owner, who was often charged with making his money from the "end of a rule." The pace of development in regions dependent on the railway and steam power made itself evident in sudden spurts of activity, but kept increasing as time went on, and as technological advances increased the capacity of mills.

The expansion of the lumber trade to the United States was hastened by the effects of the disappearance of the British preferences and the Reciprocity Treaty of 1854, and by the shift from wind, wood, and water transportation to steam and iron. The economy built up on the St. Lawrence by sailing vessels, timber, and European markets was exposed to severe strains upon the introduction of the steamship, canals, and railways.[7] Emigrants deserted the sailing vessel for the steamship.[8] Exports of dairy products and wheat began to displace timber. Lumber shifted from an export to the increasingly mature metropolitan area of Great Britain to one to the less mature and rapidly expanding metropolitan areas of the United States. An economy built up to meet the demands of Great Britain now supported the expansion of the United States. Whereas the dairy[9] and the live-stock industries migrated from the United States to further an expanding trade to Great Britain, the lumber industry shifted its support of Great Britain to that of the United States.

The long depression from the seventies to the nineties coincided in Canada with the difficulties which followed the shift to railways and steamships on the St. Lawrence. The lumber trade to the United States exposed the economy to the effects of the marked fluctuations incidental to the cyclical disturbances of American business, but it was released from dependence on the long-term credit arrangements involved in trade with Great Britain.[10] Many Canadians migrated to the United States; and, later, others moved to western Canada. In 1880 the exodus from the Ottawa district to Manitoba was "very great owing to the great commercial depression."[11] The boom of the early eighties

[7]See *Problems of Staple Production*, pp. 17–23.
[8]See *Select Documents, 1783–1885*, pp. 536–8.
[9]See J. A. Ruddick *et al.*, *The Dairy Industry in Canada*, ed. H. A. Innis (Toronto, 1937), pp. 4–5. [See this volume, p. 211.]
[10]See *Select Documents, 1783–1885*, pp. 508–9.   [11]*Ibid.*, p. 741.

in Manitoba had its roots in the depression of the seventies in Ontario. The timber trade to Great Britain in the first half of the century was marked by immigration into Canada, and the lumber trade to the United States in the second half of the century was accompanied by emigration. Population and forest products were drawn into the expansion of the United States which followed the Civil War, and which was marked by an enormous increase in railway mileage. Industrialism in England, with its demands for lumber, involved displacement of labour and emigration, while in the United States it involved the opening of a continent and a demand for labour. The occupation of the Middle West and the long determined efforts of Canada to restore the St. Lawrence by deepening canals and constructing a continental railway were followed by the pouring of population into western Canada after the turn of the century. There was an expansion of the domestic market for lumber in eastern Canada, and in western Canada from British Columbia.

On the Pacific coast lumbering had developed in response to the demands arising from the gold rush in the late fifties. Buildings, ship supplies, and shipping brought domestic and export demands. Ships bringing in population found lumber as a return product.[12] On the St. Lawrence the timber trade brought immigration and in British Columbia immigration brought the lumber trade. The construction of the Canadian Pacific Railway opened a market in the interior; and the boom which followed the Klondike gold rush, the opening of the Kootenay, and the development of an extensive market on the prairies hastened the construction of sawmills in the interior of British Columbia and on the coast. A decline in the rate of settlement on the prairies and a decline in the demand for lumber led to the search for markets. The needed shipping had been released by the ending of the war. Freight costs were low. The Panama Canal was now open. The desired markets were accessible in both the Atlantic and the Pacific. And Canada's Pacific coast lumber shifted from support of wheat production for Great Britain to support of industrialism in Japan.[13]

The size of the trees and year-round operations in British Columbia involve heavy and extensive logging equipment and large sawmills. Logging companies emerge as separate entities from companies concerned with milling. Cedar and western hemlock grow together in "mixed stands." They are logged with Douglas fir and sold to shingle and pulp and paper mills. The consequent relatively inelastic supply

[12]See ibid., pp. 797–9.
[13]H. A. Innis, "Forest Industries in Canada," Pacific Affairs, Sept. 1929.

of cedar and western hemlock tends to accentuate variations in the price of shingles, and of pulp and paper as by-products of lumber. As a result of competition from British Columbia lumber, with its extensive fixed capital and enormous resources as contrasted with eastern Canada, lumber mills tributary to the Atlantic were compelled to restrict operations. The decline of white pine and the importance of spruce facilitated the sale of limits to pulp and paper companies, made easier the shift of lumber companies to pulp and paper operations, and increased the difficulties of the pulp and paper industry. The eastern provinces competed for the establishment of pulp and paper plants. Lumber plants were closed down, or were extended by the use of large quantities of small logs in the production of a wide range of materials and in drying plants which reduced the weight and widened the market accessible by rail. The United States market for pulp and paper increased as the British market for eastern lumber declined. The heavy bulky character of the commodity continued to mean unused capacity on an important scale in incoming ships, and supported extensive imports to British Columbia in spite of the substantial protective tariff.[14]

The dominance of the St. Lawrence in the economic development of the forest first through the fur and then through the timber trade in relation to Europe and the lumber industry in relation to the United States involved contrasts and comparisons described by Professor Lower. Because of the vast areas drained by the St. Lawrence, the fur trade, the fishing industry, and the timber trade of New France came directly under the control of the Crown. Great Britain as a conqueror adopted, extended, and modified the policy of France. After the American Revolution the areas in British North America were divided politically, the timber trade was encouraged, immigration was stimulated for the purposes of defence, and, with the achievements of responsible government, the resources of Canada came under the control of each colonial or provincial political unit. "At Confederation it was decided to make of the natural resources the corner stone of provincial finance. . . . Self-government and with it certain rights and assets including the public lands had been conceded to each of the provinces by the Imperial Government."[15]

[14]See *Report on the Influence of the Panama Canal on Trade with Western Canada* (June 1930), and "Canada and the Panama Canal," *The Canadian Economy and Its Problems*, ed. H. A. Innis and A. F. W. Plumptre (Toronto, 1934), Appendix V.

[15]*Report of the Royal Commission on the Transfer of the Natural Resources of Manitoba* (Ottawa, 1929).

The significance of the fur trade in emphasizing the waterways as a boundary between British North America and the United States involved continuous adjustment in the history of the lumber industry. The shift of exports of lumber to the United States and the ease with which it took advantage of boundaries which were largely rivers and the slight difference in bulk through manufacture brought tariffs from the United States which favoured the export of logs from Canada rather than lumber, tariffs that were met by export taxes and embargoes on Canadian logs to compel American mills to migrate to the Dominion. The control of resources by the provinces after Confederation, strengthened by Privy Council decisions, limited the value of export taxes under federal direction, and the result was that in 1898, following the Dingley tariff, Ontario imposed embargoes on saw logs cut on Crown lands. This expedient was developed by the other provinces and became a flexible instrument, particularly in the pulp and paper industry. It reflected the widely varying character of the demands of the lumber industry in separate regions and the influence of that industry on the development of independent powers of the provinces.

Control over natural resources by the provinces chiefly concerned with the lumber industry, that is, New Brunswick, Quebec, Ontario, and British Columbia, involved not only the development of special instruments for the control of trade, but also the elaboration of regulations for the exploitation of forests. Revenues were collected by the provinces from those engaged in carrying on the lumber industry. The strength of private firms, particularly firms accustomed to American methods of alienation of forest land,[16] which were engaged in lumbering operations on land owned by the Crown, and the difficulties of developing effective regulations facilitated charges of corruption. The dominance of water navigation, the tendency toward centralized control in the industry, and the weakness of agriculture when so dominated by lumbering,[17] meant a type of feudalistic structure and

[16]See B. H. Hibbard, A History of the Public Land Policies (New York, 1924); Edna Ferber, Come and Get It (New York, 1935).
[17]See A. R. M. Lower, Settlement and the Forest Frontier in Eastern Canada (Toronto, 1936); also J. F. W. Johnston, Report on the Agricultural Capabilities of the Province of New Brunswick (Fredericton, 1850). The trade involved numerous handicaps to agriculture. "So many being employed in this trade, no doubt impedes the progress of agriculture and yet there are a good many settlers but they are poor and miserable—and they are kept in continual bodily fear from those villanous raftmen or shantymen who on their way to and from Quebec commit every species of cruelty and injustice on the peacable settler. The poor farmer thinks himself happy if he can escape the depredations of these un-

corrupt governments.[18] In Nova Scotia with its many short rivers, its early settlement from New England, and the importance of its fishing industry, lumber seemed less important and the forest areas were alienated from the Crown. In New Brunswick, Quebec, Ontario, and British Columbia, the importance of holdings under the Crown has necessitated the development of more efficient policies of regulation, whereas in Nova Scotia large private companies have limited the effectiveness of government policy. As Dr. Saunders has shown, lack of control raises problems of conservation policy in terms of resources and labour.

With the decline in resources of the United States, increasing urbanization, and the demands accompanying the upward swing of the business cycle the conservation movement became important[19] and attempts were made to lower the tariff on lumber. In 1909 the duty on sawed lumber was reduced from $2 per thousand feet under the Dingley tariff to $1.25, and in 1913 it was admitted free. With the beginning of the depression a duty of $1 was imposed in 1930, and it quadrupled from 1932 to 1935. Imposition of a tariff on lumber tended to accentuate the importance of imports of paper which had been admitted duty free since the Reciprocity Treaty in 1911. As a result of the tariff Canada was compelled to find an export market for lumber

principled lords at the expense perhaps of his only hen or goose or perhaps one of his two sheep. . . . Lumbermen are a mixture of Irish, Scots, English, in short you will find among them from every part of Europe, the very dregs of those respective countries, and the most depraved and dissipated set of villains on earth. For my own part the Ottawa would be the last place in America I would choose for a future residence, the Red River is a paradise compared to this river. Remember that I speak of the Ottawa from Hull upwards." Letter from Cuthbert Cumming to James Hargrave, Chats, April 20, 1829, *Hargrave Correspondence, 1821–1843*, p. 33. See Ralph Connor, *The Man from Glengarry* (Toronto, 1901). With the growth of industrialism, "there is on frontier works a fixed rotation. It proceeds from the lumber camps outward to the railway work and thence to the mines and mills of the industrial centres." E. W. Bradwin, *The Bunkhouse Man* (New York, 1928), pp. 184ff. The effect of the industry on labour has been evident not only in its direct relation with agriculture but also in a wide variety of ways. Migration following the lumber industry has been described by Professor Lower and is reflected in the mythology which has grown up about Paul Bunyan and the Blue Ox. James Stevens, *Paul Bunyan* (Garden City, 1935). Robert Dollar began in the lumber industry on the Ottawa and moved to Muskoka, Georgian Bay, Michigan, and California, where he became engaged in shipping. *Memoirs of Robert Dollar* (San Francisco, 1927), pp. 1–30. In British Columbia the shift from handlogging to machine operations displaced an individualistic type of labour. M. A. Grainger, *Woodsmen of the West* (London, 1908).

[18]See G. S. Thompson, *Up to Date or the Life of a Lumberman*, pp. 44 ff.

[19]See *Report of the National Conservation Commission* (Washington, 1909); also C. R. Van Hise, *The Conservation of Natural Resources in the United States* (New York, 1910), Introduction and part III.

in countries other than the United States. Embargoes and export taxes imposed by the provinces became largely ineffective with the attempt of other countries to develop their own sawmill industries through tariffs favouring imports of logs and the inability of the chief exporting provinces to resist during the depression. Federal policy has consequently become more important in the lumber industry. At the Ottawa Conference in 1932, Canadian lumber was given an advantage of 10 per cent on the delivered price. The imperial preference was revived on this occasion at the instance of Canada rather than Great Britain. As embargoes and export taxes, imposed by the provinces, were effective against import duties in compelling the migration of industry to Canada so imperial preferences were effective against import duties in securing a preferred position in important Empire markets such as Australia and Great Britain. Again the bulky cheap character of the commodity increased the effectiveness of governmental policy in tilting the preference for lumber to British Columbia from the adjacent areas of Washington and Oregon. The character of the commodity accentuated its sensitiveness not only to direct regulations in the form of duties and preferences, but also to broad government policies. Monetary policy in England furthered a boom in housing and a marked expansion in the demand for lumber. In turn it contributed to the prosperity of Australia. Recovery measures in the United States are responsible for an increase in the domestic market for building materials, but an advance in prices as a result of administrative control or of monetary policy weakened the position of American lumber on the export markets in competition with British Columbia. The lumber industry of British Columbia gained because of the disparity between British and American policies. The Reciprocity Treaty of 1935 and the proposed Anglo-American treaty were designed to deepen the channels of trade between Great Britain and Canada and the United States. By the encouraging of Canadian lumber imports, American prices were brought more quickly into line and the possibilities of building increased.[20]

[20]The National Lumber Manufacturers Association criticized the terms of the agreement as "harsh" but argued that in so far as it involved a restoration of world trade, it contributed to the possibilities of a restoration of an export trade in lumber. Oregon, on the other hand, complained of Canadian competition. *Extending Reciprocal Foreign Trade Agreement Act* (Washington, 1937), pp. 354–6.
"Their cheaper timber, lower timber taxes, privilege of employing a considerable percentage of low-waged Orientals, their longer working hours, and their big advantage in water transportation costs give them an edge which no American manufacturer can hope to overcome and pay his employees wages which will permit of their living up to the American standard.

The timber and lumber trade has reflected vast dynamic changes in the movement of population, and the spread of industrialism. In Canada it responded to the demands of British urbanization in the first half of the nineteenth century, of the United States in the second half, and the demands of the domestic market and the countries of the Pacific in the twentieth century. It provided the scaffolding of industrialism and has been gradually replaced by the more durable materials such as minerals. Industrialism has been poured into moulds of wood.[21] The timber and lumber trade followed the demands of industrialism based on coal in Great Britain and the United States in the nineteenth century and on coal and the new sources of power in the Atlantic and Pacific basins in the twentieth. Because of lumber's bulk and cheapness, its markets were profoundly affected by major improvements in navigation such as followed the opening of the Panama Canal. With its exhaustion the political framework built up during exploitation has remained as a mould for later developments. It has left stranded lumber mills, ghost towns, rural slums, and weak railroads. The pouring in of goods, characteristic of successive waves

---

"British Columbia mill operators run their plants 48 hours a week and thousands of their employees receive a wage which gives them a weekly pay check no greater than that paid by mills in Oregon and Washington for a 40-hour week, this alone resulting in a tremendous saving in the labor cost per thousand feet on the lumber produced.

"American mills shipping lumber from one American port to another are compelled by law to use nothing but American vessels, but the British Columbia mills have the privilege of transporting their lumber to our Californian and Atlantic coast markets in cheap tramp steamers of any flag, with the result that they have in their transportation costs an advantage in the delivered prices ranging as high as $3 per thousand feet, this alone placing them in a position to dominate our markets at will." *Ibid.*, pp. 549–50.

"In 1929 over 78 per cent of our export sales went to the British Empire. The first six months of this year our sales to the same markets were only a little over 8 per cent. . . . In 1929 the British Columbia mills shipped 41,000,000 feet to Australia. That same year the mills in Oregon and Washington sold 224,000,000 feet to Australia. As a direct result of the preferential tariffs built up against the mills in the United States at the request of the lumber industry in Canada, in 1935, the British Columbia mills sold 129,000,000 feet to Australia and the mills in Oregon and Washington saw their sales to this territory drop to the puny footage of 23,000,000 feet, a complete reversal which meant their elimination. In our trade with England the situation is even worse. In 1929 the British Columbia mills shipped to England a trifle less than 70,000,000 feet and the mills in Oregon and Washington sold 248,000,000 feet. In 1935, as a direct result of the Ottawa preferential agreement which gave the Canadian mills a 10 per cent advantage on the delivered price, the British Columbia mills sold 455,-000,000 feet to the United Kingdom and the mills in Oregon and Washington sold only 31,000,000 feet which was practically nothing." *Ibid.*, p. 553.

[21]See *Select Documents in Canadian Economic History, 1783–1885*, pp. 653–4.

of activity in the exploitation of the forest, has, again, been followed by exhaustion[22] and by the decline in imports which necessitates governmental intervention in conservation measures, concessions to pulp and paper mills, and encouragement to possible developmental projects. In Canada this heavy, bulky character of lumber stressed regionalism and emphasized the power of the provinces in the federal structure. The provinces which had been chiefly concerned with lumbering, and later with pulp and paper, defended their own interests and compelled the provinces dependent on wheat to rely on federal support. The control over natural resources which emerged from dependence on the lumber industry was supported by hydro-electric power and railroads. The problem of Canadian federalism is linked to the disparity between economies stamped with the influence of the lumber industries and economies dependent on wheat, and the provincialism of the one has accentuated the federalism of the other.

The story of the lumber trade lies on the borderline of history and economics. We have referred to some of its economic implications in this brief outline but the study is also one that is not lacking in the elements of drama. The forest wilderness that confronted the settler and furnished him not only with shelter and heat, but furniture and the possibilities of comfort, proved to be the source of profit in the world's markets as well. The interplay between the markets of England and the United States still continues although under changed conditions, and the most recent chapter of Canadian-American tariff history contains the epilogue to this long story.

[22]See C. M. Davis, "The Cities and Towns of the High Plains of Michigan," *Geographical Review*, XXVIII (1938), 664–73; also H. A. Innis, "The Economics of Conservation," *Geographical Review*, XXVIII (1938), 137–9.

The Penetrative Powers of the Price System*

ECONOMICS is an older subject than statistics, but this paper is confined to the period since statistics began to leave its impression on economics and reached that stage, fatal to economics, when it came of age. Professor G. N. Clark in *Science and Social Welfare in the Age of Newton* (Oxford, 1937) has traced the background of statistics, in the growing importance of mathematics through astronomy, surveying, and book-keeping which followed the discovery of the New World, prior to its beginnings with the publication of John Gaunt's *Observations upon the Bills of Mortality* in 1662, or four years before the census of Talon in Canada. An important statistical department was set up in England under an inspector-general to collect statistics on imports and exports about 1695. The effects of the imports of treasure from North America were becoming increasingly evident and William Fleetwood, with a strong vested interest in stability in the value of fellowships, published his *Chronicon Preciosum* in 1706. And so the snake entered the paradise of academic interest in economics. Under the stimulus of treasure from the New World the price system ate its way more rapidly into the economy of Europe and into economic thought.

"A project of commerce to the East Indies, therefore, gave occasion to the first discovery of the West."[1] The rise in prices in the late sixteenth and early seventeenth centuries stimulated the flow of trade from Europe to the New World, and to the Old World from the West Indies to the East Indies.[2] With the beginning of the seventeenth century, the formation of the East India Company was accompanied by the settlement of Virginia. Dried fish from Newfoundland provided food for the fishing industry and for shipping. It was carried to Spain

*From *Canadian Journal of Economics and Political Science*, IV (1938), 299–319; reprinted in *Political Economy in the Modern State* (Ryerson, 1946), pp. 145–67.
[1]Adam Smith, *Wealth of Nations* (Modern Library ed., New York, 1937), p. 531.
[2]See E. J. Hamilton, *American Treasure and the Price Revolution in Spain* (Cambridge, Mass., 1934); Adam Smith, *Wealth of Nations*, p. 202. Bodin wrote the *Discours sur les causes de l'extrême cherté qui est aujourd'huy en France* in 1574.

and exchanged for treasure, and used as food for ships going south of the line to the East Indies to exchange treasure for spices, calicoes, raw silk, and other East Indies goods. Exports of treasure from England evoked the protests of mercantilists and precipitated the discussion which became the basis of the interest shown by English economists in problems of foreign trade. It would be interesting to speculate on the history of economic thought if England had been an important producer of precious metals and not an importer and an exporter, and if large joint stock companies had not existed to be defended and to support arguments and publication. The defence of the East India Company by Thomas Mun in his pamphlet in 1621 was accompanied by the battle between divergent views of Misselden and Malynes. The rise in prices stimulated the trade described by Adam Smith: "The silver of the new continent seems in this manner to be one of the principal commodities by which the commerce between the two extremities of the old one is carried on, and it is by means of it, in a great measure, that those distant parts of the world are connected with one another."[3] Under its drive, the commercial system of England expanded in the New World and in the Old. With limited shipping facilities, the production and trade of light valuable commodities from the New World became evident in tobacco from Virginia and sugar from the West Indies. Manufactured products were sent to Africa for slaves and gold to be carried to sugar and tobacco plantations. New England was fostered by Virginia for the production of fish for exchange of specie in Spain rather than of tobacco. She expanded to produce not only fish for Europe, but also lumber, fish, and agricultural products and ships to carry these cheap bulky commodities for short distances to the English plantation colonies of the New World. I hope the historians will concede a claim to the effects of rising prices not only in the expansion of settlement in the New World but also in the Puritan Revolution, the passing of the Navigation Acts, the establishment of the colonial system, and the defeat of a powerful commercial rival in the Dutch.

While Adam Smith attacked the system which emerged, he was aware of its advantages in defence. He saw it as part of the spread of the price system which had swept aside the feudal system, and led to the discovery of the New World, and with his support, to the wiping

[3]Smith, *Wealth of Nations*, p. 207. "Of all the commodities, therefore, which are bought in one foreign country, for no other purpose but to be sold or exchanged again for some other goods in another, there are none so convenient as gold and silver" (*ibid.*, p. 516).

out of the inequities of the colonial system itself. "But what all the violence of feudal institutions could never have effected, the silent and insensible operation of foreign commerce and manufactures gradually brought about."[4]

A revolution of the greatest importance to public happiness was in this manner brought about by two different orders of people, who had not the least intention to serve the public. To gratify the most childish vanity was the sole motive of the great proprietors. The merchants and artificers, much less ridiculous acted merely from a view to their own interest, and in pursuit of their own pedlar principles of turning a penny wherever a penny was to be got. Neither of them had either knowledge or foresight of that great revolution which the folly of the one, and the industry of the other, was gradually bringing about. It is thus that through the greater part of Europe the commerce and manufacture of cities, instead of being the effect, have been the cause and occasion of the improvement and cultivation of the country.[5]

His predecessor, Richardson, wrote in 1750 that "the giving trade the utmost freedoms and encouragements is the greatest and most solid improvement of the value of lands."[6]

The character of trade which emerged in relation to the growth of cities in Europe was described by Nicholas Barbon in *A Discourse of Trade* (London, 1690), who wrote:

The chief causes that promote *trade*, (not to mention good government, peace and scituation, with other advantages) are industry in the poor, and liberality in the rich.

Those expences that most promote trade, are in cloaths and lodging: in adorning the body and the house, there are a thousand traders imploy'd in cloathing and decking the body, and building and furnishing of houses, for one that is imploy'd in providing food. . . . Fashion or the alteration of dress is a great promoter of *trade*, because it occasions the expense of cloaths, before the old ones are worn out: It is the spirit and life of *trade*. . . . The next expence that chiefly promotes *trade*, is building . . . it imploys a greater number of trades and people, than feeding or cloathing.

Beside, there is another great advantage to *trade*, by enlarging of cities; the two beneficial expences of cloathing and lodging, are increased; Man being naturally ambitious, the living together, occasions emulation, which is seen by outvying one another in apparel, equipage, and furniture of the house; whereas, if a man lived solitary alone, his chiefest expence would be food. (pp. 31–4)

---

[4]*Ibid.*, p. 388. For an excellent account of the decline of the feudal system in Japan as a result of the introduction of money see M. Takizawa, *The Penetration of Money Economy in Japan and its Effects upon Social and Political Institutions* (New York, 1927).   [5]Smith, *Wealth of Nations*, pp. 391–2.
[6]W. Richardson, *An Essay on the Causes of the Decline of Foreign Trade* (London, 1750).

External trade was an extension of internal trade. Commodities carried long distances under primitive conditions of navigation were necessarily light in bulk, high in value, and suited to the demands of the luxury class in metropolitan areas. Consumption goods, especially those involving the introduction of habits, created a steady demand. Tobacco consumption spread rapidly after the seventeenth century. Sugar was imported in increasing quantities to sweeten the tea and chocolate brought from the East especially in the latter half of the seventeenth century. Furs met the demands of fashion in clothing, and in the case of durable commodities, such as beaver hats, were passed down through various strata of society. The demands of the upper classes, encouraged by imports of specie and increasing fluidity of resources, stimulated production of luxury goods, expansion of trade, and the penetration of luxuries to lower classes.

The characteristics of production, distribution, and consumption of these commodities imposed strains on any colonial system aiming at comprehensiveness and the interests of the mother country. In the fur trade France sent vessels of goods to be traded with the hunting Indians of the Precambrian formation north of the St. Lawrence, and its development involved continued penetration to the interior. Settlement and agriculture were restricted and exposed to the fluctuations in the price of a commodity determined by fashion and by uncertain supplies from the Indians. The agricultural base in the St. Lawrence was consequently not adequate to the establishment of a sedentary fishery in the Maritimes and neither could be linked to the demands of the French sugar plantations of the West Indies. In the English colonial system the demands of the plantation commodities, such as sugar and tobacco, differed from those produced in the commercial colonies, such as fish and lumber for the West Indies, and those produced in Newfoundland, namely fish chiefly for European consumption. The plantations required slaves, foodstuffs to supply the slaves, lumber for buildings, and live-stock to operate the mills.[7] These cheap bulky secondary commodities supplied by New England and other colonies were extremely sensitive to regulations which affected prices of luxury goods. The colonial system encouraged the plantations through monopolies of the English market and the fisheries and agriculture as a base of supply for the plantations. "To increase the shipping and naval power of Great Britain, by the extension of the fisheries of our colonies, is an object which the legislature seems to have had almost constantly in view. Those fisheries, upon this account, have had all the

[7] C. R. Fay, "Plantation Economy," *Economic Journal*, Dec. 1936.

encouragement which freedom can give them, and they have flourished accordingly. The New England fishery in particular was, before the late disturbances, one of the most important, perhaps, in the world."[8] With the expansion of the fishery, shipping increased, larger quantities of goods were available, and protests were more vigorous against restrictions imposed at the instigation of the plantations in the interests of cheaper supplies and provisions. The colonial system had inherent contradictions stimulating production by a policy of freedom in colonies producing secondary commodities and restricting the market for those commodities by a policy of preferences for colonies producing staple commodities. New England shipping encroached consequently on the French Empire and capitalized its limitations by profitable smuggling. It supported expansion of trade from secondary bulky commodities into the luxury commodities of the New World, through the manufacture of molasses, a by-product of sugar, into rum and its exchange for furs, slaves, and fish. The difficulties of European commercial systems in North America were evident in the retreat of the French and finally in the withdrawal of the English to the St. Lawrence. The effectiveness of the commercial development of New England with the advantages of freedom of trade supported by the fishery and shipping, broke down the colonial system of France and in turn of England. Shipping implied commercial strength, naval power, and defeat of European control.

The decline of the British commercial system proceeded rapidly after the American Revolution and the publication of the *Wealth of Nations*. After the War of 1812, the Colonial Trade Acts of the twenties, and admission of the United States to the British West Indies in 1830, became landmarks in the steady trend toward free trade. The attacks of Adam Smith and the group of government interventionists, who were his disciples and followers, on the vested interests of the merchant class bore fruit in clearing away the shackles of the colonial system. Decker had written in 1744, "Restraint is always harmful to trade." "Nothing but freedom can secure trade."[9] Adam Smith declared that "Of the greater part of the regulations concerning the colony trade, the merchants who carry it on, it must be observed, have been the principal advisers. We must not wonder, therefore, if, in the greater part of them, their interest has been more considered than either that of the colonies or that of the mother country."[10] "The

---

[8]*Wealth of Nations*, pp. 544–5.
[9]Sir Mathew Decker, *An Essay on the Causes of the Decline of Foreign Trade* (Dublin, 1749).   [10]*Wealth of Nations*, p. 550.

sneaking arts of underling tradesmen are thus erected into political maxims for the conduct of a great empire; for it is the most underling tradesmen only who make it a rule to employ chiefly their own customers."[11] The slave trade was finally abolished in the West Indies, the Reform Bills destroyed the power of vested interests in Parliament, the timber preferences were reduced, the Corn Laws repealed, the Navigation Acts abrogated, and responsible government established in the colonies. The free trade system in North America was extended by the Reciprocity Treaty with the United States. The abolition of slavery in the Civil War was an important landmark in the transition from status to contract. The disappearance of the East India Company was followed by the purchase of Rupert's Land from the Hudson's Bay Company. The price system had gradually but persistently eaten out the rotting timbers of European colonial structures and as it destroyed the feudalism so it destroyed the defences of commercialism.

Commercialism left a powerful stamp on the history of the East and West. Great Britain emerged as a dominant metropolitan unit. The Americas became politically independent but continued to carry the culture of people from Spain, Portugal, France, and England. In Canada a large French population had grown up on the lower St. Lawrence in response to the demands of the fur trade. Across the northern half of the continent the aborigines had felt the powerful influence of the commercial pull. Sir George Simpson wrote, "Connubial alliances are the best security we can have of the good will of the natives," and half-breeds are evidence of the policy. Religious practices detrimental to the trade were replaced by Christianity. Of one tribe Simpson wrote: "They have made a poor hunt in consequences of the death of a relation and in the agony of grief according to ancient usage rent their garments so that they are now destitute of every necessary." Again he wrote:

There may be a difference of opinion as to the effect the conversion of the Indians might have on the trade; I cannot however forsee that it could be at all injurious, on the contrary I believe it would be highly beneficial thereto as they would in time imbibe our manners and customs and imitate us in Dress; our Supplies would thus become necessary to them which would increase the consumption of European produce & manufactures and in like measure increase & benefit our trade as they would find it requisite to become more industrious and to turn their attention more seriously to the Chase in order to enable to provide themselves with such supplies; we should moreover be enabled to pass through their Lands in greater safety which would lighten the expence of transport, and supplies of Provisions

---

[11]*Ibid.*, p. 460.

would be found at every Village, and among every tribe; they might likewise be employed on extraordinary occasions as runners, Boatsmen, etc., and their Services in other respects turned to profitable account.

The Honble Committee I am satisfied will take this view of the subject and there are a few of the most enlightened in this Country who would do so likewise but there are others (and I am almost ashamed to say Members of our Council) who would condemn it as being wild & visionary and ruinous to the Fur Trade without even taking the trouble of thinking seriously thereon or looking at the question in all its bearings and important consequences.[12]

Duncan McGillivray wrote: "For the prairie Indians the love of rum is their first inducement to industry; they undergo every hardship and fatigue to procure a skinful of this delicious beverage, and when a nation becomes addicted to drinking, it affords a strong presumption that they will soon become excellent hunters."[13] With monopoly control Simpson reduced imports of spirits to a minimum. The fur trade left a framework for the later Dominion. The timber trade, based on preferences and the specific gravity of white pine, hastened English settlement in Upper Canada. The fishing industry left a region divided between four national interests, France, Newfoundland, Canada, and the United States. These divisions in northern North America illustrate the general divergent effects of commercialism.

Into the moulds of the commercial period, set by successive heavier and cheaper commodities, and determined by geographic factors, such as the St. Lawrence River and the Precambrian formation; by cultural considerations, such as the English and French languages; by technology, such as the canoe and the raft; by business organization, such as the Northwest Company and Liverpool timber firms; and by political institutions peculiar to France and England, were poured the rivers of iron and steel in the form of steamships and railways which hardened into modern capitalism. Improved transportation, increasing specialization in Great Britain, the spread of machine industry in relation to coal and iron, and migration of population to urban centres involved imports, of wheat, live-stock, and dairy products from North America for foodstuffs, cotton from the United States and wool from Australia for clothing, timber from Canada and New Brunswick for housing, and raw materials for manufacturing, and exports of manufactured products. Steamships and railways lowered costs of transportation and hastened the shift to bulky imports of low value, and perishable commodities from more adjacent regions. The discovery of gold in the Pacific basin, in California and British Co-

[12]Frederick Merk, *Fur Trade and Empire* (Cambridge, Mass., 1931), p. 108.
[13]A. S. Morton, *The Journal of Duncan McGillivray* (Toronto, 1929), p. 47.

lumbia, and in Australia and New Zealand, was followed by immediate migration of population, exports of gold and, later, of bulky commodities, and rapid extension of transportation facilities. The Suez Canal and the Union Pacific Railway were opened in 1869, the Canadian Pacific Railway in 1885, and the routes from Great Britain via the East and the West to the Pacific drastically shortened in space and time.

The rise of industrialism in the first half of the nineteenth century was hastened by the demands of the Napoleonic Wars[14] for iron and steel and by the increasing effectiveness of the price system. It was the reverse side of the decline of the commercial system. The emergence of free trade by the middle of the century reflected and enhanced the efficiency of the price system and the growth of industrialism. The ebb of commercialism was the flow of industrialism. The establishment of responsible government in Canada marked the collapse of the colonial system and the beginnings of capitalistic development. Government was unified in the Act of Union and broadened in Confederation. The divisive trends of the United States disappeared with the success of the North in the Civil War.

Again war was followed by rapid expansion of the iron and steel industry, rapid construction of railways, and improvement of steamships. What Geddes has called palæotechnic society,[15] emerged in full bloom with its coal mines, industrialism, and urbanization. Credit facilities were improved with additional supplies of gold, completion of the Atlantic cable, development of financial structures, especially during the Civil War and after the improvement of political structures, and the improvement of the exchanges for handling commodities and securities.[16] Legislation improved the position and effectiveness of corporations, and new developments for the amassing of large quantities of capital and capital equipment, such as the trust and the holding company, were introduced. Institutions for the collection and direction of funds, such as banks, bond houses, and insurance companies, became more effective. Inefficiency was weeded out through ruthless competition, the long depression, and improved bankruptcy legislation. Marked increase in production and lowering of costs of transportation contributed to falling prices.[17] With the advantages of industrial leadership and lowering of the costs of raw material in

[14]T. S. Ashton, *Iron and Steel in the Industrial Revolution* (London, 1924).
[15]See L. Mumford, *Technics and Civilization* (New York, 1934). Also E. F. Heckscher, "Recent Tendencies in Economic Life," *The World's Economic Future* (London, 1938), pp. 97–110.
[16]H. M. Larson, *Jay Cooke, Private Banker* (Cambridge, Mass., 1936).
[17]"Memorandum to Royal Commission on the Depression of Trade and Industry," *Official Papers of Alfred Marshall* (London, 1926), pp. 4–5.

Great Britain and the influence of mathematics and the natural sciences, the interests in the concern of Marx with the exploitation which accompanied industrial change shifted to that of Jevons, Marshall, Walras, and Pareto in the development of equilibrium analysis. The gold standard operated in the fashion familiar to all students of textbooks of economics, and the prices between countries were automatically adjusted. The price system operated at a high state of efficiency in the occupation of the vacant spaces of the earth. In countries producing cheap and more bulky raw materials, improved transportation was dependent on funds from industrial areas. They were repaid in part in areas dominated by government activity, such as Canada, by revenue from tariffs on manufactured goods from industrial areas or were avoided in part by bankruptcy in areas dominated by private enterprise, such as the United States. Competition of manufactured goods led to the protective tariff and schools of economics which traced their origins to List in Germany, Carey in the United States, and Buchanan in Canada. Canada attempted to secure revenue and to check competition from industrial countries, and to participate in the development of more extensive projects by facilitating credit expansion.

The outbreak of the Great War has been regarded as the signal for the collapse of capitalism. Sombart has traced the history of capitalism to its final stage of *hoch capitalismus*. Geddes would describe it as the rise and decline of the palæotechnic (or coal and iron) society and the beginnings of the neotechnic (or new sources of power and base metals) society. But with the shift from commercialism to capitalism, so with the shift from capitalism to what may be called later phases or whatever the war and post-war period may be designated, the ebb of one was the rise of the other. Where capitalism followed the more rigid channels of surviving commercialism or where it arrived later in a highly centralized state, it was a part of governmental machinery. In Germany,[18] Italy, and Japan and in the British Dominions the state became capital equipment. The twentieth century was Canada's; and Germany wanted a place in the sun. In Canada the federal government supported, and engaged in, railway building on an extensive scale, and the provinces, strengthened in their power by Privy Council decisions, shared in railway construction and engaged in the development of hydro-electric power and in the expansion of mining and the pulp and paper industry. In Great Britain and the United States, on

[18]See T. Veblen, *Imperial Germany and the Industrial Revolution* (New York, 1915).

the other hand, regulatory boards were conspicuous for railways and public utilities, and control was developed to combat trusts and monopolies and to meet the problems of monetary disturbance.

The war brought a marked increase in government activities in all nations.[19] The conduct of military and naval activities over a long period brought encroachment of the state on private organization, especially in the fields of banking and transportation. In Canada the federal government became an owner of railways on a large scale. Most significant developments appeared in the field of finance and in its influence on the price system through the fixing of prices of commodities by governmental bodies set up for war purposes and the floating of loans by governments on an unprecedented scale. The end of the war found the participants with debts of astronomical figures. The Treaty of Versailles riveted a debt structure on the German nation. These debts were followed by a long series of revisions and disturbances, including ruinous inflation in Germany and Austria, the Dawes Plan, the Young Plan, the League of Nations Plan, the collapse of Austria, *de facto* cancellation of debts, depreciation of sterling, the franc, and the dollar, and increasing reliance on nationalistic measures ranging through various stages of totalitarianism.

The war and post-war period to 1929 was marked by a continuation of the prosperity which had its rise in the late nineties of the last century. The state was more effectively utilized as a monetary device,[20] and political disturbances reflected economic disturbances more directly. Capital equipment begun in the war and the pre-war periods was extended and completed. Railways in Canada, the Panama Canal (opened in 1917), and the release of shipping after the war contributed to marked expansion based on accessibility to the Pacific. These extensions of palæotechnic structure were accompanied by a marked development of the neotechnic structure. Significant inventions and new sources of power were utilized and extended. Oil displaced coal in ships and vastly increased their range, especially in the Pacific. The internal combustion engine played an increasingly important role in transportation, agriculture, and industry in the densely populated areas and in the remote areas. Roads and hotels were built on an extensive scale. Hydro-electric power was developed with and without government support in the non-coal areas and contributed to a marked

[19]See the small library on war history published by the Carnegie Endowment for International Peace.

[20]See W. A. Mackintosh, "Gold and the Decline of Prices," *Proceedings of the Canadian Political Science Association*, 1931, pp. 88–110.

increase in the supply of non-ferrous metals such as nickel, zinc, lead, aluminum, and gold. Following the stimulus of the war these neotechnic developments contributed to the expansion of Russia, Japan, Italy, France, Germany, the British Dominions, and the United States. The radio and expanding newsprint production were reinforced by the nationalistic energies released by new inventions and new sources of power.

While the palæotechnic and the neotechnic developments reinforced each other in the war and carried forward the boom of the twenties they began to diverge and to conflict in the depression. The coal areas as the basis of palæotechnic industrialism were the centres of development because of the importance of coal as a weight-losing raw material[21] which attracted other raw materials. Its significance was evident to neotechnic industry in the importation of petroleum in large quantities and in the importance of iron and steel to the automobile industry. But the difficulties of the coal industry in the twenties, evident in Great Britain especially in the depressed areas, in contrast with the emergence of the light industries, such as the automobile, radio, and electrical equipment in new locations, indicate the character of the change. The railway problem in Canada and other countries followed the emphasis on heavy equipment in rails, right-of-way, locomotives, and cars, and extensive financing for handling increasingly bulky, heavier, and cheaper commodities and the consequent effectiveness of motor competition with its stress on light valuable commodities, light equipment, and ease of finance. Wheat production was rapidly extended in the war and during the twenties by intensive and extensive cultivation, with railroad construction and motor transportation, in trucks and tractors, while industrialism centred on the coal areas was in distress and the market was narrowed. Tariffs emerged with increasing nationalism to protect agriculture in the wheat markets of the world.

Hydro-electric power is less mobile and flexible than petroleum. Distance from the power site has been an important factor but the handicap has decreased with inventions and new materials. It has facilitated the exploitation of the resources of non-agricultural areas with resistant formations and broken topography distant from coal formations. The conspicuous resources have been minerals and newsprint and pulp products, but with the depression, production of metallic minerals supported by gold has become an important com-

21C. J. Friedrich, *Alfred Weber's Theory of the Location of Industries* (Chicago, 1929).

petitor for power and has strengthened the radio against the newspaper.

The implications of neotechnical industralism have been evident in the growth of cities and metropolitan areas. On the one hand the skyscraper and increasing compactness of population in large apartment houses have been encouraged by developments in electrical equipment and on the other hand population has spread out over wide areas as a result of the automobile and metalled roads. Population has been released by machine industry in agriculture and has migrated to the more densely populated areas. Rising standards of expenditure and congestion have been accompanied by declining birth-rates. Building booms have characterized the sharp depreciation through obsolescence of housing equipment, and governments have attempted to encourage the construction of houses in the face of competition from more efficient apartment houses and at the expense of unfortunate individuals who have been encouraged to own their own homes. The demands of population in congested areas, under the direction of scientific work in nutrition, have shifted from carbohydrates to vitamins or from wheat to dairy products, live-stock, fruits, and vegetables. Improved transportation facilities, especially in the development of refrigeration, have increased the range of supply of proteins, fats, and vitamins. The wheat-coal economy, which involved hauling bulky commodities to the dominant coal areas, has been broken by the emergence of a large number of metropolitan centres dependent on new types of supplies and new types of transportation characteristic of recent industrialism. The strengthening of the Dominions and of the provinces in the Statute of Westminster and with the benefit of Privy Council decisions since the war reflected the decreasing importance of the metropolitan demand of Great Britain and the expansion of new metropolitan areas on the North American Continent. The city has sharpened the cultural background established under the influence of commercialism.

Neotechnic industrialism superimposed on palæotechnic industrialism involved changes of tremendous implication to modern society and brought strains of great severity. The institutional structure built up on iron and steel and coal has been slow to change. Governmental machinery in those regions in which palæotechnic society developed late has been extended and government intervention in regions in which it developed earlier has been intensified as a result of the rigidities of labour organization and corporate finance. Regions which continued primarily commercial, as Newfoundland, in the export of dried fish and in which capitalism, represented by the railway and the steamship, involved heavy burdens, failed to survive the effects of the new industrialism and the impact of the depression and lost responsible government. The effects of government intervention have been less severe in regions dominated by neotechnical industrialism and enhanced in regions dominated by palæotechnical industrialism. Wheat areas and coal and iron regions have been penalized. Adjustment by tariffs, railway rates, bounties, bankruptcy legislation, and other devices which characterized palæotechnic industrialism has become inadequate and compelled the intervention on a large scale of monetary devices.

The price system has been thwarted by the burden of debt hanging over from the old industrialism and stimulated by the support of government in the growth of the new industrialism as in the Ontario Hydro-Electric Power Commission. Private enterprise has been exposed to conflict and defeat in the fields of labour and capital in the old industrialism and has been conspicuously successful in the new industrialism. The search for liquidity favoured the new industrialism. Profits from tobacco were turned into the development of hydro-electric power on the Saguenay and supported substantial profits from the production of aluminum. The Ford Motor Company has been a conspicuous tribute to individual enterprise and the use of petroleum, as has also the development of Radio City. Private enterprise has been handicapped by the inconsistencies of political decisions but it has adapted itself with amazing facility. With monetary policy the state has been compelled to concentrate on vast areas and has been less effective in major undertakings such as the St. Lawrence waterways with the consequent profits which accompany disturbances on a large scale. In democratic countries with a strong labour organization or a large and vocal agricultural population, monetary policy is an important device but limited by an essentially conservative outlook.

The problem of debt in the war and the post-war period arising from this background of capitalism has had significant repercussions on the effectiveness of the price system. It was enhanced by the rise of continental economies, by the construction of transcontinental railways following the discoveries of gold on the Pacific, and by the dominance of coal and steel. Short-term credit which characterized the commercial system dominated by an island was followed by long-term credit dominated by continents. The unmanageable character of long-term credit in terms of allocation of yields in relation to costs became evident in the enormous reduction in value of railway securities in the United States, in the emergence of large fortunes through reorganizations and the formation of trusts, and in the evolution of the Canadian federal structure as an instrument capable of carrying an expanding debt. The problem of debt is the problem of Canadian federalism, as the federal structure is a credit instrument. To confine ourselves to Canada, the so-called railway problem has emerged with the problem of wheat, the competition of roads and motor transport and of new routes such as the Panama Canal, and has been evident in the disappearance of dividends on Canadian Pacific Railway stock and the continuance of deficits on the Canadian National Railways. The intensity of the problem incidental to the enormous amounts of capital involved in transcontinental railways, and the burden of overhead costs incidental to the economic, political, and geographic background has been evident in the first decade in the pronouncements of Sir Henry Thornton, and in the second decade in the pronouncements of Sir Edward Beatty. On the one hand, the Canadian Pacific Railway as the bulwark of private enterprise has shown little evidence of weakening in the struggle, and its plea for arrangements which appear to provide for operation of all Canadian railways at the expense of government is in danger of being regarded as an attempt at participation in the old game of tired business men in Canada. On the other hand, the Canadian National Railways are directly under the sovereign power of Parliament and should not be used to lay conduits under the name of co-operation from the Treasury to the pockets of Canadian Pacific shareholders, or be exposed to the subtle sabotage of maintaining an empty hotel in Vancouver and an empty hole in Montreal for nearly a decade in order not to injure private enterprise. It is the hope of democracy in Canada that both will continue to strive earnestly but that neither will succeed, and that the impossibility of running two competitive railways will continue. Dictatorship for the advantage of the Canadian Pacific Railway and a balanced budget is a prospect to be contemplated with concern. Those who argue for the abolition of the Canadian National deficit must suggest alternative and more effective devices for offsetting the burden of the tariff and the relief of depressed areas. Dictatorship proposed by the Canadian National in the form of a compulsory arbitration tribunal should be resisted as an encroachment on the powers of Parliament and on the rights of the Canadian Pacific. Both railways should be warned against talking nonsense about scientific rate structures and uneconomic costs in their attacks on road transport. Political agitation as to savings rather than earnings gives rise to the suspicion that the problem of efficient administration of transcontinental railways has not been solved or that administration, adapted to expansion, has been inadequate with its cessation. The public would like more indication of attempts to increase earnings rather than to be asked to make more sacrifices in the interest of savings. We may hope that the aggressiveness of the Canadian Pacific Railway will keep politics out of the Canadian National and that the aggressiveness of the Canadian National Railways will keep the Canadian Pacific out of politics and out of the Canadian Treasury, and that the results will permit the continuation of democratic government. The vested interests of the social scientist will suffer less from the attacks of Sir Edward Beatty than from the indifference of an amalgamated railway.

Organs of opinion reflect the increasing significance of regional and metropolitan growth, in demands for economies in the interests of finance or for protection against the possibilities of poorer service and discrimination which would accompany the various proposals for economic dictatorship. Montreal and Toronto have chiefly reflected the financial interests of the St. Lawrence in the demands for railway amalgamation, but the exceptions and western Canada support the outlook of wheat in fears of rigidities of economic dictatorship. Interests representing the new industrialism have been evident in striking fashion in control by the pulp and paper industry of the *Mail and Empire* and then by mining and hydro-electric power in the amalgamation of the *Globe* and *Mail*. Newspapers tend to reflect to an increasing extent the influence of rapid transportation and efficient distribution characteristic of metropolitan development. The pressure of overhead costs incidental to large-scale capital equipment in newspaper plants and newsprint mills has increased the importance of large-scale circulation and of good will or the stereotype of Walter Lippmann. Dependence on advertising, particularly from department stores, has become a vital issue in policy as to news, editorials, and features.[22] The cheap newspaper is subordinated to the demands of

[22]Freedom of the press and freedom of speech have always been relative terms assuming a moderate tolerance. Newspaper space involves a substantial outlay of funds as does an hour's broadcasting. In private conversation where talk is said to be cheap, one is inclined to revise Mark Twain's dictum and to say that we have freedom of speech and freedom of the press and not the good sense not to use either of them. Small talk, bores, and other terms are in constant demand. In so-called conferences freedom of speech is paraded as a special feature, but it usually amounts to common scolding or saying things calculated to get the conference into the newspapers—in other words, advertising space for nothing. See H. A. Innis, "Discussion in the Social Sciences," *Dalhousie Review*, XV (Jan. 1936), 401–13.

modern industrialism and modern merchandising. Overhead costs have contributed to lack of precision in accounting, and the allocation of costs between the purchaser of goods from department stores and the purchaser of the paper, or between the purchaser of paper and the purchaser of hydro-electric power from plants owned by paper companies, is extremely difficult to determine. In paying for electric light or for groceries one cannot be certain how much is paid for newspapers. The patterns of public opinion or the stereotypes have become blurred, and amalgamations of newspapers and the fusion of editorial policies lead to demands for general programmes which appeal to the business mind. Broad stereotypes are typical, such as the belief in the stability of governments, or—as social scientists, who have logically taken the place of millennialists, have been wont to put it—the dangers of civilization crashing, whatever that may mean. The Canadian variant points to the break-up of Confederation.

Periodicals emerge to meet the demands of any group whenever that group becomes sufficiently specialized to demand goods which warrant advertising on a sufficient scale to support the periodical. Specialization of this character is largely restricted to cities and regions. Such periodicals attempt to build up fresh stereotypes but are forced to compete with constantly improving technique designed to reach new and possibly lower levels of intelligence, especially those who prefer to look at photographs rather than to read. Those who prefer to read have hived off as supporters of pocket-book digests. Illustrations have reached a place of dominant importance and writers have been compelled to illustrate the illustrations including the advertisements. The difficulties which new parties experience in building up sharp stereotypes through newspapers or periodicals have been less evident in the publication of large editions of cheap books. New educational movements and reform programmes make the world safe for publishers. The support of religious bodies to publishing houses has weakened and been replaced by the state with its demands for educational texts. Education comes under the jurisdiction of the provinces. A substantial publisher of textbooks is not in a strong position to publish literature other than that of a strikingly nationalistic or local character. The incipient fascism of Canadian intellectuals, the group which cannot distinguish a bar association from a trade union, in Winnipeg, Toronto, and Montreal, evident in nationalism, isolationism, and the boosting of Canadian literature in the interests of Canadian publishers, has deep roots. School texts handled on a mass production basis in an off-peak period by large organizations such as mail-order houses and providing as a by-product, advertising, reduce the volume of publishing houses and, who knows, may injure the possibility of developing Canadian poetry. Abolition of standard texts in favour of the publication of a wide variety of books increases the cost of education to the publishers, the state, and the purchaser of books, but it tends to break down broad stereotypes.

The decline in value of political stereotypes which accompanies the decline of the party newspaper has been partly a result of the increase in importance of the radio as a political weapon. Competition between newspapers and the radio for advertising, as well as in the handling of news, has been evident in the concerted attack by the press on the Canadian Broadcasting Corporation following contracts with American firms. From the standpoint of the public, it is a choice between Moon Mullins and Charlie McCarthy. The radio capitalizes the disadvantage of the large newspaper in appealing to stereotypes which refuse to be blurred, as is evident in the strength of religion in the rural areas. While it has served the dictatorship of Russia, Germany, Italy, and Japan, it has assisted in escape via the provincialism of Mr. Aberhart and the federalism of Mr. Roosevelt. As a new invention the radio threatens to circumvent the walls imposed by tariffs and to reach across boundaries frequently denied to other media of communication, but like the newspaper it is adapted to the demands of metropolitan areas. Saskatchewan elections may provide a rough indication of the range of the Calgary stations.

In a political entity such as Canada in which the forces of centralization are so strong, the element of size involves powerful counteracting forces of decentralization. The wheat-coal economy and the enormous burden of debt which has accompanied its decline have involved rigid interest and transportation charges supported by broad general stereotypes involving imperialism, nationalism, demands for railway amalgamation, union of the Prairie Provinces and of the Maritime Provinces, the dangers of communism, the dangers of fascism, and the like. Adam Smith might have said of capitalists as he said of merchants: "The government of an exclusive company of merchants is, perhaps, the worst of all governments for any country whatever."[23] "I have never known much good done by those who affected to trade for the public good."[24] Wide fluctuations in prices of raw materials such as furs, fish, timber, wheat, pulp and paper, and minerals involve a large element of elasticity, in

[23]*Wealth of Nations*, p. 537.   [24]*Ibid.*, p. 423.

marketing structures as in barter and the truck system, in the standards of living of producers, and in financial structures, as reorganizations will attest. Expanding metropolitan areas dependent on the new industries such as pulp and paper, minerals, and hydroelectric power were provided with cushions in relief, in relative financial independence, and in the more direct impact of new inventions. The exposed areas have been of the wheat-coal economy and the favoured areas have gained with the new industrialism. In spite of the hard core of rigidity of the debt structure, the monetary policies of other nations, especially of Great Britain and the United States, compelled a change in monetary structure and monetary policy in Canada. A prominent Canadian banker stated at an annual meeting of a bank largely concerned with the new industrialism, in January 1931: "For the future it is absolutely essential that means should be devised to prevent the drastic changes in the price level which have been characteristic of the period since the close of the war."[25] A representative of the same bank stated in 1938: "Experience will have taught us nothing, if as a result of occurrences of the last seven years we do not conclude that positive action from a monetary point of view is the first essential in controlling excesses of both boom and depression."[26] The effects have been evident in defaults, with and without benefit of the political success of Mr. Aberhart. A monetary policy which might have softened the effects of the depression in the wheat-coal areas might have spurred on the activities of the new industrialism in the hydro-electric power, mining, and pulp and paper areas and increased the internal strain already severe as attested by the major disasters of debts necessitating the Royal Commission on Dominion-Provincial Relations. The difficulties of the wheat-coal regions are not less because of the declining sympathetic interest of the regions of the new industrialism.

The limitations of the price system in failing to overcome the handicaps of rigidities of debt burdens and in accentuating internal strains have been evident in the rise of monetary nationalism and the increasing importance of the state as a monetary instrument. Bankruptcy is no longer accepted as an effective solvent and is no longer possible with the state as a credit instrument and the possibilities of controlling inflation. It is "unthinkable." The increasing strength and influence of institutions concerned with long-term credit, such as bond

[25]*Proceedings of the Canadian Political Science Association*, 1931, p. 122.
[26]S. R. Noble, "The Monetary Experience of Canada during the Depression," *Canadian Banker*, April 1938.

houses and insurance companies, based on the application of mathematics in the calculation of mortality tables and bond yields has left no alternative. Within the state, large-scale capital equipment and the drive to operate at capacity have accentuated the importance of alternative production and intensified competition in off-peak periods. Ridges formed by buckling under competitive pressure are conspicuous in basing point systems, intensive advertising, and monopolistic arrangements. The tendency towards fixed prices has been accompanied by more intense competition in other directions as in the case of railway service and train schedules and political agitation. The realm of intangible services assumes increasing importance and the skyscaper has become the modern cathedral. Long-term credit is the new basis of modern belief. The difficulty of competition in prices compels a shift in cost items and a realignment of accounting. The rigidity of accounting systems accentuates the importance of fixed prices with the result that the accountant is bribed to present accounts with limited value for interpretation or accuracy.[27] Accounting systems have met the demands of corporations for release from control of debt by facilitating the development of policies by which reserves and surplus have been built up, and control lost to the shareholders. Dependence on the capital market for new supplies of capital has been materially lessened, with the result that it becomes more speculative. Short-term credit and the importance of liquidity intensify speculation. Concentration of control in the hands of management, with the possibilities of interlocking directorates and the like, involves possibilities of unwise developments in large organizations, and lack of information regarding their policies. The monetary system with its mathematical implications facilitates the development of mechanical control devices, ranging from improved accounting machinery to the adaptation of automatic services to the nickel and other coins and of the Canadian nickel in size and weight to the American nickel.

The price system has stimulated minor correctives in persuading the consumer to educate himself through consumers' research organizations, societies to stop propaganda (of all things), and other devices, and still permits many of us to live in comparative peace. Its handicaps have been stressed to an increasing extent by economists who have been concerned with monopoly theory and with the decline of competition or with the rise of economic warfare and what someone has called the decline of the idea of competition. The

[27]See C. A. Ashley, "Some Aspects of Corporations," *Essays in Political Economy in Honour of E. J. Urwick* (Toronto, 1938).

effectiveness of the price system within the state is evident in the attempts to reinforce pecuniary by political values. The successful politician is precluded from policies which indicate class or self-interest but he is successful in so far as he succeeds in enlisting the support of the price system. He should be the orthodontist of the social sciences pursuing his way by gradual but persistent pressure, but he continues with analogies of the machine in "pulling levers" or with violent medical treatments in giving "a shot in the arm."[28]

The effectiveness of the price system has been shown in the decline of feudalism, the decline of mercantilism, the rise of palæotechnic capitalism, and the shift to neotechnic capitalism. It has stimulated the growth of inventions and the trend in the movement of goods from light and valuable raw materials to heavy and cheap raw materials, and to light and valuable finished products. It has hastened the rise of new sources of power and of new industries and accelerated the decline of obsolete regions. The drive of the price system on the economic and social structure within the state has been accompanied by continual disturbance between the states. The role of the state in assuming the burdens of depreciation through obsolescence of the wheat-coal economy and in stimulating the development of new industrialism involves rapid expansion of public debt and necessitates the continual revision of currencies in relation to other countries. The relative lack of rigid structure in the international field has probably reduced the dangers of international disturbance. The stupidity of nationalism is tempered by the chaos of internationalism. Losses through nationalism are offset by realignments of national boundaries, trade agreements, international cartels, foreign balances, world fairs, and subsidized tourists. Monetary nationalism is a reflection of the role of the state in the expansion of industrialism and the means by which the state is compelled to rely increasingly on expanded public debt and to avoid increasingly its effects. Employment and the demands for consumers' goods must be stimulated by state activity. To obtain bread we must build a gun or lay down a stone. Monetary nationalism and the constant necessity for readjustments of exchange have become normal phases of the recent effects of the price system. Responsible government in the vital sense of control over funds has disappeared in favour of secret operation of equalization funds. The automatic system which centred on London has come under divided control with the rise of North America and the opening of the Pacific.

28V. F. Coe, "Monetary Theory and Politics," *Essays in Political Economy in Honour of E. J. Urwick.*

We seem destined in economics to follow the meteorologist in modifying equilibrium analysis and turning to what he has called the polar front theory in which the meeting of economic masses becomes important rather than trade between nations. There are serious weaknesses in the analogy of flowing from high to low pressure areas, and great advantages in discussing pressure groups. The economics of losses is not less significant than the economics of profits.

Economists have reflected the confusion introduced by machine industry. The decline of vested interests peculiar to the period after Adam Smith was a tribute to the economic value of the *Wealth of Nations*, but the emergence of vested interests (i.e., the legitimate right to something for nothing) under capitalism has reduced the value of economic theory based on Adam Smith and increased the value of economic theory adapted to nationalism. To extend the thesis of Mr. Keynes as to the influence of rising prices on literature, it may be said that they tend to correspond with free will systems of economic thought. Jevons might have added economic systems to Acts of Parliament and sun spots. Scientific advance and the application of science to industry through inventions are characteristic of periods of prosperity. The philosophic outlook based on scientific achievement leaves its stamp on economics. Periods of prosperity may be characterized by most intensive work in economics but periods of depression have been characterized by attempts at application, particularly in the field in which mathematics provides a convenient channel between science and economics, namely money. Economics becomes a branch of physics and chemistry rather than of biology. Politics has become a method of revolt. The word political has been restored to its place with economy, and equilibrium analysis must be modified and extended throughout the social sciences. A study of the elasticity of demand for autarchies is significant to a study of the elasticity of demand for wheat.[29] Depressions produce deterministic systems and arguments such as have been advanced in this paper.

[29]See *The State and Economic Life* (Paris, 1934), pp. 252–4, 289–90.

The Wheat Economy*

THROUGHOUT the long period of prosperity from the turn of the century to 1929, labour and capital poured into the prairie regions of western Canada for the production and export of wheat. With the depression the tide began to ebb. The drought years accentuated the problem of decline in prices.[1] There has been a retreat from land, an outward migration of labour, a sharp decline in interest payments, particularly through writing down of debts, and a decline in railway earnings and in sales of goods from eastern Canada and British Columbia.

The region is located on the indeterminate height of land between the St. Lawrence and the Pacific coast. Wheat may flow to Vancouver or to Montreal, and manufactured goods may be imported from the east or the west, depending on the varying rates of shipping and tariff levels. Emigration of labour and lower standards of living have reduced the demands for manufactured goods and have been the concern of the Canadian economy from the Atlantic to the Pacific.

World trade in wheat has expanded with the rise of industrialism.[2] Adaptability to transport and storage gave it a strategic place in the extension of production of foodstuffs in the plains regions to meet the demands of the densely populated industrial seaboard areas. With the support of more recent industrialism characterized by the tractor and the combine, wheat production has penetrated to the continental climatic fringes. Fluctuations[3] have been accentuated and the soil has been exposed to rapid deterioration. Labour and capital equipment

---

*From G. E. Britnell, The Wheat Economy (University of Toronto Press, 1939), pp. vi–xiv.

[1] Professor J. L. McDougall estimates that from 1929 to 1936, 60 per cent of losses have been due to price changes and 40 per cent to changes in volume of production. Canadian Journal of Economics and Political Science, IV (Aug. 1938), 430.

[2] See W. A. Mackintosh, "Western Agriculture in the Canadian Economy," Proceedings of the Conference on Markets for Western Farm Products (Winnipeg, 1938), pp. 8ff; also pp. 153–4; K. W. Taylor, "The Commercial Policy of Canada," Canadian Marketing Problems, ed. H. R. Kemp (Toronto, 1939); F. W. Burton, "Wheat in Canadian History," Canadian Journal of Economics and Political Science, III (May 1937), 210–17.

[3] See Isaiah Bowman, The Pioneer Fringe (New York, 1931).

retreat with difficulty.[4] In a letter to Edgeworth, Marshall characterized the wheat industry as follows: "Under some circumstances it is
a complete industry; and then it responds slowly to price. Under others
it is a mere department of general agricultural industry; and then it
responds almost instantaneously."[5] With the second alternative, governments concerned with programmes of self-sufficiency have been conspicuously successful in increasing the production of wheat.[6] Industrialism based on new sources of power and scientific advance has
not only meant a decline in international trade in wheat through production in new regions but also through changes in nutritional habits
with less dependence on carbohydrates. More bulky food products
characteristic of changes leading to a more balanced diet involved
higher transport charges and consequently more local production.[7]
These developments restrict the market for wheat produced in regions
where it is a "complete industry," and lower prices necessitate governmental support in those regions. A community which emerged from a
background of rapid growth of international industrialism has been
faced with the effects of rapid emergence of national industrialism. It
has been concerned with a commodity essential to international industrialism and a commodity which has responded quickly to national
industrialism. The population of western Canada dependent on wheat
production has been compelled to submit to the effects of fundamental
cultural readjustments in Western civilization as well as to the effects
of variations in seasons. The wheat policies of European governments
largely determine the policies of governments in other wheat-producing regions.[8] The response to price in western Canada has varied
with the capital resources, background, and training of settlers, and
geographic features such as climate and soil, but the wide areas

[4]The Regina Board of Trade claimed that "if the great open plain . . . in the
centre of which Regina stands cannot make a place for itself in the world's
economy by the production of hard wheat it is doubtful if it has any place in the
world's economy." *Proceedings of the Conference on Markets for Western Farm
Products*, p. 163. Mr. J. H. Wesson stated that when the farmer has produced
"a lot of wheat and sells it lower than the cost of production, he feverishly
proceeds to try to produce more to offset his losses." *Ibid.*, p. 77. See also the
Hon. J. G. Taggart, "The Possibilities of Shifting from Wheat Growing to Other
Types of Farming in Western Canada and the Implications of Such Changes,"
ibid., pp. 201ff.

[5]A. C. Pigou, ed., *Memorials of Alfred Marshall* (London, 1925), p. 440.

[6]See *Proceedings of the Conference on Markets for Western Farm Products*,
pp. 48ff.

[7]See C. J. Friedrich, *Alfred Weber's Theory of the Location of Industries*
(Chicago, 1929).

[8]*The State and Economic Life* (Paris, 1934), pp. 252–4.

affected by drought preclude the extensive development of mixed farming. The extreme difficulties in formulating an effective government policy under these conditions without previous experience have been evident in problems of relief, farm credit,[9] political revolution, and political stagnation.

If we accept the conclusion that population flows "from an area of low standard of living to an àrea of high standard of living" and that rate of flow is "a gradient of standards of living,"[10] we can regard the migration from the prairie regions eastward[11] as an indication of a sharp decline from a high to a low standard of living. The significant problem is not the standard of living but the rate of its change. Rapid change in standard of living has disastrous effects on population and has involved governmental measures of an emergency character. Professor Hope has characterized one measure, a guaranteed price of wheat, as "about the most unfair kind of bonus you can possibly give Western agriculture because it gives a definite bonus to the man with a big crop, and nothing to the man with a crop failure. There is no bonus on course grain."[12] Suggested policies include reducing costs through such expedients as lowering the tariff[13] and the cost of marketing both wheat and manufactured products,[14] and thereby possibly increasing production; enhancing prices by monetary policy and thus probably maintaining the rigidity of such fixed charges as debt and increasing production; stimulating consumption by reducing the spread

[9]W. T. Easterbrook, *Farm Credit in Canada* (Toronto, 1938).

[10]Carl Alsberg, "Standards of Living as a Factor in International Relations," *International Affairs*, Nov.–Dec. 1937, pp. 920–1; also "The Food Supply in the Migration Process," *Limits of Land Settlement* (Paris, 1937).

[11]W. B. Hurd, "Population Movements in Canada, 1921–1931, and Their Implications," *Proceedings of the Canadian Political Science Association*, 1934, pp. 220ff; S. W. Alty, "The Influence of Climatic and Other Geographic Factors upon the Growth and Distribution of Population in Saskatchewan," *Geography*, March 1939, pp. 10ff.

[12]*Proceedings of the Conference on Markets for Western Farm Products*, p. 240; see also R. W. Gardner, "Wheat Production Costs," *Canadian Chartered Accountant*, March 1939, pp. 165ff.

[13]See A. R. Upgren, "Monetary Policy in Relation to Farm Income," *Canadian Chartered Accountant*, March 1939, pp. 131ff. Premier Bracken claims that tariff and monetary policies imposed a burden of $47,000,000 annually on western Canada. *Canadian Chartered Accountant*, March 1939, p. 239. See F. J. Westcott, "An Approach to the Problem of Tariff Burdens on Western Canada," *Canadian Journal of Economics and Political Science*, IV (May 1938), 209ff.

[14]See J. E. Lattimer, "Recent Developments in Co-operative Marketing," *Canadian Marketing Problems*, ed. H. R. Kemp, pp. 112–25. While Professor Lattimer argues that increased co-operation has been a result of high costs of marketing, in so far as co-operation may involve difficulties of bankruptcy it may contribute to rigid costs of marketing.

between the price of wheat and the price of bread,[15] especially in Canada; reducing production and exports by fostering alternative products[16] such as beef, pork, mutton, and butter, and, as Professor Lattimer advocates, cereals for export to other provinces more favourably situated for the raising of live-stock and the manufacture of dairy products; maintaining labour and capital equipment in the drought areas[17] to take advantage of favourable years by such devices as relief and crop insurance; and withdrawing population from the most distressed areas. These policies cannot be regarded as a solution to the problems of marked fluctuations in price or in volume. They may even accentuate the fluctuations, and they may become contradictory as more favourable conditions for wheat production limit the possibilities of production of alternative commodities.

The complexity of the problem involves difficulties not only for western Canada but also for British Columbia and eastern Canada. Widely fluctuating income in western Canada involves periodic bombardments on eastern Canada and British Columbia.[18] Low prices of wheat lead to increased production of live-stock and dairy products in western Canada and more direct competition with other regions. Farming technique in the St. Lawrence is necessarily flexible. Intense specialization is more difficult to achieve, and competition in export markets is handicapped. Limited shipments of high-grade products to the export markets involve flooding the domestic market with lower-grade products and in turn reducing the possibilities of domestic consumption.

The effects of sharp fluctuations are particularly severe with the closed system built up under the Canadian tariff[19] and American immigration restrictions. Migration from Canada to the United States and from Europe to Canada[20] was effectively checked by 1930. The other regions have been affected by variations in immigration from

[15]For a discussion of the control of flour mills over the baking industry, see *Investigation into an Alleged Combine in the Bread-Making Industry in Canada* (Ottawa, 1931), pp. 38ff.

[16]A. M. Shaw, "The Problem of Export Markets for Canadian Cattle"; L. W. Pearsall, "The Problem of Export Markets for Canadian Hogs"; and G. W. Tovell, "Markets for Creamery Butter": *Proceedings of the Conference on Markets for Western Farm Products*, pp. 265ff.

[17]See W. J. Waines, "Problems of the Drought Area in Western Canada," *Essays in Political Economy in Honour of E. J. Urwick* (Toronto, 1938), pp. 205ff.

[18]See J. A. Ruddick *et al.*, *The Dairy Industry in Canada* (Toronto, 1937).

[19]See H. A. Logan, "Labour Costs and Labour Standards," *Labour in Canadian-American Relations* (Toronto, 1937), chap. x.

[20]See H. R. Kemp, "Notes on the Population Problem," *Commerce Journal*, March 1939, pp. 31ff.

western Canada as well as by variations in trade. Natural increase in population in the St. Lawrence region plus immigration from western Canada, with no outlet to the United States, has enhanced the difficulties of unemployment, relief, lower standards of living, and increasing stress on self-sufficient agriculture.[21] The Maritimes, with a population drained by emigration over a long period to the interior of the continent, with a fishing industry compelled to meet tariffs and competition from other countries in foreign markets, with a lumber industry faced with competition from British Columbia through the Panama Canal, and with agriculture, restricted in its local markets, forced to meet competition from the St. Lawrence and compelled to bear with other industries losses incidental to a closed system, have continued to face a low standard of living.[22] They have been affected by the difficulties in western Canada through a decline in demand for railway equipment, coal, and manufactured products. These repercussions of disturbances in western Canada on other regions have increased the difficulties of unified approach to a common problem. The lowering of prices of raw materials in the depression contributed to the increasing importance of the gold mining and the pulp and paper industries in relation to the American market, and of industries such as agricultural implements and motor cars in relation to other markets. The latter industries sustain possible losses in the markets of western Canada by profits in foreign markets. Access to the American market[23] may soften the severity of repercussions but the task of government is difficult.[24]

The persistent difficulty of adjusting institutions combining feudalism and modern capitalism, which characterizes the federal governments of the North American continent,[25] in placing, according to feudal principles, control over natural resources and land in the hands of the provinces and the states, and, according to capitalistic demands, control of interstate and foreign trade in the hands of the federal

[21]See E. C. Hughes, "Industry and the Rural System in Quebec," *Canadian Journal of Economics and Political Science*, IV (Aug. 1938), 341ff.

[22]See *The Maritime Provinces since Confederation* (Ottawa, 1927), chap. II.

[23]It has been estimated that the United States will require fifteen to twenty million additional acres of land to meet the demands of increasing population by 1950. See O. E. Baker, "The Agricultural Prospect," *Our Natural Resources and their Conservation*, ed. A. E. Parkins and J. R. Whitaker (New York, 1936), chap. IX.

[24]F. W. Burton, "Staple Production and Canada's External Relations," *Essays in Political Economy in Honour of E. J. Urwick.*

[25]See H. A. Innis, "Significant Factors in Canadian Economic Development," *Canadian Historical Review* XVIII (Dec. 1937), pp. 374ff [see this volume, p. 200]; also "Notes on Problems of Adjustment in Canada," *Journal of Political Economy*, Dec. 1935, pp. 800ff.

government, involves a drain on economic energies and inability to direct them effectively. The British North America Act was designed to foster trade and commerce and to enable the provinces to defray their expenditures by subsidies and direct taxes. The advance of technology, which created paper from spruce and balsam and converted the vast waste areas of the Precambrian formation into a region with paper plants, power sites, and mines producing chiefly for the American market, accentuated the feudalistic character of federalism. Construction of railways and canals with federal support for the development of trade and commerce contributed to the exploitation of the extensive northern areas belonging to the provinces of Ontario and Quebec and to the rapid development of the prairie resources belonging to the federal government. The consequent debt of the federal government and the problems of wheat in the prairie regions in relation to European markets are in sharp contrast with the advantages of the provinces of the St. Lawrence. A federal tariff structure linked to the transportation system provides further assistance to the industrial regions of the St. Lawrence. With rigid railway rates, and relatively rigid prices of manufactured products, and sharp decline in income, the pressure for debt revision in the prairie regions has been direct and pronounced. Taxes in the form of debt and debt reduction have fallen heavily on the debtor and on the creditor. The tariff possibly increases the burden of western Canada and thereby the burden of the federal government through relief, assumption of provincial debt, and lower railway earnings, and penalizes those concerned with farm credit. These inherent constitutional inconsistencies contribute to the difficulties of escape from a lower standard of living. They are fostered by confusion of economic thought in western Canada which emphasizes freedom of trade because of the importance of wheat on the one hand, and statements that "fair price is the cost of production" and the just price is that which enables people "to buy the goods and services they need to carry on their labour in their service," on the other hand. In eastern Canada feudalism and physiocratic ideologies stress the importance of return to the land and the spiritual advantages of rural life and a lower standard of living. Professor Britnell has perhaps made his most important contribution in hastening a decline in the rigidities of these phases of agricultural fundamentalism[26] by compelling a consideration of the problems of the wheat economy.

[26]See J. S. Davis, "Agricultural Fundamentalism," *Economics, Sociology and the Modern World*, ed. N. E. Himes (Cambridge, 1935), pp. 3–22; also "The Spectre of Dearth of Food: History's Answer to Sir William Crookes," *Facts and Factors in Economic History* (Cambridge, 1932), pp. 733ff.

The Canadian federal structure is wrenched between the influence of British policies and their effect on wheat, and of American policies and their effect on minerals and newsprint and on the rigidity of such important costs of wheat production as railway rates and interest charges. The policy of damping down speculative activity restricts the possibilities of lifting wheat prices and increases reliance on government intervention. Disparities between the policies of Great Britain and the United States have been felt most acutely in the regions of widely fluctuating income and the problems of standards of living have necessitated dependence on arbitrary transfers between regions in the Canadian federal structure.

The Changing Structure of the Canadian Market*

A LFRED MARSHALL has described a market "in all its various significations" as "a group or groups of people some of whom desire to obtain certain things and some of whom are in a position to supply what the others want."[1] Elsewhere he writes: "The more nearly perfect a market is, the stronger is the tendency for the same price to be paid for the same thing at the same time in all parts of the market."[2] Within these broad definitions this study is more directly concerned with the institutions, such as the various forms of retail stores, designed to bring products immediately to the consumer, and less directly concerned with other institutions, such as the grain exchange, designed to bring raw materials to the manufacturers. In new countries such as Canada, the relations between these institutions are necessarily close, since their economic development is a result of the demand of more highly industrialized areas, first of Europe and later of the United States and the Orient.

The character of the relationship has varied with the improvement of transportation and communication and has shown a strong tendency to widen. In the fishing industry merchants were concerned with the sale of the product, and the allocation of returns in the purchase of provisions and supplies such as salt; the hire of the vessel; and the payment of shares. Since they sent out ships from ports scattered along the coast line of France and the west country in England, competition favoured specialization for various markets. The innumerable elements responsible for variations in the extent of the returns involved arrangements in which the interests of the fishermen, who conducted operations far from the supervision of the merchant, were directly enlisted, and by which the variations should be shared proportionately. Responsibility for the venture was shared roughly on the basis of a third each for the ship owner, the supplier, and the fishermen, who had and still have elaborate share arrangements.

*From Jane McKee, ed., *Marketing Organization and Technique* (University of Toronto Press, 1940), pp. vii-xiii.
[1]*Industry and Trade* (London, 1923), p. 182.
[2]*Principles of Economics* (London, 1910), p. 325.

In the fur trade this intimate relationship gradually disappeared. Fishing vessels participated in the fur trade in the Maritimes and the Gulf of St. Lawrence but monopolies were granted by the state to merchants with vessels which penetrated up the river. Merchants agreed to establish settlements, but the costs were heavy and the agreements were disregarded. Competition between the nations of Europe was extended to North America, and the Dutch prior to 1664 traded with the Iroquois on the Hudson. The government of France was compelled to abandon monopolies and to assume direct control in 1663. The inadequacies of monopoly trade were evident in the slow growth of settlement and in the emergence of individual merchants in the colony as a result of the necessity of extension of the trade to the interior. "Of all the expedients that can well be contrived to stunt the natural growth of a new colony, that of an exclusive monopoly is undoubtedly the most effectual."³

Competition between merchants in the colony thrived on the increase in settlement which followed direct government control. Attempts were made, at their insistence, to persuade the Indians to pay annual visits to the fairs at Montreal and elsewhere and to prevent foreign merchants, that is, those trading directly each year from France, from participation.⁴ The government protected the French trade by military activities against the Iroquois to the south, including the establishment of a post at Cataraqui (Kingston), and the Hudson's Bay Company to the north and by providing a valorization scheme by which furs were purchased at a fixed price. Paris tended to dominate the trade in furs but made little impression on the trade in merchandise which centred about La Rochelle.⁵ The division between fur merchants and supply merchants was sharpened.

The division became more pronounced after the Treaty of Utrecht (1713) as a result of the increasing importance of agriculture and the prosperity which followed the first opening up of the West by La Vérendrye. Resident merchants protested more vigorously against "foreign" merchants with agencies in Quebec and Montreal and against pedlars who carried on trade throughout the country districts. The authorities resisted their demands and insisted on the advantages of freedom of trade in increasing the consumption of goods throughout the French Empire.⁶

³Adam Smith, *Wealth of Nations* (Modern Library ed., New York, 1937), p. 542.
⁴H. A. Innis, *The Fur Trade in Canada* (New Haven, 1930), pp. 55–7; *Select Documents in Canadian Economic History, 1497–1783*, ed. H. A. Innis (Toronto, 1929) pp. 311–13.
⁵*Select Documents, 1497–1783*, pp. 325–6.   ⁶*Ibid.*, pp. 402–6, 408–11.

The concern of France with the fur trade and the fishing industry checked the effectiveness of the merchants. Merchants in New France were hampered by the limited resources of the colony and its obsession with the fur trade, with all that it implied in uncertainties of supply and of demand and of price, by attempts within the colony to establish the rigid mercantilism of the mother country in such institutions as the guilds and local regulations of prices and markets, by restrictions on Protestantism, by the attempt to develop an integrated colonial empire, and by the costs of military activities including two periods of inflation. Louisburg was established as a basis for the sedentary fishery after the Treaty of Utrecht, but it was forced to rely on the marketing organization of the English colonies in spite of the opposition of France.

Anglo-American merchants who followed the French merchants after the conquest had the advantage of freedom of access by the Hudson and the Great Lakes, of support from a strong marketing organization in the English colonies, of a more closely integrated empire, and of an expanding marketing structure concentrated on London and based on English industrialism. The emergence of competition between the marketing organization of the English colonies[7] with its widening interest in the markets of the Atlantic basin and beyond, supported by wooden sailing vessels and a diversity of products, and the London organization, contributed to the American Revolution and to the dominance of London merchants on the St. Lawrence. Anglo-American merchants succeeded in extending the fur trade far beyond the limits reached by the French. A powerful organization of merchants in the Northwest Company pushed the trade to the Mackenzie and the Columbia rivers. As in the case of the French merchants from the St. Lawrence, it came into competition with the Hudson's Bay Company. Formed in 1670 through the support of French traders from the St. Lawrence, Radisson and Groseilliers, who had resisted governmental direction, the latter suffered from attacks by the French prior to the Treaty of Utrecht, from French competition from the St. Lawrence under La Vérendrye and his successors, and from the energetic competition of the Northwest Company. The advantages of the Hudson Bay route were again evident in the merger of the Northwest Company with the Hudson's Bay Company in 1821. Merchants' organizations concerned with the fur trade were

7A. M. Schlesinger, The Colonial Merchants and the American Revolution (New York, 1917).

amalgamated in London to trade through Hudson Bay to western Canada.

The shift of the fur trade of western Canada from the St. Lawrence to Hudson Bay accentuated on the other hand the division on the St. Lawrence between a marketing organization concerned with imports of manufactured products and a marketing organization concerned with exports. The spread of English population to Upper Canada with the Loyalists, soldier settlements, and migration from Great Britain, increased the importance of marketing concerned with the purchase and export of agricultural products and imports of manufactured goods. Encouragement of the timber trade by imperial preferences during and after the Napoleonic Wars hastened the growth of settlement and involved demands for a wider range of imports and a specialization of marketing structure for timber.[8] The increased extent of the market warranted specialization and the beginnings of financial institutions such as the Bank of Montreal (1817) to link together the various marketing organizations. The element of distance and seasonal considerations involved regional specialization and the increasing importance of marketing centres such as Kingston and Toronto in Upper Canada. British export centres such as Glasgow began to compete more effectively with London and to strengthen competition. After completion of the Erie Canal from New York to Buffalo and of the Welland Canal, western Ontario and Toronto had an alternative import route. As a result, merchants in Lower Canada and in Upper Canada pressed more vigorously for canals on the upper St. Lawrence. With the Act of Union in 1840 financial support was available for their construction and they were completed by 1850.

In Nova Scotia, the establishment of Halifax (1749) facilitated the extension of the fishing industry from New England. Retreat of the French from Cape Breton and the St. Lawrence enabled Halifax merchants to increase their range of trade. Wooden sailing vessels enabled merchants from the ports along the coast to compete with Halifax, and merchants from the Channel Islands dominated the bilingual centres of the Gulf of St. Lawrence. The timber trade of the St. John and the Miramichi rivers restricted the growth of specialized marketing structures in New Brunswick. The merchants of Nova Scotia demanded and obtained modifications of the British colonial system enabling them to compete with New England. Where New England

8A. R. M. Lower et al., The North American Assault on the Canadian Forest (Toronto, 1938).

merchants had been unable to secure a modification of the colonial system within the Empire, the effects of their competition outside the Empire made possible the success of Nova Scotia merchants.[9]

The growth of competition between ports in the United Kingdom, the effects of increasing industrialism in the demand for raw materials, including timber and food stuffs, and the demands of merchants in North America, made the strictures of Adam Smith increasingly effective. In his vigorous and stout attacks on the colonial system he left memorable sentences. "The sneaking arts of underling tradesmen are thus erected into political maxims for the conduct of a great empire; for it is the most underling tradesmen only who make it a rule to employ chiefly their own customers. A great trader purchases his goods always where they are cheapest and best, without regard to any little interest of this kind."[10] "In every country it always is and must be the interest of the great body of people to buy whatever they want of those who sell it cheapest. The proposition is so very manifest, that it seems ridiculous to take any pains to prove it; nor could it ever have been called in question had not the interested sophistry of merchants and manufacturers confounded the common sense of mankind."[11] "The government of an exclusive company of merchants is, perhaps, the worst of all governments for any country whatever."[12] "To found a great empire for the sole purpose of raising up a people of customers, may at first sight appear a project fit only for a nation of shopkeepers. It is however a project altogether unfit for a nation of shopkeepers; but extremely fit for a nation whose government is influenced by shopkeepers. Such statesmen, and such statesmen only, are capable of fancying that they will find some advantage in employing the blood and treasure of their fellow-citizens to found and maintain such an empire."[13]

The rapid industrialization of Great Britain, with construction of railways, urbanization of population, the introduction of free trade, increasing imports of raw material, and increasing exports of finished products, supported demands in Canada, especially on the part of the merchants in Montreal, for railways to supplement canals. This extension of capital equipment necessitated financial assistance by the government of Canada and in turn the development of devices such as the tariff for the collection of revenue.

[9]See J. B. Brebner, The Neutral Yankees of Nova Scotia (New York, 1937); H. A. Innis, The Cod Fisheries (New Haven, 1940). For the St. Lawrence see D. G. Creighton, The Commercial Empire of the St. Lawrence, 1760–1850 (Toronto, 1938).
[10]Wealth of Nations, p. 460.   [11]Ibid., p. 461.   [12]Ibid., p. 537.   [13]Ibid., p. 579.

Increase of settlement in Ontario followed improvement in transportation. Wheat production expanded and was followed by dairying
and the export of cheese. Wholesale merchants in Montreal, Kingston,
and Toronto imported goods from Great Britain and distributed them
throughout western Ontario through the general store.[14] Credit was
given by firms in Great Britain to wholesale houses in Canada and by
these to general stores. Competition among wholesale houses[15] was
evident in the increasing number of commercial travellers who visited
the rural districts. The general store merchant purchased the country
produce and sold it to commission merchants to be sold locally or
exported.[16] Success in the general store was a result of economy, a
judicious knowledge and balancing of credit risks, and the use of barter
through book accounts. Fluctuations in the price of exports strengthened the position of the barter system as they compelled the merchant
to protect himself in the purchase of agricultural products and in the
sale of manufactured products.

Improvement in transportation increased the range of exports to
Great Britain to include live-stock and apples and demanded specialization in the export marketing structure. Moreover, it increased competition between importing merchants. Finance became more important as the link between exports and imports, and the banking
structure became more effective. Completion of the Atlantic cable
(1866) narrowed the range of fluctuations between Great Britain and
North America and facilitated the establishment of a world price,
especially for such a commodity as wheat. Improvement in transportation and communication involved financial support and increase
in tariffs. Competition from lower costs of transportation and expanding industrialism in the United States led to demands on the part of
Canadian manufacturers for modifications in a tariff for revenue which
would provide protection for manufactured products.[17] Importers in
Toronto were forced to compete with an expanding local industry, and
the wholesale trade from Great Britain began to decline.[18]

[14]See Herbert Heaton, *History of Trade and Commerce* (Toronto, 1928),
pp. 233–4.
[15]See H. Johnston, *A Merchant Prince: Life of Hon. Senator John MacDonald*
(Toronto, 1895).
[16]See a memorandum by Sir Joseph Flavelle, in J. A. Ruddick *et al.*, *The Dairy
Industry in Canada* (Toronto, 1937), pp. 34–6.
[17]See S. D. Clark, *The Canadian Manufacturers' Association: A Study in Col-
lective Bargaining and Political Pressure* (Toronto, 1939).
[18]C. C. Taylor, *Toronto Called Back from 1886 to 1850* (Toronto, 1886),
pp. 247–9; see also *Select Documents in Canadian Economic History, 1783–1885*,
ed. H. A. Innis and A. R. M. Lower (Toronto, 1933), pp. 662ff.

With increasing industrialism and urbanization heavier demands were made on the retail trade. It was significant that active general store merchants moved from small Ontario towns and established department stores in Toronto.[19] The sale of goods for cash and a fixed price for large quantities of uniform goods provided the basis for the introduction of large-scale marketing. Reduction of fire hazards, improvement of street railway systems, a steady decline in the price of newsprint, an improvement in methods of advertising, and the extension of postal facilities enabled department stores not only to dominate the retail trade of the large cities but also to extend their trade to rural areas through the mail-order catalogues. The barter system of the general store was exposed to the ruthless efficiency of cash trading.

With the opening of the West following the construction of the Canadian Pacific Railway and the enormous increase of population after the turn of the century, the demand for manufactured products brought a marked expansion of markets in eastern Canada and in western Canada. The monopoly of the Hudson's Bay Company invited and became exposed to competition from the United States.[20] Merchants became established in Winnipeg and other centres and the Hudson's Bay Company entered the retail trade on an extensive scale.[21] Merchants in Regina and other western centres demanded railway rates enabling them to compete with Winnipeg.[22] In British Columbia the early importance of placer mining gave the banks an important position as merchants of gold, the raw material. The marketing structure responded to the demands of a sudden increase in population scattered over a wide area. Development of mining in the Kootenay areas and later in the Yukon in the nineties imposed tremendous demands on the trade of Victoria, Vancouver, Calgary and Edmonton.[23] The latter city felt the effects of the opening of the Peace and Mackenzie districts.

Maritime merchants suffered from the effects of the long depression from the seventies to the nineties in the sharp decline of wooden sail-

[19]Timothy Eaton moved from a small general store in St. Mary's to Toronto in 1869. Robert Simpson moved from Newmarket to Toronto in 1871. G. G. Nasmith, *Timothy Eaton* (Toronto, 1923).

[20]Innis, *Fur Trade in Canada*, pp. 345ff.

[21]Stores were opened at Winnipeg in 1881, Fort William, Lethbridge, and Nelson in 1892, Vernon and Kamloops in 1912. Large stores were established at Calgary and Edmonton.

[22]See the Regina Rate Case in D. A. MacGibbon, *Railway Rates and the Canadian Railway Commission* (Boston, 1917), pp. 177–8.

[23]H. A. Innis, *Settlement and the Mining Frontier* (Toronto, 1936).

ing vessels as well as the handicap of protection which weakened the importers of the St. Lawrence. Expansion of the Prairie Provinces and British Columbia had less direct but more serious implications for the Maritimes than for the St. Lawrence basin, since they responded to the peak activities of the early part of the century and collapsed with their disappearance, especially in the post-war period.

In the war and the post-war period transportation facilities were enormously extended by canals, railroads, automobiles and roads, and aeroplanes, and communication improvements ranged from the development of rural mail delivery to the radio. Railroad and road extension in the non-agricultural areas was followed by tremendous growth in the mining, pulp and paper, and hydro-electric power industries. A large industrial population in the mining camps and pulp and paper towns provided a large cash market not only in the immediate vicinity but also in the large cities, especially of Ontario and Quebec, and of such provinces as Manitoba, Alberta, and British Columbia.

With these developments relations between the marketing structure for exports and the marketing structure for consumers' goods, whether imports or domestic, were steadily widened. The increasing importance of cash in the production of wheat, pulp and paper, and minerals involved increasing efficiency in marketing. The truck and barter system gradually declined with increasing competition. The general store was compelled to meet competition from pedlars who carried packs from farm to farm,[24] from wagons which were miniature general stores on wheels, and from the mail-order catalogue. In more remote areas in which the fur trade and the fishing industry remained dominant the truck system declined slowly, although the radio has made price information continually accessible. The Hudson's Bay Company is still controlled from London and is the oldest joint stock company in the world. Robin Jones and Whitman, originally a Jersey Island firm, transferred its headquarters to Canada in 1904. In Newfoundland, dependence on the fishing industry narrowed the possibilities of a break between the marketing structure for imports of manufactured

---

[24]These pedlars exchanged articles for board and room and for the profit available. Since they did not necessarily revisit the routes the articles were in many cases defective. They were often foreigners and in the country districts were referred to as "Italians." The writer has strong reminiscences of abuse heaped on the head of a pedlar who followed the trail of defective articles traded by a forerunner. Sam Slick represented a type of Yankee pedlar in the Maritimes. His formula was "human nature and soft sawder." See T. C. Haliburton, *The Clockmaker, or the Sayings and Doings of Samuel Slick of Slickville* (London, 1843).

products and the marketing structure for exports, with the result that the debt system has tended to prevail.[25]

In the separation between marketing structures, finance played an increasingly important role. The varying effects of the depression on an economy producing minerals and newsprint, especially in eastern Canada, for the markets of the United States, wheat in the Prairie Provinces for Europe, and lumber in British Columbia for markets in the Pacific and the Atlantic, were evident in complex economic, political, and social problems. Readjustments in the economy in response to these varying effects involved an emphasis on elements of the institutional machinery providing for flexibility in which marketing organization was significant. Retailers were compelled to bring the rigid prices of manufactured products into line with the flexible prices of exports, and department stores occupied a strategic position because of extensive buying power and ability to reach a wide market. The extent of the political boundaries of Canada as developed under commercialism implied dependence on a wide variety of staple exports with varying returns as a result of prices, yields, and rigidity of costs characteristic of high transportation changes and a protected system. As a result of the extensive market and the fluctuating character of the economy, department stores have attempted to deploy by establishing branches in large centres.[26] Their activities serve as a balance-wheel to an economy covering a vast area and constantly tending toward disequilibrium.[27]

The Canadian economy has been profoundly influenced by its geographic background, which has involved dependence on Europe and later on the United States and the Orient. Its characteristics are reflected in the peculiarities of its marketing structure. Consequently, the problems of marketing in Canada differ from those of the United States. While the decline in the price of newsprint, the rise of ad-

[25]The debt system had its own protective devices. Goods were sold at a high price to the local purchaser on a book account and products were purchased similarly at a high price on a book account. A purchaser from outside the district was compelled to pay the same high price but in cash. Consequently it was cheaper to purchase the product outside than in the district. Competition became effective with improved transportation for imports. See H. A. Innis, *The Fur Trade of Canada* (Toronto, 1927).

[26]The T. Eaton Company opened a store in Winnipeg in 1905, Montreal in 1925, Hamilton in 1927, Saskatoon in 1927, Calgary in 1929. In 1928 the Canadian Department Stores Ltd. was purchased and the T. Eaton Company Ltd. Maritimes was formed.

[27]*The Canadian Economy and Its Problems*, ed. H. A. Innis and A. F. W. Plumptre (Toronto, 1934).

vertising agencies,[28] the rise of the radio, and the decline in the number of newspapers have been evident in both countries, technical advances in the United States have been transferred to Canada and have been characterized by differences in rate of development. Marketing organization has been influenced by these and other features. Mail-order houses preceded department stores in the United States and followed them in Canada. The sharp fluctuations of the Canadian economy have exercised severe pressure on marketing structure.[29] The Royal Commission on Price Spreads reflected the difficulties to which department stores were subjected during a period of depression. The sensitive position of department stores in Canada has been responsible for the emphasis on goodwill. Reluctance on their part to reach back to the control of industries follows an appreciation of the importance of goodwill. Competition tends to shift from prices to services as a form of competition. The size of marketing units in the department stores involved limitation in the numbers of organizations and a tendency toward imperfect competition (duopoly?). American marketing with its large-scale demands assumes the importance of complementarity[30] in the extension of control over industry in a sense which could not be realized in Canada. Marshall stated that "the marketing side of the work of a business is an integral process and not a series of independent transactions."[31] The pattern of metropolitan growth in the United States, outlined by Professor N. S. B. Gras,[32] needs substantial modification in Canada. A metropolitan area which begins as a trading centre, becomes a centre of transport routes, and then develops as an industrial and finally a financial centre in the normal

[28]H. E. Stephenson and F. C. McNaught, *The Story of Advertising in Canada* (Toronto, 1940); also R. M. Hower, *The History of an Advertising Agency* (Cambridge, Mass., 1939).

[29]Financial problems arise from the same phenomenon chiefly because of the greater flexibility involved. The results are evident on the one hand in major liquidations in more exposed areas and in the extension of government debt. See A. F. W. Plumptre, *Central Banking in the British Dominions* (Toronto, 1940); also K. W. Taylor, "The Commercial Policy of Canada," *Canadian Marketing Problems*, ed. H. R. Kemp (Toronto, 1939); *Canadian Investment and Foreign Exchange Problems*, ed. J. F. Parkinson (Toronto, 1940).

[30]In the salmon fishing industry large marketing organizations of food products reach back to control the smaller organizations engaged in the production of salmon. See H. E. Gregory and K. Barnes, *North Pacific Fisheries* (Honolulu, 1939). Drug stores are notorious illustrations of attempts to increase the range of stocks to take advantage of complementarity.

[31]*Industry and Trade*, p. 20.

[32]N. S. B. Gras, *An Introduction to Economic History* (New York, 1922), chap. VI.

character of its growth, will be affected in Canada by the varying demands of Europe for staple products from definite regions over varying periods of time and under varying conditions of production. The demands of the Canadian economy on the marketing structure fluctuate widely from conditions of very onerous character to conditions of an extremely favourable character. Flexibility becomes extremely important and specialization is more limited.

The problem of marketing in Canada is of fundamental importance and has ramifications which necessitate an appreciation of the characteristics of the economy as a whole. The slow division between the marketing institutions concerned with exports and those concerned with imports reflected the importance of staple products. Separation between these institutions involved heavy strains on the marketing organizations concerned with finished products.

Marketing organizations reflect the influence of increasing specialization in production of finished goods. In turn, industry reflects the peculiarities of commodities. Nickel production dependent on large ore bodies and extensive capital equipment presses relentlessly on secondary industries. The newsprint industry and the hydro-electric power industry combine in the competitive struggle against the radio. The increasing complexity implies the necessity for greater sensitivity in advertising. Department stores evade costs of newspaper advertising by an extensive use of handbills. Decline in numbers of newspapers has its effect not only on the advertising policy of large organizations but also on politics. The problems of marketing have far-reaching ramifications in a democracy.

Recent Developments in the Canadian Economy*

THE attempt to control and direct our own destinies since we emerged from the intense baptism of fire of the 1914–18 war has been evident in every phase of economic life. The growth of nationalistic determinism has not been peculiar to Canada but has reflected a general trend of the war and post-war period throughout the world. The war speeded up the prosperity which began with the turn of the century, following the long period of depression from 1846, and which ended with the severe crisis of 1929. Those who believe in the regularity of cyclical activity describe a long wave from 1896 to 1933, a shorter wave from 1922 to 1933 and a very short wave from 1929 to 1933. All of these coincided to produce the unprecedented severity of the latter year. Those who are concerned with a more detailed description of cyclical activity regard the long depression as one characterized by extensive construction of railroads or as industrial capitalism with dependence on coal, and the long period of prosperity as one characterized by new sources of power such as gasoline and electricity or as marked by the entrenchment of metropolitanism and the growth of finance capitalism. The crisis and the depression exposed the limitations of finance capitalism and were followed by the spread of national capitalism.

The sources of the material for this paper reflect perhaps more effectively than any other index the growth of nationalism. One may point to the amazing growth of the Dominion Bureau of Statistics under Dr. Coats who assumed direction in 1918, registered in an ever widening range of census material, an ever increasing stream of publications, and the ever expanding size and weight of the *Canada Year Book*. Provincial governments have followed—two of them, strikingly enough at the extremities of the Dominion, have established economic councils. Universities have increased the size of departments concerned with the social sciences. The revival of the Canadian Political Science Association was followed by the publication of the *Canadian*

*From Chester Martin, ed., *Canada in Peace and War* (Toronto, Oxford University Press, 1941), pp. 58–85.

291

Journal of Economics and Political Science. The *Canadian Historical Review* developed into a quarterly immediately after the war. American foundations have supported Canadian scholarship in facilitating research and the publication of the results in volumes in the Canadian Frontiers of Settlement series and the Canadian–American Relations series. The man on the street has been persistently educated in the patter of economics by the daily press and the development of a more efficient specialized press in such media as the *Financial Post*. Large-scale production of paper, the extension of printing presses, and the development of the aeroplane and the radio have speeded up communication and made it possible for electorates to be swayed by the new gospels of social credit, poverty in the midst of plenty, production for use and not for profit, and all the rest.

The character and extent of economic literature have been profoundly affected by secular and cyclical activity. It is not the point of this paper to present an economic interpretation of economic bibliography, but the decline of immigration, the disappearance of free land, and the onset of the depression have brought a wide range of problems which are reflected in the reports of the commissioner of the Combines Investigation Act, of the Tariff Board, and of Royal Commissions on regional problems, particularly in the Maritimes and the Prairies, on banking, railways, and price spreads, and on special industries such as wheat, coal, and textiles. These documents have the smell of political bias, the evidence presented to the bodies concerned reeks with the claims of special interests, and the debates about them are designed to catch every conceivable political breeze. Provincial governments have made extensive inventories of their resources and supported directly and indirectly numerous Royal Commissions and investigations.

The voice of the economist is heard throughout the land. In every investigation economists of quality and quantity have contributed substantially either by giving evidence or by stuffing the shirts of their betters, that is, writing the final reports. The rise of economists has been an important political trend of the post-war period. They have captured crucial positions in the civil service, especially with the Bank of Canada, and the discussion of the problems of Canadian recovery has taken on the air of rational calculation. Every large organization concerned with business has its economist. A new religion has emerged. The acute religious controversies of the past generation have given way to economics. One would like to believe that the continuous and rapid growth was important to the extension of knowledge.

But men at whiles are sober
And think by fits and starts. (Housman)

All of this is presented by way of credentials and to show that I am aware of the relatively slight but important role which economics has to play. While we have established the new priesthood to which every venture must in some way pay tribute, our religion is sufficiently young to permit of disputation, and I may be permitted for this reason to point to some trends which may not be in every way conceded.

They answered, as they took their Fees
"There is no Cure for this Disease." (Belloc)

The 1914–18 war hastened a trend of rapid exploitation which began early in the century and slowed down in 1929. A brief description of the major developments in separate regions will indicate more clearly the place of various industries. The stimulus of the cyclonic economic activities of the Pacific in the early part of the century to transcontinental traffic and industrial development in eastern Canada began to show striking signs of decline. The centre of the spectacular outburst in the Yukon had declined to the point in 1926 where empty houses were conspicuous and the only evidences of activity were the operations of a few large dredges systematically exploiting the remaining placer gold of the large rivers and the small-scale operations of individuals and partnerships on the creeks. The engine which had run on the short railway of the district in the height of its prosperity stood in its stall with little prospect of being moved until the crack of doom. A tourist trade attracted by the log cabin in which Robert Service formerly lived brought money into a region which formerly produced it. Fur farming and shipments of concentrated ore from the silver lead camp at Mayo emerged from a scene of desolation and wreckage. Church and state retreated on all fronts. That pioneer of missionary efforts in the Arctic and the Yukon, Bishop Stringer, was leaving to become Archbishop of Rupert's Land with his headquarters at Winnipeg. A community which thought only of dollars as the smallest units had gradually become reconciled to quarters and finally to dimes. The high price of gold during the depression and the low price of commodities brought a revival, but the pulse beat was feeble.

Completion of four railways from the Prairies to the coast of British Columbia immediately before the war, two by the Yellowhead Pass and one each by the Kicking Horse and the Crow's Nest Pass, three to Vancouver and one to Prince Rupert, unlocked the resources of the province. Fresh halibut was sent by express from Prince Rupert to the markets of eastern Canada and the United States. Canadians and

Americans pushed to more distant fishing grounds of the Pacific and eventually reached the point when exhaustion compelled the adoption of mutually restricted operations in the Halibut Treaty of 1923—significantly enough the first to be signed by Canada with the United States without the intervention of Great Britain. The salmon fishing of the Fraser River was subject to the same trends toward depletion and a later convention between Canada and the United States pointed to the need of a mutual policy of conservation.

The lumber industry after the turn of the century flourished in relation to local demands, to the demands of an expanding market in the Prairies, and to the demands of Pacific regions, especially the Orient. Completion of the Panama Canal immediately after the war opened the industrial regions of the Atlantic to the lumber producers of the Pacific. Lumber pushed its way into the markets of eastern Canada and responded to the housing boom in England. Cheap water navigation extended the range of markets for a heavy bulky commodity and the new industrialism based on oil and hydro-electric power lowered costs of transportation and created markets on the Pacific and the Atlantic. Similar rapid expansion of the pulp and paper industry assumed expansion of hydro-electric power. Ships were attracted to British Columbia ports for enormous quantities of raw materials, including wheat from Alberta, and they brought as ballast manufactured products which penetrated far to the interior.

As in the Yukon the mining boom of the Kootenay area in the late nineties suffered a temporary collapse but interest shifted from the precious metals to the more permanent development of base metals. In the war period, copper deposits were exhausted and intensive experiments solved the problem of handling complex Sullivan ores and led to the enormous investment of capital in hydro-electric power, concentrators, refineries, and fertilizer plants at Trail. Coal mines in the Crow's Nest Pass area and Vancouver Island suffered from the competition of hydro-electric power, and oil from the Pacific states. Specialized agriculture responded to the demands of the Prairies, the urban population of British Columbia, and the markets accessible by the Panama Canal. Irrigated fruit farming of the Okanagan and dairy production of the Fraser valley were faced with intensive competition on the export markets, and there emerged a demand for systems of control and, in the case of fruit, exposure to inquiries and prosecutions under the Combines Investigation Act.

Exhaustion of resources, the increasing importance of large-scale capital equipment, and the attractions of a pleasant climate to labour from the prairie regions led to demands for restriction of Oriental immigration and to the enactment of legislation barring both Chinese and Japanese. Oriental labour was driven by regulations from the mines, the lumber camps, and the fishing industry and took refuge in agriculture and commercial activities. We shall leave the Pacific coast conscious of an intensely specialized economy developed at great cost in the face of topographical restrictions but expanding under the stimulus of new sources of power and the advantages of enormous improvements of navigation. Depletion of resources, exposure to the effects of fluctuations in the prairie markets, and competition in the export markets have contributed to the demands for controls and to the difficulties of controls. A marked concentration of population in the area of Vancouver and Victoria facilitates the organization of local demands.

In the vast area east of the Rocky Mountains and west of Fort William and north from the 49th parallel to the Arctic we have suggested the effects of expansion on the Pacific in the shipment of wheat from Alberta and of products from the Pacific coast to the interior. Settlement was extended to the Peace River and wheat was grown in larger quantities. The high prices of the war and the sharp decline after the war were followed by gradual improvement under the influence of speculative activity in North America prior to recovery in the wheat-producing regions of Europe. Construction of branch lines, the efficiency of new sources of power in tractor, truck, and combine, the introduction of new varieties, and the expansion of the pooling system facilitated concentration on wheat. Collapse of the boom in 1929, low prices of wheat, and years of drought converted an area of high purchasing power to one marked by emigration, drastically reduced standards of living, relief, and debt with serious repercussion for railways, industry, and finance. The tragedy of the wheat-producing areas was offset in part by a shift to dairying and live-stock and was accompanied by phenomenal expansion in the vast area dominated by the Canadian Shield. In 1924 the Peace, the Slave, and the Mackenzie rivers flowed serenely to the north with only the disturbance of the ordinary routine of the summer season. The Hudson's Bay Company had just completed another amalgamation with its rival the Lamson Hubbard Company after the difficulties of fabulous prices of fur during the war and the disastrous collapse which followed. Fur-trading posts had been extended among the Eskimo along the Western Arctic following up the Canadian Arctic expedition in the search for supplies of white fox. More efficient transportation had been introduced, Imperial Oil had discovered petroleum at Fort Norman but it was not developed until the discovery of radium ore in Bear Lake created new demands.

The Panama Canal not only lowered costs to the Pacific and to northern Alberta but it also hastened the development of the mineral resources of coal and oil in southern Alberta. Moreover, it hastened the development of trade to Bering Sea and around the north of Alaska. Its effects in opening the north were reinforced by a further major development of transportation, the Hudson Bay Railway. The discovery of a successful flow sheet by Mining Corporation led to the development of Flin Flon and Sheritt Gordon by the Hudson's Bay Mining and Smelting Company and to construction of branch lines of railway, a smelting plant, and a hydro-electric power plant on the Churchill River. Experience gained in constructing the railway to Flin Flon led to the rapid construction of the Hudson Bay Railway to Churchill in the winter season of 1928–9. The Hon. Frank Oliver, who had long cherished the dream of the West for an outlet by Hudson Bay, was one of the first to visit the new port in 1929. The firm of James Richardson sent the first small consignment of wheat via the Hudson Bay route in the same year. Completion of the railway was followed immediately by prospecting activities by air from points along the west coast of Hudson Bay, the Western Arctic, and the Mackenzie. Many will remember the dangerous adventure of Col. McAlpine in the fall of that year. The extensive prospecting investigations were followed by discovery of the mineral wealth of Bear Lake and of Slave Lake. The Mackenzie River became a centre of intensive prospecting and mining for minerals and oil and contributed materially to make Canada the most important country in the world in the handling of freight by air. The fur trade was extended to the extreme eastern part of the Arctic at King William Land and in the Boothia Peninsula. Final evidence was collected on the tragedy of the Franklin expedition. The Hudson's Bay Company established contact with the last band of Eskimos, and concluded an activity which began with the first landing of Europeans on the shores of temperate North America and finally completed the northwest passage as a commercial route. Governmental activity was in evidence in scientific investigations and conservation. Depletion of animal life led to steps which involved the heroic and successful undertaking of driving a reindeer herd from Alaska to the Mackenzie delta.

The movement of the economic height of land eastward from the Pacific coast, in which the influence of the Panama Canal penetrated far into the interior and encroached on the sphere of the St. Lawrence, meant intensification of industry along the Atlantic seaboard at the expense of industry in the heart of the continent, and had implications direct and indirect for eastern Canada, particularly in the depression. Enlargement of the Welland Canal, improvement of the Erie Canal, and improvement of harbours in Canada and the United States in part offset the effects of the pull of the Pacific coast, but the St. Lawrence canals have still to be deepened. Through the Panama Canal came butter from New Zealand to harass the Canadian dairy industry and to lead to the demand for, and the introduction of, protective tariffs. Lumber from the Pacific coast was sold in the markets of eastern Canada in competition with the local product. Fruit from British Columbia came into competition with fruit from eastern Canada. Railway expansion in the prairie regions no longer created demands for rails and equipment from the steel mills and car plants of Ontario, Quebec, and Nova Scotia. Decline in demand for steel meant decline in the demand for Nova Scotia coal. Companies were reorganized, and subventions were paid to increase the market for coal in Ontario.

The Canadian lumber industry had long felt the effects of demand from the increasingly urbanized markets of the United States. Control of land, timber, minerals, and power-sites by Ontario enabled her to engage in reprisals against tariffs imposed by the United States by embargoes on logs and pulpwood cut on Crown lands. Ontario attempted to compel American capital to establish plants in Canada but, with exports permitted from private lands and without an embargo in Quebec and New Brunswick, was only partially successful. Depletion of American supplies of pulpwood, the demand of American newspapers for cheaper raw material, and the imposition of an embargo in Quebec in 1910 and in New Brunswick a year later were followed by a lowering of the tariff on newsprint in the Reciprocity Treaty of 1911 and a further lowering in 1913. The way was prepared for migration of the industry to Canada. The demand for newsprint during the war and the cutting off of supplies of sulphite pulp from Scandinavia were followed by a sharp rise in prices. The investment of large profits from war undertakings in advertising rather than in payment of profit taxes supported a continuation of high prices, but ultimate readjustments brought a drastic decline. Bankrupt sulphite plants came on the market as a result of renewed Scandinavian competition. The necessity of lower costs hastened the construction of large plants such as that of the International Paper Company at Three Rivers. Newsprint mills were closed down in the United States and the power sold to industries and municipalities. Power sites were acquired in Canada to support the newsprint industry and ultimately, as in the United States, municipalities and industries. The Duke fortune from tobacco was invested in the Duke Price power and paper developments on the Saguenay. On the Ottawa, the St. Maurice and the Saguenay, and even on the rivers of the Hudson Bay drainage basin made accessible by the National Transcontinental, forests of spruce and balsam, cheap navigation, power sites, labour conditions, and a short rail haul to New York and the Atlantic seaboard combined to encourage numerous and enormous undertakings. The upward swing of the business cycle gathered momentum and brought increased demands for advertising space and for newsprint, and a widespread familiarity with bonds, arising from the war, made funds available for construction. The crisis of 1929, the depression, and the development of new methods of communication in the radio were followed by low prices, disaster, reorganization, and the end of the period of colossal undertakings. Paper companies became increasingly concerned with power with the result that it tended to become the main product and newsprint the by-product. The difficulties of Abitibi in the development of power plants and the advantages to newsprint mills on the Ottawa of power contracts with the Ontario Hydro-Electric have been a centre of intense political interest in Ontario. With high prices during the last war large numbers of newspapers like the *News* and the *World* in Toronto disappeared, and with the difficulties of the depression the *Globe* and *Mail* were amalgamated. Partisanship becomes less conspicuous as the traditional dichotomy of the Liberal and Conservative press disappears. Advertising returns from department stores become a more important source of revenue. The significance of the radio has been evident on all sides. We have witnessed a revolution in the technique of communication far more significant in its implication than the change from the movies to the talkies or the vogue of Charlie McCarthy.

A discussion of the problems of newsprint and hydro-electric power is drawn irresistibly into a discussion of another major industry which has depended on power development, namely, mining. The *Globe and Mail* has been supported by capital from mines. As in British Columbia mines have been opened, exploited, and exhausted, but the industry has shown greater evidence of continuity and expansion. The enormous nickel deposits at Sudbury were rapidly exploited during the 1914–18 war and a refinery was built at Port Colborne. The end of the war, naval limitation agreements, and the demand for lighter battleships with the use of new sources of power such as oil, compelled the industry to concentrate on the discovery of new uses. New alloys were worked out and industry was provided with more efficient raw materials. A world monopoly was strengthened in the amalgamation of the International Nickel and Mond in the late years of the twenties. Cobalt emerged as a great poor man's silver camp early in the century but its properties were exhausted by capitalistic devices in the war and the post-war period. We know of the wealth which poured from this region through the benefactions of the late Col. Leonard, the O'Briens, and others. Companies transferred their activities from Cobalt to Porcupine and began the development of such gigantic properties as Dome, McIntyre, and Hollinger. From the rich mines of Kirkland Lake we have had Dr. J. B. Tyrrell, Mr. Wright of the *Globe and Mail*, and Sir Harry Oakes. Capital from Hollinger contributed to the construction of the smelter at Noranda. As companies accumulated surpluses, and mines were exhausted, there came the search for other properties, with the success we have described in Flin Flon in northern Manitoba, and the development of properties in northern Quebec. Nipissing, Mining Corporation, Dome, Hollinger, and the others have ceaselessly examined possible developments in the whole of the vast Precambrian area. Moreover, a widespread interest in penny stocks, the financial interests of Toronto, Buffalo, and New York, independent financiers, brokers, and governments have been responsible for large numbers of developments such as those in the Patricia District and elsewhere. Hydro-electric power has kept pace. Power released from exhausted mining camps, such as Cobalt, power developed with the newsprint industry, power supported by private enterprise and governments directly and indirectly concerned with mining met the demands of the industry. Island Falls, Abitibi, Quinze, and numerous other sites have emerged. The effects of the demands of expanding industries in mining, pulp and paper, and hydro-electric power have been evident in the growth of a more highly integrated industrial region in eastern Canada, shown in the establishment of the Ontario Research Foundation and the National Research Council. A divergence of interest has grown up within Canada—the Prairies with wheat dependent on Great Britain, the East with less dependence on the Prairies and with greater dependence on new industrial products for the markets of the United States.

The pull of the densely populated areas of the eastern states has been evident not only on the regions tributary to the St. Lawrence but also in the Maritimes. After the war mine sweepers were converted into trawlers and the production of dried cod was enormously increased in Iceland. This increase in production pushed cod from Newfoundland out of European markets to the markets of the West Indies and South America. In turn Nova Scotia was unable to compete with Newfoundland and she sought protection in the sheltered market of the St. Lawrence region and in the United States. She was compelled to turn from the dried fish industry to the fresh fish industry. Salt gave way to ice. Refrigeration and rapid transportation involved capital equipment in the form of trawlers, freezing plants, and fish-meal plants. The American market became more important with exhaustion of resources, increased population, and speeding up of transportation. The live lobster trade extended from western to eastern Nova Scotia and the Magdalen Islands. American capital became dominant in the Maritime fresh fish industry in the late twenties. Retreat from European to North American markets imposed tremendous strains on the Atlantic industry. These were evident in the greatest of all tragedies for democratic populations—the disappearance of responsible government in Newfoundland and in St. Pierre and Miquelon. In the Canadian Maritimes direct and indirect subsidies, and a healthy interest in their own problems as shown in the active co-operative movement, have relieved the starkest aspects. All around the shores of Nova Scotia, New Brunswick, Gaspé, the Canadian Labrador, Newfoundland, and the Newfoundland Labrador, disturbances in the economic life in the countries bordering the Atlantic were felt directly and immediately. War in Spain, the imposition of sanctions on Italy, the collapse of the coffee market in Brazil, the problems of sugar in the West Indies—each of these was registered in the price of cod. Nova Scotia apples were faced with competition from British Columbia. New Brunswick and Nova Scotia became concerned with the pulp and paper industry as a result of competition from the Pacific. Iron and coal suffered from higher costs of production and the decline of markets for rails in the prairie regions.

Throughout Canada, but particularly in the more densely populated regions of the East adjacent to the United States, petroleum as a new source of power became the basis of an enormous programme of road construction on the part of the provinces. The construction industry, the automobile industry, and a host of subsidiary industries flourished. The tourist trade was encouraged by favourable exchange rates, and we capitalized on the "noble experiment" by repealing prohibition. The fishing fleets converted their schooners into rum runners. Encouragement in the use of new sources of power by the provinces increased the difficulties of the railroads dependent on coal and in turn of the Canadian Pacific Railway and the federal government.

To summarize, the 1914–18 war intensified the demand for fur, for fish, wheat, and other food products, for newsprint and minerals. In the post-war period lowering of costs of transportation through the use of the Panama Canal and the use of oil in travel by air, water, road, and railroad brought an extension of production in the vastly extended area tributary to the Pacific coast. It became possible to travel to Moosonee and to Churchill by pullman and to cover the vast areas of the Mackenzie and the Yukon by plane. We have seen these developments, most of us, in our own time. Cheaper products from the Pacific coast hastened the growth of industries and the concentration of population along the Atlantic seaboard. New sources of power, and the significance of technological change in transportation to the movement of cheap bulky commodities such as timber and of light valuable manufactured products, implied profound disturbances to the industries of North America. The framework of the industrial structure of the pre-war period was subjected to terrific bombardment by a revolution affecting heavy staple products. Economists have paid insufficient attention to the specific effects of these changes on specific commodities and specific industries. In Canada as in the United States population began to move eastward rather than westward. The quota imposed by the United States hastened urbanization of population and a decline in the birth rate. It was significant that the Anglo-Saxon population ceased to be a majority in Canada. I shall not discuss the implications of a declining birth rate in European populations to problems of labour, trade, and strategy during the present war. We must be content to point to the increasing importance of the markets of the United States to eastern Canada as a result of increasing population and exhaustion of resources.

II

The United States in the pre-war period was a debtor nation; in the post-war period a creditor nation. With large supplies of gold, a population trained in the use of securities as a result of war finance, a powerful financial centre in New York, and an agricultural and industrial plant fresh from the war effort, she was reluctant to face the effects of competition from the imports which characterized a creditor position. High import tariffs and enormous loans enabled her to increase exports and to participate in the task of European reconstruction. To a large extent loans were made by which reparations were paid by Germany to pay the Allied debts to the United States. Moreover, the disappearance of debts in Germany through the drastic effects of inflation enabled cities and towns and industrial plants to secure new mortgages for extensive renovations and improvements. The Versailles Treaty prohibited the draining of funds into armaments and led to concentration on commercial aviation, and development of the electrical, chemical, lignite, and iron and steel industries. Germany purchased Wabana iron in Newfoundland in competition with Nova Scotia.

The intense speculative boom in the late twenties in the United States supported by the technological advances we have described, and evident in the loans for Canadian pulp and paper plants, roads, hydro-electric power plants, and skyscrapers of the cities of North and South America, began to reverse the process and to drain funds from Europe. Wheat, newsprint, minerals, commodities and securities, governments, private traders, and wheat pools were carried along in the upward sweep. The effects of the crash in 1929 and the depression which followed spread rapidly throughout the entire world. The collapse of speculative markets was marked by the sharp fall in prices of securities and commodities. Governmental credit felt the effects. The long series of attempts to reinstate Austria, after the vast empire of 1914 had been dismembered and carved into separate states centring about Prague and Budapest, eventually faced defeat. The bankruptcy of one of the largest banks in Vienna in May 1931 and attempts to check disaster forced one country after another off the gold standard and finally England was pushed into the arms of a National Government in September. The Ottawa Agreements of 1932 and the election of President Roosevelt were a part of the attempts at recovery in the British Empire and the United States. The banking crisis in the United States in 1933 was followed by the ill-fated World Economic Conference.

The significance of the refusal of the United States to participate effectively in the World Economic Conference warrants careful study. The long period of the wars of the last half of the eighteenth and the early nineteenth centuries in some sense solved the problems of commercial capitalism, since the American Revolution was followed inevitably by the trend toward free trade in Great Britain, and by the second Empire. But it was precisely the contributions of the United States to the solution of the problems of commercial capitalism which made it impossible for her to solve the problems of finance capitalism.

Active governmental intervention in a European war involved enormous loans to the Allies, a strong creditor position, and marked technological advance. High tariffs and private loans to enable Europe to repay the interest on government loans contributed to the impasse of 1929 and 1933. The United States following the traditions of commercial capitalism repelled political entanglements in Europe, but the war and finance capitalism brought entanglements of a more subtle character. Nevertheless President Roosevelt continued the policy of his predecessors and where loans had been made to finance exports he raised the price of gold to $35 an ounce in order to compel other countries to sell that commodity in return for American dollars with which they could purchase American goods.

The effects of this policy varied widely. With the end of the period of reconstruction in Europe, nations imposed tariffs on wheat and other commodities, partly on grounds of retaliation against the United States and partly in the interests of self-sufficiency for military purposes and to check the drain of gold. Russia, with the assistance of European and American engineers and five-year plans, had reached the point where she became a competitor in European markets. Gold bloc countries were forced off the gold standard. Finally, attempts were made to re-establish certainty in exchange by the development of exchange equalization funds and the introduction of the Tripartite Agreement between France, England, and the United States in 1936 and the addition of other countries at a later date.

The immediate effects on Canada became evident in marked activity in gold mining, and in base metal mining where gold was a by-product. The pulp and paper industry gradually recovered from the low point of the depression. The indirect effects were more difficult to trace. The long series of devices of the United States to maintain a relatively rigid continental price structure had its effects on the more elastic price structure of maritime areas. The 1914–18 war weakened the dependence of the Orient on Europe and hastened the industrialization of Japan. The disastrous effects of the fall in prices in 1920 on the silk industry were followed by the earthquake of 1923 and the financial panic of 1927, but in spite of these difficulties Japanese textiles began to extend their markets in the Far East and India was compelled to raise her tariffs. Lancashire was severely affected and began to press for a share of the markets of Canada and the other Dominions. Wheat and wool moved in large quantities from Australia to Japan. The depression was accompanied by determined efforts to extend markets in China by conquest.

The Antipodes were closely tied to the price structure of Great Britain and reflected its difficulties. Great Britain had suffered from attempts to catch up with the gold standard in the twenties. A temporary boom in coal mining, following occupation of the Ruhr by the French in 1923, was marked by higher prices, and the difficulties after its evacuation were followed by the general strike of 1926. With the crash in the United States and the drastic fall in prices of raw materials Great Britain was at last in a position to gain. The light industries had expanded rapidly in the south with the difficulties of the heavy industries in the north. A housing boom created demands for British Columbia lumber. The dominant position of Washington and Oregon in the world's lumber market was lost and British Columbia took their place. There was a dramatic reversal of positions as a result of the price-lifting policies of the United States and the higher costs. While the lumber industry flourished, the dairy industry felt the effects of competition from the Antipodes and took refuge behind tariffs and the creation of boards designed to support the fluid milk industry and to increase the consumption of that product. There were attempts to gain access to the American market. Low prices of grain favoured a shift to the production of bacon for export to Europe.

It is picturesque to describe the United States as an island of dollars floating in a sea of sterling but it is not accurate. It was rather a centre of disturbance in the wide sea of the world's economy sending out currents affecting at various points the centres of Canadian life depending on whether they produced minerals, especially gold, and newsprint, or wheat and lumber. To widen the channels of influence of the American price-lifting policy and to narrow the discrepancy between American and world prices the Hull treaties were designed to provide a series of sluiceways or an anchorage for the American economy. These sluiceways enabled Canadian products to penetrate the American market at certain points.

The discrepancies between sterling and the dollar introduced innumerable strains between the areas affected in Canada, and compelled a resort to various expedients. We adopted a wheat board and guaranteed a minimum price for wheat. We defaulted on debts and introduced various adjustment schemes. Railway rate legislation improved the position of the extremities of the Dominion, the Maritimes and British Columbia. The Bank of Canada emerged to cope with the problems arising from our dependence on staple products for export to Great Britain and the United States. The old provinces with control over their own mineral and pulpwood resources felt immediately the effects of the New Deal and were more advantageously situated than the new wheat-producing provinces with more direct dependence on Great Britain. To adjust these problems it was necessary to appoint the Rowell Commission.

Adjustments between Canada and the United States have involved not only the introduction of internal machinery. Specially designed arrangements such as the Halibut Treaty and the Salmon Treaty were concerned with conservation. The International Joint Commission, among other tasks, made extensive investigations leading to the proposals for deepening the St. Lawrence waterway. But the problem of reaching agreements was complicated by the character of the constitutional framework. Constitutions designed for defence are not adaptable to co-operation. The Senate of the United States is a notorious stumbling block to treaties. It is paralleled by the position of the old provinces in the Confederation of Canada. Nationalism is entrenched in constitutional handicaps. The extent of its influence has been evident in the difficulties of co-operation between labour organizations of the United States and Canada. Strict avoidance of political activities has facilitated affiliation between the Trades and Labour Congress and the American Federation of Labor and the relatively rigid relationships between railway wages in Canada and the United States, but it has not prevented the isolation of the unionism of the French Canadians and the unpleasantness over the C.I.O.

Rigidities in some relationships between Canada and the United States have accentuated concentration on flexibilities in others. Labour is largely restricted from migrating to the United States but the tourist trade is an object of intense interest on the part of Canada. Capital movements have been encouraged in every possible way. American firms not only have responded to encouragement but have been quick to see the implications of differences in price levels or of instability in American policy and have set up branch plants to take advantage not only of the Canadian market but also of the diverse markets provided by imperial and other agreements. The automobile and the agricultural implement industries will serve as illustrations. The aluminum industry on the Saguenay was a result not only of the search for investment in hydro-electric power development by the Duke interests but also of the search for a means by which the Aluminum Company of America could participate effectively in a world cartel. American industry has recognized the importance of maintaining a position in other countries to offset the effects of disturbances in the United States. Properties are bought in Canada to hedge against inflation in the United States. The state prohibits us from owning gold, but we can still buy gold stocks and gold mines. The state has resorted to control over gold as a means to security and has made insecurity more inevitable.

Economic trends, or perhaps we should say political trends, in Canada have been and will be powerfully influenced by political trends in the United States. These are primarily concerned with internal problems and it would be dangerous to predict their solution. National finance capitalism in other countries has followed the path of direct governmental control of exchanges and of the direction of economic and political energies to military ends concerned with immediate or ultimate conquest or resistance to conquest. Colonies have become important as a means of expenditure to support policies of full employment and not as a direct means to wealth. They have come to serve as economic balance wheels. Ethiopia could scarcely be regarded as an asset under any other circumstances. Colonies as a means of expenditure have not been thought of by the United States although the vacillating policy toward the Philippines might be regarded as partaking of that character. The same could not be said of military and naval expenditures including bonuses to veterans. The interest in less tangible forms of conquest such as spheres of influence in South American republics and in China may become more important. Canada in her own interests as well as in those of the United States should be constantly alert to the implications of American policy. In a world in which nations and particularly the United States concentrate on their own problems and the use of the new machinery of the modern state, Canada is in a very dangerous position. European civilization has moved from an emphasis on land under feudalism, to an emphasis on trade under commercialism, to an emphasis on money under finance capitalism. We have not yet solved the problem of working with gold or working without it. The democratic countries have gone so far as to co-operate in agreements and the struggle at the moment is between co-operation and coercion. Those words of Lewis Carroll assume ominous import.

> He thought he saw a banker's clerk
> Descending from a bus,
> He looked again and saw it was
> A hippopotamus.
> "If this should stay to dine" he said
> "There won't be much for us."

It may seem preposterous that Canada should entertain the alternative of coercion but there is all too much evidence that the dangers to which we have been exposed have led us to follow precedents created elsewhere and to establish new ones. Compulsion has reared its ugly head where co-operation was the pass word. In British Columbia in the fruit industry and in the dairy industry Supreme Court decisions have been invalidated by legislation compelling numbers outside the co-operatives to abide by the decision of the majority. In the Prairie Provinces compulsory legislation has found its way onto the statute books. Even in the federal field the Natural Products Marketing Act was prevented by a Privy Council decision. In the West and the East, boards have emerged with a powerful element of compulsion. One expects manufacturers to follow merchants, who in the words of Adam Smith are "silent with regard to the pernicious effects of their own gains. They complain only of those of other people." "People of the same trade seldom meet together, even for merriment and diversion, but the conversation ends in a conspiracy against the public, or in some contrivance to raise prices. It is impossible indeed to prevent such meetings by any law which either could be executed or would be consistent with liberty and justice. But though the law cannot hinder people of the same trade from sometimes assembling together, it ought to do nothing to facilitate such assemblies; much less to render them necessary." The commissioner of the Combines Investigation Act regards all this as a normal course but he does not consider political compulsion. Nationalism is still the last refuge of scoundrels. There are well-meaning leaders of large organized religious bodies who argue for toleration and compulsion in the same breath. The dangers of national finance capitalism have been acute in Canada. With the construction of boards and the complicated machinery which has emerged in Ottawa since the war the dangers are not less, and considering the inexperience of those who man such recently installed devices, are much more.

> Oh! let us never, never doubt
> What nobody is sure about! (Belloc)

Nor is the British Empire a final bulwark. With scarcely a word of dissent responsible government was dismissed in Newfoundland as a constitutional nicety by a Royal Commission presided over by a labour peer. Good government is no substitute for self-government.

At the moment we are concerned with the immediate world problem of resisting coercion by force of arms. It is a second effort and the more important for that. It is essentially a part of the inevitable tradition of Canadian life—one would hope—of neither accepting nor imposing domination. Only in such a world could we of all countries have lived and only in such a world can we live. It may seem strange that the United States should have blazed the way to this freedom and that we should be compelled to participate in a struggle to maintain it. But it is more vital to us than to her since she has grown into other ways.

> And how am I to face the odds
> Of man's bedevilment and God's?
> I, a stranger and afraid
> In a world I never made. (Housman)

The Canadian Mining Industry*

THE increasing significance of minerals to modern civilization gives a study of the mining industry in the more recent nations of the New World a place of crucial importance. The discovery of America by Europeans was a result of the search for precious metals, and the character of its occupation was profoundly influenced by their exploitation. The universal demand for liquidity preference heightened the intensity of the search. Policies favouring their exploitation and acquisition were planned to increase the commercial strength of nations. Even Adam Smith wrote that "of all the commodities, therefore, which are bought in one foreign country for no other purpose but to be sold again for some other goods in another, there are none so convenient as gold and silver. In facilitating all the different roundabout foreign trades of consumption which are carried on in Great Britain, consists the principal advantage of the Portugal trade; and though it is not a capital advantage it is, no doubt, a considerable one."[1] The Spanish conquests were directed to the capture of stores of precious metal built up by Indian civilization and to extraction from mines. The obsession of Spain with military occupation was accompanied by imports of enormous quantities of treasure, by a rise in prices, a decline in industry, and the attraction of goods from other European countries with small supplies of precious metals, such as England. "We have no treasure but by trade, for mines we have none." The policies of such countries were elaborated to foster types of trade which brought large and continuous imports of specie. The fisheries were encouraged in Newfoundland and New England to secure exports for Spain and the production of tobacco and sugar in Virginia and the West Indies was given support to check imports from Spain. The Navigation Acts excluded foreign shipping and ensured control over freights and insurance.

The expansion of English commercialism as a result of these policies supported, and was supported by, the growth of English industrialism based on coal. Governmental authority over industry and trade was

*From E. S. Moore, *American Influence in Canadian Mining* (University of Toronto Press, 1941), pp. v–xvii.
[1]*Wealth of Nations* (Modern Library ed., New York, 1937), p. 516.

steadily weakened in England and the colonies.[2] The effectiveness of Dutch and English trade restricted French expansion and encouraged the extension of governmental authority in France and the French colonies. In the fishing industry, the fur trade, and the West Indies trade, France was hampered by the Crown and its companies, and her limitations were the opportunities of England. She fostered shipbuilding and the iron industry on the St. Lawrence[3] and the production of coal in Cape Breton but at the expense of imperial strength. The retreat of the French Empire from North America in 1713 and in 1763 in the face of the expansion of the British Empire contributed to the revolt of the colonies in America and hastened the decline of authority in England.

The withdrawal of the American colonies and the later stages of the industrial revolution in England, which followed the use of coke in the manufacture of iron and the use of steam, were accompanied by modifications in the second Empire in the growth of responsible government in the British American colonies and the emergence of free trade. As a part of the second Empire, Nova Scotia attempted to strengthen her position with relation to Newfoundland and the West Indies by asserting control over trade with the regions formerly belonging to the first Empire. Short distances, cheap water navigation, and wooden sailing vessels made it possible to export cheap heavy commodities such as coal, grindstones, granite, paving stones, and gypsum[4] (plaster of Paris) to restore the exhausted fields of New England. In spite of the demands of expanding industry and trade in the United States for coal, the imposition of a duty and the completion of the Schuylkill navigation in 1825, which enabled Pennsylvania anthracite to reach the seaboard, brought handicaps to Nova Scotia. Coal was admitted duty free during the period of the Reciprocity Treaty (1854–66) chiefly for the manufacture of gas, but the end of reciprocity brought fresh difficulties.

The achievement of responsible government in Nova Scotia was followed by attempts to secure control of mineral resources and in 1858 an agreement was reached between the government and the

²See J. U. Nef, Industry and Government in France and England, 1540–1640 (Philadelphia, 1940), and J. U. Nef, The Rise of the British Coal Industry (London, 1932).

³J. N. Fauteux, Essai sur l'industrie au Canada sous le régime français (Quebec, 1927), chaps. I–III.

⁴G. S. Graham, "The Gypsum Trade of the Maritime Provinces," Agricultural History, July 1938, pp. 209–23; also Richard Brown, The Coal Fields and Coal Trade of the Island of Cape Breton (London, 1871); H. A. Innis, The Cod Fisheries (New Haven, 1940), chap. IX.

General Mining Association which removed the monopoly of the latter over coal. The government of Nova Scotia became immediately concerned through interests in royalties in the acquisition of new markets. Railroad construction was fostered in the Maritimes Provinces, and Confederation was regarded as a means not only of relieving the problem of debt which accompanied the railroads but also of increasing the market for coal by construction of the Intercolonial Railway and by providing a sheltered market in the St. Lawrence. In New France, in the second Empire, and in Confederation, coal mining was an object of governmental concern.

The decline of policies designed to secure gold under the mercantile system, and the emergence of independent states in the New World and of responsible government and free trade in the second Empire, were followed by the gold rushes to margins of the Pacific Ocean. The direct effects of the discovery and exploitation of placer gold replaced the indirect effects of acquisition by conquest and trade policy. The gold rush to California in 1849 was followed by gold rushes to Australia, New Zealand, and British Columbia. Prospectors pushed out from placer areas which were occupied and being exhausted, and in 1857 a rush began to the Fraser River and later to the Cariboo country. The marked increase in population on the edges of the Pacific basin was accompanied by improved navigation, increased trade and domestic industry. Coal was mined on Vancouver Island for domestic consumption and for export to California. The demands of population on the Pacific coast hastened the industrialization of the eastern states, evident in the construction of railways and in the expansion of coal mining and of the iron and steel industry, especially after the completion of the canal at Sault Ste Marie in 1855, the opening of the Minnesota iron deposits, and the Civil War. A transcontinental railway was completed to California in 1869. Partly as a means of checking possible encroachments from the United States on the Red River and the Pacific coast, and partly as a result of the demands of population in British Columbia, new provinces were added to Confederation on condition that "construction of a railway from the Pacific toward the Rocky Mountains" should be started in two years and should be connected with the Canadian railway system in ten years. Placer mining on the Pacific coast had enormous significance to the economic and political history of North America.

The British North America Act was designed deliberately to support construction of the Intercolonial Railway and of the Canadian Pacific Railway as a result of the demands of Nova Scotia and British

Columbia and of attempts to check American competition. The possibilities of the St. Lawrence region as a market for coal from the Maritimes were limited. The *Royal William* crossed the Atlantic in 1833 with Pictou coal, and steamships to and from the St. Lawrence depended on Nova Scotian coal for their bunkers. Deepening of the upper St. Lawrence canals, including the Welland, to nine feet by 1850 and improvements of the channel below Montreal enabled ocean-going steamers to compete more effectively for Great Lakes trade. Construction of railways to supplement the canals and to compete with American lines created demands for iron and coal. The iron industry in the province of Quebec met demands for domestic consumption, including car wheels, and began to draw on Nova Scotian coal. But the mineral deposits of the St. Lawrence in the geological formations suited to lumbering and agriculture were inadequate as a basis for industrial expansion. Copper was shipped from Bagot County, Leeds County, and the Bruce and Wellington mines through the St. Lawrence canals, to Boston and England. The Montreal Mining Company turned from the production of copper at the Bruce and Wellington mines to the production of silver at Silver Islet on Lake Superior. Oil was shipped from Petrolia to Europe. In the search for new oil fields, salt was discovered but, faced with competition from the product brought from England as ballast in the timber ships, it was exported to meet the demands of the packing industry in the United States. Construction of railways for the development of the timber trade north of Lake Ontario was followed by the shipment of phosphate to meet the demands for fertilizer in Europe and of iron from the counties of Leeds, Frontenac, and Lanark through the Welland Canal to Cleveland. The mining industry of eastern Canada was confined to areas accessible to navigation and to railways built chiefly over sedimentary formations. Only the fringes of the Precambrian formations were touched, as on Lake Superior. Non-metallic and base metal ores were exported in spite of their weight to more highly industrialized regions, coal, salt, and asbestos to the United States, copper to England and the United States, oil to Europe, gypsum and apatite to the exhausted agricultural areas of New England and Europe. Gold had been found in small quantities in Quebec and Nova Scotia.

The demands of Nova Scotia for markets for coal and the limited possibilities of industrial expansion based on coal and iron and steel in the St. Lawrence region hastened the adoption of Confederation and construction of the Intercolonial Railway and a transcontinental railway to the Pacific coast. Concentration of the St. Lawrence region on the timber trade and agricultural exports and the entrenchment of the Hudson's Bay Company behind the vast stretch of Precambrian formation against encroachment from the St. Lawrence necessitated enormous governmental expenditures. Federation [5] was a device to secure ample supplies of capital for the construction of railways from the Atlantic to the Pacific in a region handicapped by concentration on staples such as fur, timber, and agricultural products and without an iron and steel industry. The Hon. Charles Tupper, former Premier of Nova Scotia, effectively represented the coal interests of that province when as Minister of Railways he pressed for energetic construction of the Canadian Pacific Railway and supported the introduction and operation of the National Policy as a means of stimulating industrial growth. The problems of the mining industry of the Appalachian region were solved in part by adaptation of the political structure of British North America to support construction of a transcontinental railway across the Canadian Shield and the Prairies to the Cordilleran region and the Pacific coast. Resistance of the Hudson's Bay Company was broken by the introduction of gold mining and other industries on the Pacific coast and by the necessities of the St. Lawrence and the Maritimes.

The enormous demands of extensive railway construction absorbed the energies of government and private enterprise. The mineral resources of the Precambrian shield discovered in the course of construction were exploited by American capital. S. J. Ritchie extended his interests from the iron mines of southeastern Ontario to the copper-nickel deposits of Sudbury. The large reserves supported an intensive campaign for the use of nickel as an alloy with steel for the manufacture of armaments and after World War I for industrial purposes. On the Pacific coast precious metals (especially gold) dominated the mining industry, and important lode mining began with copper-gold. American capital was attracted to the more easily extracted deposits in close proximity to the railways near the boundary.

Completion of the main line of the Canadian Pacific Railway released Canadian energies, and Toronto interests became concerned in the Rossland mines. With the assistance of the government the Canadian Pacific Railway built the Crow's Nest Pass line west from Lethbridge and linked the Crow's Nest coal mines with the smelter at Trail. Canadian control was strengthened in the extension of smelter capacities and the addition of refineries and plant for the handling

[5]H. A. Innis, "Iron and Steel, Wheat and Finance," *Problems of Staple Production in Canada* (Toronto, 1933).

of the more complex ores producing lead and zinc. The dominance of Canadian control in British Columbia through the Consolidated Mining and Smelting Company contrasted sharply with American control in eastern Canada through International Nickel. American control over International Nickel was established in the construction stage of the Canadian Pacific Railway and Canadian control over Consolidated Mining and Smelting in the developmental stage. The coal deposits of British Columbia supported Canadian control over the more easily extracted metals in that area whereas the coal and iron industry of the eastern states supported American control over the complex base metals of eastern Canada.

As the gold rush to British Columbia hastened the construction of the Canadian Pacific Railway, the gold rush to the Klondike on the Yukon after 1896 created the feverish activity which hastened the construction of two additional transcontinental railways north of the Canadian Pacific Railway after 1900. The interest in the fabulous yields of the Yukon was evident in the bitter controversies in the House of Commons in Ottawa and in the contention between Canada and the United States over the Alaska boundary.[6] Railways were built along the northern edge of the vast plains area to the north of the main line of the Canadian Pacific Railway and eventually penetrated the Precambrian formations by a line from The Pas to Churchill on Hudson Bay. Mineral deposits in the Precambrian shield were tapped by the railway from The Pas to Flin Flon and from Edmonton to Waterways, especially after the war of 1914–8.

In the vast area opened by the new transcontinental railways Canadian interests were active in exploration and development, but American capital supported exploitation. Canadian capital gained enormous advantages from construction by the Ontario government of the Temiskaming and Northern Ontario Railway from North Bay. The discovery of precious metal ores, silver at Cobalt and gold at Porcupine and Kirkland Lake, was followed by the development of hydroelectric power for their exploitation. Freedom from dependence on coal, richness of the ore deposits, ease of extraction as a result of the rapid advancement of technique in the precious metal industry, and substantial profits strengthened Canadian possibilities of control. The profits obtained from silver mining at Cobalt enabled Canadians to dominate the gold mines of Porcupine with the exception of Dome. The more extensive demands for elaborate technique and capital which followed the exhaustion of the more accessible silver deposits in-

[6]See J. W. Dafoe, *Clifford Sifton in Relation to His Times* (Toronto, 1931).

creased American importance, especially in such mines as Nipissing, and in turn, as a result of the dominance of Canadians in Porcupine, in mines of Kirkland Lake. Strong Canadian control in precious metal mining and the accessibility of Nova Scotian coal enabled Canadians to participate actively in the exploitation of copper-gold deposits at Noranda in Quebec. Canadians were aggressive in the development of precious metal mining in northern Quebec, the Patricia district, northern Manitoba, and the Northwest Territories. In base metals such as copper and zinc, enormous demands for capital and for elaborate technique and preoccupation of Canadians with precious metals gave Americans decided advantages in the case of the Hudson Bay Mining and Smelting Company. American capital provided strong support for the successful development of radium on Bear Lake.

The limitations of the Appalachian region in supplies of minerals and the inability to compete with American coal on the Atlantic seaboard accentuated the importance of a national policy which combined protection for Canadian manufacturers and railways and Nova Scotian coal. The addition of two transcontinental railways and the opening of the West favoured the rapid expansion of the iron and steel industry in Nova Scotia, after strong initial support from American capital, and in Quebec. American capital and skill took advantage of the increase in demands for steel, especially after the discovery of the iron resources of the Mesabi Range, and of accessibility to American coal, to support the Hamilton Blast Furnace Company at Hamilton in 1893, its amalgamation with the Ontario Rolling Mill Company in 1899, and the formation of the Steel Company of Canada in 1910, and to initiate the Consolidated Lake Superior Company in 1899, including the Algoma Steel Company in 1901. American iron ore and coal were combined in the manufacture of steel in Ontario.

The importance of cheap supplies of coal in the United States has been evident in the political and economic history of Canada. The heavy, bulky, and cheap character of coal gave it a dominant place in the location of industrial growth. A commodity consumed in the process of utilization,[7] it had a decided tendency to pull raw materials toward the place of its extraction. Metallic ores moved more cheaply to coal than coal to ore. Limited coal resources in eastern Canada favoured the export of ores to Great Britain and to the United States. Coal in Nova Scotia attracted iron from Newfoundland but the industrial expansion of the St. Lawrence region based on cheap water

[7] See C. J. Friedrich, *Alfred Weber's Theory of the Location of Industries* (Chicago, 1929).

navigation and a policy of protection attracted coal from Nova Scotia to Montreal and from the United States to Ontario. Rich silver ore from Cobalt and rich gold ore from Kirkland Lake were shipped to American smelters, but the increasing importance of lean ores and hydro-electric power led to the growth of concentrating and refining plants in precious metal mining areas. Base metals were also shipped to American smelters, but the cheap heavy ore and hydro-electric power favoured construction of smelters which attracted coal.

The policy of the federal government in its concern for coal fostered the growth of secondary industries by subventions to coal movements, protection of the iron and steel industries, construction of railroads, and the development of preferential rates of duty in Empire countries, and tended to favour Quebec at the expense of Ontario. Hydro-electric power as a substitute for coal supported the movement of secondary industries to the ore deposits and the movement was hastened by policies of the provincial government of Ontario in its support of the development of hydro-electric power, the construction of railways, and the erection of refining plants, as in the case of nickel, at Port Colborne.[8] In Quebec, accessibility to Nova Scotian coal involved a less aggressive governmental policy. Private enterprise was more effective and American capital was concerned with the development of power sites on the Saguenay and the large-scale utilization of power in the manufacture of aluminum. The advances of electro-chemistry increased the importance of electric power in the extraction of metals, encouraged the location of refining plants near ore deposits, and strengthened the influence of hydro-electric power sites in the location of secondary plants.

Weakening of the importance of coal in the mining industry as a result of the increasing use of hydro-electric power complicated the problems of modern industrialism. Cheap supplies of iron and coal in eastern North America provided the framework of industrialism which supported the construction of transcontinental railways to the region of the Pacific coast opened up by the gold rushes and consequent economic activities. The enormous expansion of capital equipment characteristic of machine industry stressed the limitations of iron as a metal and created demands for alloys. While iron in combination with coal was effective in the creation of power, copper became important for the transmission and effective utilization of power. The growth in use of hydro-electric power greatly increased the demands for transmission metals and the limitations of copper, particularly as to weight,

[8]*Report of the Royal Ontario Nickel Commission* (Toronto, 1917).

brought an increasing use of aluminum. The efficiency of new metals reduced the demands for old metals and, accompanied by substitution, increased supplies of the old metals in the form of scrap. The copper cartel was broken in part as a result of the competition of aluminum. The problem of changing demands was complicated by the problem of changing supplies. Construction of transcontinental railways through extensive geological formations favourable to the existence of base and precious metals was followed by an enormous increase in production, particularly with continual improvements in methods of extraction and new sources of power. Discovery and exploitation of transmission metals and of alloys, of precious metals and of base metals, were profoundly affected by geographic accident, as in the case of nickel at Sudbury and silver at Cobalt. The supplies of metals met demands which arose from the limitation of iron and steel but in an irregular fashion. Though the price system favoured exploitation in terms of the value of metal and costs of extraction including costs of transportation, the accidents of geography, particularly in the existence of rich placer areas in the Pacific region, frequently introduced violent disturbances. Although most disturbed by gold, the price system was also affected by accidental developments of other precious and base metals.

The importance of hydro-electric power and of base metals to the coal and iron industries has been complicated by the effects of the oil industry and of the non-metallic minerals. The internal combustion engine has contributed to the rapid expansion of discovery by aviation and of exploitation by aviation, trucks, gasoline boats, and Diesel engines. Oil has encroached on the position of coal in transportation in the densely populated regions. The demands of power sites for cement have been accompanied by the enormous demands of road construction. Federal and provincial governments have supported road construction and they have encouraged the tourist trade and the establishment of branch plants of American automobile companies. Oil and hydro-electric power reinforced the coal and iron industrialism at some points and subjected it to obsolescence at others.

The bombardment of the steel and coal industrial structure by non-ferrous metals and new sources of power has been particularly acute in Canada as a result of the geographic background in which vast areas of mineral-bearing formations were rapidly opened by transcontinental railways. The political and economic structure of the federation of Canada with its emphasis on coal and iron, rigid debts, and protectionism has tended to conflict with the political and economic structure of the provinces with their emphasis on the new industrialism of hydro-electric power, oil, and minerals. The results have been evident in the financial and labour problems of the iron and steel, coal mining, and railroad industries, of federal debts, and of interprovincial and international constitutional stalemates. The disequilibrium which marked the extensive intervention of the federal government in the construction of transcontinental railways to overcome the handicaps involved in the absence of an iron and steel industry enormously stimulated the production of minerals and hydroelectric power and the use of oil. It strengthened the position of provinces with mineral resources in a progressively industrial civilization and weakened the position of provinces in which wheat production had been stimulated. The dead hand of an old industrial system is particularly menacing to new industrialism. In both Canada and the United States, labour and capital have organized defences against new competitors. The United Mine Workers and the Railway Brotherhood are significantly international organizations.

The difficulties in Canada have been enhanced by the increasing importance of neo-mercantilism in the United States. The indirect influence of gold on industrialism in the United States evident in the construction of transcontinental railways from the iron and steel and coal mining regions of eastern North America to the Pacific coast was accompanied by its direct and indirect influence through the support of a political structure in Canada to the construction of the Canadian Pacific Railway. The direct influence of gold on policies of the mercantilist systems was followed by indirect influences in the industrial system in the United States and in turn by direct influences in the new mercantilism. The price-lifting policy which increased the price of gold to $35 an ounce stimulated economic activity in the gold-producing regions, particularly of eastern Canada. The prosperity of these regions was in sharp contrast with the federal problems of wheat and railways in the prairie regions with their dependence on Europe.

The increasingly important position of minerals in the advance of modern industrialism has stressed their significance in trade with the United States. The secular trend has implied closer relations between cyclical trends in the two countries. The importance of refractory combination ores as a source of gold and of improved technology in its extraction has brought an increase in output of other metals combined with gold. The latter metal tends to shift from a position as by-product to one as main product. The base metals tend to become by-products[9] and consequently less sensitive to changes in price and more effective in the drive of the new industrialism. The international problem of trade in mineral products complicates the intranational problem.

The results of these and other policies have been registered in trade directly in minerals and mineral products and indirectly in all items. Protection and the establishment of industries in Canada foster imports of raw materials such as coal, petroleum, and iron ore and discourage imports of manufactured products. They discourage exports of mineral ores and encourage exports of manufactured products. American capitalists have attempted to take advantage of Canadian policies and of American policies by establishing industries in Canada. To avoid the effects of governmental policy they have searched assiduously for mining properties (hedging against inflation), and to strengthen their own position in the United States and to participate in world cartels they have built Canadian plants.[10] As exhaustion of mines proceeded in the United States increasing demands for capital brought increasing centralization of control. The mining industry in part became entrenched behind tariffs and cartels and in part migrated to new countries. In countries which have shifted from a position of producers and exporters to a position of importers, tariffs have been imposed as a means of protecting high-cost producers faced with low prices due to supplies of scrap and supplies from low-cost producers in new countries. American protectionist policies, on the other hand, have encouraged the development of secondary industries in the United States at the expense of Canada as a producer of ore in the case of asbestos and gypsum.

The attempt to secure supplies of gold by trade policies which characterized the mercantile system implied an emphasis on consumers' goods to sell to the specie-holding country or to prevent purchases from the specie-holding country. Mercantilism implied concentration on certain types of commercial activity. The attempt to secure supplies of gold by extraction from placer beds implied an immediate demand for consumers' goods and mining supplies and an ultimate demand for producers' goods in the form of transcontinental railways and steamships and an enormous increase in production of raw material for the manufacture of consumers' and producers' goods

[9]See W. Y. Elliott *et al., International Control in the Non-ferrous Metals* (New York, 1937).
[10]D. H. Wallace, *Market Control in the Aluminum Industry* (Cambridge, 1937).

—specifically, in the case of Canada, wheat, minerals, lumber, and fish. These activities have implied state capitalism in Canada and have strengthened the trend toward nationalism and the new mercantilism in the United States.

American industrialism supported the establishment of an iron and steel framework in Canada; the enormous drain on Canadian energies left the task of exploiting mineral resources to an important extent to Americans; and Canadians were effective in the exploitation particularly of precious metals, and of base metals in relation to traffic development. Exhaustion of mines in Canada, the highly technical demands of base metal ores, and the importance of the American market favoured American capitalists and technicians.

Imperfect Regional Competition and Political Institutions on the North Atlantic Seaboard*

THE fishing industry has been conducted on the Atlantic seaboard of North America for centuries through small units of capital equipment—the ship or the small boat. It is essentially dependent on individual initiative and enterprise and was particularly so prior to the introduction of large-scale units of capital in the nineteenth century. Various devices depending chiefly on the size of the unit of equipment were developed to reward the fisherman in proportion to his catch and to stimulate his interest. The dependence on individual initiative was tempered by the necessity of co-operation since it was only rarely that an individual fisherman could command and direct his own capital equipment. The small boat required three to five men, and the ship a crew which was disciplined in relation to its operations. It required, moreover, the support of capital interests whether in providing the ship or the supplies and provisions, but the risks of the industry compelled a wide division of capital interests as a means of insurance. If conducted within narrow geographical limits such as a single port or a number of small ports in a definite region these capital groups had large common interests. The industry was therefore characterized by individual enterprise which was sharply competitive and by types of co-operation ranging from the fishermen of a small boat to the group of merchants in definite regions. The common interests of the group were concerned with finance, markets, and political control over areas of production. The power of each group became concentrated in separate geographic regions in the Atlantic basin, the west country, Newfoundland, Nova Scotia, and New England, and the effectiveness of the power varied in part with the element of monopoly and imperfect competition. Each community became a centre of aggressiveness and of

*From the *Commerce Journal*, 1942, pp. 21–6; reprinted in *Political Economy in the Modern State* (Toronto, 1946), pp. 229–35.

governmental expansion with the emergence of a centralized merchant group.

The west country (Cornwall, Devon, Dorset) was a region with a large number of ports which sent out ships to prosecute the fishing industry in Newfoundland. It was able to exercise powerful influence in a mercantilist state and to plead with effect the unity of its prosperity with that of the nation, since, as a result of its efforts, treasure was brought from the Catholic countries of Spain, Portugal, and the Mediterranean, and trained seamen were available for the navy. Attempts made by London interests representing the carrying trade to establish a colony through a joint stock company were defeated through attacks by west country interests in England and in Newfoundland. Their powers were limited, however, to a definite region of the New World and their determined efforts to maintain control of the fishing industry of the Avalon Peninsula hastened the migration of settlers to New England on the mainland. West country ships to Newfoundland took out settlers and their effects to New England as a means of increasing revenue for the voyage. Small units of capital facilitated rapid adjustment in the migration between regions along the Atlantic seaboard. Flexibility of economic organization based on technology accentuated the significance of liquidity preference in the demands of a mercantilist state for specie. Long-term capital interests, defeated in attempts to establish a settlement in Newfoundland, moved to New England.

The growth of settlement, the development of the fishing industry, and increase in shipping led to the emergence of a new centre in New England. It began to compete with the west country in the markets of Europe but its effects were less direct. Sheltered by the Navigation Acts, shipping flourished and trade expanded from New England to the West Indies and to Europe. Provisions were shipped to the West Indies to be exchanged for sugar, molasses, and rum and these with other provisions were shipped to Newfoundland to be exchanged for bills. By insisting that Newfoundland was not a colony the west country enabled New England interests to argue that it could be used as a warehousing centre under the Navigation Acts. Their insistence made Newfoundland conspicuously the centre of attention in Parliament after 1688 and emphasized more sharply the view that the mainland colonies were creatures of the Crown and not of Parliament. Demands for liquidity preference in England which fostered the exchange of fish for specie in Spain and Portugal were paralleled and in part thwarted by the demands for liquidity preference in New England which fostered the exchange of provisions and supplies for bills in Newfoundland. The more skilled fishermen migrated from Newfoundland to New England but others remained in Newfoundland through the support of New England in spite of protests of the west country. The influence of New England in the British Parliament was weakened by the increasing interest of its fishing industry in the West Indies, where again it came into conflict and was overshadowed by the dominance of the planters of the British West Indies. New England was exposed in Parliament to attack on the one hand from the west country as a competitor in Europe and as a support to settlement in Newfoundland, and on the other hand from the British West Indies as a support to settlement in the French West Indies. The influence of New England was evident in the cession of Nova Scotia to Great Britain in 1713 and in the capture of Louisburg in 1745, and the limits of its influence in the return of Louisburg to France in 1748. In the Treaty of Paris the influence of the West Indies rather than New England was instrumental in leaving Guadaloupe with France. In this it offered no threat as a competitor within the Empire and the fur trade of Canada offered a wider market for British West Indies molasses and rum.

France in contrast with the west country and New England had no single region dominated by the fishery. It was scattered among a large number of ports on the Channel and in the Bay of Biscay which sent vessels to widely scattered regions in North America including the Banks. The deliberate attempt to offset the handicaps of decentralization in the Old and the New World by the establishment of Placentia, and, after the Treaty of Utrecht in 1713, Louisburg, was defeated by the absence of an agricultural base. The inability to establish a base was a result of the agricultural limitations of the St. Lawrence region, the handicap of seasonal navigation, the smuggling with the Acadians of the Bay of Fundy, the inability to develop a colony on Prince Edward Island, and the dependence on the English colonies. A centralized fortified area could not survive against the opposition of England and the English colonies. The establishment of Halifax in 1749 and the capture of Louisburg and Quebec brought to an end the effort of France to dominate the New World.

With the fall of France the antagonism between New England and England was no longer tempered by the existence of a common enemy. New England thrived under the protection of the Navigation Acts and the evasion of legislation designed to favour the West

Indies planters at her expense. The direct influence of the West Indies planters and of the west country in the corrupt Parliaments of Walpole rendered the influence of New England ineffective. Parliament reflected the direct pressure of the West Indies and the west country but not of New England. As we have seen, her ineffectiveness was evident in the Treaty of Paris and in later legislation in which her markets for rum and molasses were widened by the acquisition of Canada but her supplies were narrowed by the influence of the West Indies in leaving Guadaloupe under French control. The rapid and effective activities of New England and the other colonies in resisting a Parliament which was under the influence of the West Indies and the west country was apparent in the short period between the Treaty of Paris and the outbreak of revolution and the Treaty of Versailles.

The sharpness of the break between New England and England facilitated the emergence of new fishing interests from the Channel Islands to Cape Breton and the Gulf of St. Lawrence to take the place of the French, and of a new mercantile group centring about Halifax which was quick to press for the advantages of exclusion of New England from the colonial system. Seizing concessions, notably in the Act of 1778, which England had made too late to save the colonies, Nova Scotia pressed for advantageous modifications of the colonial system at the expense of the West Indies. The latter were no longer able to dominate colonial policy in Parliament but they succeeded eventually in 1830 in gaining access to the cheaper provisions of the United States whereupon Nova Scotia was compelled to turn (1) to the trade of Newfoundland vacated by New England and (2) to the pursuit of more vigorous tactics in excluding American fishermen from her inshore waters. The growth of autonomy in Nova Scotia was rapid in relation to England and to the United States, compared with New England, and extremely rapid compared with Newfoundland. Expansion of New England was the reverse side of restrictions on Newfoundland by the west country but the rise of Nova Scotia and difficulties in the West Indies hastened settlement in Newfoundland.

Increased trade from Nova Scotia to Newfoundland favoured the growth of settlement and weakened the position of the west country. Parliament after the Reform Acts was more pliable and provided a less certain shelter in which the influence of the West Indies and the west country could be exerted at the expense of Nova Scotia and Newfoundland. The growth of settlement in Newfoundland led to the emergence of representative institutions. But these institutions flowered more quickly as a result of renewed efforts from France in St. Pierre and Miquelon to revive the fisheries by improved techniques and generous bonuses. Newfoundland seized upon control of her natural resources, which came with responsible government, to press steadily toward weakening the French by depriving them of supplies of bait and by excluding them from the French shore in 1904.

Representative institutions in Newfoundland were used to oppose not only France but, with parliamentary reform, the decline in influence of vested interests in England, free trade, and responsible government, also the west country, the Channel Islands, Nova Scotia, and New England. With the abrogation of the Reciprocity Treaty in 1866 Nova Scotia enlisted the support of Canada under Confederation to secure the Washington Treaty. The retreat of New England to the shelter of an expanding internal market under the tariff and the *modus vivendi* arrangement reflected resistance to pressure from Nova Scotia and Canada. Newfoundland resented efforts of Nova Scotia to use her in attempts to secure better arrangements with the United States after the termination of the Washington Treaty in 1885.

The long delay in the growth of representative institutions in Newfoundland incidental to the protracted decline of control from the west country prior to parliamentary reform in Great Britain was in sharp contrast with the rapid growth of Nova Scotia through the support of a modified colonial system after the American Revolution. Nova Scotia, pressing on New England, sought support in Confederation, and New England, pressed from Nova Scotia, sought shelter on the continent. The aggressiveness of Nova Scotia left Newfoundland with no alternative but resistance through accentuation of local autonomy. The burden of industrialism, especially in the construction of railways, carried for Nova Scotia by the Dominion was carried in Newfoundland by herself.

Control by the west country delayed growth of settlement and in turn of governmental and judicial institutions in Newfoundland. This control in turn hastened growth of settlement and acquisition of governmental institutions in New England. The accentuated local autonomy of New England contributed to the American Revolution and to the attempt of Nova Scotia to secure advantages under the colonial system. The rapid growth of Nova Scotia led to the support of settlement in Newfoundland and in turn to decline of control from the west country. The eventual emergence of strong local autonomy in Newfoundland, following the struggle between the accentuated autonomies of New England and Nova Scotia in which each turned for support to the continent, led to industrialism, debt, and the loss of responsible government.

Liquidity preference became less effective as a stimulus to trade and competition, and political institutions lost the flexibility essential to adjustment. The effectiveness of the demands of the west country for control over Newfoundland through its dependence on short-term credit and its ability to emphasize the importance of imports of specie from Spain and Portugal, and the increasing demands of New England and the colonies for short-term credit to support an expanding trade, and of an expanding trade for supplies of short-term credit, were factors leading to the break up of the French Empire and in turn of the first British Empire. The importance of short-term credit in the American Revolution and the United States increased the burden of long-term credit essential to the staple trades of Great Britain and supported the trend toward the Reform Acts and the constitutional changes which destroyed protection for interests in timber, shipping, sugar, fur, and other long-term credit trades. Liquidity preference had its implications in the changes in political structure in the west country, New England, Newfoundland, and England. The power of finance was steadily increased. Destruction of the shelter for staple trades as a result of the trend toward free trade led to a search for new expedients in the development of governments in areas producing staple commodities. The Act of Union and the British North America Act emerged as bases for lowering costs of transportation and to provide support for an accompanying expanding debt structure. The new mercantilism was embedded in constitutional structures.

The significance of liquidity preference in the trend toward free trade in Great Britain was paralleled by the expansion of government finance in Canada. Governmental institutions in Newfoundland, unlike those of Canada, were unable to meet the test of debt expansion under conditions of prosperity and depression, nor will they be exposed to the same problems of international adjustment incidental to Canadian success. Political institutions have become less flexible with devices facilitating the handling of credit, and the prospects of international adjustment less promising.

Liquidity Preference as a Factor in Industrial Development*

THE last half of the nineteenth century was characterized by a series of erratic outbreaks of economic activity along the Pacific coast of North America and in Australia which suddenly transformed vast, scantily populated areas into regions producing enormous quantities of raw materials for a highly industrialized Europe. Traffic to the Pacific had been restricted to commodities of high value and light bulk, such as furs, wool, and tea. The encircling movement of world trade which surrounded the globe first in the fur trade in which traders from Russia met traders from Europe and North America in Alaska was strengthened by the sudden economic cyclones which followed the gold rushes. The discovery of placer gold in California in 1848 was followed by the rush of 1849, and the opening up of other areas in the Pacific region. Possibilities of enormous wealth, the enhanced value of gold following depression and a secular decline in prices, and the uncertainty of yield, led to the immigration of large numbers, chiefly young men, with at least sufficient funds to pay the expensive passage and to buy large quantities of expensive supplies. The influx of labour and capital into regions chiefly mountainous in character, and with restricted economic development, necessitated importation of goods and supplies on a large scale. High prices as a result of sudden increase in demand and the addition of large supplies of gold provided enormous profits on imports and on shipping. The profit motive in its most intense form was in evidence in the rush of labour and supplies to new gold fields.

Influx of population was followed by rapid exhaustion of the accessible gold fields and the necessity of searching for new regions or of developing alternative natural resources. The return of prospectors from California, and the intimate knowledge of the peculiarities of the country which accompanied the spread of sheep-raising over wide areas in Australia, led to the discovery of gold in New

*From *Transactions of the Royal Society of Canada*, Third Series, vol. XXXVII (1943), Section II, pp. 1–31; reprinted in *Political Economy in the Modern State* (Ryerson, 1946), pp. 168–200.

South Wales and in Victoria and to an influx of immigrants in 1852. The hope of the Chief Secretary who wrote, "If this is a gold country it will stop the Home Government from sending us any more convicts and prevent emigration to California" at Sydney in 1851 was fulfilled. Population increased rapidly from 437,665 in 1857 to 1,168,149 in 1871, and gold production in the period totalled £124,000,000. Decline in the yield of the placer fields and the introduction of capitalistic methods of exploitation and displacement of labour were followed by migration, search for gold in other regions, and the rush to New Zealand (Otago in 1861, and Westland in 1865). The arrival of large numbers of young men equipped with supplies and with experience in Australian fields led to rapid exploitation.

On the Pacific coast of North America, miners pushed northward from California in searth of new fields and in 1858 "about 10,000 foreign miners" were attracted to the bars of the Fraser River. Large numbers of disillusioned, among them Henry George, turned back, but others pushed up the Fraser to make the important discoveries on its tributaries in the Cariboo in the early sixties. The total yield of gold from 1858 to 1876 was estimated at $40,000,000. The population of British Columbia totalled 36,247 in 1871, when it entered Confederation.

The effects of the discovery of gold in the Pacific regions were evident in the demand of large numbers in relatively densely populated areas for ships to carry them to the gold fields. The discovery of gold in California quickened the demand for American sailing ships. Clipper ships carried passengers around the Horn for San Francisco and thence proceeded to China for a cargo of tea to be taken to London. The increasing demands for raw materials and for markets for manufactured products from Great Britain were met by the migration of ships and trade. News of the gold strike of 1851 in Australia was followed by a demand for fast, comfortable ships from England and the abandonment of the miserable emigrant ships of the forties. The Blackwallers employed from London to India were diverted to Australia. The fast sailing ships of New England and Nova Scotia were in demand in Liverpool for the Australian route. James Baines, with the Black Ball Line, purchased the famous ships of Donald McKay, a native of Nova Scotia; and his rival, the White Star Line, joined in competition for mail contracts, landing mail in Australia in from sixty-five to sixty-eight days, and for passengers. The Marco Polo (1,625 tons), pioneer of the Black Ball Line, built in Saint John, New Brunswick, in 1851, and her Master, Captain James Nicol Forbes, became famous in the Australian trade with a record passage by the Horn from Melbourne to Liverpool of fifty-six days, and a round trip of five months and twenty-one days. Time was reduced as a result of the theories of M. F. Maury as to wind directions and as to routes. New England and British North American ships were in demand as larger, better sailing vessels and built of softwoods of cheaper construction. As the timber trade of British North America contributed to support industrial change in Great Britain in the first half of the century, the softwood ships of North America supported commercial change in the Pacific. But steamers to Colon, a railway thence to Panama, completed in 1855, and steamers thence to California almost displaced sailing ships by Cape Horn.

The increase in settlement along the coast of Australia, following the gold rushes, created a demand for more efficient services between the ports and from the ports to the interior. The Australian Steam Navigation Company and other companies established services in 1851 and later dates between Melbourne and Sydney, Sydney and Brisbane and Melbourne and Adelaide, and Melbourne and New-castle. Railway mileage in Victoria and in New South Wales increased from two miles in 1854 to 171 miles in 1859 and total railway mileage in Australia to 1,042 in 1871. In 1854, a mail service was established between Melbourne and Wellington, New Zealand. Steamers ran from Melbourne to Dunedin, and Sydney to Auckland, and, after the gold rush in New Zealand, from Melbourne to Otago. New Zealand coastal steamers ran between Wellington and Dunedin, and in the gold rush to Hokitika. Steamships engaged on short runs were extremely mobile and capable of being shifted according to demands. They were taken as troopships for the Crimean War, and were engaged after 1860 in the Maori Wars in the North Island of New Zealand. Telegraph communication was established between Sydney, Melbourne, and Adelaide in 1858, and a line was opened from Perth to Fremantle in 1869. A submarine cable was laid from Tasmania via Circular Head and King Island to Cape Otway in 1859 and in the Cook Strait in 1866. In New Zealand a wooden tramway was built from the Bluff to Lake Waktipu and a railway was built from Christchurch to Lyttleton early in the sixties, and from Invercargill to Bluff Harbour in 1867. In 1870, 1,887 miles of telegraph line had been laid.

The entrance of the steamship in the Pacific transoceanic trade was infrequent and slow to develop in spite of assistance through mail contracts. In 1853, mail was taken by the Peninsula and Oriental Company from Singapore to Sydney, but the Crimean War necessitated withdrawal of steamships and cancellation of the service. After considerable difficulty the P. and O. began a monthly service from

England to Australia via Mauritius in 1859 but this was abandoned for connections at Galle in Ceylon. After several unsuccessful efforts, a steamship service was started from Panama to Sydney. The island of Rapa was selected as a coaling station in 1866, but the service disappeared with the completion of the Union Pacific to San Francisco in 1869 and the establishment of a line from San Fancisco to Sydney in 1870.

On the American coast, steamers were employed to run from Panama to San Francisco, and to Oregon and British Columbia. Steamboats were brought up from California to be employed on the route from Victoria to Langley, and from Langley up the Fraser River to Emory's Bar. The rapidity of development of British Columbia placer mining was hastened with the plant and technique which had been developed in the California gold fields. Location of placer gold fields tended to concentrate in the upper reaches of the swift waters of relatively mountainous regions. In British Columbia, discovery of gold on the bars of the Fraser River was followed by discoveries in the Cariboo, with the result that improved land transportation was essential since navigation was not feasible. Goods were handled from Emory's Bar to Yale by smaller craft and eventually the Cariboo Road was extended to Barkerville.

The effects of placer mining on the movement of population and on transportation facilities were cyclonic in character. Rapid increase in population created demands for shipping and improved transportation, and led in the distant regions of the Pacific to the development of numerous subordinate industries. Funds brought out by immigrants from densely populated industrial areas, supplies of gold obtained from the gold fields, and a scarcity of manufactured products and provisions, led to a sharp rise in prices. The intensely speculative character of gold mining with the uncertainty of returns, the disturbances created by new discoveries, and the decline of production in relation to primitive methods, necessitated a high rate of depreciation and reinforced the trend toward high prices. The short life of a placer camp involved fabulous charges.

I

Gold mining introduced an advanced state of monetary organization which accentuated flexibility in the specialization of production. It brought a reversal in the trend of a spread of money from the centre to the circumference in the sudden emergence of money on the fringes. Mercantile systems which favoured devices increasing imports of specie and accentuated the importance of liquidity were outstripped by the production of large quantities of gold. The demand of a large population for foodstuffs was followed by agricultural expansion. The total land under crop in Australia increased from 491,000 acres in 1850 to over a million acres in 1858: New South Wales, 223,000; Victoria, 299,000; Tasmania, 229,000; South Australia, 264,000; and Western Australia, 21,000. "All wages rose, all accessible good land was in great demand, the dealers in produce found the advantage of prices rising in the article as it passed through their hands, live stock increased in value, shipping was profitably employed."[1] The dominance of the wool trade in both Australia and New Zealand became less conspicuous. Labour was attracted to the gold fields, and wages of shepherds increased. A rise in the price of meat led to emphasis on the production of mutton. Cattle became increasingly important.

Labour was released from gold mining with the exhaustion of shallow diggings, and the displacement of primitive technique by capitalistic devices which could be adopted with the improvement of transportation. In 1861, the Victoria gold fields employed 711 steam engines (10,782 horse-power). Alternative employment was limited. Shipping in relation to gold mining implied a heavy outbound cargo and a light, highly valuable, return cargo. Ample space was available on ships returning to England and improved transportation to the gold fields facilitated a return to wool production and wool exports. Lower freights and higher prices contributed to strengthen the position of wool following the disturbances of the gold rush. But wool production did not involve a substantial demand for labour. Industries which emerged in relation to the demands of the large population of the gold fields offered greater possibilities for absorption of labour, provided new markets for manufactured products were available. In 1861, Victoria had 403 factories employing 3,830 persons. Attempts to encourage industry were accompanied by attempts to increase revenues and to stimulate agricultural development in addition to wool production.

Placer mining, with its emphasis on labour and on supplies of funds, stressed individualism, but continued exploitation necessitated capital equipment including roads which implied governmental machinery for the collection of revenue and the carrying of debt. An immediate and strong popular demand arose for improved transportation to the difficult regions of the gold mining areas. While the outlay for im-

[1]Cited, *Cambridge History of the British Empire*, vol. VII, part II, p. 151.

proved transportation was heavy, miners were extremely reluctant, as a result of high prices, to contribute to the support of transportation.

Placer mining strengthened and consolidated the trend toward democratic government. The Australian Colonies Government Act of 1850 was followed, with the stimulus of a rapid increase in population, by responsible government in New South Wales, Victoria, and Tasmania, in 1855. Self-government implied control over lands and of revenue[2] from land sales.

Following the abolition of the preference on goods from the United Kingdom in 1851, and the demands for revenue, import duties were imposed by Victoria in 1855. Under the determined and energetic leadership of David Syme, a policy of protection was adopted in 1866 and employees increased to 28,000 in 1874. This development involved industrialism, protection, and extension of agriculture. The struggle between the wool producer and the agriculturist which characterized Australian land policy became severe and was followed by the Land Act of 1862 with its emphasis on settlement.

New South Wales had been less seriously influenced by the gold rush. Population had been drained to Victoria and industrial development was weakened. In 1852 duties[3] were imposed on selected commodities. The importance of wool exports and dependence on a staple product precluded attempts to develop manufacturing by protection. The free trade policy of New South Wales was in striking contrast to the protectionism of Victoria. South Australia responded to the demands of the gold fields with increased production of wheat. With relative decline in local demand, and the introduction of agricultural machinery, particularly the stripper, exports of wheat were sent to Great Britain in 1866. The area under crop increased to 801,571 acres in 1870–1. Robert Torrens contributed to the solution of the land problem of agricultural expansion through the system which was introduced in 1858, and the Strangeways Act (1868) gave further en-

[2]Licence fees were introduced in New South Wales and in Victoria, but at rates which were inadequate and which became increasingly unpopular with attempts at rigorous collection and exhaustion of the goldfields. As a result of determined protests, fees were reduced in Victoria in 1853, and following the Ballarat riots of 1854, miners' rights, conferring the franchise, displaced the licence fee, and an export duty of 2s. 6d. per ounce on gold was imposed in 1855. Local courts were established in the gold fields to settle disputes.

[3]Miners were forced to pay licence fees but, with the example of Victoria, an export tax was introduced in 1857 and licence fees abolished. Wool production increased in importance, and the number of sheep increased from 5,615,054 in 1861 to 16,278,697 in 1871. The position of the squatter tended to defeat, through "dummying," the efforts of the farmer in the Land Act of 1861. Land under crop increased to 378,592 acres in 1870–1.

couragement. Tasmania, Western Australia, and Queensland increased the area under crop during the period, but the total advance was not relatively important.

The diverse economic development of the colonies of Australia involved conflicts in policies. The contrast in tariff policy between New South Wales and Victoria, and their limitations in treaty-making power, caused the failure of numerous conferences. In 1867 an agreement was reached between the two colonies, but it was not until 1873, in the Australian Colonies Duties Act, that the imperial authorities conceded the right to make trade agreements.

Agreement was conspicuous, on the other hand, in the exclusion of Chinese. Migration of Oriental labour was a result of the immediate demands for labour in the gold fields, of the high costs of labour in temperate areas of the Pacific coast with light density of population and at long distances from the Atlantic seaboard,[4] and of the existence of areas of intense population density along the Asiatic fringe.

Expansion of transport facilities and improvement of navigation, particularly the iron clippers and the beginning of regular steam traffic, supported the rapid economic growth which followed the gold rush to the distant areas of Australia. Concentration on wool as a commodity adapted to the demands of distant transportation was accentuated. Public borrowings accompanied improved transportation facilities and expansion of production. All the states had appeared on the London market to secure loans to finance capital improvements: Victoria, 1859; New South Wales, 1855; South Australia, 1854; Queensland, 1861; Western Australia, 1845; and Tasmania, 1867. Free trade in Great Britain and development of Australia through staple products in relation to the demands of that area were accompanied by financial support from Great Britain and in turn by responsible government and the institution of suitable financial machinery designed to secure adequate revenue. The geographical characteristics of Australia with its exten-

[4]Prospects of profitable occupation induced Chinese brokers to provide capital to pay the costs of transportation (the ticket credit system) to the gold fields. It was estimated that 2,000 Chinese coolies were employed in the Victoria goldfields in 1854. The Restriction Act in 1855, prohibiting the arrival of Chinese by vessels, was followed by migration to South Australia and immigration to Victoria by land. In 1857, Chinese in the Victoria goldfields had increased to 26,370, and South Australia was persuaded to pass a restriction Act. Victoria, in the same year, imposed heavy taxation on the Chinese population. In spite of legislation, population totalled 42,000, with the result that previous Acts were replaced by legislation imposing still heavier taxation. Chinese population declined with exhaustion of the goldfields, and in 1864 restrictive legislation was repealed. In New South Wales, 12,988 Chinese were engaged in the goldfields in 1861 and a bill similar to the Victoria Act of 1855 was enacted.

sive coast-line implied decentralization of governments and competition for labour rather than for capital, whereas in Canada concentration on the St. Lawrence implied centralization and competition for capital for construction of canals and railways. Confederation appeared early in Canada as a result of competition from the United States and later in Australia as a result of difficulties between decentralized states.

The effect of the gold rush of Australia on New Zealand in the fifties was to provide a base to support the expansion which followed the gold rush to New Zealand in the early sixties. As in Australia, high prices of agricultural products stimulated production and decline in gold production released labour for the development of other industries. Canterbury and Otago, as the chief centres of sheep-raising, and the South Island generally, increased in importance with demands for provisions, supplies, labour, and shipping. The number of sheep increased from one and a half million in 1858 to nearly ten million in 1871, wool exports from nearly four million pounds to nearly thirty-eight million, and land under cultivation from one hundred thousand acres to one million, two hundred thousand acres. Grain exports declined from 118,740 bushels in 1859 to 3,238 bushels in 1863, but increased to 1,032,092 bushels in 1871. South Island definitely established economic supremacy until the end of the century over North Island which had been harassed in the sixties with the Maori Wars. In 1871 population in South Island totalled 159,918, and in North Island 96,875. The development of railways and public works followed the increase in revenue incidental to the gold rush. In 1870 the debt of the government totalled £4,543,316, and of the provinces, £3,298,575.

The effects of the gold rush in British Columbia were similar to those in Australia and New Zealand. Rapid increase in population created demands for provisions and supplies. The immediate demands and high prices of foodstuffs led not only to a rapid increase in imports, but also to local production. In spite of geographical limitations of soil and climate the colony was self-sufficient in its supply of wheat by 1866. Salmon were caught in large numbers for local consumption. Timber and planks were imported from American mills during the early building boom in Victoria, but local sawmills were rapidly introduced and by 1870 were installed on the Fraser and in the Cariboo to meet the demand of towns, and of miners for construction of flumes and sluice boxes. As placer creeks were exhausted and capitalistic methods of extraction increased in importance, surplus population moved outwards to new creeks or contributed to the more stable development in the support of new industries. Built up to meet the immediate demands of gold mining, industries served as a basis for expansion in the production of exports. As ever, gold mining involved a heavy inbound cargo and a light outbound cargo, and the lumber industry provided the raw material for an outbound cargo and for the rapid development of various regions in the Pacific. Operations begun at Alberni and Barclay Sound in 1861 were sufficient to support exports of over eleven million feet in 1862 to New Zealand, Australia, Hawaii, the Orient, South America, and even to England and Italy. Cheap lumber was essential to support the rapid transient changes in the economies of Pacific countries. The importance of industrialism as shown in the coastal steamers led to the development of the coal resources of Vancouver Island. A first shipment of 1,840 tons from Nanaimo to San Francisco in 1852 was followed by an increase of sales to a peak of 44,005 tons in 1868.

The inrush of immigrants in 1857 and 1858 led to the cancellation of the Hudson's Bay Company's licence to trade in British Columbia in 1858. Various forms of taxation were necessary to finance local construction to the interior, and included mining licences, a head tax, a tonnage tax, an import tax, and tolls. Decline of gold mining and difficulties of taxation led to an increase in the debt of the colony. A free trade policy abandoned by Vancouver Island involved higher duties, union of the colonies in 1866, and union with Canada in 1871 in which a debt of $1,666,200 was assumed by the Dominion. Like Australia, British Columbia was faced with the Oriental problem, and as early as 1864 about two thousand Chinese were employed in the gold fields, but it was not until a much later date that restrictive legislation was enacted. The cycle of sudden immigration, exploitation and the use of capital equipment, the emergence of government and debt, and the shift to new natural resources continued in British Columbia as in other placer mining regions.

The expansion and later contraction of the gold fields of British Columbia were followed by increasing interest from the Atlantic. The long and difficult route overland began to compete with the long route by the Panama or the Horn. Milton and Cheadle crossed the Rocky Mountains in 1862 in the footsteps of fur traders and miners. Construction of an overland telegraph to Asia was brought to an abrupt stop with completion of the Atlantic cable in 1866. Alaska was added to American territory in 1867. These developments were the forerunners of the agreement by which British Columbia joined Confederation on condition that a transcontinental railway be built. The gold rush of British Columbia, the expansion of the United States, and the problem of debt in Canada precipitated the demand for political unity across the northern half of the continent and in turn for economic unity. Gold mining and its consequent economic development was a powerful factor pulling the westward extension of Empire to meet extension eastward.

II

Economic development in the Pacific prior to the completion of the Suez Canal and particularly in Australia emphasized the importance of the Cape of Good Hope and South Africa. The need of regular steam communication from England to Cape Town was increased by the internal difficulties in South Africa and by the requirements of a squadron based on Cape Town for the suppression of the East Africa slave trade. Better harbour accommodation for troop ships and passenger ships proceeding to India and Australia, and the use of Durban coal supported steamship development and traffic to the Far East. The Union Steamship Company began monthly mail service from Southampton to Cape Town in 1857. It was extended to Durban in 1865 and made semi-monthly in 1868. A telegraph was completed from Cape Town to Simonstown in 1860 and to Grahamstown in 1864. Railways were built from Cape Town to Wellington (57 miles) in 1863, and to Wynburg in 1864. The Cape Town harbour works were completed in the decade from 1860 to 1870 and the Castle Steamship Company established a line in 1872. Extension of government accompanied improvement of communications. In 1853 representative government was established in Cape Colony, but responsible government was delayed until 1872. Natal continued as a Crown colony and Basutoland came under a protectorate in 1869. As a result of the rush to the diamond fields of Kimberley in 1867–8, the British government assumed responsibility for maintaining order among the mining population in 1871, and annexed the Transvaal in 1877.

Expansion in the gold regions of the Pacific and improvement of transportation facilities strengthened extension to India and the Far East. Steamships had shortened the route to Suez, and from Suez to India. The Peninsula and Oriental Company signed a contract in January 1853 for a fortnightly service between England and Alexandria, between Marseilles and Malta, and between Suez, Calcutta, and Hong Kong with a service every two months from Singapore to Sydney. A supplementary contract in 1854 provided for a service from Suez to Bombay, but the outbreak of the Crimean War reduced a fortnightly service from Bombay to China to a monthly service. The Indian

Mutiny was followed by an extension of the line between Bombay, Aden, and Suez, and with a fortnightly service from Marseilles to Alexandria and arrivals and departures alternating from Calcutta and Bombay, a weekly service was given to India. Completion of the railway from Alexandria to Cairo in 1857 and its extension to Suez facilitated the change from Marseilles to Alexandria rather than to Malta. In 1864, a telegraph line with cable was completed from London to Karachi and in 1870 a cable was completed under British control. In 1867 a weekly service was provided to Bombay, and a fortnightly service to and from China and Japan. The Suez Canal was completed in 1869 and in the same year Marseilles as the port of arrival and departure was displaced by Brindisi. With this extension of steamship service, coaling stations were established and facilities for handling steamships were developed. Coastal steamship services were extended with the formation of the British East India Navigation Company in 1857, and included the coast from Singapore to Zanzibar in 1862. Interlocking directorates with the Netherlands East India Company formed in 1866 extended a line from Singapore to the Dutch East Indies and to Brisbane, Sydney, and Melbourne by Torres Strait.

As in North America improvement of navigation contributed to the development of railways and canals in the interior, so in India, railroads extended from terminal ports, canals, and river steamships reduced costs of transportation, and involved increasing government support. The energy of Lord Dalhousie prepared the way for capital expenditures in numerous directions. Lower Burma was annexed in 1852, Jansi and Nagpur in 1853, and Oudh in 1856. The pressure of industrialism and the Indian Mutiny in 1857 were to be followed by final surrender of governmental control on the part of the East India Company in 1858. The Ganges Canal was completed in 1857, and the Kistna delta canals in 1855, and the Ravi Canal in 1859. The programme of energetic railroad construction outlined by Lord Dalhousie in 1853 was followed, particularly after the Mutiny, by rapid progress. In 1853 a road was completed from Bombay to Lhana, in 1854 from Calcutta to Raneegunje (37 miles), and in the following year 120 miles were built in Madras. The depression in North America in 1857 and the importance of development of transportation facilities after the Mutiny led British contractors and capitalists to turn their attention to India. In 1858, Brassey began construction of a railroad from Calcutta to Khoostea on the Ganges (112 miles; completed 1862). In the following year one was built from Nulhattee to Azimgunje (27 miles) and in 1864 from Arkonam to Conjeveram (18 miles). The Delhi railway from Ghazeaabad to Umritsir (304 miles) was completed in 1870. Railway mileage in India increased from 35 in 1853–4 to 4,771 in 1870. In spite of government guarantees and other privileges, development was slow, but the serious famines of 1860 and 1866 led to active participation by the state in railway construction in 1869. The capital invested in railways in India has been estimated as follows:

(*in thousands of pounds*)

1858	£5,500	1864	£3,800
1859	7,150	1865	5,400
1860	7,580	1866	7,700
1861	6,500	1867	7,000
1862	5,800	1868	4,500
1863	4,750	1869	4,400

The telegraph preceded and accompanied the railroad. In the suppression of the Indian Mutiny it was said that "The electric telegraph has saved India." Before the advent of railway troops could be moved only about ten miles a day, whereas by rail they could cover four hundred miles in a day.[5]

The railway provided cheap transportation for raw materials from, and for manufactured products to, the interior. Access to the Raniganj coal fields by railway in 1854 contributed to the spread of industrialism. Wars in Russia and America accentuated the development of trade in tropical products from new sources, such as India, and had effects similar to gold in other regions. Imports of wheat in Great Britain following the abolition of the Corn Laws, and prior to the development of bulk handling, required extensive use of jute bags and the importation and manufacture of jute. The Crimean War cut off supplies of grain from Asia and necessitated increasing reliance on America for grain and on India for jute. The manufacture of jute in India began in 1855, the first power loom was introduced in 1859, and several mills were opened in the sixties. The average annual export from Calcutta from 1858 to 1863 was nearly 1,000,000 hundredweight. The cotton famine in Lancashire precipitated by the American Civil War was accompanied by high prices of textiles and increased exports from Bombay and from Egypt. The value of exports of cotton from Bombay increased from £5,500,000 in 1862 to £35,000,000 in 1866. The first cotton mill was established at Bombay in 1853, but the high price of cotton during the Civil War period, and the collapse of the

[5]L. C. A. Knowles, *Economic Development of the Overseas Empire* (London, 1924), p. 300n.

speculative period of the cotton boom, hampered industrial expansion. Egypt owing to her advantages in nearness and in the production of a long staple cotton could outbid India, and her exports to England increased rapidly.

Cultivation of Indian tea increased rapidly in the sixties in Assam, Bengal, southern India, and Ceylon. According to one account, a plantation of 1,876 acres in 1850 produced 216,000 pounds, and 295 plantations of 31,303 acres produced 6,251,143 pounds in 1870. After the boom of the early sixties and the crash of 1866, cultivation expanded slowly and about 10,000,000 pounds were exported to the United Kingdom in 1869. Coffee exports from the Wynaad in South India totalled nearly 20,000,000 pounds in 1860-1. In 1865, 14,613 acres were under cultivation in this region. The district of Coorg began production in 1854 and had 73,306 acres under cultivation in 1870.

As a result of the increasing consumption of coffee, 176,000 acres were planted in Ceylon from 1853 to 1869 and produced a crop valued at £4,000,000 sterling. Exports reached a maximum of 1,054,030 hundredweight in 1870. Unfortunately the spread of the coffee blight began in 1862 and eventually ruined the industry, but after a few years of sharp strain it was replaced by tea and cinchona. Cinnamon production increased in the latter part of the period but chiefly at the expense of quality. As a result of active government intervention and substantial expenditures on irrigation canals after 1856, the production of rice increased. Roads were built throughout the island and products were brought to the markets at lower costs. In 1867 a railroad was completed from Colombo to Kandy (75 miles) and in 1871 from Peradanuja to the important coffee district at Nawalapituja. Decline of coffee production in the Far East brought a shift to Brazil as at a later date decline in rubber production in Brazil followed the shift of rubber to the Far East.

Extension of steamship navigation to the Far East produced an expansion of trade. The cession of Hong Kong and the opening of treaty ports in 1842 was followed by persistent efforts to extend trade, and the treaties of Tientsin of 1858 were extended and enforced in 1860. Similarly, treaties with Japan in 1859 were extended and enforced in 1865, and supplemented by a tariff convention of 1866. The way was opened for rapid expansion after 1868. The strategic importance of Singapore and the Malay States on the route to the Far East was evinced by the creation of the Crown colony in 1867.

The extent of development of trade between the United Kingdom and the Pacific is suggested in an increase in imports of India and Ceylon from £9,094,349 in 1850 to £30,055,138 in 1860, and to £31,856,422 in 1870, and in exports from £7,874,584 in 1850 to £13,811,961 in 1860, and to £30,705,844 in 1870. British shipping entered and cleared to India and Ceylon increased from 1,081,511 tons in 1860 to 4,701,765 tons in 1870. Imports of Australia and New Zealand from the United Kingdom increased from £2,744,671 in 1850 to £16,316,853 in 1860, and amounted to £14,102,897 in 1870, and exports to the United Kingdom increased from £2,622,762 in 1850 to £12,502,378 in 1860, and to £13,343,356 in 1870. British shipping entered and cleared, exclusive of coastal trade, increased from 310,161 tons in 1850 to 2,355,399 tons in 1860 and 3,912,429 tons in 1870. British shipping entered and cleared to Hong Kong increased from 724,693 tons in 1860 to 1,649,250 tons in 1870. Imports of the Cape of Good Hope from the United Kingdom fluctuated from £1,165,624 in 1850 to £2,187,207 in 1860 and £1,956,305 in 1870, and exports to the United Kingdom from £611,817 in 1850 to £1,547,351 in 1860 and £2,123,061 in 1870. British shipping entered and cleared increased from 300,937 tons in 1850 to 388,217 tons in 1860 and 314,063 tons in 1870.

III

Attraction of the remunerative passenger traffic to the gold fields of California and Australia hastened the decline of sailing vessels and the development of the steamship in the Atlantic. The clipper ship in the United States accompanied the boom days of shipbuilding in the fifties in Quebec and New Brunswick, and of shipbuilding and shipping in Nova Scotia in the sixties. The application of steam to navigation lagged behind its application to land transport, but received a strong impetus from the demand for cheaper and faster service, the influence of invention, and government subsidies. The liberal subsidies granted by the United States to their steamships (1845–7) contributed to the breakdown of the British Navigation Acts. The repeal of these Acts in 1849 and the admission of foreign ships to the coasting trade of Great Britain in 1854 increased the mobility of shipping. Areas with advantages in abundance of shipbuilding material, and in skill and technique, responded to the demand for wooden sailing vessels. But such advantages were eventually offset by the superiority of iron, coal, and steam, and the industrial development of the United Kingdom. The pressure of industrialism based on railroads and ports was evident in the transformation of shipping. The displacement of American softwood by British hardwood, and of British hardwood by iron, prepared the way for the iron steamship. Wooden and iron steamships were at first concerned primarily with passengers and mail and superseded even the fastest clippers. The reduction in the thickness of the hull with the use of iron actually reduced the weight of ships, provided space for more cargo, involved less danger from fire, permitted the construction of larger ships to carry coal, enabled them to stand heavy driving in head seas, and overcame the handicap of spars and masts in limiting the size of ships. The increasing efficiency of marine engines, the introduction of the screw, and the decline in fuel consumption[6] widened the range of steamships. Steamships from Great Britain began to penetrate the non-coal areas of Africa, South America, and the Pacific.

The effect of the Pacific gold rushes was evident first in the rapid extension of steamship services to the West Indies and the Panama. A contract with the Royal Mail West India Steam Packet Company was extended to include a monthly service to the Brazils in 1852. Later contracts in 1857 imposed a faster schedule and development of the service to Rio de Janeiro and River Plate. In 1866 and 1868 the time from England to the Panama was reduced. The Pacific Steam Navigation Company developed a coastal trade between Panama and Valparaiso. In 1868 a profitable monthly service was established from Liverpool via the Straits of Magellan to Valparaiso. This became a fortnightly service and was extended to Callao in 1870. Additional steamship lines were organized, particularly from Liverpool to the West Indies and the Panama with the energetic activities of Alfred Holt beginning in 1855. With the Limited Liability Act of 1862 amalgamations were formed, the West India and Pacific Steam Navigation Company in 1863, and the Liverpool, Brazil and River Plate Steamship Company in 1865. In that year a steamship of the Holt Line made an 8,500-mile non-stop trip from Liverpool to San Francisco.

Sailing ships were challenged further by completion of the Suez Canal, and of the Union Pacific Railway in 1869, which cut the continents in half and removed support from sheltered routes. The 1850's was a most interesting decade in the history of Atlantic shipping

[6]The decline is illustrated by the following chart from C. E. Fayle, *A Short History of the World's Shipping Industry* (London, 1933), p. 241:

	Gross tons	Coal per day in tons	Bunker capacity	Cargo capacity
1855, *Persia*, iron steamship, paddle, simple side lever engines	3,300	150	1,640	1,100
1865, *Java*, iron steamship, screw, simple inverted engines	2,697	85	1,100	1,100
1874, *Bothnia*, iron steamship, screw, compound engines	4,556	63	940	3,000

for it saw the steamer making real headway against the sailing ship, principally because iron construction and screw propulsion obtained recognition. It was, too, a period of cut-throat competition, which in addition to providing excitement for the lookers-on who did not stand to lose dividends by it, invariably meant technical development.[7] Steamship lines supported by mail subsidies were organized for regular schedules. Following the disappearance of the Collins Line, keen rivalry continued beween the Cunard, Inman, Allan, and Dominion lines in the fifties and sixties. Competition for passengers penetrated to the immigrant trade. The percentage of immigrants arriving in Canada by steamships increased from 45 in 1863 to over 95 in 1869. Finally, steamships encroached on bulk cargo traffic and extended development from coastwise to ocean traffic. Improvements in navigation on the Atlantic were significant in strengthening the position of the more highly industrialized areas by lowering the costs of the cheapest form of carriage, that by water. The improvements were hastened by the advantages resulting from the increased size of the unit employed and from rapid depreciation, accentuated by losses, from mobility as to routes, and from the severity of competition between large capitalistic organizations. The early improvements were concentrated on speed and were designed to increase the mobility of labour. Improvements in relation to the movement of labour hastened the production and movement of raw materials in new areas and enlarged the demand for the manufactured products of Great Britain.

The increasing importance of iron and coal contributed to the strength of the merchant marine of Great Britain. In the depression of 1857 large numbers of American vessels[8] were sold to Great Britain, and with the outbreak of the Civil War and the ravages of Confederate cruisers half a million tons of shipping were transferred to British registry. Total shipping cleared and entered in ports of the United Kingdom increased from 24,700,000 tons in 1860 to 36,600,000 tons in 1870, and the percentage of British tonnage from 56 to 68. Shipbuilding activity in the United Kingdom was great in 1863–5, when the Civil War checked American industry, and reached its peak of 275,000 tons in 1864. By the end of the sixties the steamship had surpassed the sailing vessel in Great Britain.

[7]F. C. Bowen, A Century of Atlantic Travel, 1830–1930 (London, n.d.), p. 53.
[8]In the decade from 1850 to 1860 the tonnage of the American merchant marine increased from 3,535,000 to 5,049,000, and in 1861 a maximum of 2,494,984 tons were engaged in foreign trade. As a result, the percentage of British tonnage entering and clearing United Kingdom ports declined from 69 as an average from 1847 to 1849 to 56 in 1860.

	Total number of vessels		Total tonnage
In 1860	Sail	818	168,420
	Steam	198	93,590
In 1870	Sail	541	123,910
	Steam	433	364,860

The iron steamship capitalized the advantages of Great Britain in her possession of iron and coal and of ports accessible all the year round. Her striking competitive advantages in shipbuilding bound her formal and informal Empire more closely to her. The advantages of areas which produced wooden sailing vessels rapidly depreciated and the expansion of canals and railways to the interior of new lands was encouraged with a consequent increase in the production of raw materials and demand for finished products. The supremacy of Great Britain in shipbuilding hastened this shift of energies in the outer Empire to internal exploitation. Shipbuilding and shipping were the basis of her expansion. Thus the increasing importance of British shipping, particularly with the development of the iron steamship on the Atlantic, and the migration of about two and a half million people in each of the decades from 1850 to 1870,[9] coincided with the internal development of North America and other regions.

The Sault Ste Marie Canal, completed in 1855, gave access to the iron ore resources of Lake Superior, and the Civil War and railways created demands for iron and steel. Shipbuilding tonnage on the Great Lakes increased from 212,000 in 1851 to 547,267 in 1866, and railways extended inland from Atlantic ports to Chicago in 1852 and the Mississippi in 1854. Mileage in the United States increased from 9,021 in 1850 to 52,922 in 1870. The Homestead Act of 1862 opened up new lands for rapid occupation, and exports of wheat from the United States, particularly with rise in prices to the peak of 1867 and the increasing use of machinery which accompanied scarcity of labour in the Civil War, totalled 188,000,000 bushels in 1870. The Civil War was in part a result and in part a cause of concentration on western expansion. It involved a profound disturbance to trade. Exports of cotton were practically wiped out from 1862 and reached about three-fourths of the total of 1860 in 1870. The financial drain of the war weakened the monetary and credit structures of both North and South and contributed to the sharp upward trend of protection in the post-

[9]W. A. Carrothers gives a total of 2,844,512 emigrants from the British Isles from 1853 to 1870 of which 61 per cent went to the United States and 28 per cent to Australia in the eight years 1853–60, and 72 per cent to the United States and 17 per cent to Australia in the ten years 1861–70.

war period. With the end of the Civil War, restrictions on settlement in the West were removed and settlement was encouraged. Destruction of the influence of the South was favourable to an increase in the tariff in the North. Reciprocity, which had served as one of the compromises between the North and South to delay the Civil War, since Canada was expected to offset for the North the extension of slavery to Texas in the South, came to an end. Free land, loss of revenue from land sales, and war debt involved higher tariffs and protection as new sources of revenue. The South was no longer a factor restraining the tendency toward protection.

Internal expansion in the United States created a demand for capital and labour, and increased competition with less fortunate areas. These areas were consequently drawn more closely to the United Kingdom through the production of raw materials and the demand for finished products, and were forced to adopt a definite policy of encouragement of capital and labour. The Reciprocity Treaty, during its existence from 1854 to 1866, created an immediate relationship between expansion in the United States and Canada. But the Civil War marked the end of the break between the South and the North, between staple production and industrialism, and between free trade and protection, and sharpened the contrast between an economy built up around the St. Lawrence, with its emphasis on water transportation, on staples and on the markets of Great Britain, and an industrialism with its emphasis on railroads, and led to abrogation of the Reciprocity Treaty. The election of Lincoln from the marginal free soil state of Illinois marked the end of compromise and the supremacy of the North.

In Canada the improvement of transportation facilities by canals and railways was stimulated by the possibility of sharing in the rapidly expanding traffic of the Middle West and thereby reducing overhead costs. The Welland Canal and the St. Lawrence canals, enabling steamships from the upper lakes to descend to Montreal, were completed by 1850, and were intended to reduce costs of transportation from Upper Canada[10] and to compete with the Erie Canal which carried traffic from Buffalo to New York.

[10]Attempts to strengthen the position of the St. Lawrence included a contract in 1852 with the Canadian Steam Navigation Company requiring a fortnightly service to Quebec in summer and a monthly service to Portland in winter. Difficulties led to cancellation in 1855 and a new arrangement with Messrs. Allan of the Montreal Ocean Steamship Company for similar service. Weekly sailings winter and summer to Portland and Quebec respectively were begun in 1859 but it was not until 1864 that a satisfactory postal route was introduced on the St. Lawrence. Lighthouses were installed on the river and on the gulf, and telegraph lines were extended from Quebec to Father Point

Handicaps of seasonal navigation on the St. Lawrence necessitated the construction of railways to ports on the Atlantic seaboard open all the year round. Reciprocity and the Civil War brought a marked increase in trade with the United States. A railway was built from Portland to Montreal in 1853, and from Montreal to Toronto in 1856, and to Sarnia (1855). Portage roads to offset the limitations of the St. Lawrence system were built across the Welland Peninsula and to Collingwood (1855). The completion of the Victoria Bridge at Montreal in 1859 provided a through line not only to develop traffic in Canada, but also to tap the traffic of the Middle West.

The Suspension Bridge (1855) provided a shorter route for American lines to New York, and the importance of propellers on the larger vessels of the upper lakes in the sixties rendered the Welland Canal increasingly obsolete. In spite of the construction of the Welland Railway in 1858, Montreal failed to increase materially its share of traffic. In 1871, three-fourths of the tonnage could not be taken through to Lake Ontario. Shipments of flour and wheat, reduced to bushels, increased to 11,425,167 in 1869, but the total was slight compared to exports from New York. In spite of a lower rate from Chicago to Montreal, "such has been the commanding influence of that great commercial metropolis New York in drawing trade to itself and in keeping down the price of ocean transport that those efforts, though not fruitless, have not been so successful as at first anticipated."[11] High rates of ocean freight to Quebec and Montreal, partly as a result of insurance and other costs, but particularly of the inability of Montreal to provide a balanced cargo and of the seasonal character of navigation, were a serious drawback.

Inability to compete with American routes reduced long-haul traffic on the canals and railways, and necessitated increased reliance on local traffic. Revenue was reduced and the interest charges on capital invested in canals, and to a less extent in railways, were paid by increasing demands on the government. The importance of water navigation, competition from the United States for capital, labour, and traffic, and importation of skill and capital from Great Britain for construction purposes, involved government assistance on a substantial scale. The completion of the major railway systems in England

---

in 1859. The channel to Montreal was steadily deepened to 22 feet in 1878. In turn, as railways were built to New York, construction of railways to Montreal to obtain a larger share of traffic was essential. Insurance charges were gradually reduced on the St. Lawrence and the competitive position strengthened.

[11]*Canada, Sessional Papers,* 1863, no. 3.

by the middle decades of the century increased the demands for raw materials, and released railway contractors alert to the possibilities of guarantees from the colonial governments. The achievement of responsible government facilitated credit arrangements but involved difficulties with Great Britain and the United States.

The repeal of the Corn Laws and Navigation Acts involved the loss of preferences on colonial wheat and, coinciding with depression, led to the annexationist manifesto of 1849 and the demands for reciprocity with the United States.[12] The Reciprocity Treaty of 1854 was designed to increase trade between Canada and the United States, this is, to create a free trade area in North America, and to encourage traffic on the St. Lawrence. It hastened the migration of American technique through opening a market for sawn lumber and other products. The position of the square timber trade and of wooden shipbuilding for the British market was weakened and the advantages of the St. Lawrence in the production and export of white pine as square timber and wooden ships became less conspicuous with the increasing importance of the American market for sawn lumber. Removal of the preference in Great Britain, and competition from Baltic lumber and iron steamships, coincided with increasing demands for foodstuffs and especially wheat. During the Crimean War, the cessation of imports of wheat from the Black and Baltic seas, which had become important after the abolition of the Corn Laws, accentuated demands from Canada and the United States, and contributed to the rise in the price of wheat and to increasing emphasis on railroads and the steamship. The proportion of lumber and timber to total exports from land was below 50 per cent in the fifties, and the trend, with wide fluctuations, continued downward to below 30 per cent in 1870.[13] Dependence on wheat and heavy fixed charges incurred with the introduction of railways and steamships precipitated difficulties in finance. The depression of 1857 brought a sharp decline in the price of wheat which was followed by fluctuations in price and yield. In spite of the abolition of seigniorial tenure and of clergy reserves in 1854 the want of good land in Upper Canada in the early sixties was accompanied by difficulties of wheat production incidental to exhaustion of virgin soil, by the introduction of agricultural machinery from the United States, especially after the Civil War, and by increasing diversification of agriculture. The demand for live-

[12]See *Cambridge History of the British Empire*, VI, 382–4; also H. A. Innis, *Problems of Staple Production* (Toronto, 1933), chap. II.

[13]A. R. M. Lower, "The Trade in Square Timber," *Contributions to Canadian Economics*, VI (University of Toronto Studies, History and Economics, 1933).

stock and live-stock products during the Civil War and the migration of dairying technique from the United States contributed to increasing exports of dairy products (particularly cheese) to Great Britain after the abrogation of reciprocity. In the late seventies, the steamship contributed to the development of substantial exports of live-stock.

Problems of wheat and lumber exports were reflected in the crisis of 1857 in decline in imports, decline in revenue, and government deficits. The financial structure was profoundly affected by fluctuations in exports and by the shift in economic life shown particularly in the growth of towns which accompanied the railroad and the steamship. Speculation in real estate, difficulties with exports, and expansion of credit affected private as well as public finance. The more important banks of Upper Canada collapsed after 1863 and legislation restricting banks to commercial credit and to new developments followed.

An important step in meeting these problems was taken in 1858 with an increase in the tariff of 20 per cent. In 1855, Great Britain opposed negotiations for free trade between Canada and the West Indies, but a rise in the tariff was more serious.[14] Galt argued that the improvements in transportation paid for by revenue received from customs were more than sufficient through lowering of rates to offset the addition of duties. and that in this sense customs duties were designed to stimulate free trade.[15]

[14]The Duke of Newcastle, with the support of the Sheffield Chamber of Commerce, protested in a letter dated August 13, 1859, and Alexander Galt, the Minister of Finance, replied on October 25, 1859: "Self government would be utterly annihilated if the views of the Imperial Government were to be preferred to those of the people of Canada. It is therefore the duty of the present Government distinctly to affirm the right of the Canadian legislature to adjust the taxation of the people in the way they deem best, even if it should unfortunately happen to meet the disapproval of the Imperial Ministry. . . . The fiscal policy of Canada has invariably been governed by considerations of the amount of revenue required. . . . It is certainly ungenerous to be reproached by England, when the obligations which have caused the bulk of the indebtedness of Canada have been incurred either in compliance with the former policy of Great Britain, or more recently assumed to protect from loss those parties in England who had invested their means in our railway and municipal bonds." (Canada, Sessional Papers, 1860, no. 38, cited in E. Porritt, The Fiscal and Diplomatic Freedom of the British Overseas Dominions, Oxford, 1922, pp. 455–6.) See also Cambridge History of the British Empire, VI, 349.

[15]"All these improvements have been undertaken with the twofold object of diminishing the cost to the consumer of what he imports, and of increasing the net result of the labour of the country when finally realized in Great Britain.

"If by an increase of five per cent. on the duty, a reduction of ten per cent. on the other charges were produced, the benefit would accrue equally to the British manufacturer and to the consumer, and the indirect but legitimate protection to the home manufacturer would be diminished; the consumer would pay five per cent. more to the Government, but ten per cent. less to the merchant

The Tariff Act was not disallowed, nor was it adequate to meet the problem. In 1866, with a debt of $77,020,082, the government was "unable to raise more than half of a moderate loan even when offering eight per cent. interest" as a result of "the disastrous effect on Canadian credit of the experience of British investors." The solution of the problem consisted in part in increasing traffic by intensive economic development, and more particularly by extensive economic development. Mr. E. W. Watkin, representing the directorate of the Grand Trunk, advised extension of the railway eastward to the Maritimes and westward to Rupert's Land. With the encouragement of the British government, he succeeded in securing a reorganization of the Hudson's Bay Company in 1863, with a view to arrangements for construction of the railway, but it was not until 1869 that the Dominion government extinguished the rights of the Hudson's Bay Company and not until 1870 that Manitoba was added to Confederation. British Columbia, seriously injured by decline in gold production, joined Confederation in 1871 on condition that a connecting railway should be built within ten years. The debts of both provinces were taken over by the Dominion, arrangements were made for the payment of subsidies to contribute to the costs of local administration, and the Canadian Pacific Railway was completed in 1885.

In the Maritimes, railways were designed as portage railways to give Halifax short connections to Windsor on the Bay of Fundy and to Pictou on the Gulf of St. Lawrence, and to give Saint John a short connection to Sheliac on the Gulf of St. Lawrence; and totalled 365 miles in 1866 costing $15,000,000. Confederation between United Canada and the provinces of New Brunswick and Nova Scotia involved arrangements by which the debts incurred, chiefly as a result of transportation, were assumed by the Dominion. Moreover, capital was made available through a guarantee of a loan by the Imperial government for extension of the Grand Trunk Railway through British territory to the winter ports of Halifax and Saint John, and the Intercolonial Railway was completed in 1876.[16] The new Dominion served as a credit structure by which capital became available with government support, and transportation facilities were extended. The St. Lawrence route, with its dependence on extensive

and forwarder. In this illustration lies the whole of the Canadian customs." (*Canada, Sessional Papers*, 1862, no. 23.) This argument had been developed by Adam Smith. See H. A. Innis, "Significant Factors in Canadian Economic Development," *Canadian Historical Review*, XVIII (1937), 374–85. [See this volume, p. 200.]

[16]See *Cambridge History of the British Empire*, VI, 444ff, 460ff.

governmental intervention in the reduction of transportation charges, and its inability to compete with American roads for through traffic, was forced to rely on fresh government support for the development of new sources of traffic. The political structure was adapted to these demands.

The establishment of fiscal autonomy in relation to Great Britain involved similar changes in relation to the United States. The competition of American manufactured products during the depression of 1857 coincided with the demand for revenue and, with the pressure of Canadian industrial interests, reinforced the trend toward higher tariffs. Protests arose from the United States against a violation of the spirit, if not the letter, of the Reciprocity Treaty. The outbreak of the Civil War brought a marked increase in trade with the United States, but the end of the war and the financial difficulties of the United States and removal of the South as a free trade influence led to increasing protests against the treaty, and to its abrogation in 1866. The Civil War, and especially the *Trent* affair and the Fenian raids, were accompanied by increasing attention on the part of Great Britain to the North American colonies, and hastened Confederation.

The trend toward centralization which characterized the economic development of the St. Lawrence was in contrast to the trend towards decentralization in the Maritime Provinces, particularly Nova Scotia. Confederation was in some sense imposed by the needs of the St. Lawrence. The Atlantic steamship on the St. Lawrence, industrialism in Montreal, and the railroad in the Maritimes, created demands for coal from Cape Breton and the Pictou fields, while reciprocity encouraged trade, particularly from the Atlantic coast of Nova Scotia and the Bay of Fundy, to the United States. Confederation and a compromise between a high Canadian tariff and a low Nova Scotian tariff involved additional burdens to the western portion of the Maritimes which were not entirely offset by the advantages of new markets in the St. Lawrence to the eastern portion. Reciprocity permitted American fishermen to fish in inshore waters and to compete with Maritime fishermen, but the advantages to the United States were lost through the dearth of shipping during the Civil War. The fishery and settlement extended from Gaspé and from Newfoundland to the north shore of the St. Lawrence and Labrador with the result that Nova Scotian vessels were compelled to search new grounds and Lunenberg vessels went for the first time on the Grand Banks in 1873. The Washington Treaty encouraged the Canadian industry.

Reciprocity between the United States and the colonies of British

North America included Newfoundland and coincided roughly with the introduction of responsible government in that area in 1855. Competition from the French had effects similar to the effects of competition on Canada from the United States. Introduction of the seine in the cod fishery along the French shore and of the trawl on the banks adjacent to St. Pierre and Miquelon was followed by determined efforts to restrict their operation by Newfoundland. Conservation measures and control over sales of bait to the French were designed to check French competition stimulated by bonuses and large-scale operations. A treaty of 1857 arranged between Great Britain and France as to the disposal of the Newfoundland fishery was not enforced as a result of the hostility of Newfoundland and its insistence on responsible government and the recognition of its implications by Great Britain. Control was extended through the customs to the Labrador, with the result that the position of St. John's was strengthened at the expense of Nova Scotian, American, and British fishing interests. In spite of her proximity to Great Britain the effects of steam navigation were not evident until a late date. As a result of success with a submarine cable between Carleton Head, Prince Edward Island, and Cape Tormentine on the mainland completed November 22, 1852, F. N. Gisborne introduced the telegraph in St. John's in the same year and planned construction of a transatlantic cable. In 1856 a cable was completed and telegraphic communication established with North America but it was not until July 27, 1866, that a permanent transatlantic cable was laid by the *Great Eastern* from Valentia to Heart's Content. In 1869 a French cable was laid from Brest to St. Pierre, and in 1873 extended to Canso, Nova Scotia. Mail was carried under contract from St. John's to Halifax in winter months, and direct steamship lines to Galway began in 1856 and to England under the Allan Line in 1873. Internal development was fostered by responsible government, protection, and the spread of industrialism. The steamship was introduced in the sealing industry in 1863, and improved methods of extracting seal oils were introduced in the fifties. The herring and salmon fisheries became increasingly important. Abrogation of the Reciprocity Treaty was a logical development in Newfoundland as it had been in the other colonies. Commercial credit continued of dominant importance and the Union Bank was established in 1854 and the Commercial Bank in 1857. The demand for roads and capital improvements involved insistence on the part of the Newfoundland government on the right to impose duties and collect revenue. While the Maritime Provinces had joined

United Canada in spite of differences in economic and political structure, Newfoundland, less influenced by the railway, had found the differences too great to permit of political union with the continent. Capital demands were not adequate to stamp the economic life of Newfoundland in a mould adapted to the requirements of Confederation, and the dispersion of economic life, characteristic of the fishery extending along the coast, precluded political unity.

IV

The series of gold rushes hastened the trend toward increasing mobility of labour. The effects of industrialism, particularly through the steamship and the railway, contributed to expansion of free trade and responsible government in the temperate areas and to the spread of freedom of contract in the tropical regions. Further, the spread of the humanitarian movement led to protracted and finally successful efforts to suppress the transatlantic slave trade. These, however, were complicated by the decline of preferences on sugar with the adoption of free trade. West Indies planters attempted to meet the difficulties by encouraging immigration of Chinese coolies. Capital was supplied by the planters, and labour was brought out under the contract system. "By judiciously promoting emigration from China and at the same time vigorously repressing the infamous traffic in African slaves, the Christian governments of Europe and America may confer benefits upon a large portion of the human race, the effects of which it would be difficult to exaggerate." So wrote Lord Russell to Earl Cowley on July 11, 1860.[17] Chinese officials were not impressed by the advantages, and emigration to tropical countries was restricted. Emigration beginning in 1852 was checked until 1859 and carried on with numerous difficulties after that date. British Guiana brought in about fourteen thousand Chinese in the period 1853 to 1879. For the more tropical West Indies, Indian coolies were more promising. In 1844, the East India Company granted permits to Jamaica, British Guiana, and Trinidad and in 1847 to Ceylon, to recruit coolie labour; also the British government granted similar permits in 1858 to St. Lucia, in 1860 to St. Vincent and St. Kitts, and in 1867 to Grenada. Many liberated slaves were brought to the West Indies, especially from Sierra Leone; also a large immigration came from Madeira.

In 1851 Lagos was captured from a powerful slavery gang with

[17]Cited, P. C. Campbell, *Chinese Coolie Emigration to Countries within the British Empire* (London, 1923), p. 129.

heavy losses and the rightful king restored. His successor, being under the control of slaves, was deposed and in 1861 Lagos was annexed. From this beginning Great Britain checked the slave trade on the Slave Coast. Also mercantile efforts on and near the Niger secured a basis for expansion of control over Southern and Northern Nigeria.

In Cape Colony, representative government in 1853 tended to emphasize equal political rights for blacks and whites. The contrast with the policy of the neighbouring Dutch republics involved difficulties with native tribes, which forced Great Britain to assume an increasingly strong position as a means of assuring order. The shift to free trade coincided with the spread of industrialism in the coal-bearing formations of the temperate regions and with the disturbance of economic life in the tropical regions. Mobility of labour and capital which accompanied the trend toward freedom of trade was of profound significance to the relatively unpopulated areas of the temperate regions, and of serious implication to the densely populated areas of the tropical zones. The abolition of slavery through the Civil War in the United States was a part of the general trend among countries dominated by Anglo-Saxon races. The long struggle of the British Navy off the coast of West Africa to put down the slave trade, with little or no support for a long time from other powers, ended successfully in 1863–6 owing to the annexation of Lagos, to the efficiency of screw steamers in capturing slavers, and to the complete abolition of slavery in 1862 by the United States, and, later, by Brazil and Cuba. The migration of Oriental labour to the gold fields of the Pacific and of coloured labour to the tropics were indications of the far-reaching changes of the period.

The tremendous impact of the gold discoveries of the Pacific was evident in the enormous demands for capital equipment and manufactured products and also in the contributions of gold imports toward the changes of British capital structure. With increasing industrialism, the ample resources of commercial credit in Great Britain became inadequate to meet the internal and external demands for long-term credit. The crash of Overend Gurney and Company in 1865 was in part a result of the depression and in part of far-reaching changes in the financial structure. More effective organization of long-term credit facilities was evident in the extension of legislation to provide for limited liability companies in 1855 and 1862, and in the emergence of a holding company such as the International Financial Society in 1863. The completion of the Atlantic cable in 1866, the extension of cables, telegraphs, and mail steamships linked the financial structures of North America to Great Britain and to the Far East and facilitated capital movements and more direct control of economic and political development. Improvement of financial machinery hastened the decline of the East India Company and of the Hudson's Bay Company, and the development of industrialism in Great Britain and within and without the Empire. Responsible government and the realignment of political structure in the temperate and in the tropical regions provided efficient credit instruments by which shipping and transport were revolutionized with industrialism. Political control from Great Britain declined in importance, but its decline was essential to the expansion of economic control. Guarantees and bonuses were provided by colonial governments with and without the support of the Imperial government for the construction of railways; for example, the Grand Trunk Railway, under private or government construction. The weak position of Empire countries through their dependence on staple products, the timidity of capital which had suffered losses in foreign countries in the forties, and the competition of expanding industrial areas such as the United States, implied dependence on governmental support. The vested interests which characterized an Empire dependent on Navigation Acts, staple products, and commercial credit were weakened with the emergence of the Reform Acts in Great Britain, responsible government, and the progress of industrialism. The shift to navigation and land transport linked to steam was followed by the demand for, and the supply of, new staples more essential to the increasing industrialism of Great Britain, such as wheat and wool. Public finance and private finance, and political and economic institutions alike, reflected the expansion of industrialism in the Empire and the Western world.

The downward trend of duties of the period ending in 1850 continued practically to vanishing point. The British budget of 1853 abolished the duty on cotton yarn, the excise tax on soap, and the advertisement tax, and halved the duties on fruits and dairy products. In 1855 the stamp duty on newspapers was removed, and in 1860 all duties on imported manufactures. The excise duty on paper was abolished in the following year. The Cobden agreement with France was negotiated in 1860. The timber duty followed in 1866, and the sugar duty, after a series of gradual reductions, disappeared in 1874. These changes completed the movement toward free trade, and the removal of protection from the vested interests which had grown up in the colonies producing the staples, sugar and lumber, and they encouraged internal trade dependent on advertising and newspapers.

With the repeal of the Navigation Acts (1849) the advantages of industrial maturity and leadership were practically unhampered by governmental restrictions.

Advantages accruing through removal of duties and taxes, and increasing efficiency of the fiscal mechanism, were supplemented by technical improvements, particularly as applied to shipping. Commodities were imported cheaply, and with improved railways, ports, and ships were carried over longer distance and at lower costs. The stream of goods and commodities moving toward and away from an enlarged metropolitan centre increased in speed and ran with less friction. The completion of a railway and canal system in the United Kingdom by the middle decades of the nineteenth century created an industrialism based on iron and coal, with the growth of an urban population, an increasing demand for raw materials, and an expanding market for finished products.

Extension of the influence of Great Britain in the Pacific and Atlantic under the impetus of technological advance, particularly in relation to navigation and transport in the Atlantic regions, and the impetus of the profit motive, particularly in the gold regions of the Pacific, implied an economic balance in which disturbances of one area were offset by advances in the other. The Civil War and the opening up of a continent in the United States involved its retreat from the sea and opened the door more widely to Great Britain. The Crimean War checked Russian exports of wheat and stimulated production and exports from Canada and the United States. The depression of 1857 in North America and the Civil War were followed by a shift of British interest to Central Africa, India, and the Pacific. The Civil War and the Crimean War forced extension outwards of empire. The shifting of interests strengthened the position of Great Britain. The possibilities of increasing traffic reduced overhead costs on expanding industrial equipment. Improved technique, such as the introduction of steel, hastened the process of expansion. The increasing efficiency of industrial Britain was accompanied by the increasing efficiency of financial and fiscal Britain. The impact on Great Britain of wide fluctuations in the economic activity of regions producing raw material, exposed to shifts from gold to wool and to variations in the yield and price of raw materials, as in the case of wheat, was softened by the balancing of regions. The costs of shifting to the more permanent base of industrialism in terms of iron and steel were borne largely by the obsolescence of areas supplying quantities of raw material, such as timber and wooden ships, and were offset in part by lower costs of transportation and the development of new staples. Agriculture in England felt the impact of competition from new areas and arable land was converted into pasture. Diversity of demands for capital as a result of the economic and political divergences of regions producing raw materials, ranging from New Zealand to the United States, involved competition for labour and capital from the aggressive, rapidly expanding, continental area of the United States, with the weaker areas of the old Empire, and the evolution of types of government and guarantees adequate to secure metropolitan growth. Canada felt more directly the effects of American expansion and of British demands for guarantees, with the result that her experiences with tariffs and political structure were destined to establish precedents for later developments in the other Dominions. The period from 1849 to 1870 was a watershed in imperial history in the spread of industrialism to new regions.

The impact of free trade and industrialism, particularly in relation to steam navigation, accentuated the emphasis on specialization of production of raw materials in new countries and on the production of finished products in more highly industrialized regions. Water transportation and the increasing distances of the Pacific stressed production of specialized raw materials. Gold production emphasized the advantages of a highly industrialized area in its ability to supply promptly and abundantly supplies of finished products. The heavy cost of production, particularly in terms of transportation of raw materials, such as wheat and wool, suited to the demands of an increasingly industrialized area, and the enormous costs involved in the shift to new staples, implied in the pressure of free trade and industrialism and of gold rushes, involved extensive government support. Free trade in Great Britain brought increasing emphasis on staple products in new countries and in turn the introduction of capital equipment, steamships, canals, roads, and railroads, and problems of finance and governmental activity along the lines of responsible government, federation, and protection. Dependence on staples involved more sweeping fluctuations of price, yield, and returns, and accentuated reliance on governmental intervention. Limited liability in its relations to the growth of corporate activity in Great Britain was paralleled by government guarantees in the regions producing raw materials. Commercialism began to give way to capitalism.

Expansion of trade brought improvement in transportation, the emergence of public debt, responsible government, and nationalism. Capital became relatively immobile and inflexible in the government securities of the Dominions. Access to bankruptcy which characterized more mature regions was denied. Political institutions were elaborated in relation to the increasing problems of debt. Dominions, provinces, and municipalities resorted to conversions and even to bankruptcies. Monetary policies were widened on an extensive scale, nationalism was intensified and capital rendered still less mobile.

The cyclonic effects of the gold rushes in the Pacific region were evident in the expansion of shipping and trade on the Atlantic and the Pacific and in the development of Great Britain as a metropolitan centre of the world. It is significant that Marshall suggested that after 1873 the economic history of one country could not be written. At a later date the gold rushes had profound effects on continental development. Transcontinental railways were built to San Francisco and in turn from Montreal to Vancouver to link up the economic areas based on the discovery of gold with the eastern seaboard of North America. Construction under private enterprise in the United States hastened railway construction with substantial government support in Canada. The Klondike gold rush had its effect in hastening construction of two additional transcontinental railways which became the basis of the Canadian National Railways. The vast resources of a continent were opened up with transcontinental lines. The discovery of placer gold reversed the basic trends of liquidity preference which favoured the growth of metropolitan areas particularly with the support of mercantilistic policies. The discovery and production of gold on a large scale shifted the impact of liquidity preference from trade to production, from established areas to new areas, and enormously widened the bounds of production and trade.

The significance of liquidity preference in economic history extends far beyond monetary policy. It was not confined to the place of gold in trade and production. Improvements in communication had the same effects. The phenomenal expansion of newspapers following the displacement of rags by wood accentuated the intensification of trade, enormously extended the sensitivity of modern economic society, and enhanced the role of liquidity preference.

The effect of liquidity preference was evident in the distortion of economic development in relation to staple production. The attractive power of gold hastened the opening of the Pacific and in turn contributed powerfully to the rapid expansion of wheat production following the construction of transcontinental railways on the North American Continent and of animal products, wool, mutton, and dairy products, in Australia and New Zealand. The pressure of agricultural products on the markets of Europe hastened industrial development and contributed to the rise of protection in industry and agriculture.

Distortion by the gold rushes of more normal trends of metropolitan development—in which improved techniques in transportation and communication gradually led to changes in types of product from the hinterlands, more easily handled products being replaced by less easily handled products, fur by timber and timber by grain—by the speeding up of transportation improvement with construction of transcontinental railways was offset in part by their effectiveness in stimulating changes in staple production. Concentration on staples implied a highly specialized economy, changes from which were accomplished with great difficulty and with distress. The Napoleonic Wars and high preferential duties brought the shift from fur to timber in the St. Lawrence. The Rebellions of 1837 were in part a result of the difficulty of shifting from timber to grain.

The gold rushes hastened the shift to new staples and contributed to the difficulties of the long depression, but once the shift was made the basis was provided for the great boom. There were no gold rushes to soften the depression of the thirties, and the shift from wheat to live-stock and dairying in western Canada was accomplished with intense difficulty.

Decentralization and Democracy*

THIS paper is concerned with the changes in types of power in the Atlantic basin following the discovery of America. Direct control from Europe under the French, Dutch, Spanish, and British empires has gradually changed with emergence of independent states in North and South America and of the British Commonwealth of Nations. In Canada European institutions were more strongly entrenched and feudalism continued to exercise a powerful influence, latterly, for example, in the control of natural resources by the provinces. The provinces have become landlords with great disparity of wealth varying with federal policy, technological change, and provincial policy. The changing disparity enhances the complexity of democracy in Canada.

The advantages of the British Empire in its struggle with the French Empire were in part a result of the implications of imperfect competition between drainage basins in the interior as contrasted with more effective competition between the maritime regions of the Atlantic seaboard. In the latter region, imperfect competition was reflected in the slowness with which adjustments were made between the west country in England, Newfoundland, Nova Scotia and New England. In the interior of the continent competition was less effective in the struggle between traders of various nationalities or of the same nationality as it was carried on between drainage basins. Trunk rivers and tributaries with low heights of land between drainage basins facilitated the tapping of vast regions. The relative effectiveness of competition on the seaboard and in the interior of the continent had implications for the struggle of empire.

In the sixteenth century the French Empire was concerned with the extension of the fishing industry in the New World as a means of strengthening self-sufficiency with access to new supplies of food and to an industry promising naval strength. The English Empire was concerned with the acquisition of specie flowing from the New World of Spain. It concentrated on the dry fishery in Newfoundland and

*From *Canadian Journal of Economics and Political Science*, IX (1943), 317–30; reprinted in *Political Economy in the Modern State* (Ryerson, 1946), pp. 236–50.

exports to Spain. By the end of the century the French were also influenced by the high prices of Spain only to find that the more accessible sites for the prosecution of the dry fishery were occupied by the English and that it was necessary to penetrate to more distant sites such as the Gaspé region in the Gulf of St. Lawrence. The interest of France in development of the fishery in relation to her own needs and of England in trade with Spain involved the delay of a century in penetrating the northern part of the continent. In the seventeenth century, France, after comparative failure on the sea-board, established a foothold at Quebec in the protected region of the St. Lawrence, and built up connections with the Hurons of Georgian Bay by the Ottawa route. The Hudson River was occupied by the Dutch after Hudson's voyage of 1609, and the Iroquois, driven from the St. Lawrence by the hunting Indians and the French, received support for vigorous counter-attacks. Fortifications were extended up the St. Lawrence to Three Rivers, Montreal, and the mouth of the Richelieu, and trade with the agricultural Indians of the Georgian Bay region by the Ottawa route was protected. In turn the Iroquois were pressed to the interior and proceeded across the east end of Lake Ontario and north to destroy the Huron villages in 1648–9. Concentration on military activity and the restrictions on the fur trade under company control necessitated governmental intervention. The fur trade involved heavy outbound cargo and a light return cargo with the result that settlement was discouraged and that vigorous efforts by the government to encourage immigration were made. The difficulties of the fur trade stimulated the interest of traders such as Radisson and Groseilliers in the alternative outlet by Hudson Bay. The necessity of concentrating on the St. Lawrence precluded the development of the route and Radisson and Groseilliers deserted to the English to assist in the formation of the Hudson's Bay Company in 1670.

The active interest of the French government in the St. Lawrence was accompanied by a determined effort to build up an integrated Atlantic empire. Placentia in Newfoundland was established as a basis of the fishing industry in 1662 and attempts were made to link the St. Lawrence as an agricultural base to the sugar plantations of the West Indies. The effort failed because of the increasing demands of the St. Lawrence. Energy was dissipated in efforts to check competition by the destruction of English posts in Hudson Bay and by the construction of forts along the Great Lakes. Destruction of the Huron villages compelled the French to build up their own trading organization to the interior. Dissipation of resources was evident in the abandonment of Fort Frontenac in 1689 with the capture of posts on James Bay, and its re-establishment in 1694 after their loss in 1693. The uncertainty of returns from furs which followed the success or failure of military and naval activity and the changes in fashion combined, with the increasing debt incidental to expansion in the interior, to produce inflation and the disorganization of economic life in the St. Lawrence. The French West Indies were compelled to rely on the English colonies and on Ireland for supplies and provisions. In the Treaty of Utrecht in 1713 France recognized defeat in retreat from Nova Scotia and Hudson Bay.

Penetration of the St. Lawrence by the French involved restriction of the English to the regions along the Atlantic seaboard. In the seventeenth century, with the exception of the conquest of Quebec from 1629 to 1632, and of Nova Scotia for a short period, England confined her activities to the establishment of colonies along the southern seaboard and in the West Indies. In 1664 New York was captured from the Dutch. Mercantilist policy involved not only the export of dried fish from Newfoundland as a means of securing specie from Spain but also the production of tropical products in the British West Indies as a means of restricting the purchase of those commodities from Spain. The resources of the Atlantic seaboard enabled the colonies to provide supplies for the British West Indies and even for the French West Indies. The limitations of French integration imposed strains on an inclusive British Empire. Attempts of the west country to maintain control over Newfoundland and to check settlement facilitated the migration of labour from Newfoundland to New England. On the other hand, the increase in the production of agricultural commodities, lumber, and fish in the English colonies and restrictions on exports to the French West Indies lowered the price of exports to Newfoundland and supported the growth of settlement in spite of west country hostility. Concentration on the Atlantic seaboard emphasized the importance of naval strength and encouragement of the fishing industry and carrying trade as nurseries for seamen and reserves for ships. The construction of military fortifications was discouraged and the English Empire was never cursed with the problem of dependence on a staple commodity such as fur and the heavy burden of fixed charges incidental to the construction of forts in the interior, and the consequent devastating effects of inflation.

With retreat from Hudson Bay, Nova Scotia, and Newfoundland after 1713, France consolidated her position at Louisburg on Cape

Breton and renewed efforts were made to rebuild an empire on a more solid base. But the basic problems of integration were accentuated rather than alleviated. The establishment of a settlement on Cape Breton was handicapped by the limited resources of the area, by the limitations of the St. Lawrence region, and by the difficulty of attracting Acadians from the dyked lands of the Bay of Fundy to the forest lands of Prince Edward Island or of encouraging them to raise grain, rather than live-stock to be smuggled from the Bay of Fundy. The French West Indies were unable to rely on French supplies and provisions and a smuggling trade with the English colonies increased in the West Indies and in Cape Breton. Cheap supplies and provisions from the English colonies were exchanged for rum through both channels. French policy favoured consumption of French brandy in New France, and French West Indies rum was sold to the English.

The St. Lawrence was handicapped by the loss of Hudson Bay, which compelled French traders to extend their trade from Lake Superior to Lake Winnipeg and the Saskatchewan under La Vérendrye and his successors. The long and difficult voyage around the arc of a circle along the edge of the Hudson Bay drainage basin, in competition with the Hudson's Bay Company on Hudson Bay at the centre of the circle, imposed heavy burdens on the colony. Moreover, the development of trade from the mouth of the Mississippi meant encroachments on the trade of the St. Lawrence. Fortifications were extended along the Great Lakes to check competition from the English and the Iroquois from Albany and Oswego. In spite of efforts to encourage the iron industry and shipbuilding on the St. Lawrence, France was unable to develop an agricultural and an industrial base to meet the demands of Louisburg and the West Indies and of Saskatchewan and the Great Lakes. Inflation again broke out and the Seven Years' War brought the collapse of Louisburg, Quebec, and the French Empire in North America.

Again the inability of the French to develop an integrated Empire had implications for the British Empire. Expansion of production and trade in the English colonies involved an increase in the smuggling trade to the French West Indies. Continued encouragement to the fishing industry and to shipbuilding involved a clash with British West Indies planters anxious to check trade with the French West Indies. The influence of the planters in Great Britain secured the Molasses Act of 1733, which was designed with other legislation to create a monopoly market in Great Britain and to check the trade of surplus tropical products of the French West Indies with the surplus products of the temperate English colonies of the seaboard. The legislation stimulated the smuggling trade through Louisburg and enhanced the interest in Nova Scotia and Newfoundland. Settlement continued to increase in Newfoundland and the influence of the west country to decline. With the defeat of France it was expected that the markets of the St. Lawrence would be opened to the products of the British West Indies and that more rigid control would be exercised over the trade between the English colonies and the French West Indies.

Destruction of the French Empire profoundly disturbed the equilibrium of the Atlantic and was followed by the collapse of the British Empire and the loss of the colonies. The Treaty of Versailles recognizing the independence of the United States followed the Treaty of Paris in two decades. Anglo-American traders pushed rapidly into the territory vacated by the French and quickly occupied the region northwest of the Saskatchewan. The English colonies extended the fishing industry to the Gulf of St. Lawrence and participated, in spite of protests from the British West Indies, in smuggling to the French West Indies, which were no longer able to draw even meagre support from the St. Lawrence. Conflicts emerged between the colonies and the British West Indies, between the colonies and Newfoundland, which under west country influence attempted to check the colonial fishery, and among the colonies themselves, since traders from Albany dependent on the Iroquois middleman organization demanded restriction of trade to the posts, and the St. Lawrence region and traders from Quebec and Montreal, following the organization built up by the French after the destruction of the Huron middlemen, insisted on extending the trade among the Indians. Pallisser's Act in 1775 encouraged the Newfoundland fishery at the expense of the colonies, and the Quebec Act of 1774 enlarged the province of Quebec to extend the control of the St. Lawrence at the expense of Albany. The Hudson's Bay Company in the year of the Quebec Act made its first important move inland in the construction of Cumberland House to check the encroachments of the Anglo-American traders. The complexity of an empire including the West Indies and Newfoundland with strong influential groups in England, the colonies including Nova Scotia in possession of a powerful tradition of assemblies, a conquered territory in Quebec, and a charter company in Hudson Bay, imposed too severe a strain on the constitutional resources of Great Britain, taxed by the addition of Scotland in 1707 and the corruption of Parliament under Walpole and George III. Removal of colonial fears of a major hostile power after the Seven Years' War brought disaster.

The fall of New France and the French Empire had been a result of the inadequacies of control by France with a continental background, and the dependence on military participation and consequent rigidities. The fall of the British Empire was a result of the inadequacies of control by England with a maritime background and her dependence on naval strength and consequent elasticities.

After the Revolution United Empire Loyalists followed earlier New England immigrants into Nova Scotia, and migrated to the province of Quebec in the Eastern Townships and north of the Great Lakes. The Maritimes were divided into separate colonies, Nova Scotia, New Brunswick, Prince Edward Island, and Cape Breton. Nova Scotia made a deliberate effort to establish a place for itself within the British Empire comparable to that formerly occupied by New England and the American colonies. The influence of the West Indies was weakened, particularly with legislation against slavery, as the influence of Nova Scotia became stronger. The latter opposed the re-establishment of trade between the West Indies and the region which had now become the United States, and attempted to develop her own resources, and to build up an *entrepôt* trade from the St. Lawrence and from New England. Protests from the West Indies eventually led to the opening of trade with the United States. As the French had failed to build up an integrated trade between the St. Lawrence, the Maritimes, and the West Indies, so Nova Scotia failed. The difficulties of Nova Scotia in relation to the West Indies were in part a result of the increase in population in Newfoundland. The American Revolution and wars between England and France weakened the control of the west country and hastened the growth of a resident population. The demands of an increasing population attracted trade from Nova Scotia and weakened her possibilities in relation to West Indies trade. The aggressive influence of Nova Scotia in the second Empire became more effective in contrast with the West Indies in the first Empire. Efforts to prevent the loss of the American colonies by such measures as the Colonial Tax Repeal Act of 1778 were exploited by Nova Scotia through an Assembly inherited from the old Empire. Whereas Massachusetts was willing to recognize the Crown but refused to recognize the supremacy of the British Parliament, Nova Scotia accepted supremacy and secured modifications in Imperial legislation enabling her to strengthen her autonomy. The dependence of Nova

Scotia on the fishery, shipping, and trade was in contrast with the limited possibilities of the St. Lawrence.

Anglo-American traders driven to the Northwest by the extension of immigration to the interior of the United States developed an effective instrument for the command of increasing capital which came with increasing distances. The Northwest Company emerged with the support of rum from the West Indies restricted in the American market after the Revolution, the development of shipping on the Great Lakes, the organization of food supplies, and extension to the Athabaska and the Mackenzie rivers. Organization of the American fur trade and the Jay Treaty compelled Anglo-American traders to withdraw and to penetrate the Northwest as the XY Company. Intensive competition brought amalgamation in 1804. To offset the effects of organization of trade from the St. Lawrence, the Hudson's Bay Company was compelled to reorganize a structure developed in relation to the fur trade on Hudson Bay. The organization of a base for supplies of food and a determination to exact recognition of the ownership of land drained by rivers flowing into Hudson Bay provided the background for the Selkirk settlement. As on the St. Lawrence the French government had been compelled to intervene to prevent retardation of settlement by companies, so on Hudson Bay competition from St. Lawrence traders compelled the Hudson's Bay Company to provide a base for settlement in the Selkirk scheme. The Northwest Company extended its organization across the continent to the mouth of the Columbia River but was handicapped in the development of Pacific trade. New England, restricted after the Revolution in trade with the British Empire, became active in South America and the Pacific, and built up extensive connections with the Sandwich Islands and the Orient. While the attempt of the Northwest Company to build up trade on the Pacific failed because of inability of Nova Scotia to build up a trading organization in relation to the St. Lawrence, the West Indies and Newfoundland, but succeeded in developing a transcontinental organization, American traders succeeded in the Pacific regions but failed to develop a transcontinental organization by the Missouri across the plains to the Columbia. The Hunting Indians of the north supported the Northwest Company but the Plains Indians of the south restricted American organization. Astoria was taken over by the Northwest Company but arrangements were made to trade with the Orient through Boston firms to avoid the monopoly of the East India Company. Limitations of the Northwest Company on the Pacific contributed to its difficulties in the competitive struggle with the

Hudson's Bay Company. In 1821 the two companies were amalgamated and Hudson Bay became the dominant route with the elimination of the St. Lawrence.

As in the French Empire, the St. Lawrence was inadequate as a continental base to support Nova Scotia in relation to the West Indies and Newfoundland, and the fur trade to the interior. In the French Empire brandy was sold in the St. Lawrence at the expense of West Indies rum, and in the British Empire settlement was followed by grain production and concentration on whiskey rather than rum. With supremacy of Hudson Bay, settlers on the lower St. Lawrence and in the Great Lakes region turned to the timber trade which emerged through the efforts of Great Britain to build up an alternative supply during the Napoleonic Wars. The demands of United Empire Loyalists in the Great Lakes region and of traders in the lower St. Lawrence and the importance of military strength led to the adoption of the Constitutional Act of 1791 and the division of the province of Quebec into Upper and Lower Canada. The resources of Upper and Lower Canada were in the land and of Nova Scotia in the sea. Nova Scotia developed her autonomy in relation to the trade of the Empire whereas Upper and Lower Canada were concerned with the occupation of land by settlers and the exploitation of the forests. The Crown's control over land strengthened the position of the executive, and the Assembly, without the long traditions of Nova Scotia, was less effective in its struggle for responsible government. Military control and settlement in the St. Lawrence, in the British Empire as in the French Empire, strengthened the interest of Europe in finance, while naval control and trade in the Maritimes facilitated the growth of independence. Rebellion broke out in Upper and Lower Canada but Nova Scotia achieved responsible government with peace.

The Reform Act in Great Britain hastened the destruction of shelters which protected the vested interests of staple trades with long-term credit, such as sugar, thus contributing to the break-up of the second Empire. The emergence of free trade compelled realignments in the St. Lawrence essential to the lowering of transportation costs to offset the loss of protection. Canals were built, the provinces of Upper and Lower Canada were united, and credit was provided to strengthen a transport system to compete with the alternative New York route. Canadian tariffs replaced the tariffs of the colonial system. In Nova Scotia, following defeat in checking trade between the United States and the West Indies, determined efforts were made to hamper the American fishery. Success was partially achieved in the opening of American markets in the Reciprocity Treaty. In the St. Lawrence and in Nova Scotia advantages were gained in American trade during the difficult period of compromise between North and South in the United States. With the success of the North in the Civil War, the Reciprocity Treaty came to an end and American tariffs were imposed. New schemes were essential on the St. Lawrence to strengthen its position with the increasing difficulties of the American market and in Nova Scotia to compel a reopening of the market for fish.

In the territory under the control of the Hudson's Bay Company after 1821, monopoly was strengthened and barricades were built along the Precambrian formation against competition from the south. Signs of strain were evident in the most distant area, in the retreat from the Columbia to Victoria on Vancouver Island after the settlement of the Oregon boundary dispute. In the Red River free trade was conceded by the Hudson's Bay Company to traders from the Mississippi drainage basin to the south in 1849. A major breach in the system came with the discovery of placer gold in the Fraser River in 1857 and the rapid occupation of the Pacific coast region. The monopoly of the Hudson's Bay Company with that of the East India Company came under attack, and colonial government emerged in British Columbia and Vancouver Island. The entrenchment of the Hudson's Bay Company in the territory drained by rivers flowing into Hudson Bay, held by it under the charter from the Crown, yielded only after the joining of the provinces of Ontario, Quebec, Nova Scotia, and New Brunswick in Confederation, and the demand for a solution of their transportation problems by extension of the trunk railway of the St. Lawrence. The policy of imperial defence, which created divisions in British North America after the Treaty of Versailles, successful in the War of 1812, was reversed in the interests of unity and centralization after the Civil War. The policy of division and defence after 1783 left a legacy of control by the provinces over their natural resources in the federal structure which checked the trend toward centralization.

In Newfoundland, revival of the French fishery after the Napoleonic Wars was accompanied by determined efforts to hamper it comparable to those of Nova Scotia against the United States. The struggle for responsible government brought control over natural resources and a gradual pressure for exclusion of the French by such measures as were involved in the bait legislation and later in the removal of the French from the French shore, and for exclusion of American, Nova Scotian,

Canadian, and English traders and fishermen. The aggressiveness of Canada, supported by Nova Scotia, especially after the abrogation of the Washington Treaty, embittered Newfoundland and made federation impossible.

Throughout the history of northern North America the Maritimes, and especially Nova Scotia, had served as an unsuccessful base of empires. In the French régime, first in Nova Scotia and after 1713 in Cape Breton, attempts to link the St. Lawrence and the French West Indies failed because of the high prices of the St. Lawrence incidental to the drain of westward expansion in pursuit of the fur trade. In the British régime, Nova Scotia was again unable to take the place of the English colonies in relation to the British West Indies, but she effectively developed a position in the British Empire and assumed an aggressiveness which enabled her to enlist the support of Canada against encroachment from the United States. The price of the enlistment was recognition of Canadian tariffs and acceptance of the high price system of the St. Lawrence. Higgling was evident in the free port policy in the Gaspé region and after Confederation in construction of the Intercolonial Railway and its extension to Sydney, tariffs and subventions on coal and iron, upward revisions of federal subsidies, and the Maritime Freight Rates Act.

Confederation emerged in relation to the problems of the St. Lawrence and the Maritimes and of the Pacific. The resistance of the Hudson's Bay Company, weakened in Red River and on the Pacific, yielded under pressure from the Atlantic and the Pacific. But it was felt in the location of the Canadian Pacific Railway along the southern border, its extension through British Columbia by the Crow's Nest Pass line, and its monopolistic measures. The long delay which accompanied the monopoly position of the Hudson's Bay Company was followed by rapid occupation of the prairie regions. Disequilibrium as a result of resistance of the Hudson's Bay Company, characterized by large-scale migration from the St. Lawrence and the Maritimes to the United States and by widening of the gauge of the Grand Trunk Railway to link up with the American system at Chicago, was followed by disequilibrium with the sudden opening of the prairies by construction of a transcontinental railway and completion of the St. Lawrence canals to fourteen feet. The long depression was followed by the great boom. The monopoly position of the Canadian Pacific Railway, evident in a favourable capital structure and large dividends, was followed by the pouring in of capital into the region north of the

Canadian Pacific Railway, and in the construction of two additional transcontinental railways by the Yellowhead Pass to Vancouver and Prince Rupert. These developments followed support from newly created credit instruments in the Prairie Provinces and from the interest of the provinces of Ontario and Quebec in the development of natural resources especially after the Privy Council decision of 1898. The Temiskaming and Northern Ontario Railway, expansion of the mining industry in Cobalt, Porcupine, and Kirkland Lake, exploitation of hydro-electric power, particularly in the Ontario Hydro-Electric Power Commission, fostered by protection of Nova Scotian coal, and construction of pulp and paper plants through the active intervention first of Ontario and later Quebec and the other provinces, accompanied the extension of transcontinental systems east from Winnipeg.

Rapid occupation of the prairie regions from the late 1890's to about 1930 accompanied the construction of railways and canals to the Atlantic seaboard and after the war the completion of the Panama Canal. As a result of the latter, freight rates were lowered in the areas with high freight rates to the St. Lawrence and the resources of Alberta and British Columbia were developed with striking rapidity. The St. Lawrence was strengthened in its struggle with the Pacific by deepening of the Welland Canal.

The depression coincided with the decline in influence of major technical developments in transportation. Regionalization became more pronounced with competition between the Panama and the St. Lawrence and the development of natural resources, hydro-electric power, pulp and paper and minerals, particularly in the provinces of Ontario and Quebec. Provincialism has paralleled the new industrialism. The increasing demands of the United States with expanding population and declining resources shifted the direction of trade from an east-west to a north-south route particularly in regions other than the Prairie Provinces.

Regionalization has brought complex problems for an economy developed in relation to the St. Lawrence. It has been strengthened by the growth of automotive transport and roads in competition with coal and steam and water and rail. Confederation as an instrument of steam power has been compelled to face the implications of hydro-electric power and petroleum. Confederation has been to an important extent the creation of private enterprise represented by the Canadian Pacific Railway, supported by the federal government in a tariff and railway rate policy, and in the Canadian National Railways. The direct interest of the federal government in the Canadian National Railways cannot be separated from an indirect interest in the Canadian Pacific Railway. The burden of a political structure developed in relation to exploitation of the prairie regions has rested to an important extent on those regions and adjustment involves a struggle between regions which have become concerned with new types of power and the American rather than the European market, and regions which have suffered directly from the difficulties of the European market and costs of a system of transportation facing obsolescence from new types of transportation.

Strains on the political structure have been evident on all sides as problems of adjustment have become more acute. Demands on party organization as the basis of government have been almost insuperable. The Senate, in contrast with second chambers in Great Britain and the United States, was created in a period with limited political capacity and little effort has been made to adjust its membership to the increase in talent available. Necessities of party organization have made it a pasture for old party war horses which old age pensions render unnecessary. Regions favoured by the British North America Act with a large number of senators are able to build up powerful party organizations with the promise of tangible rewards.

With limitations of the Senate the strain imposed on the courts has not been lessened. Reform of the civil service has increased the necessity of patronage in judicial appointments. Not only has the foundation of the courts been weakened by patronage but division of authority between the Privy Council and the Supreme Court of Canada has meant lower prestige for the latter. A strong Supreme Court insistent on avoiding an attempt to follow the elections is an essential bulwark to a democracy. We are hearing far too much about peace by power and far too little about equality before the law.

In the House of Commons the exacting demands of party organization have the effect of increasing the power of the Cabinet and of a small group within the Cabinet. Patronage has been increasingly restricted to this group and taken out of the hands of the members. Not only have members of Parliament less power but they are selected from a weaker group. Decline in the influence of the press and particularly the amalgamation of newspapers since the last war precludes intense party activity and effective discussion. Editors are compelled to follow a neutral policy without endangering the interests of either party. The radio becomes more effective in the hands of a central party organization but the character of discussion is lowered because of the necessity of appealing to large numbers.[1] Discussion is restricted in the constituencies and in turn in the House of Commons. The increasing dictatorial powers of a small group in the Cabinet and the lowering of the calibre of members of Parliament have contributed to the unprecedented breaches in the British tradition of anonymity in the civil service. Members of the civil service are becoming almost as well known to the public as ministers. A new civil service has emerged with much looser responsibilities to ministers in charge of departments. Ministers are able to evade responsibility by using the pronouncements of members of the civil service as kites to test public opinion, or by throwing individuals to the wolves when the chase becomes too warm. The power of opposition has been reduced enormously during the war period. Members of the opposition oppose the government in arguments and vote with it. Union government almost prevails in fact if not in name. Opposition consequently becomes effective in separate provinces, and provincial parties[2] have emerged on a large scale, most obviously in Alberta and Quebec.

The emergence of new parties favours the growth of ideologies and the neglect of practical problems of government. These ideologies range through free enterprise, production for use and not for profit, new democracy, *bloc populaire,* and the like. Bureaucracies give rise to parties with ideologies because they prevent groups from facing immediate problems and leave them with no alternative but party activity. The economics of parties is by no means clearly understood but the supply of parties is associated with the demands of the professions, particularly the legal profession, for advertising, and the demand for parties with the inability of groups to register their views effectively. The complex problems of regionalization in the recent development of Canada render the political structure obsolete and necessitate concentration on the problem of machinery by which interests can become more vocal and their demands be met more efficiently. It is imperative that serious attention should be given to the problem of revising political machinery so that democracy can work

[1]"Then Tom Corcoran (assistant to the President) offered me a little advice. The day of the printed word, he announced, was over. 'You have no idea what a good thing it is for your soul to have to address yourself to a big radio audience. You've got to clarify your meaning, make things simple, reduce them to their ultimate essentials if you want to get them over to a big audience, because human beings are a hell of a lot stupider than you would ever think.'" (Raymond Moley, *After Seven Years,* New York, 1939, p. 355.)

[2]See J. B. Crozier, *History of Intellectual Development on the Lines of Modern Evolution,* III (London, 1901), 258–9, on parties in France.

out solutions to modern problems. The danger that bureaucracies, including Royal Commissions, will suggest legislation rather than devices by which the demands of interests can be reflected and discussed previous to the enactment of legislation has been evident. The dangers of an obsolescent political structure cannot be avoided by patchwork solutions and plans of the bureaucracies. Each region has its conditions of equilibrium in relation to the rest of Canada and to the rest of the world, particularly in relation to Great Britain and the United States. Manipulation of a single instrument such as monetary policy implies a highly elaborate system to determine how far transfers between regions or provinces are necessary. Otherwise full employment will become a racket on the part of the central provinces for getting and keeping what they can. The provinces will require elaborate machinery to protect themselves against exploitation of haphazard federal policies. Provincial finances will reflect the influence of federal activity. The result of neglect of interrelations between the provinces and the Dominion will be evident in increasing division and greater reliance on bureaucracy.

The argument developed in this paper assumes that the end of the second thirty years' war is in sight and that the Pax Britannica will be followed by an effective Pax Americana-Britannica. It assumes that the political scientist[3] can escape from the hocus-pocus of the economist and concentrate on the extremely difficult problems of his own field. He can best make a contribution to economic development by suggested modifications to political machinery.

[3]"A similar revolution of ideas is very rare in the West, and indeed experience shows that innovating legislation is connected not so much with Science as with the scientific air which certain subjects, not capable of exact scientific treatment, from time to time assume. To this class of subjects belonged Bentham's scheme of Law-Reform and, above all, Political Economy as treated by Ricardo. Both have been extremely fertile sources of legislation during the last fifty years." (Sir Henry Sumner Maine, *Popular Government*, London, 1885, p. 146.) "We Englishmen pass on the Continent as masters of the art of government; yet it may be doubted whether, even among us, the science, which corresponds to the art, is not very much in the condition of Political Economy before Adam Smith took it in hand" (*ibid.*, p. 58). "Popular Government and Popular Justice were originally the same thing. The ancient democracies devoted much more time and attention to the exercise of civil and criminal jurisdiction than to the administration of their public affairs; and, as a matter of fact, popular justice has lasted longer, has had a more continuous history, and has received much more observation and cultivation than popular government." (*Ibid.*, pp. 89–90.) On the problems of government in Great Britain, and, one might add, the more acute problems of government in Canada, see the discussion of the machinery developed in the United States to check the usurpation of the Cabinet (*ibid.*, pp. 196ff).

The Political Implications of Unused Capacity*

THE implications of economic development on the North American continent to the economic history of Europe have been traced in detail and in general and broad generalizations have emerged to describe their character. An attempt has been made to suggest effects of concentration on specific staple products in Canadian economic expansion, particularly in the confused period of shifts to new staples. Unused capacity involved in exploitation of staples had its effect in prolonging the dominance of one staple or in hastening its decline, and contributed powerfully to the disturbance of equilibrium in Canada and in Europe. The heavy outbound cargo from Europe characteristic of the fur trade restricted immigration, and the heavy return cargo characteristic of the timber trade hastened immigration. The role of unused capacity in determining the characteristics of economic development was weakened or strengthened by peculiarities of particular staples.

North America was settled by immigrants crossing from Asia by Bering Strait. The blocking of the polar ice by this narrow gateway left the Pacific Ocean to exercise a moderating influence on the climate of the western part of the continent and to favour the migration of population to Central and South America. Aboriginal culture in North America reflected a marked adaptation to geographical environment worked out over an extended period and consequently had a profound effect on the character of relations with Europe. Migration from Europe was halted by the accessibility of the Atlantic to the Polar Sea and by the inhospitable Greenland ice cap and the Labrador current with the result that the first approach of the Norsemen met defeat. The Pacific had its moderating influence on the vast portion of northwestern America in Arctic Felix, Alaska, and the Mackenzie River, whereas the Atlantic lowered the temperature of the eastern part of North America in Arctic Deserta. In the second effort contact was made from Spain in the subtropical areas of Europe with the highly elaborated aboriginal culture in the tropical regions of Central

*From *Political Economy in the Modern State* (Ryerson, 1946), pp. 218–28.

372

America. Europeans attacked aboriginal culture in areas in which it was most highly developed and brought its abrupt collapse. Reserves of precious metals were looted in Mexico and Peru and the booty taken to Europe.

Concentration on imports of precious metals brought a sharp rise in prices in Spain and the shrivelling of industry and trade. Other countries seized the opportunity to meet the demands of Spain and to secure the advantages of high prices. England with "no treasure but by trade" elaborated mercantile policies designed to attract precious metals. The fishing industry was encouraged in the New World as a means of gaining access to the Spanish market and, after the Armada, England established a foothold on Newfoundland. Early in the seventeenth century she restricted imports of sugar and tobacco from Spain in order that she might produce them in her colonies in the New World and thus secure specie rather than these commodities. Control by Spain of the more densely populated aboriginal territory in the New World compelled English expansion in the Atlantic basin to depend on the migration of English labour in Newfoundland and the northern colonies and the movement of slaves from Africa to the plantation colonies in the south and the West Indies. Trade to India was supported by exports of specie obtained through trade from Spain.

France as a country adjacent to Spain found it unnecessary to establish a foothold in the New World to prepare dried fish for the Spanish market until the latter part of the sixteenth century when the Channel ports became more directly concerned. Finding the English entrenched along the Atlantic coast the French developed the industry in the Gulf of St. Lawrence, notably on the Gaspé Peninsula and thus established a base for the expansion of the fur trade up the St. Lawrence and its tributaries. As Spain was profoundly influenced by her contacts with the aborigines of Central and South America through the supplies of precious metals, France was profoundly influenced by her contacts with the hunting Indians of North America through supplies of furs. France and Spain were directly concerned with the effects of contrast between aboriginal and European cultures whereas England was indirectly concerned. In France and Spain the demands of the upper classes determined the character of relations with the aborigines of North America; in England the supply of English and African labour was significant.

The vast, angular-shaped area of Precambrian formation in North America had its implications for drainage systems in the large rivers which flowed along its edge, the St. Lawrence and the Mackenzie, and in the difficult shorter rivers which crossed it in flowing to Hudson Bay. In this area flora and fauna moulded the culture of the hunting Indians while in the later formations to the south soil conditions and climate favoured the agricultural Indians, the Huron Iroquois of the upper St. Lawrence, southern Ontario, and northern New York. The Dutch and later the English moved from the Atlantic seaboard south of the St. Lawrence approach and traded with the agricultural Indians by the Hudson River. The French were dependent first on the agricultural villages in the Georgian Bay area but with their annihilation by the Iroquois they were compelled to develop the St. Lawrence areas with their own agricultural base. The English, restrained by the agricultural Indians and the Appalachians, took full advantage of the possibilities of expansion in trade with the area bordering on the Atlantic. The enormous handicaps of seasonal migration in the more northernly areas drained by the St. Lawrence hastened the discovery and occupation of the Mississippi across a narrow height of land. La Salle overcame the handicaps of navigation on the upper St. Lawrence, established posts on the Great Lakes, and exploited the fur trade of the head waters of the Mississippi. The flood of lower-grade furs from this area was an important cause of the development of inflation.

Attraction of the French to the south led to the establishment of a post at the mouth of the Mississippi early in the eighteenth century and to competition for trade in the interior between New Orleans and Montreal. With the success of a trade unhampered by seasonal navigation the French under La Vérendrye turned from the St. Lawrence to the northwest of Lake Superior. In this direction they came into more direct competition with the Hudson's Bay Company. In New France company control broke down particularly after the destruction of the Huron villages, and after 1663 the Crown intervened with active measures hastening settlement and trade. Traders such as Radisson and Grosseilliers persuaded the English Crown shortly after the Restoration to grant a monopoly to the Husdon's Bay Company in 1670. With little possibility of agricultural development in the vicinity of Hudson Bay, posts were established at the mouths of rivers draining into James Bay and Hudson Bay and controlled effectively from London. The problem of smuggling peculiar to commodities of small bulk and high value proved insoluable on the St. Lawrence but it was solved by the highly centralized control from London as apparently it was solved in the shipment of treasure from the New World to Spain.

The interest of France in the fur trade of the St. Lawrence involved dependence on a commodity which fluctuated widely in supply as a result of competition from the Dutch, and later the English, from the Hudson River, and the English from Hudson Bay; of wars between Europeans and aborigines; of geographic characteristics evident especially in the size and peculiarities of drainage basins; and of the character of aboriginal cultural traits in relation to the demand for European goods. Fur was a commodity in which not only supply but also demand fluctuated widely. As a luxury product it was exposed to the fluctuations incidental to changes of fashion in the courts of Europe and to the immediate effects of prosperity and depression. The difficulties were shown in the organization of military defence of the St. Lawrence and the consequent centralization of policy in institutions of state and church, and in the inability to control the price of furs, shown in the collapse of the financial structure after 1700 through inflation. The burdens imposed by the system of defence and centralization led to the emergence of the Hudson's Bay Company in Hudson Bay, and to the failure of the St. Lawrence as a base for provisions for the fishing industry on the Atlantic coast and for sugar plantations of the French West Indies. An integrated Atlantic empire became impossible and the English colonies became a source of provisions for the French in both north temperate and tropical regions.

Collapse of the French Empire in North America brought repercussions which led to collapse of the first British Empire. The extension of the fishing industry from Newfoundland to New England early in the seventeenth century was followed by competition between the west country and the colonists. Adjustments within the British colonial system were hampered by the political influence of the west country and of the sugar planters in the British West Indies. The latter resisted trade between the coastal colonies and the French West Indies and supported the Treaty of Paris, which left Guadaloupe in the French Empire and added Canada to the British Empire, thereby accentuating the disturbance in the balance, between an extended market within the British Empire for molasses and rum in the fur trade, and a narrow supply from the British West Indies. The disappearance of Louisburg and the Sugar Act made smuggling more difficult and Imperial restrictions more burdensome. Anglo-American traders reorganized the fur trade of the St. Lawrence after the fall of New France and rebuilt a defence system depending on London instead of Paris. The Northwest Company solved the problem of the French régime by combining agricultural development in Ontario, to support shipping on the Great Lakes for the handling of bulk cargo, with the canoe route of the Ottawa for return shipments of furs. It extended trade from the Atlantic to the Pacific.

The second British Empire was profoundly modified by the changes involved in the withdrawal of the American colonies and the collapse of the first Empire. Flexibility was substituted for the rigidity which brought collapse of the first Empire. The supremacy of Parliament was recognized, but Lord Mansfield in Campbell vs. Hall (1774) strengthened the position of the Assembly in the colonies, and consequently in Nova Scotia. The Colonial Tax Repeal Act (1778) further strengthened Nova Scotia by providing for control over revenues secured from taxes collected under the colonial system. Nova Scotia was able to press more effectively for revisions of the colonial system to enable her to compete with the United States, particularly as the British West Indies had suffered a decline in influence with the abolition of slavery and the competition of sugar from the East Indies. Moreover, the support of Nova Scotia brought an increase in population which enabled Newfoundland to escape the domination of the west country. On the St. Lawrence, Parliament through the Quebec Act of 1774 denied an assembly to the colony and it was not until 1791 that assemblies were granted to Upper and Lower Canada. The merchants lost control of the fur trade to the northwest after the amalgamation of the Northwest Company and the Hudson's Bay Company in 1821, but the effects of the loss were offset, and along with New Brunswick the regions gained, as a result of the substantial imperial preference given to the timber trade. The struggle of Wilkes and others in securing freedom to report the proceedings of Parliament opened the door to reform and the destruction of control by vested interests. With the destruction of vested interests representing fish, sugar, timber, and ships in the colonial system the way was clear to free trade and responsible government. Whereas New England was hampered by the influence of vested interests operating from the west country in Newfoundland, and from the West Indies, Nova Scotia was able to take an active part in the defeat of those vested interests.

British North America included the French in the lower St. Lawrence region who had lost their contacts with the mother country except through the Church, population which had migrated from New

England to Nova Scotia after 1713, and the Loyalists who migrated from the United States and were settled in pockets from the Atlantic seaboard to the Great Lakes. The region contained groups with the pre-revolutionary background of France steeped in the traditions of the Church in Quebec and with the loyalist traditions of the state, particularly in New Brunswick and Ontario which escaped the influence of revolutionary tradition in the United States. British North America was a young country with the oldest pre-revolutionary ideas of Europe. Expulsion of the Loyalists from the United States weakened the centralizing tendencies of the colonies and contributed to the trend which culminated in the Civil War, and, reinforced by the British military tradition, strengthened the centralizing tendencies in British North America. The military system with its division of British North America into separate colonies dominated by military power restricted the growth of responsible government. Construction of the Rideau Canal as a military route delayed the construction of other canals.

The subordination of the executive to the Assembly which characterized responsible government involved control over revenues which meant control over funds received from lands. Newfoundland with control over land and trade continuously and effectively pressed for exclusion of French, English, Canadian, and American fishermen. Responsible government was interpreted as implying "that the consent of the Community of Newfoundland is regarded by Her Majesty's government as the essential preliminary to any modification of their territorial and maritime rights."[1] From this interpretation the legislature not only waged an effective battle against the French but also resisted efforts on the part of Canada to secure control of her natural resources in proposals for admission to Confederation. Nova Scotia insisted on her rights to the extent of compelling the United States and Great Britain to concede the Reciprocity Treaty from 1854 to 1866, and of persuading Canada to adopt a permissive system, and under Confederation a compulsory system, to exclude American fishermen to the point that the United States conceded the Washington Treaty. With control over natural resources she was able to break the monopoly of the General Mining Association over coal in 1858. Confederation of the colonies left the control over land with the provinces but placed the control over the coastal fisheries under the federal government.

Competition in western Canada from the French and later the Anglo-American merchants and the North West Company from the

[1]Henry Labouchere in a dispatch of March 26, 1857.

St. Lawrence with the Hudson's Bay Company from Hudson Bay assumed an intense form, characteristic of duopoly, and led to monopoly in 1821. The vast era under the control of the Hudson's Bay Company after that date included land owned by virtue of the charter granted in 1670 or that drained by rivers flowing into Hudson Bay, and regions beyond to the Pacific coast under a licence for twenty-one years. Under a monopoly, a large surplus population was moved from numerous posts to Red River and to Canada and attracted fresh competition from Americans which weakened the company on the Columbia and on the Pacific coast. The Oregon boundary was finally settled at the 49th parallel in 1846. Vancouver Island was granted to the Hudson's Bay Company in 1849, and, on the insistence of the Imperial government, an assembly was elected in 1856. On the mainland the licensing arrangement was brought to an end with the gold rush to the Fraser River and in 1858 a colony was organized. An area which had been systematically organized in defence against settlers from the United States was suddenly overrun by large numbers of people pushing northward in the search for gold. In the following year Vancouver Island was repurchased by the Imperial government. In 1864 a council was set up in British Columbia, but an assembly was refused. The character of the gold rush led Newcastle to write that "the fixed population . . . is not yet large enough to form a sufficient and sound basis of representation, while the migratory element exceeds the fixed and the Indian far outnumbers both together."[2] In 1866 the government of the mainland was united with that of Vancouver Island and the Assembly of the latter disbanded. Problems of finance which arose from the sudden development of a community dependent on placer gold hastened the adoption of an arrangement involving the construction of a transcontinental railway and the inclusion of British Columbia in the federal structure. Immediately before the united colony joined Confederation in 1871 an assembly was elected and responsible government was achieved. The natural resources were left in the hands of the province.

The discovery of gold speeded up the construction of a transcontinental railway and in turn had important effects for the prairie region across which it had to be built. The territory under control of the Hudson's Bay Company by virtue of charter was organized, more effectively than that under the licensing arrangement, against encroachment from the St. Lawrence across the Canadian shield but was

[2]Cited in A. S. Morton, *A History of the Canadian West to 1870-1* (Toronto, n.d.), p. 785.

eventually sold to the Dominion of Canada. The resistance of the Company and the delay in admitting the region to Confederation involved the defeat of efforts to secure responsible government in its full implications. Manitoba became a province but gave up land "for the purposes of the Dominion." The boundaries of Manitoba, Saskatchewan, and Alberta were determined along astronomical lines and the provinces of Alberta and Saskatchewan were created in 1905, again without control over land. The "purposes of the Dominion" having been served, and the lands largely alienated for the construction of transcontinental railways, the natural resources were given to the Prairie Provinces in 1930. Attempts to secure compensation for misuse of the lands by the Dominion have not been completely successful.

With the exception of Nova Scotia, assemblies emerged at a late stage in the second Empire and responsible government was slow to mature as a result of slowness in the adoption of parliamentary reform and of the geographic background with its emphasis on waterways and on exports of staples and the creation of vested interests centring about them. The organizations of defence in the French régime on the St. Lawrence in opposition to English trade from the south and the north implied a legacy of defence in the English régime. especially after the American Revolution. Occupation of New France by conquest and the insistence on defence delayed the introduction of assemblies on the St. Lawrence until 1791 and of responsible government until 1849. The organization of the Hudson's Bay Company for defence against competition from Canada and the United States in western Canada paralleled the organization for defence on the St. Lawrence. Entrenchment of the Hudson's Bay Company in the fur trade and the sudden changes wrought by the gold rushes on the Pacific coast contributed to the indefinite delay of responsible government in the Prairie Provinces.

The bitterness of the struggle for responsible government on the St. Lawrence had repercussions in western Canada. The provinces which took the place of the colonies in Confederation continued with such important characteristics of responsible government as control of their natural resources. The federal government was concerned primarily with customs for revenue to support transportation improvements in railways and canals, to pay subsidies largely on a population basis and thus avoid controversies over religion, and to pay interest on debts incurred chiefly in building railways and canals and taken over from the provinces. The exclusion of the federal government from control over natural resources in eastern Canada and the dominance of the Hudson's Bay Company over a long period checked the growth of assemblies and the achievement of complete responsible government in the prairie region.[3] Land was reserved by the Dominion for the support of railway construction to carry out the agreement with British Columbia.

The use of lands "for purposes of the Dominion" was accompanied by control over competition from the United States in the tariff and in restrictions on the construction of railways to the American boundary. Location of the Canadian Pacific Railway along the southern route left vast areas to the north to be occupied. The recovery following the long depression from the seventies to the nineties was accompanied by important new discoveries of placer beds on the Klondike in the Yukon region. As the Canadian Pacific followed the gold rushes in British Columbia, the Canadian Northern and the Grand Trunk Pacific followed the gold rushes of the Yukon in the territory north of the Canadian Pacific, but exhaustion of land led to dependence on bonds for their construction. The effectiveness with which the Dominion realized its "purposes" was evident in the enormous increase in the production of wheat in the period from 1900 to 1929. The problems which have followed concentration on wheat have been evident in western and eastern Canada in the depression and the war. Deprived of control over natural resources, the attention of the West was concentrated on federal problems such as railway rates, grain marketing, prices, tariffs, and debts.

With control over natural resources under the British North America Act and Privy Council decisions, the province of Ontario began an active policy of development by imposing embargoes on logs and pulpwood cut on Crown lands, by supporting public ownership of hydro-electric power, and by constructing the Temiskaming and Northern Ontario Railway. Cobalt, Porcupine, and Kirkland Lake poured out riches of gold and silver and hydro-electric power sites were developed. The policies were less effective in the pulp and paper industry and it was not until the demand of newspapers in the United States for cheap newsprint brought a reduction of the American tariff, and the province of Quebec and other provinces imposed an embargo after 1910, that the pulp and paper industry migrated with startling rapidity to Quebec, Ontario, and British Columbia and later to New Brunswick, Manitoba, and Nova Scotia. The problems of wheat which

[3]See Chester Martin, "Dominion Lands" Policy (Toronto, 1938); also Morton, A History of the Canadian West to 1870–1, pp. 914ff.

characterized the policies of the Dominion in fulfilment of its "purposes" in the Prairie Provinces after 1929 were accompanied by the problems of newsprint which characterized the policies of the provinces with control over their natural resources. Gold mining in Quebec, Ontario, and Manitoba offset in part the effects of the depression on wheat and newsprint. Fish, minerals, lumber, pulp and paper, hydroelectric power, and the favourable effects of the Panama Canal softened the blow of the depression in British Columbia.

In areas in which responsible government had not been achieved because of control over natural resources by the Dominion government, the position of provincial administrations reflected the maladjustment of political machinery. It has become obvious that the constitutional arrangements imposed too heavy a burden on the Prairie Provinces in that numerous makeshifts have been arranged by which the Dominion has attempted to relieve the burden and that the political atmosphere has become disturbed and confused. Manitoba, Alberta, and Saskatchewan have shown signs of achieving political maturity. In the area in which responsible government was achieved and control over natural resources was acquired at the expense of exclusion from Confederation, the problem of finance has been scarcely less acute. Newfoundland abandoned responsible government and accepted Commission government. Absence of federal control in Newfoundland has been as disastrous as excessive federal control in the Prairie Provinces.

The first Empire was concerned with the significance of land and the second Empire with the significance of trade. Gradually land has assumed increasing importance in the second Empire and the Statute of Westminster coincided closely with the return of natural resources to the Prairie Provinces. The Canadian federal structure has assumed a closer parallel to that of the United States as the feudalization of the second Empire approached the feudal character of the first. The dominance of trade in the second Empire and concentration on staples imposed heavy burdens on Great Britain until through parliamentary reform she was able to free herself from the control of vested interests in a policy of free trade and in the granting of responsible government to the colonies. The problems of trade in staples evaded by Great Britain became more acute for the colonies. But the colonies resorted to feudalism as the mother country emphasized trade. They began to concentrate on machinery designed to meet internal problems, ranging through Confederation to protection and construction of transcontinental railways. The political machinery was closely adapted to meet the severe economic demands of dependence on staples with their sharp changes in prices and income. Governmental devices stabilized in part and accentuated in part the fluctuations. Support to improvements in transportation was achieved with low interest rates secured by the government, and low costs of transportation provided a tremendous impetus with an increase in prices. The disturbances incidental to dependence on staples, including the essential importance of governmental support, created difficulties within Canada and without. Concentration on large-scale production of single staples involved sharp fluctuations in output which bombarded with violent intensity the international economy, to mention specifically the case of wheat. The study of the Canadian economy becomes of crucial significance to an understanding of cyclical and secular disturbances not only within Canada but without. In a sense the economies of frontier countries are storm centres to the modern international economy.

The Church in Canada*

MODERN civilization, characterized by an enormous increase in the output of mechanized knowledge with the newspaper, the book, the radio and the cinema, has produced a state of numbness, pleasure, and self-complacency perhaps only equalled by laughing-gas. In the words of Oscar Wilde, we have sold our birthright for a mess of facts. The demands of the machine are insatiable. The danger of shaking men out of the soporific results of mechanized knowledge is similar to that of attempting to arouse a drunken man or one who has taken an overdose of sleeping tablets. The necessary violent measures will be disliked. We have had university professors threatened with the loss of their positions for less than this. But I have little hope of making any impression with what I have to say.

I have made a slight study through unhappy experiences with meetings of this sort and I have always been impressed by the success which attends meetings addressed by Americans or Englishmen. Speakers of both groups are quickly made aware of our sensitiveness and spend much of their time commenting on how much better things are done in Canada than in Great Britain or the United States. Such speakers are very courteous, and are generally equipped with a great fund of stories carefully interspersed throughout the speech, and a peroration which emphasizes the absence of political boundaries between Anglo-Saxon peoples. The demand for this type of speech implies a lack of interest in a Canadian speaker who might say something distasteful about domestic affairs.

THE CANADIAN CHURCH PROBLEM

The problem of the Church is the problem of Western civilization and for that reason is all the more dangerous to discuss. Our position in Canada is perhaps more serious because of our counter-revolutionary tradition. In Quebec the French population largely escaped the influence of the French Revolution and in the older English-speaking provinces immigrants arrived from the United States because

*From *In Time of Healing* (Twenty-Second Annual Report of the Board of Evangelism and Social Service of the United Church of Canada; Toronto, 1947), pp. 47–54.

of their definite hostility to the revolutionary tradition. The position of the Roman Catholic Church in Quebec is paralleled by the concern of Protestants and of Roman Catholics in English-speaking provinces with control over the activities of the state. Gibbon wrote that "the various methods of worship which prevailed in the Roman world were all considered by the people as equally true, by the philosopher as equally false and by the magistrate as equally useful," and this might be paraphrased by saying that "the various political groups which prevailed in Canada were all considered by the people as equally true, by the philosopher as equally false and by the Church as equally useful." Students of cultural development in Canada have failed to realize the extent to which religion in English-speaking Canada has been influenced indirectly by the traditions of the Gallican Church in Quebec. Nor do we appreciate the significance of the political background of the France of Colbert and Louis XIV. State and Church under an absolute monarchy in France was State and Church under an absolute monarchy in New France. Great Britain failed in the first Empire because Englishmen are alike, but succeeded in the second Empire to a greater extent than is generally realized because French bureaucracy had become solidly entrenched in New France. It was this bureaucracy which enabled the British to govern New France and which enabled Canadians through governmental activity to develop their natural resources by construction of canals, railways, hydro-electric power facilities, and other undertakings. It was this bureaucracy in Church and State which was reflected in the place of Quebec in Confederation and in turn of English-speaking provinces. Clemenceau once remarked that England was a French colony gone wrong. He might have felt that in Canada the French colony had followed expected traditions.

The absence of a revolutionary tradition in Canada assumes relative stability and continuous repression with the result, as Professor J. B. Brebner[1] has shown, that we have been largely concerned with the training of our best students for export to countries with a revolutionary tradition. The Erastian character of religion assumes that the Church has been largely concerned with the development of organization and in turn with ecclesiasticism and links with other interests notably in business. I am told that church union was to a very important extent a response to economic demands. Separate churches could not maintain activity in a large number of communities in the West, and it seemed wiser to follow the example of the banks, the railroads, and the

[1]*Scholarship for Canada* (Ottawa, 1945).

elevators and to emphasize the branch system and avoidance of duplication. The results were evident in fact in the breaking away of radical elements, to cite only the case of the late J. S. Woodsworth and the rise of separate parties in the West. It is significant that the late William Aberhart seized on the relations between the Church and the money-changers in his speeches to his Bible Institute. It was a disturbing sight to see the United Church among the creditors who could lose through its position as a holder of Alberta's bonds.

The lack of a revolutionary tradition continually implies the dangers of compromise which have become conspicuous in Canadian life. In spite of the work of my friend Professor C. B. Sissons on the life of Egerton Ryerson it is difficult to evade the impression that his connection with education brought the school system of Ontario and of other provinces which followed its lead too close to the Prussian bureaucratic system. The results have been evident in an emphasis on the formalities of religious instruction in the schools and a neglect of the basic problem of character. We have been much concerned in academic circles with the decline of Greek, but I am afraid we do not realize that this is a symptom of an unwillingness to face the exacting demands implied in a study of Greek civilization. We have neglected the philosophical problems of the West and have not realized that the Greeks were fundamentally concerned with the training of character.

THE HAND OF PURITANISM

A counter-revolutionary tradition implies an emphasis on ecclesiasticism and the *ipsissima verba* of the Scriptures, particularly of the Old Testament with all the dangers of bibliolatry and of Puritanism. The hand of Puritanism is evident in our literature, in our art, and in our cultural life. This implies neglect of the interrelation between reason and emotion. Religion is a good servant but a bad master, or to cite Pattison: "Those periods when morals have been represented as the proper study of man and his only business have been periods of spiritual abasement and poverty."[2] Puritanical smugness has had a sterilizing influence on the cleansing effects of art and other expressions of cultural life.

The cause of this is, says Shelley, that statesmen and manufacturers have not learnt from the poets the art of recognizing and retaining the significance of that which they see:

The cultivation of poetry is never more to be desired than at periods when, from an excess of the selfish and calculating principle, the accumulation of

[2]*Essays by the Late Mark Pattison* (Oxford, 1889), II, 82.

the materials of external life exceed the quantity of the power of assimilating them to the internal law of human nature.[3]

Whilst the mechanist abridges, and the political economist combines labour, let them beware that their speculations, for want of correspondence with those first principles which belong to the imagination, do not tend, as they have in modern England, to exasperate at once the extremes of luxury and want. They have exemplified the saying, "To him that hath, more shall be given, and from him that hath not, the little that he hath shall be taken away...."[4]

As one reads the last pages of the *Defence of Poetry* one begins to see light on that dark saying of Aristotle, "Poetry, therefore, is more philosophic and a higher thing than history, for poetry tends to express the universal and history the particular."[5]

The implications of ecclesiasticism to political life have been evident on every hand. We have had political leaders who have been notorious for breaking records for longevity in political life. When Oliver Mowat was introduced to a prominent statesman in England with a comment on the length of time he had been Premier of Ontario he was greeted with the comment, "Have you no public opinion in that province?" The late J. W. Dafoe is said to have stated that all great public questions in Canada were settled on the basis of personal prejudices, and that political leaders on the whole have lacked the virtue of magnanimity. Lord Acton's comment that "no public character has ever stood the revelation of private utterances and correspondence"[6] has particular significance for the fundamental corruption of Canadian public life.

THE VICISSITUDES OF AN ECONOMIST

Oscar Wilde wrote an essay on the decay of lying but I am not sure that it would bear reading in this country. We are all too much concerned with the arts of *suppressio veri, suggestio falsi*. "The inexorable isolation of the individual is a bitter fact for the human animal, instinctively so social, and much of his verbalizing reflects his obstinate refusal to face squarely so unwelcome a realization. The great maxims and social inventions are so drawn as to minimize this realization, and are often framed in terms which taken at their face value are operationally footless."[7] I am reluctant to make speeches in public for various

[3]Shelley, *Prose Works* (London, 1912), "Defence of Poetry," p. 31.
[4]*Ibid.*, pp. 28–9.
[5]Graham Wallas, *The Art of Thought* (London, 1926), pp. 130–1.
[6]Lord Acton, *Historical Essays and Studies* (London, 1919), p. 506.
[7]P. W. Bridgman, *The Intelligent Individual and Society* (New York, 1938), pp. 142–3.

reasons, and one reason for accepting your generous invitation was the feeling that this was an eminently suitable body to which I might present a personal dilemma. The Department of Political Economy, if I may judge from personal experience, is under constant surveillance by a wide range of individuals. If in the course of an article I make a reference to a large government department or a large business organization, I will receive in an incredibly short time after the article has been published a personal letter, possibly directly from the public relations officer of the organization concerned or indirectly from the president or head of the organization, explaining that my remarks are liable to misinterpretation and inferring that the head of such an influential department in a large university should be very careful about the way in which his views are expressed. I plan to leave in my estate a valuable collection of autographs of prominent men in this country. For these reasons I am largely compelled to avoid making speeches in public and to resort to the careful preparation of material to be made available in print. In most cases this involves writing in such guarded fashion that no one can understand what is written or using quotations from the writings of authors who stand in great repute. I have often envied the freedom of my colleagues in other subjects. On the rare occasions on which I read the reports of their speeches I am always impressed by the ease with which they make statements largely because no one will pay much attention to what they have to say, or because they speak about subjects which do not affect people's direct interests. I am unhappily too aware of the fact that I am the first Canadian to be appointed to the position which I have the honour to hold and that such an appointment coming at so late a date reflects the very great fear of pronouncements made by the holder of my chair. My predecessors have been regarded as safe since as non-Canadians they could not make statements on Canadian affairs which would be taken seriously. But even they, partly because they were not Canadians, were subjected from time to time to the most bitter attacks in the press. Members of the department have been harassed inside and outside the University by protests from representatives of various interests, including political parties.

CHURCH WEAKNESSES

The Church has been rather too intent on losing its life and having it too. It has not been sufficiently philosophical, nor raised sufficient questions as to its limitations. The following quotations are to the point:

This absence of a professional public, and not the restraints of our formularies, seems to me the true reason why a real theology cannot exist in England. Every clerical writer feels himself bound to decide every question of criticism or interpretation in favour of the orthodox view. It is demanded of him by public opinion that he shall be an advocate and not a critic. Science or knowledge cannot exist under such a system; it requires for its growth the air of free discussion and contradiction. . . .[8]

As poetry is not for the critics, so religion is not for the theologians. When it is stiffened into phrases, and these phrases are declared to be objects of reverence but not of intelligence, it is on the way to become a useless encumbrance, the rubbish of the past, blocking the road.

Theology then retires into the position it occupies in the Church of Rome at present, an unmeaning frostwork of dogmas, out of all relation to the actual history of man. In that system, theological virtue is an artificial life quite distinct from the moral virtues of real life.[9]

The heresy trials which have littered the annals of the history of Canadian churches point in the same direction. The blood of the martyrs is the seed of the Church and the Church has apparently always demanded its share of blood. Over the doorway of one of your large colleges there are the words "the truth will make you free," but the heresy trials suggest that the search for truth may mean the loss of your job. The Church is always in danger of overstepping the bounds of moderation. Following Dean Inge, "In religion nothing fails like success."

The social sciences in which I happen to have an interest may be used as an illustration of the limitations of the Church. So, too, modern business has not been educated in terms of its limitations and responsibilities. The Church has been too apt in its acceptance of the claims of other interests because it has not been sufficiently critical of its own position. Instead of checking the pretensions of the social sciences it has accepted them and used them and even exaggerated them. Or it has regarded such subjects as sociology as dangerous and to be avoided, which in turn makes for over-emphasis on such subjects as economics and politics. The Church is in part responsible for a tendency in the social sciences to neglect the importance of training and character. With great pretentiousness they pronounce on questions of exceeding complexity in the social sciences and belittle the necessity of a long period of intense training and the development of character essential to an appreciation of the danger of interfering in other people's lives. They are very apt to assume an active role in the

[8]Mark Pattison, *Memoirs* (London, 1885), p. 317.
[9]*Essays by the Late Mark Pattison*, II, 86–7.

direction of education and in political and even military activity because of what appears to be their overwhelmingly Erastian character. While there is evidence of improvement in the attitude of the Church for example toward conscription in World War I and World War II, it has been all too supine in accepting the pretensions of bureaucracy in Ottawa to solve all problems and in its acceptance with little protest of the encroachments which have been made on civil liberties. Has the Church taken any active stand on the position of Jehovah's Witnesses? Has it given attention to the incipient totalitarian dangers of adult education programmes in this country? Does it appreciate the significance of the interest of the totalitarian state in science and its abhorrence of philosophy?

SOME POINTS FOR DISCUSSION

I would like to present to the members of this body the problem not of telling the truth, because I am aware that I do not know what the truth is, but of presenting considerations which will lead to discussion and to a closer approximation to the truth without leading to bitter public controversy. The discussion of questions which affect people's lives must be carried on with great circumspection. I have had occasion recently to come in contact with two professions, the nursing and the medical profession, and to be impressed again with the assumption that a long period of intensive training is essential to the preparation of individuals who are to be concerned throughout their careers with the handling of problems affecting people's lives. I have been appalled on the other hand and by comparison with the cavalier fashion in which great numbers of people discuss the problems of managing people's lives with almost no intensive training. Dale Carnegie's *How to Win Friends and Influence People* is a symptom of a widespread interest in the technique of pushing people around. In universities the rise of the social sciences and in particular the emphasis on business subjects, personnel management, industrial relations, social work, applied anthropology, and so on point to the danger of forgetting that no one can undertake the task of pushing people around without adequate discipline and training, though in fairness it should be said that there is a widespread appreciation of this danger. But we would do well to follow the example of the medical profession based on centuries of experience and tradition in emphasizing the importance of respect for the individual, evident as early as the oath of Hippocrates, and to realize that decisions affecting the lives of individuals should be made only on the basis of intensive training and on character such as comes from a combination of work with the hands as well as the brain. The social sciences in the main suffer from the lack of physical training which is so important in medicine and are apt to become a part of that system of exploitation by which so-called brain workers exploit those who work with their hands. Socrates and Greek philosophers in general were profoundly impressed with the example of the medical profession and with the need for comparable selection and training in the social sciences.

I have sometimes wondered whether ecclesiastical Christianity has not tended to suppress the Greek point of view of the New Testament and to over-emphasize the Hebrew point of view of the Old Testament and to neglect an emphasis on training and character. In swinging from one point of view to the other and in allowing fanaticism to thrive, Christianity has tended to foster an anarchistic society. This view was expressed some years ago by Santayana, from whom I quote:

Nothing is accordingly more patent than that Christianity was paganized by the early Church; indeed, the creation of the Church was itself what to a Hebraizing mind must seem a corruption, namely, a mixing of pagan philosophy and ritual with the Gospel. . . . By this corruption it was completed and immensely improved, like Anglo-Saxon by its corruption through French and Latin; for it is always an improvement in religion, whose business is to express and inspire spiritual sentiment, that it should learn to express and inspire that sentiment more generously. Paganism was nearer than Hebraism to the life of Reason because its myths were more transparent and its temper less fanatical; and so a paganized Christianity approached more closely that ideality which constitutes religious truth than a bare and intense Hebraism, in its hostility to human genius, could ever have done if isolated and unqualified.[10]

What was condemnable in the Jews was not that they asserted the divinity of their law, for that they did with substantial sincerity and truth. Their crime is to have denied the equal prerogative of other nations' laws and deities, for this they did, not from critical insight or intellectual scruples, but out of pure bigotry, conceit, and stupidity. They did not want other nations also to have a god. . . . What the moral government of things meant when it was first asserted was that Jehovah expressly directed the destinies of heathen nations and the course of nature itself for the final glorification of the Jews.

No civilized people had ever had such pretensions before. They all recognized one another's religions, if not as literally true (for some familiarity is needed to foster that illusion), certainly as more or less sacred and significant. Had the Jews not rendered themselves odious to mankind by this arrogance, and taught Christians and Moslems the same fanaticism, the

[10]George Santayana. *The Life of Reason,* III, *Reason in Religion* (London, 1906), pp. 106–7.

nature of religion would not have been falsified among us and we should not now have so much to apologize for and to retract.[11]

Yet what makes the difference is not the teaching of Jesus—which is pure Hebraism reduced to its spiritual essence—but the worship of Christ—something perfectly Greek. Christianity would have remained a Jewish sect had it not been made at once speculative, universal, and ideal by the infusion of Greek thought, and at the same time plastic and devotional by the adoption of pagan habits. The incarnation of God in man, and the divinization of man in God are pagan conceptions, expressions of pagan religious sentiment and philosophy. Yet what would Christianity be without them? It would have lost not only its theology, which might be spared, but its spiritual aspiration, its artistic affinities, and the secret of its metaphysical charity and joy.[12]

RELIGION AND FANATICISM

Denominationalism does not help to avoid this tendency toward fanaticism. It would be difficult to make any statement on the subject of religion which would not give rise to protests from a particular group. Newspaper editors are constantly aware of the increasing vigilance of various denominations and carefully avoid the subject, and it would not be wise for me to rush in where newspaper editors fear to tread. The churches must be regarded with other groups as always on the alert for an unguarded comment.

In universities one finds a reflection of this fanaticism in that individuals advance in all seriousness the proposition that civilization can be saved by having everyone take their specific subject. That such fanatical points of view can find expression in such an institution as a university points to very grave weaknesses in Western society, as Frederic Harrison in the following quotations makes plain:

This mania for special research in place of philosophic principle, for tabulated facts in lieu of demonstrable theorems and creative generalizations, attenuates the intelligence and installs pedantic information about details, where what man wants are working principles for social life. The grand conceptions of Darwin and of Spencer are too often used by their followers and successors as a text on which to dilate on microscopic or local trivialities which mean nothing. And even Spencer's Synthesis, the only one yet attempted by any English thinker, proves, on being closely pressed, to rest on a substructure of hypotheses, and to ignore two-thirds of the entire scale of the sciences viewed as an interdependent whole. The enormous accumulation of recorded facts in the last century goes on as blindly in this, quite indifferent to the truth that infinite myriads of facts are as worthless as infinite grains of sand on the sea-shore, until we have found out how to apply them to the amelioration of human life.

[11]*Ibid.*, pp. 76–7.   [12]*Ibid.*, pp. 84–5.

It was obvious that the literature of the first half of the nineteenth century greatly surpassed that of the second half. And it is sadly evident that literature in the twentieth century is far inferior even to that of the second half century.[13]

Historical study today is far more scientific, and is grouped and classified into elaborate sections, periods, and nations. But like almost every other study, it is overwhelmed with its infinite details, and its unity is lost in interminable special subdivisions, "periods," and subsidiary "ologies." Girls and lads in their teens are so deep in "diplomatics," numismatics, and the Manor system, that they are too learned to know anything of common things like the Punic Wars or the French Revolution. Science, too, suffers from the incoherent specialization which is bound up with modern research. The study of science, of course, must be said to be far more widely popularized today, and to be a much higher order of thought. But biography, the typical literature of our age, feels the reaction of the ceaseless multiplication of lives to record, until the best and the greatest lives are too often overwhelmed in the flow of the obscure and the commonplace.[14]

It is not only dangerous in this country to be a social scientist with an interest in truth but it is exhausting. You will remember the remarks of the Persian at a banquet in Thebes noted by Herodotus. "This is the most cruel pang that man can bear—to have much insight and power over nothing." On a wider plane it is a source of constant frustration to attempt to be a Canadian. Both Great Britain and the United States encourage us in assuming the false position that we are a great power and in urging that we have great national and imperial possibilities. From both groups we are increasingly subjected to pressure and in turn to bureaucratic tendencies dictated by external forces. We have no sense of our limitations. On the question of Russia we are constantly pushed into a position in which it is assumed that we take sides. We have little chance to raise questions as to the dominance of military authorities in the United States or as to the political needs of the Labour party in Great Britain. We seem destined to occupy in North America the place of Czechoslovakia as a show window in relation to Russia in Europe, first as to the British Empire and second as to the American Empire. But I am in danger of assuming that I may make an impression in what I have to say. I would conclude with an additional word about the Church.

I have attempted to underline certain facts. In common with many observers, I believe that the Church has ceased to have an intellectual interest for people because the Church has lost its curiosity for ideas. Failing to have an interest in ideas the Church has of necessity found

[13]Frederic Harrison, *Autobiographic Memoirs* (London, 1911), II, 322–3.
[14]*Ibid.*, I, 22–3.

an outlet for its energies in social action. This has led to a vast congeries of good works and a vast amount of planning for others and pushing others around. We have developed an amazing aptitude for knowing what the other fellow ought to be doing. If the Church can not return to an interest in ideas, and must therefore express itself exclusively in social action, we ought to insist upon a higher quality of discipline. I have indicated the physician and the nurse as types of special disciplines that are necessary, people who respect the individual and know when to leave him alone, but first of all they know their subject thoroughly. But skill and discipline are of little value unless the practitioners of good works are selected for their integrity and the high quality of their characters.

Great Britain, The United States and Canada[1]

CANADIANS have reason to remember industrial cities in the Midlands for their protests against the imposition of a protective tariff in Canada in 1858 and later dates, following the introduction of free trade in England in the forties. Free trade was accompanied by factory legislation at home and by protective tariffs in the colonies. Thorold Rogers wrote that "a protective tariff is to all intents and purposes an act of war,"[2] and its introduction in Canada undoubtedly appeared to Nottingham and other cities as an act of war on the part of the colonies against the mother country. The complaints led Canadians such as A. T. Galt to present arguments showing that the protective tariff was not an act of war but was adapted to the demands of a new country and that it was a fiscal device by which improvements in navigation and transportation could be financed, and the cost of moving industrial goods from Great Britain to new markets, and raw materials to Great Britain, could be lowered. British investors were thus insured of a return on capital loans. According to Galt, "The fiscal policy of Canada has invariably been governed by considerations of the amount of revenue required." Moreover, he insisted, "Self government would be utterly annihilated if the views of the imperial government were to be preferred to those of the people of Canada." But the arguments probably made little impression on England. Robert Lowe is stated to have said to Lord Dufferin following his appointment as Governor-General of Canada in 1872, "Now you ought to make it your business to get rid of the Dominion."[3]

[1]A revision of the twenty-first Cust Foundation Lecture delivered at the University of Nottingham on May 21, 1948. [Printed in *Changing Concepts of Time* (University of Toronto Press, 1952), pp. 109–33.]

[2]J. E. Thorold Rogers, *The Economic Interpretation of History* (New York, 1888), p. 339.

[3]Herbert Paul, *The Life of Froude* (London, 1906), p. 253. "The Canadians, or rather the Maritime Provinces, seem likely to give some trouble, and the British Government may perhaps have an illustration of the difficulties and dangers incident to the retention in diplomatic dependence of communities which are otherwise independent, and which, naturally enough, look to no interest but their own." Goldwin Smith to Gladstone, May 14, 1871, *A Selection from Goldwin Smith's Correspondence* (Toronto, n.d.), p. 39. In the United States, Sumner intended to press "every possible American claim against England, with a view of compelling the cession of Canada to the United States." *The Education of Henry*

I

Throughout the history of Canada, the St. Lawrence River has served as an outlet from the heart of the continent for staple products and as an entrance for manufactured products from Europe. Consistently, political and economic considerations have directed its improvement by the construction of canals and the building of railways. The constitution of Canada, as it appears on the statute book of the British Parliament, has been designed to secure capital for the improvement of navigation and transportation. Railways have been extended from the St. Lawrence to the Atlantic and to the Pacific, and canals have been deepened as a means of increasing the commercial importance of the river. Reliance on the tariff in the Galt tradition has become a crude instrument in the use of which there has been some waste, particularly in duplication of railways, and constant friction over the adjustment of the burden, evident in controversies about freight rates and subsidies to provinces.

To an important extent the emphasis has been on the development of an east-west system with particular reference to exports of wheat and other agricultural products to Great Britain and Europe. However, since the turn of the century, the United States has had an increasing influence on this structure. The construction of the Panama Canal, through the energetic efforts of Theodore Roosevelt, has been followed by the development of Vancouver as a port competitive with Montreal and by a weakening of the importance of the St. Lawrence.[4] The exhaustion of important industrial raw materials in the United States has been followed by the growth of the mineral industry and of the pulp and paper industry in Canada. The Precambrian Shield, which has been a handicap to a system built up in relation to Europe, has become a great advantage as a centre for the development of hydroelectric power and for the growth of a pulp and paper and of a mineral industry in relation to the United States. American imperialism has replaced and exploited British imperialism. It has been accompanied

---

Adams (New York, 1931), p. 275. Motley as American ambassador in London in 1870 opposed construction of the Canadian Pacific Railway. Allan Nevins, *Hamilton Fish: The Inner History of the Grant Administration* (New York, 1936), p. 421. "Our relations with England are of far greater importance to us than those with Germany—there being more points at issue, more chances of friction and greater difficulty in almost every question that arises on account of the irresponsibility and exacting temper of Canadian politicians." Whitelaw Reid to President Roosevelt, June 19, 1906; cited by Royal Cortissoz, *The Life of Whitelaw Reid* (London, 1921), II, 331.

[4]See H. A. Innis, "Economic Trends," *Canada in Peace and War*, ed. Chester Martin (Toronto, 1941), pp. 58–85. [See this volume, p. 291.]

by a complexity of tariffs and exchange controls and a restriction of markets, with the result that Canada has been compelled to concentrate on exports with the most favourable outlets. Newsprint production in Canada is encouraged, with the result that advertising and in turn industry are stimulated in the United States, and it becomes more difficult for Canada to compete in industries other than those in which she has a distinct advantage. Increased supplies of newsprint accentuate an emphasis on sensational news. As it has been succinctly put, world peace would be bad for the pulp and paper industry.

II

The dangers to Canada have been increased by the disturbances to the Canadian constitutional structure which have followed the rise of new industries developed in special relation to the American market, and to imperial markets notably for the products of American branch plants. The difficulties have been evident in the central provinces, Ontario and Quebec, and in provinces which continue to be largely concerned with the British market. A division has emerged between the attitude of provinces which have been particularly fortunate in the possession of natural resources in which the American market is interested and that of provinces more largely dependent on European markets. This division has been capitalized on by the politicians of the respective provinces and by those of the federal government. American branch factories, exploiting nationalism and imperialism in Canada, were in part responsible for agitation in regions exploited by the central area and for regional controversies.

The strains imposed on a constitution specially designed for an economy built up in relation to Great Britain and Europe have been evident in the emergence of regionalism, particularly in western Canada where natural resources were returned to the provinces in 1931, and in regional parties such as Social Credit in Alberta and the C.C.F. in Saskatchewan. In regions bearing the burden of heavy fixed charges and dependent on staples which fluctuate widely in yield and price, political activity became more intense. Relief was obtained by political pressure. A less kindly critic might say that currents of hot air flowed upwards from regions with sharp fluctuations in income. Regional parties have gained from the prestige which attaches to new developments. They have arisen in part to meet the demands of regional advertising, which in turn accentuates regionalism. They have also enjoyed the prestige which attaches to ideas imported from Great Britain, notably in the case of Social Credit and of socialism. The achievement of Canadian autonomy has, then, been accompanied by outbursts of regional activity. Small groups have emerged to combine, disband, and re-combine in relation to protests against the central provinces, notably in the matter of railway rates. Large parties have found it extremely difficult to maintain an effective footing and have tended to break up into provincial parties or into small back-scratching, log-rolling groups within the party.

Provincial regional parties have been in part also a reflection of the influence of new techniques in communication. The radio station, the loud speaker, and the phonograph record enormously increase the power of the regional politician. The radio, for instance, proved a great advantage to skilful preachers in the political field in both Alberta and Saskatchewan. In Alberta, with its vast potential resources, the late William Aberhart, during the period of severe depression and drought, built up a large audience throughout the province using this medium. The influence of Social Credit in Saskatchewan is said to have varied directly with distance from Alberta, the strength of receiving sets, and the power of broadcasting stations. Its success warrants detailed consideration since it points to the elements responsible for the break-up of large political parties. As a teacher Aberhart had acquired an extensive vocabulary. Graduates from his school were scattered throughout the province and his influence persisted as a factor facilitating effective appeal. His Bible Institute and appeals to the Bible and to religion were used with great effect. Bible texts and hymns and semi-biblical language were designed to attack usury, interest, and debts. The conversations and parables of the founder of Christianity were repeated with great skill, notably in attack on the money changers. Audiences throughout the province were held together by correspondence. Large numbers wrote in and subscribed small amounts. Their names were read over the radio and comments were made on their letters. There were attacks on older types of communication such as the chain newspapers dominated by eastern control. The Calgary *Albertan* was purchased as a means of carrying these attacks into the newspaper field itself.

In the East, Nova Scotia had regarded Confederation as a device for opening American markets, whereas the St. Lawrence region thought of it as a basis of protection against American goods. The Maritimes felt the full impact of capitalism in the destruction of wooden shipbuilding and in expensive transportation to central Canada. Their iron and steel and coal industries, developed to answer the demand for rails and the needs of industrial expansion in Canada, were among the first to feel the effects of a decline in the rate of that expansion. With strong political traditions, born of a maritime background, it might be expected that the Maritimes would be among the first to voice complaint against injustice. Newfoundland has entered Confederation with a great instrument for political intrigue in the federal system, namely, admission without responsible government.

The appearance of a large number of small parties in Canada suggests an obvious incapacity of a party or of two parties to represent effectively the increasing number of diverging interests. Provincial boundaries have become important considerations in determining party growth: to mention Social Credit in Alberta, C.C.F. in Saskatchewan, coalitions in British Columbia and Manitoba, Liberals in the Maritime Provinces, Mr. Frost in Ontario, and Mr. Duplessis in Quebec. The consequent complexity suggests a new type of politics or the disappearance of an old type of politics.

The effects of this complexity have been evident in the federal field. At one time government was said to be determined by the longevity of the Walpole Administration. The length of life of one administration became an argument for the greater length of life of another. As evidence of the futility of political discussion in Canada, there were Liberals who deplored the activities of the federal administration in no uncertain terms but always concluded with what was to them an unanswerable argument—"What is the alternative?" In one's weaker moments the answer does appear conclusive, but what a comment on political life, that no one should vote against the administration for fear of worse evils to come! One forgets that it probably matters little how one votes so long as one votes against the government or for the party one expects to see defeated in order to secure a healthy minority. All this is in part a result of the exhaustion which accompanies a long term in office, particularly in a trying period, and in the demands of provincial politics. A distinguished federal civil servant once told me that no administration should be in office more than five years. At the end of that time members have ceased to have new ideas or at least are not expected to have any ideas. The exhaustion becomes evident not only among members of the administration but also in the body politic generally.

A further evidence of political lethargy has appeared in an infinite capacity for self-congratulation. Invariably we remark on the superiority of Canadian institutions, Canadian character, and Canadians generally, over Americans. This, of course, is our common North American heritage but in Canada it appears to lead to little more than a congenital tendency toward long arms with which we can slap our own backs. It is a commonplace, of course, that we are encouraged in this by our polite friends from the United States and Great Britain.

III

Our constitution has proved inadequate in the face of the demands made upon it. The Senate, that unique institution, has lent itself to political manipulation. As a guarantee of maritime rights the Maritime Provinces were given a substantial number of senators. They have supported the growth of a strong party organization. Politicians have before them as their reward for activity an appointment to the Senate for life. The active part of a politician's life is guaranteed to the party by postponement of appointment. It may be that the Liberal party will fear an eventual revival of political life and appoint senators who are younger in age so that in case of a political reverse the Senate will continue to be filled for a reasonable length of time with senators loyal to the cause. A careful medical check could be made of senatorial possibilities; the late W. L. Mackenzie King favoured only a general convention that an appointee must be under seventy and have fought an election.

The relation of the Senate to party organization has been inadequately studied. The Senate not only provides a useful anchorage for the Liberal party in the Maritimes but also a support to party organizations throughout Canada. A federal party organizer can be appointed to the Senate and the cost of secretarial expenses charged to services to the country. The procedure has disadvantages in that once senators are appointed they may lose interest in party work since they cannot easily be dislodged, but another senator can be appointed and may bring in new blood. A senatorship is also a reward for journalists[5] who have been active in the party's interest and who will presumably continue active after their appointment. A senator stands as a guard over the party's interest and is expected to be continually alert to the improvement of the party's position in the region from which he is appointed. The entrenched position of the party in the Senate contributes to inflexible government, makes political instruments less sensitive to economic demands, and possibly contributes to the rise of new provincial parties.

Parties are held together to an important extent by patronage and the judicious (not a pun) use of patronage. For the legal profession

[5]Mackenzie King prided himself on journalistic appointments to the Senate. Arthur Ford, *As the World Wags On* (Toronto, 1950), pp. 175–6.

there remains control over appointment to the bench. Ample salaries, security, retiring arrangements, and prestige tend to make the judiciary a preferred alternative to the Senate. The legal profession and to some extent the medical and other professions are handicapped by professional ethics which prohibit advertising, and the political field is admirably designed to offset this handicap. Lawyers presumably are expected to be concerned with law and it seems eminently fitting that lawyers should be selected by the party to run as members. The substantial advertising developed during the course of a campaign may be followed by the most coveted of all political positions, that of a defeated candidate. The lawyer will not be forgotten by the party when it becomes necessary for the government to select individuals to handle the enormous amount of its legal business. The position of the legal profession in and out of Parliament provides great opportunities for the distribution of patronage. Lawyers will do well, however, to support the party discreetly and strongly since a fanatical loyalty may weaken their prospects of appointment to the bench.

The lack of industrialism in French Canada has meant an emphasis on the church and the law. "Of all the roman provincials the French have been the ones who inherited most of that organizing capacity of the Romans." "It was the French culture of the English ruling caste that made England's power possible."[6] British governors took over the French bureaucratic administration after the conquest of New France and installed members of the English aristocracy in the civil service. The struggle for responsible government was essentially a struggle for jobs for the native born, a struggle which still continues in Ottawa in the interest of positions for French Canadians in the civil service. To an important extent the history of Canada has been that of a struggle between French and English, and the struggle over patronage has been particularly intense in the legal profession in Quebec.

The importance of the legal profession to party strength necessitates discussion of the calibre of men attracted to it and of legal education, which is hampered in Canada by the broad division of common law and code law, and more seriously by divisions between the universities and educational institutions controlled by the profession, particularly the bench. It is difficult to build up great law schools such as are to be found in the United States, Great Britain, or even Australia. Great legal philosophers have been conspicuously absent. Appointments to important positions such as the deanship of a law faculty have been determined by political prejudices. Consequently the legal profession

6Wyndham Lewis, *The Art of Being Ruled* (New York, 1926), p. 371.

has lacked confidence and there has been reluctance to take final measures for abolishing appeals to the Privy Council. A strong supreme court is essential to the effective operation of written constitutions, but this has proved to be difficult to obtain, partly because of the necessity of appealing to the Privy Council and partly also because of the handicaps imposed by the British North America Act on systems of legal education through placing education under the jurisdiction of the provinces.

As a result of its lack of prestige political parties have been able to exploit the legal profession in a fashion which has been the subject of much discussion in legal literature. Legal patronage has been described as "injurious to the independence of both bench and bar." Members of the Supreme Court have been selected to act on Royal Commissions on subjects in which the government finds itself in an embarrassing position, such as the Hong Kong investigation, the Halifax investigation, and the Communist trials. This use of members of the Supreme Court has fortunately not always met with success, to cite only Mr. Drew's attacks on the Hong Kong investigation, and the failures to secure conviction in the spy trials. Embarrassment to the rights of Canadian citizens has been obvious. A Canadian citizen whose rights may be imperilled by the report of a Royal Commission which includes members of the Supreme Court will not feel happy about the prospect of appearing before the Supreme Court in a possible appeal from lower courts. The citizen's rights against police interference have been seriously weakened. The use of the legal profession to whitewash political activities of the government is only possible in a country in which the profession has suffered in prestige. The Supreme Court ought not to be in a position in which the government can use it as a doormat on which to wipe its muddy feet.

The lowering of the prestige of the legal profession has implied a heightening of the prestige of the academic profession, with unhappy results for both. The tradition begins perhaps with the late Prime Minister, W. L. Mackenzie King, who came into his position armed with that great academic weapon, a doctorate from Harvard. It would be tedious to trace the steps by which various parties have enlisted the prestige of the academic profession but we can note that members of it were employed on a large scale during the depression, conspicuously with the appointment of the late Norman Rogers as Minister of Labour, and that the trend reached a great climax in the report of the Sirois Royal Commission and in the great trek of the academic profession to the Ottawa salient during the war. Royal Commissions have become a device for exploiting the finality characteristic of academic pronouncements as well as of legal statements. The Sirois Report with its length and the number of its appendices was calculated to bring to a focus all the light and leading of the legal and the academic professions in order to produce the great solution to the Canadian problem, and to guarantee the life of the Liberal Administration in Ottawa for an indefinite period. It has been used with devastating effect to divide what are called the have-nots and the haves among the provinces and to strengthen the Liberal party in English-speaking regions. The use of the class struggle as an instrument of politics has been developed to a high point and we could possibly show the Russians a few details in the higher dialectics. The other parties have been paralysed by a situation in which large numbers of voters support Liberals in the federal government, notably in Ontario and Quebec, and at the same time another party in the provincial government, in order that the dominance of any one group may be checked and that a strong opposition may be maintained against the bureaucracy.

During the war period large numbers of the academic profession joined the civil service. Government became extremely complex and the academic profession thrives on complexity. Complexity was suited to patronage, particularly after the war. We may well be concerned with the change in the attitude toward government in Ottawa, since general appeals are made to it for the solution of every conceivable problem, reflecting a belief that governments are omnipotent. We are again thrown back on the limitations of the legal profession in that legislation itself has been used to an enormous extent to strengthen the position of the party and to extend the one-party system in the federal administration.

IV

Heinrich Bruening, former Chancellor of Germany, has described basic changes in government and their causes.

I think that the greatest hindrance to constructive political action in the last thirty years has been the influence on final decisions of experts, especially of experts obsessed with the belief that their own generation has gained a vantage point unprecedented in history. No quality is more important in a political leader than awareness of the accumulated wisdom and experience handed down not only in written documents but also by word of mouth from generation to generation in practical diplomatic, administrative and legislative work. . . . The more we work with mass statistics and large schemes the more we are in danger of neglecting the dignity and value of the human individual and losing sight of life as a whole.[7]

[7]The Works of the Mind, ed. R. B. Heywood (Chicago, 1947), pp. 116–17.

Increasing centralization and control by federal civil servants, which have accompanied political difficulties, explain the violation of British traditions of the civil service by which civil servants make pronouncements which are perhaps taken more seriously than those by members of the Cabinet. During the war new civil servants, unaccustomed to these traditions, were apparently encouraged to abandon anonymity and to draw fire away from the government. Such pronouncements have been made in the field of foreign policy and reflect the increasing influence of conventions of the United States, particularly as centralization facilitates co-operation or collaboration with that country.

The emergence of the civil service to authoritarian control or, to use the German expression, development of *Gruppenführer* and *Übergruppenführer* has had an important influence on politics. The press is compelled to change its attitude in the news since the facts of governmental intervention are inconceivably dull. Nor is the dulness alleviated by the unrelieved monotony of photographs. Complexity compels the press to emphasize nonsensical subjects or to retreat to issues of the utmost simplicity. The hypothesis may be suggested that the tendency has also made for mediocrity in political leadership. It would be interesting to learn whether calculated stupidity has become a great political asset, but a careful study of the political leaders of Canadian parties leaves little doubt of the existence of the appearance and of the reality. Perhaps political talent is inadequate to the demands of a large number of parties. In any case it would be difficult to find greater political ineptitude than exists in Canadian parties. I must ask to be excused from giving specific examples. Cabinet-making becomes "a thoroughly unpleasant and discreditable business in which merit is disregarded, loyal service is without value, influence is the most important factor, and geography and religion are important secondary considerations." Sir John A. Macdonald regarded the ideal cabinet as one over which he held incriminating documents such as might place each member in the penitentiary. Broderick referred to the "malicious credulity of Canadian party spirit and the extreme lengths to which party warfare is carried at the instigation of a most virulent and unscrupulous press."[8] "Comprehensive representation . . . has deprived and will continue to deprive the Dominion of the possible maximum of efficiency in its growing bodies."[9] The demands of the present century have contributed to

[8]Hon. G. C. Broderick, *Memoirs and Impressions, 1831–1900* (London, 1900), p. 287.
[9]Paul Bilkey, *Persons, Papers and Things* (Toronto, 1940), p. 100.

the exhaustion of political capacity. During World War II the conscription issue destroyed the Liberal party in Ontario since Mr. Hepburn, the leader of the provincial Liberals, was compelled to oppose Mr. King in the hope of securing Conservative votes. In Quebec the provincial Liberal party was destroyed by supporting conscription. Political parties have become bankrupt in regionalism.[10]

Provincial parties, or, in the words of Professor C. B. Macpherson, quasi-parties, hampered in the federal field, have been compelled to undertake measures in their respective provinces which are unacceptable to the federal government. Disallowance of provincial legislation has been a measure of the political necessity felt by the provinces to intensify friction between themselves and the federal government. The difficulties of the British North America Act have been met over a long period by appeals to the Judicial Committee of the Privy Council. The British North America Act has produced its own group of idolators and much has been done to interpret the views and sayings of the fathers of Confederation in a substantial body of patristic literature. But though interpretations of decisions of the Privy Council have been subjected to intensive study and complaints have been made about their inconsistency, inconsistencies have implied flexibility and have offset the dangers of rigidity characteristic of written constitutions.

V

The change from British imperialism to American imperialism has been accompanied by friction and a vast realignment of the Canadian system. American imperialism lacked the skill and experience of British imperialism and became the occasion for much bitterness. American foreign policy has been based on conditions described by Mahan, who quoted the advice of a member of Congress to a newly elected colleague, "to avoid service on a fancy committee like that of foreign affairs if he wished to retain his hold upon his constituents because they cared nothing about international questions." In the Alaskan boundary dispute Canadians felt that they had been exploited by the United States and Great Britain, with results that were shown in the emphatic rejection of the reciprocity proposals of the United States in 1911. But the tide had turned to the point where even those gestures against the United States operated to the ad-

---

[10]Sir Wilfrid Laurier argued that the calibre of members of the House had declined as business attracted men from politics and law but that the Maritimes continued to send able individuals because of the small character of business there. Arthur Ford, *As the World Wags On*, p. 126.

vantage of American capital. Branch plants of American industries were built in Canada in order to take advantage of the Canadian-European system and British imperialism.[11] As part of her east-west programme, Canada had built up a series of imperial preferential arrangements in which Great Britain had felt compelled to acquiesce and which proved enormously advantageous to American branch plants. Paradoxically, the stoutest defenders of the Canadian tariff against the United States were the representatives of American capital investors. Canadian nationalism was systematically encouraged and exploited by American capital. Canada moved from colony to nation to colony.

The impact of American imperialism was eventually felt by Great Britain. It began with the spread of American journalism in the latter part of the nineteenth century, and continued notably in the campaign of R. D. Blumenfeld and Lord Beaverbrook in the *Daily Express* for British imperial preference. The campaign was supported with great vigour by the late Viscount Bennett when he became Prime Minister of Canada, and ended in a compromise, as British resistance was gradually mobilized and stiffened.

Participation of the United States in the First and Second World Wars has greatly increased the power of American imperialism and given it a dominant position in the Western world. The shift of Canadian interest towards the United States and the influence of this on Great Britain were brought out sharply in the work of the Right Honourable Arthur Meighen, then Prime Minister of Canada, in persuading Great Britain to abandon the Anglo-Japanese alliance. Canada has had no alternative but to serve as an instrument of British imperialism and then of American imperialism. With British imperialism, she had the advantage of understanding a foreign policy which was consistent over long periods and of guidance in relation to that policy. As she has come increasingly under the influence of the United States, she has become increasingly autonomous in relation to the British Empire. Her recently acquired autonomy, marked conspicuously in the first instance by the signing of the Halibut Treaty, has left her with little time in which to develop a mature foreign policy, with the result that she has necessarily felt the effects of the vacillating and ill-informed policy of the United States.

Autonomy following the Statute of Westminster has been a device

[11]The older type of craft unionism avoided politics and facilitated an international labour movement, but in the newer types of industrial unionism direct intervention in politics in the United States is paralleled by direct intervention in Canada.

by which we can co-operate with the United States as we formerly did with Great Britain. Indeed the change has been most striking. We complained bitterly of Great Britain in the Minto affair, the Naval Bill, and the like, but no questions are asked as to the implications of joint defence schemes with the United States or as to the truth of rumours that Americans are establishing bases in northern Canada, carrying out naval operations in Canadian waters, arranging for joint establishment of weather stations, and contributing to research from funds allocated to the armed forces of the United States under the direction of joint co-operative organizations.

The ease with which such co-operation is carried out is explained in part by the opposition to socialistic trends in Great Britain. Central and eastern, in contrast with western, Canada have had essentially counter-revolutionary traditions, represented by the United Empire Loyalists and by the church in French Canada, which escaped the influences of the French Revolution. A counter-revolutionary tradition is not sympathetic to socialistic tendencies and is favourable to the emphasis on private enterprise which characterizes the United States. Opposition to socialistic devices has been particularly important because large sectors of Canadian economic life have come under government ownership, notably the Hydro-Electric Power Commission of Ontario and the Canadian National Railways. Indeed the large-scale continental type of business organization in private enterprise reflects the influence of governmental administration, in its emphasis on seniority rules and the general sterility of bureaucratic development. Large administrative bodies are compelled to recognize the importance of morale as essential to efficiency. Mobility within the hierarchy can be achieved only with an enormous outlay of energy devoted to the appraisal of capacity. A large number of private enterprises and organizations assume constant attention to the capacities of individuals and are stoutly opposed to the restriction of choice involved in the expansion of large-scale organization. Their concern with private enterprise is reinforced by the views of American branch plants and facilitates American domination.

The abolition of titles has perhaps reflected American influence. The remarks of E. L. Godkin, a native of the north of Ireland, "the most intellectual among American journalists," have been to the point.

To a certain class of Canadians, who enjoy more frequent opportunities than the inhabitants of the other great colonies of renewing or fortifying their love of the competition of English social life, and of the marks of success in it, the court, as the fountain of honour, apart from all political significance, is an object of almost fierce interest. In England itself the signs of social distinction are not so much prized. This kind of Canadian is, in fact, apt to be rather more of an Englishman than the Englishman himself in all these things. He imitates and cultivates English usages with a passion which takes no account of the restrictions of time or place. It is "the thing" too in Canadian society, as in the American colony in Paris, to be much disgusted by the "low Americans" who invade the Dominion in summer, and to feel that even the swells of New York and Boston could achieve much improvement in their manners by faithful observance of the doings in the Toronto and Ottawa drawing rooms.[12]

"There is nothing in the universe lower than the colonial snob who apes the English gentleman." "These fellows are the veriest flunkies on earth; they are always spouting loyalty and scrambling for small titles and all the crumbs that fall to them from the tables of the aristocracy." (Goldwin Smith.) The weakening of the position of these symbols, unfortunate as their effects may have been, has not been without implications for American influence.

American imperialism has been described as "latent and fundamentally political." It has been made plausible and attractive in part by the insistence that it is not imperialistic. Imperialism which is not imperialistic has been particularly effective in Canada with its difficulty in dealing precisely and directly with foreign problems because of division between French and English.

A commercial society in a newspaper civilization is profoundly influenced by the type of news which makes for wider circulation of newspapers—"For God, for country and for circulation." Advertising, particularly department store advertising, primarily demands circulation. Circulation becomes largely dependent on the instability of news and instability becomes dangerous. Effective journalists are those most sensitive to emotional instability. Lack of continuity in news is the inevitable result of dependence on advertisements for the sale of goods. The influence of advertising in the United States spread to Europe, notably to Germany, before the First World War. Bertrand Russell has said with much truth that "the whole modern technique of government in all its worst aspects is derived from advertising."[13] "The intellectual level of propaganda is that of the lowest common denominator among the public. Appeal to reason and you appeal to about four per cent of the human race."[14] "You cannot aim too low. The story you present cannot be too stupid. It is not only impossible to exaggerate—it in itself requires a trained publicist to form any

12*Reflections and Comments* (New York, 1895), p. 270.
13Cited by Denys Thompson,*Voice of Civilization* (London, 1943), p. 180.
14*Ibid.*, p. 201.

idea of—the idiocy of the public."[15] The radio has tended to dominate the news presented in the newspaper, selecting spot news and compelling the newspapers to write it up at greater length because of the feeling that people will wish to know more about the items even though they are not news.

American foreign policy has been to a large extent determined by domestic politics. Publishers of newspapers were rewarded in the patronage system with appointments to ambassadorial posts. The secretary of state has generally played an active role in party politics. An attempt under the second Roosevelt to establish a bi-partisan basis for foreign policy has given greater stability, but foreign issues are all too apt to be dominated by the immediate exigencies of party politics. Under these circumstances a consistent foreign policy becomes impossible and military domination of foreign policy inevitable. The limitations of American foreign policy are largely a result of its lack of tradition and continuity and its consequent emphasis on displays of military strength.

Partly because of the instability of its political system,[16] the United States has shown considerable partiality for generals as presidents throughout its history. The sword has been mightier than the pen, to cite only the defeat of Greeley by Grant. Even in the United States there have been complaints of the pervasive influence of the armed forces, but no signs of abatement are in evidence. Conscription implies a strengthening of their influence. George Ticknor, an American writing in the latter part of the nineteenth century, stated: "Nothing tends to make war more savage than this cruel, forced service, which the soldier who survives it yet claims at last as his great glory because he cannot afford to suffer so much and get no honour for it. It is a splendid sort of barbarism that is thus promoted, but it is barbarism after all; for it tends more and more to make the military character predominate over the civil."[17] De Tocqueville described military glory as a scourge more formidable to republics than all other evils combined. An American has described Washington as becoming

---

[15]Lewis, The Art of Being Ruled, p. 91.

[16]"By the Constitution, the Executive may recommend measures which he may think proper, and he may veto those he thinks improper, and it is supposed he may add to these certain indirect influences to affect the actions of Congress. My political education strongly inclines me against a very free use of any of these means by the Executive to control the legislation of the country. As a rule I think that Congress should originate as well as perfect its measures without external bias." Lincoln in a speech at Pittsburgh, Feb. 15, 1861. D. A. S. Alexander, History and Procedure of the House of Representatives (Boston, 1916), p. 358.

[17]Life, Letters and Journals of George Ticknor (Boston, 1880), II, 475.

the centre for those impelled by the power rather than the profit motive. Bureaucracy assumes a hierarchy, and thus the problem of power.

Formerly it required time to influence public opinion in favour of war. We have now reached the position in which opinion is systematically aroused and kept near boiling point. Strong vested interests in disagreement overwhelm concern for agreement. With control by military men and the difficulties of a constitution which places power in the hands of the public it may become difficult to check the swings of public opinion. American "candour, good temper, immediate and fearless experimentation, sense for fact, etc., is the positive role of their incapacity for discussions and ideas." "Any fact interests them and *no idea* except as it can be shown to be in direct relation to fact." (Lowes Dickinson.) The United States has been described by John Gunther as "the greatest, craziest, most dangerous, least stable, most spectacular, least grown up and most powerful and magnificent nation ever known."[18] Her attitude reminds one of the stories of the fanatic fear of mice shown by elephants.

The Department of Economic Affairs of the United Nations in *A Survey of the Economic Situation and Prospects of Europe* described the trade problem in these words: "The European import-surplus problem is essentially the same as the export-surplus problem of the United States, and the alternatives facing the United States are those facing Europe with the signs reversed; sooner or later the United States must either increase its imports or decrease its exports or do both. But the danger exists that if adequate remedial measures are not taken to work out a tenable balance, the economic structure of both Europe and the United States may become so adjusted to the disequilibrium as to create strong pressures tending to perpetuate it." As suggested by the *Economist* there is a prospect of a "United States dollar shortage forever."[19] Nor does Europe gain much comfort from the United States. Professor J. H. Williams, a judicious observer, writes: "Deepseated in the whole process has been the growing predominance of the United States: resting on the cumulative advantages of size and technological progress and expressing itself in the so-much discussed

---

[18]William James referred to "the exclusive worship of the bitch-goddess success." Lloyd Morris, *Postscript to Yesterday* (New York, 1947), p. 330. The vices were "swindling and adroitness, and the indulgence of swindling and adroitness, and cant, and sympathy with cant—natural fruits of that extraordinary idealization of 'success' in the mere outward sense of 'getting there' and getting there on as big a scale as we can, which characterizes our present generation."

[19]See F. A. Knox, "The March of Events," *Canadian Banker*, autumn 1948, for a most useful discussion.

chronic dollar shortage. . . . We must think of the objectives of the Marshall Plan in terms of reshaping the European economy and adjusting it to its changed world position, and of making the necessary adjustments in our own. We must also regard it as the beginning rather than the end of the adjustment process."[20]

The tariff is an important instrument in American imperialism, described, in the words of Mr. Dooley, as taking up the white man's burden and handing it to the coon. "The mind that thinks in terms of the protectionist symbol is equally at home in the imperialistic symbol."[21] It is as much a contradiction in terms "to speak of protective tariffs as instruments of free enterprise as to speak of militarism or imperialism as instruments of free enterprise."[22] Trade barriers and monopolies become deadly enemies of free enterprise capitalism.[23] Reductions in the American tariff which might widen an outlet for European goods and alleviate the problem have been proposed on a limited scale, but discussion of the tariff in general will not be raised even to the high level of the argument advanced by Mr. Dooley. "The tariff! What difference does it make? Th' foreigner pays th' tax anyhow. He does," said Mr. Dooley, "if he ain't turned back at Castle Garden." There is little prospect of discussion of the tariff in the United States and Canada since European countries cannot expect to have much influence on this subject and, again in the words of Mr. Dooley, "Them that the tariff looks after will look after the tariff."

European countries feel more directly exposed to American influence and to the threat that "the cumulative advantage of size and technological progress" of the United States may enforce uniformity and standardization with disastrous implications for the artistic culture of Europe and for Western civilization. The effects have been evident in the emergence of developments which reflect a profound determination to maintain the supremacy of European culture against the threats of Americanization and communism. Civilization can hardly survive a dumbbell arrangement with its energies drawn to two centres of power, nor an arrangement dominated by one or other power group. Yet it is exceedingly difficult for an Anglo-Saxon trained in a common law tradition to understand the point of view of a European trained in the Roman law tradition.

Canadians can scarcely understand the attitude of hostility of

[20]"The Task of Economic Recovery," *Foreign Affairs*, July 1948, pp. 14–15.
[21]E. M. Winslow, *The Pattern of Imperialism: A Study in the Theories of Power* (New York, 1948), p. 203.
[22]*Ibid.*, p. 234.   [23]*Ibid.*, p. 237.

Europeans towards Americans because of the overwhelming influence upon them of American propaganda.[24] Americans are the best propagandists because they are the best advertisers.[25] Whatever hope of continued autonomy Canada may have in the future must depend on her success in withstanding American influence and in assisting the development of a third bloc[26] designed to withstand the pressure of the United States and Russia. But there is little evidence that she is capable of these herculean efforts and much that she will continue to be regarded as an instrument of the United States. The tariff has long since been forgotten in Canada. We too have our mild imperialist ventures, as shown in our acquisition of Newfoundland. "War is self-defence against reform."[27] Neither a nation, nor a commonwealth, nor a civilization can endure in which one half in slavery believes itself free because of a statement in the Bill of Rights,[28] and attempts to enslave the other half which is free. Freedom of the press under the Bill of Rights accentuated the printed tradition, destroyed freedom of speech, and broke the relations with the oral tradition of Europe.

We may dislike American influence, we may develop a Canadian underground movement, but we are compelled to yield to American policy. We may say that democracy has become something which Americans wish to impose upon us because they say that they have it in the United States; we may dislike the assumption of Americans that they have found the one and only way of life—but they have American dollars. It may seem preposterous that North America should attempt to dictate to the cultural centres of Europe, France, Italy, Germany, and Great Britain how they should vote and what education means— but it has American dollars. Yet loans or even gifts are not a basis for friendship. The results are expressed in the remark: "I cannot understand why he is so bitterly opposed to me. I have never done anything for him." Even in the United States a slight appreciation of the definition of gratitude, as a keen sense of favours to come, exists.

In our time we have seen the over-running of Czechoslovakia by Germany with the concurrence of the Allies and on a larger scale the

[24]"Says the New York Times' Hansen Baldwin: 'Canada must arm.'" *Time*, Jan. 3, 1949, p. 20, section on Canada—an illustration of the crude effrontery of American imperialism.

[25]G. S. Viereck, *Spreading Germs of Hate* (New York, 1930), p. 168.

[26]See B. S. Keirstead, "Canada at the Crossroads in Foreign Policy," *International Affairs*, spring 1948, pp. 97–110. The problem has not been simplified by the change in the position of the Canadian exchange rate.

[27]Emery Neff, *Carlyle and Mill* (New York, 1930), p. 168.

[28]See M. L. Ernst, *The First Freedom* (New York, 1946); also O. W. Riegel, *Mobilizing for Chaos: The Story of the New Propaganda* (New Haven, 1934).

overrunning of Europe in spite of their opposition. But culture and language have proved more powerful than force. In the Anglo-Saxon world we have a new mobilization of force in the United States, with new perils, and all the resources of culture and language of the English-speaking peoples, including those of the United States, will be necessary to resist it. In the crudest terms, military strategy dominated by public opinion would be disastrous.

The future of the West depends on the cultural tenacity of Europe and the extent to which it will refuse to accept dictation from a foreign policy developed in relation to the demands of individuals in North America concerned with re-election. American foreign policy has been a disgraceful illustration of the irresponsibility of a powerful nation which promises little for the future stability of the Western world. In the words of Professor Robert Peers, Canada must call in the Old World to redress the balance of the New, and hope that Great Britain will escape American imperialism as successfully as she herself has escaped British imperialism.

Index